A Message of Truth

The History, Science, and Politics of Christianity

SECOND EDITION

Andrew V. Barber, PhD

© Copyright 2019, 2020 Andrew V. Barber

All rights reserved. No part of this publication may be reproduced, transmitted, or distributed in any form or by any means without expressed written permission from the copyright owner.

Verses paraphrased and quoted from the King James Version (KJV) of the Holy Bible, which is public domain, are not restricted under this copyright.

Published by Special Delivery Press
7121 Tierra Alta Ave.
El Paso, TX 79912
www.andrewvbarberphd.com

ISBN: 9780966970272
LCCN: 2020939779

Dedicated to the Triune God

Books of the Bible and Abbreviations

Biblical citations support many arguments being advanced. The reader is urged to consult his or her Bible and verify the applicability of scriptures.

Old Testament (OT)

BOOK	ABBREV.	BOOK	ABBREV.
Genesis	GEN	Ecclesiastes	ECC
Exodus	EXO	Song of Solomon	SOS
Leviticus	LEV	Isaiah	ISA
Numbers	NUM	Jeremiah	JER
Deuteronomy	DEU	Lamentations	LAM
Joshua	JOS	Ezekiel	EZE
Judges	JDG	Daniel	DAN
Ruth	RUT	Hosea	HOS
1 Samuel	1 SA	Joel	JOE
2 Samuel	2 SA	Amos	AMO
1 Kings	1 KI	Obadiah	OBA
2 Kings	2 KI	Jonah	JON
1 Chronicles	1 CH	Micah	MIC
2 Chronicles	2 CH	Nahum	NAH
Ezra	EZR	Habakkuk	HAB
Nehemiah	NEH	Zephaniah	ZEP
Esther	EST	Haggai	HAG
Job	JOB	Zechariah	ZEC
Psalms	PSA	Malachi	MAL
Proverbs	PRO		

New Testament (NT)

BOOK	ABBREV.	BOOK	ABBREV.
Matthew	MAT	1 Timothy	1 TI
Mark	MAR	2 Timothy	2 TI
Luke	LUK	Titus	TIT
John	JOH	Philemon	PHM
Acts	ACT	Hebrews	HEB
Romans	ROM	James	JAM
1 Corinthians	1 CO	1 Peter	1 PE
2 Corinthians	2 CO	2 Peter	2 PE
Galatians	GAL	1 John	1 JO
Ephesians	EPH	2 John	2 JO
Philippians	PHP	3 John	3 JO
Colossians	COL	Jude	JDE
1 Thessalonians	1 TH	Revelation	REV
2 Thessalonians	2 TH		

CONTENTS

INTRODUCTION 1
Fallacies of Logic 2
Belief Systems 9
THE GREAT DEBATE 15
Proof 16
Causality 31
Things Not Seen 34
Morality 39
Miracles 42
Exclusivity 47
Comfort 51
Prophecy 54
Conclusions 56
THE PROBLEM OF EVIL 57
Temptation 64
The Conscience 69
Who Am I to Judge? 71
Justice 74
Government 79
Accountability 83
Legacy of Corruption 88
Sexual Confusion 91

CONTENTS

This Is War 97
SPIRITUAL WARFARE 106
As a Matter of Fact 107
The Power of Discovery 113
Show Me the Evidence 118
Political Correctness Run Amok 124
Attacks on Christianity 129
Tyranny 135
Strange Alliances 141
Economic Disaster 145
The Apocalypse 149
THE GOSPEL MAKES THE DIFFERENCE 154
Entitlement 161
Destiny 165
Freedom 167
Connecting 170
Service 173
It Is Personal 176
The Holy Trinity 181
Holy Week 185
Watch and Wait 188
The Presence of the Lord 191

CONTENTS

YOU ARE SPECIAL 196
The Universe 197
How Old Is the Universe? 202
Intelligent Design or Random Unguided Processes 206
Experience 211
Bias 215
What Is Truth? 219
Absolution 224
Diversity and Division 229
THE ESSENTIALS 243
Nature Versus Nurture 246
The Price of Your Soul 250
Eternity 255
The Real Jesus 258
The Resurrection 263
Imputation 268
Looking Forward 271
Revival 285
Fate 288
The End 292
REFERENCES 298
INDEX 305

About the Author

Andrew Barber has had successful and prosperous careers as a research psychologist, academician, counselor, psychotherapist, and consultant. He has authored over thirty-five technical publications and books (nonfiction and fiction), has conducted high-level briefings, and has presented research papers at professional conferences. He is a lifetime Christian and has served at his church in many capacities to include instructor, musician and vocalist, committee chairman, counselor, and usher captain.

After honorably completing his military service as an airborne infantryman with the 82nd Airborne Division, Andrew enrolled in college as an art student, earning his Bachelor of Arts and becoming a certified teacher. Next, he worked as a caseworker during which he completed his Master in Education. His knowledge of experimental design and statistics, and his investigation and work with adolescent runaways landed him into the field of psychological research. While working as a military scientist and statistician, he obtained his Doctorate in Psychology, progressing to the level of senior evaluator. Eventually he became a consultant to the defense industry. He held Top Secret and NATO Secret security clearances.

Dr. Barber returned to academia and counseling. He became a professor of psychology, counseling, statistics, religion, management, and human resources at graduate and undergraduate levels. He served as campus chair for the College of Social and Behavioral Sciences at a nationwide university before becoming the director of academic affairs for two campuses. His next position was director of clinical support services at a community health center, where he served as lead psychotherapist, director of mental health and health education operations, and corporate compliance officer.

Later he became the lead therapist and program manager of adult units at a large psychiatric hospital. He progressed to director of the addiction unit, the psychiatric intensive care unit, the pain management program, and the department of intake and assessment. Dr. Barber also maintained a private practice in counseling and consulting for thirty years. He mentored and supervised professionals, interns, and students in the areas of therapy, psychiatric care, and unit operations; he specialized in faith-based counseling and taught continuing education workshops. He is now focused on his research, writing, consulting, public speaking, and Christian apologetics.

INTRODUCTION

"To be, or not to be—that is the question." You may recognize this statement to be the opening line of Shakespeare's *Hamlet*. If you continue reading Hamlet's monologue, you will discover his ultimate question entailed life versus death; but it did not address the question of life after death. The crucial question is "To believe or not to believe" because that answer will address the first question as to whether you will be or won't be. As Mortimer Adler put it (1952), "More consequences for life and action follow from the affirmation or denial of God, than from any other basic question." Those who affirm God, or believe, are inclined to anticipate life after death; those who deny God, or refuse to believe, pursue worldly causes that do not lead to eternal life. Notice, it is one thing to believe in God and quite another to believe God. He speaks to anyone who will listen, through his words and through his creation (namely, the universe).

This book was produced to help the reader defend his or her views about the universe, God, life, death, and religion. It is sort of a primer for grooming one to be an apologist. An apologist is a defender of his or her belief system. For example, a lot of people believe in God and many refer to themselves as Christians. But when people of faith are asked why they believe, or how they know that the Bible is true, or what makes Christianity unique, many cannot provide a satisfactory answer. Maybe after reading this book you will feel more confident giving an answer to those who ask about your beliefs, dreams, or hopes. Possibly, you can prompt others to ponder your viewpoint, and why you believe, and how you know.

It is important to be knowledgeable, thorough, reasonable, and open-minded. Careful thought, close examination, objective analysis, factual information, pleasant demeanor, and coherent argumentation: these are advantageous if one is to persuade others convincingly. With evidence in hand you can confidently present a case, while also being equipped to deconstruct what people purport to be true.

It is prudent to research all sides of an argument before defending any one position. This requires an understanding of underlying assumptions, definitions, generalizations, and expectations associated with points-of-view other than your own. Extensively study topics, conduct thought experiments, develop viable theories, perform practical investigations, formulate alternative explanations, test hypotheses, collect, integrate, and analyze data, then draw cogent inferences. This process, in essence, constitutes the scientific method. We all are scientists to some degree (Kelly, 1955); we experiment with different strategies, attempting new things, learning by trial and error, and discovering what is real and what is true. We want to solve problems and find answers, recognize who is right and who is wrong, and discriminate the hero from the villain. We need to know the truth, what to believe, and who to trust.

This book is about exploring possibilities with the ultimate objectives being discovery and enlightenment. That pathway is paved with experience, which alone does not count as proof. Proof requires truth, and it the goal of this book to convey it. Before embarking on this excursion, however, I would like to educate the reader a little on how to be an astute observer, inspector, examiner, and evaluator.

Fallacies of Logic

Be prepared to ask informed questions, challenge incomplete answers, unmask ulterior motives, and dismantle weak arguments. In order to be an adept and critical thinker, it is necessary to determine when arguments defy logic, accuracy, sensibility, and consistency. Alert yourself to errors in analysis and thought processes; contradictions in statements, judgments, and opinions; redundancies, rambling, and tautologies; incomplete and incredible suppositions; disjointed presentations, definitions, and word usages; and misrepresentations of data, statistics, evidence, and truth.

In this subsection, some terms and concepts applicable to reasoning and logic are presented. Those who are well-versed in the following terms and concepts may wish to refresh themselves with this material. The definitions will be helpful for identifying if fallacies are being employed, because they exemplify when an argument being proffered is not based on real proof.

For starters, consider the syllogism, a form of deduction employing a practical sequence. The syllogism begins with a major premise, followed by a minor premise, and then a conclusion. A famous syllogism posed by Aristotle went like this: All men are mortal; Socrates is a man; therefore, Socrates is mortal. Premises are propositions formulated from an examination of evidence and found to be empirically valid or universally accepted. The conclusion is a decision, finding, or relationship based upon one or more premises.

An antecedent is an event or finding that occurs first or prior to another event or finding. The consequent occurs after the antecedent(s) and is explained by prior events, antecedents, or findings. Such relationships in the sequoce can imply causality. The establishment of cause-effect relationships is a fundamental objective of science or any other investigative inquiry, for it enhances insight into possible future events as well as prior motives.

Objectivity involves performing unprejudiced search, assessment, and verification; probing, examining, assembling, processing, synthesizing, and scrutinizing information. The components of intellectual development and advancement are many, and too numerous to dissect in this exposition. It is recommended that those who wish to become seasoned investigators, forecasters, apologists, and orators study topics such as critical thinking, basic data reduction and analysis, probability and statistics, experimental methodology, and fallacies of logic such as those presented below (listed alphabetically). This presentation will assist the reader in recognizing when an otherwise persuasive argument is actually based upon warped judgment, innuendo, opinion, deceit, or a spin of the facts. The list below is lengthy but is by no means exhaustive. With practice, you will come to realize when an argument being advanced to convince, persuade, or influence is flawed. Think twice, for the claims people make often run contrary to truth, indicated by their distorting, subduing, and confusing of the facts, problem, or concern.

Ad Hominem involves verbally attacking the person instead of his or her argument. For example, "Senator Smith is an idiot and doesn't know what he's talking about." (Perhaps Smith made a valid point that the challenger was not prepared to debate or discuss.)

Affirming the Consequent is an argument based on the finding that, when *a* occurs then *b* occurs; if *b* occurred it is assumed that *a* should have occurred. For example, "Wet roads cause accidents; up ahead is an accident so the roads must be wet." (Ignoring the fact that many conditions can cause accidents, like when people are impaired or distracted, which can occur anytime, anywhere.)

Amphiboly is when ambiguous grammar obscures the message (similar to equivocation which introduces ambiguous words or phrases). For example,

"The assignment was to create something artistic, so I painted my dog." (Did I apply paint to my dog, or did I produce a painting portraying my dog?)

Appeal to Association is an assumption that two people or two events possessing commonalities are connected in purpose. For example, "They both voted against the initiative; I bet they conspired together to stifle it." (Guilt by association does not permit a valid accusation.)

Appeal to Authority involves ascribing relevance to someone's opinion who is a subject matter expert, but in an unrelated field. For example, "I am going to prescribe for you a mood stabilizer." (That would be a reasonable decision for a psychiatrist but not for a proctologist).

Appeal to Emotion is an argument that elicits a strong feeling to persuade. For example, "Donate now if you care at all about abused animals." (This statement occurs after showing you graphic pictures of emaciated dogs and cats so you will feel pity.)

Appeal to Force is an argument that uses a threat to manipulate. For example, "If you break up with me, I will kill myself." (If you are suicidal you need to speak to a professional, not your ex.)

Appeal to Ignorance is an argument raised to persuade someone who is assumed to lack knowledge. For example, "There is no scientific evidence for miracles." (Science deals with the observation and measurement of natural phenomena; but sometimes an observed effect can be attributed to a cause that cannot be observed, especially if the cause is supernatural.)

Appeal to Motive is when a statement is rejected by questioning the motive of the speaker. For example, "You are saying we could be good together just to get me to sleep with you." (Well, perhaps not.)

Appeal to Popularity is the ascribing of relevance to a generally held opinion which is not based on real evidence. For example, "All politicians are compulsive liars." (Have you never met an honest one in your life?)

Begging the Question is when circular reasoning is applied whereby the premise points to a conclusion which is the basis for the premise. For example, "The fossil record indicates succeeding time periods with which we can establish geologic columns where particular fossils are likely to be found." (The premise and the conclusion cannot be one and the same; therefore, causality is not evident.)

Cherry Picking is the tendency to dismiss disconfirmatory evidence in favor of confirmatory evidence (also information bias); this is reflected in the suppression of evidence. For example, "I found research on the Internet proving that I am right." (An Internet search might generate dozens of reports of varying reliability, which are contradictory regarding their conclusions.)

Cognitive Conceit involves overestimating one's personal knowledge or experience. For example, "If you want to know anything about baseball, ask me." (It would be prudent to substantiate opinions coming from self-proclaimed experts.)

Correlation Fallacy is an argument in which causality is assumed from a correlation or relationship between variables. For example, "If *a* is statistically correlated with *b*, then *a* must cause *b*." (What if *b* causes *a*? What if the two have a cause or an effect in common, like anxiety and depression? Correlations do not imply causality and are not employed statistically to predict outcomes.)

Denying the Antecedent is an argument based on the finding that, when *a* occurs then *b* occurs; so, if *a* doesn't occur then *b* won't occur. For example, "Wet roads increase accidents, but it's not raining today so it should be perfectly safe to drive." (One must always be cautious when driving regardless of the conditions, but especially during inclement weather.)

Equivocation is using words or phrases that are ambiguous in order to mask the truth or meaning, if not to deliberately deceive. For example, "I did not have sexual relations with that person." (This does not exclude the possibility that he or she may have engaged in sexual acting out with that person.)

Error of Composition is assuming a group characteristic must be present in every component within the group. For example, "All Asians are good at Chinese checkers" (Ignores individual talent, practice, and the fact that people of any nationality can be equally talented at the same thing).

Error of Context is taking something that has been said or written from one context and applying it in a different way or to another context in an attempt to alter the original meaning. For example, "I thought you liked champagne, you did last time." (Maybe last time was a wedding and this time is a funeral.)

Error of Division is assuming that, if any component of the whole has a characteristic, it must be true of the whole. For example, "The Tigers have a great quarterback, so the team will probably make the playoffs." (Ignores the fact that team members vary in their excellence, and the fact that teamwork is a winning attribute regardless of how superior the individual players are.)

Error of Repetition is the idea that repeating the same argument over and over lends credibility to its accuracy. For example, "The government always has your best interest in mind." (This is the tactic of propaganda, trying to convince through repetition.)

Error of Silence is an argument where a lack of available evidence presupposes no evidence. For example, "Since nobody has produced physical evidence to prove the existence of God, then obviously, God does not exist." (If that is true then atheism must, by presupposition, be unequivocally false.)

False Analogy is an argument based on an illogical comparison. For example, "The candidate behaves like a Nazi." (Really? With whom can you reasonably compare Adolf Hitler, except maybe Joseph Stalin?)

False Dilemma is an argument posing limits to the available conclusions. For example, "You either agree with me on this, or we are in total disagreement." (This would negate the possibility of a compromise, which is an alternative not being allowed or considered.)

False Prediction is an argument that predicts an outcome not corroborated by any historical data. For example, "All of the computers in the world are going to crash on 01/01/2000 (Y2K)." (Guess what, nothing out of the ordinary happened.)

Gambler's Fallacy is based on the premise that several previous events changes the probability of a future event. For example, "Since I lost the last five hands, I should bet the farm on the next hand." (The likelihood of getting a good hand does not change once the cards are adequately reshuffled.)

Loaded Question is when a question is raised that assumes facts not in evidence or not settled, thereby constricting any reply to one that affirms the assumption (the respondent will be unable to agree or disagree). For example, "Are you still as hard-headed as you used to be?" (Obviously, this implies you are hard-headed whether you answer yes or no.)

Loaded Statement is when words or phrases are used that connote radical opinions or outcomes. For example, "Those supporting immigration laws are racist." (Maybe they support enforcement of laws, period.)

Misrepresenting the Data is when statistics, findings, or interpretations are quoted inaccurately to bolster a position or opinion. For example, "The unemployment rate has dropped to five percent." (What about the other five percent that gave up looking for a job and were not counted in that statistic?

INTRODUCTION

Politicians and the news media are notorious for misrepresenting the facts. Further, many studies do not produce reliable results because they are not methodologically sound, such as political polls.)

Missing the Point is when an argument, however valid, is introduced that is irrelevant to the topic being discussed. For example, "I don't understand your trauma, because I had a great upbringing." (If you have nothing relevant to contribute to the discussion, why not remain silent?)

Moving the Goalposts is when more evidence is demanded after sufficient evidence has been presented which supports the counterargument or which resolves an issue (a form of exclusion or discrimination). For example, "We are looking for teachers that are bilingual. Oh, did I fail to mention that we intend to hire more Hispanics?" (I actually experienced this when I became a certified teacher. I had applied for a job in a predominately Latino school district and reassured the supervisor that I spoke Spanish as a second language.)

Non-Sequitur means "doesn't follow" and is used as an argument in which the conclusion does not follow the premise. For example, "Real men drink beer." (Whatever that means. Besides, women are known to drink beer, even dogs sometimes. And how about real men who prefer whiskey?)

Over-Embellishment is when excruciating detail is added in an attempt to make an argument or observation appear plausible or acceptable. For example, "You could tell she was out of control, because her eyes were popping out, her head was steaming, there was smoke coming out of her ears, and she was foaming at the mouth." (Sounds like she was inhuman.)

Overgeneralization is an argument in which the conclusion is based on an inadequate or unrepresentative sample (also jumping to conclusions). For example, "If it happened to me it will happen to you." (A sample of one cannot be generalized; just as your experience and mine will likely be different, even if we are experiencing the same event at the same time.)

Oversimplification is when an argument assumes a limited number of possible causes (one or two), narrowing the possible contributing factors to few rather than many. For example, "The quarterback blew the game." (But what about the front line that didn't provide enough pass protection?)

Poisoning the Well involves countering an argument before it is raised. For example, "Nobody with half a brain supports that proposal." (It is ridiculous to assume that everybody believes the same way about the same things. Does anyone in the world think like you?)

Post Hoc Fallacy is where a cause-effect relationship is presumed from a weak association or superstition. For example, "I just broke a mirror so I'm going to have seven years of bad luck." (This is the classic "after that, therefore because of that" argument implying an unverifiable correlation. Just because two events follow in sequence does not mean they are related at all, like rain and menstruation.)

Red Herring is an erroneous suggestion about a controversial issue which detracts from the real issue at hand, in order to change the focus. For example, "Sure there is a lot of violence in the ghetto, but stricter gun control laws would reduce the crime." (Guns are not the cause of crime but they are often an instrument used by criminals, including in the ghetto.)

Reification Fallacy is when an abstract or hypothetical idea, opinion, or possibility is not concrete but is claimed to be. For example, "I know you want to go the movies tonight; can't you smell the popcorn?" (I probably could if I was at the cinema.)

Retrospective Determinism is when a suggestion is made that something happened because it was inevitable (related also to 20/20 hindsight and the knew-it-all-along effect). For example, "The Wildcats were destined to lose." (Would you have said the same thing had they won?)

Shifting the Burden involves arguing that a person must be proven wrong, rather than having to prove that he or she is right. For example, "I don't have to prove that I am right, because you can't prove me wrong." (Well maybe I can if I have time to do the research. But a lack of evidence for one position doesn't imply the other is true.)

Slanting is when a fact is presented in such a way as to suggest it is false. For example, "No way you're having a baby." (Depending on circumstances, that statement might hint it could be true but the speaker doesn't want it to be.)

Slippery Slope is when an argument is made that the occurrence of a particular event will eventually lead to a catastrophe. For example, "It only takes one drink to make an alcoholic." (I guess one mustn't walk along the seashore lest they drown.)

Straw Man is when the person will misinterpret another's viewpoint and then attack the misrepresentation. For example, "That judge advocates traditional marriage, which discriminates against homosexuals, and we cannot be appointing homophobes like her to the court." (For all you know, the woman has a child whom she loves dearly who has a same-sex partner.)

Two Wrongs Make a Right is an argument that justifies one wrong after comparing it to another wrong. For example, "It is okay to use torture on terrorists because they are evil." (There might be alternative methods of obtaining information.)

Unlikely Hypothesis is when an argument is based on an implausible theory. For example, "She slept her way to the top." (Maybe she is smarter than you give her credit.)

Verbosity Protocol is an attempt to make an argument plausible as a result of longwinded testimony and convoluted technicality; it seems impressive but is difficult to follow (one might perceive the concept too advanced to be understood). For example, "Now that I have expounded on the entire anthology of evolution theory, are there any questions?" (Only one, are you finished?)

Weasel Words is a counterargument that changes the meaning of a key word to alter the facts (also related to hedging, where words are used to imply a meaning, and then redefined afterwards). For example, "It depends on how you define the word is." (The teller's intention was to appear honest while being deceptive, using a twisted interpretation of the word "is".)

Wishful Thinking is an argument that presents a perfect or pleasing outcome regardless of how improbable. For example, "Vote for me and there will be free healthcare for everyone." (Unfortunately, practically nothing in this world comes without a cost.)

Belief Systems

There are a number of beliefs, religions, and philosophies presented in this book which may overlap, conflict, or complement one another. The following glossary is provided to enable the reader to determine which viewpoints, if any, are deemed reasonable or believable. Again, this list is far from exhaustive given the innumerable "isms" that exist nowadays.

Agnosticism is a philosophy or position that the existence of God cannot be known with certainty because it cannot be proven or disproven. The agnostic is uncommitted to believing in the existence or nonexistence of God or gods.

Altruism is an attitude or disposition founded on positive regard for fellow human beings, demonstrated by charitable acts and self-sacrifice; an unselfish devotion to the wellbeing of others.

Anarchism is a political movement to overthrow governmental rule, in favor of self-organization; a voluntary compliance with imposed laws results in unconstrained freedom, lawlessness, and disorder.

Animism is the belief that spirits reside in animate and inanimate objects alike; that there is an immaterial element to matter, life, natural things, and celestial bodies.

Atheism involves disbelief in the existence of God, a supreme being, a creator, or multiple gods; also, a belief that there is zero proof of God.

Capitalism is an economic and political system that promotes the rights of private citizens to own property, goods, and capital; and to engage in, run, or invest in any business, corporation, or commodity within a free-market society.

Collectivism is an economic and political system emphasizing group actions and benefits over that of individuals, imposing centralized control over production of goods by, and distribution of assets to, the collective.

Communism is an economic and political system suggesting that the community at large owns the property, resources, and capital; but these are distributed by a centralized government to sustain, placate, and promote the cooperative. Ultimately, control, power, ownership, and organization are governed by a single party, with services and products determined and distributed by the political state, such that the proletariat really owns nothing (see also *Collectivism*).

Conservatism is a political position based on traditional values, precepts, and institutions; the promoting of individual responsibility, accountability and enforcement of rules, economic stability, national security, and public safety. Belief that the reach and power of government should be limited, so the authority to self-govern remains with the people.

Constitutionalism is a devotion to the rule of law and the principles of our constitutional system of government, which is dedicated to liberty and justice for all. Strict adherence to the original words of the framers of the Constitution of the United States.

INTRODUCTION

Deism is a philosophy that God exists but does not intervene or interfere with nature or humanity, and which denies divine revelation as a path to enlightenment.

Determinism is a belief that all human actions and worldly events are predetermined beforehand as a consequence of preceding events; disbelief in free will or accountability.

Fascism is a political system based on an authoritarian government or dictatorship, which controls the economy, the society, and the people with a strong arm, suppressing any form of opposition or dissent (see also *Totalitarianism*).

Fundamentalism when pertaining to a religion, is a faithful adherence to doctrines, beliefs, and associated holy books.

Globalism is a political movement or policy that promotes the interests of the entire world above that of individuals, parties, and nations, whereby the sphere of influence and the powers of government extend worldwide.

Hedonism is the view that the ultimate objective in life is to please or placate oneself, such that personal pleasure is considered the greatest virtue.

Humanism is a philosophy emphasizing the importance, dignity, values, decisions, and reasoning of humanity as the supreme principle. Humans can discover knowledge for themselves and are self-sufficient, thereby rejecting supernatural influences, explanations, or reasons (see also *Naturalism*).

Imperialism is a policy in which the objective is to expand the realm of political power and influence abroad via coercion or force.

Interventionism is the practice or tactic of deliberately interfering in another nation's economy, politics, or society.

Isolationism is a policy in which the objective is to remain completely separated from the influence, concerns, pursuits, and control of outside parties or nations.

Liberalism is a political position based on beliefs in the inherent goodness and the progressive development of humanity, and the corresponding utility of activism to promote social, political, and economic reform. A view that government is responsible for protecting civil liberties and for correcting social injustices and inequalities.

Libertarianism is a political position emphasizing personal autonomy and responsibility, with unbridled freedom that doesn't impede upon others, and minimal government involvement in social and economic affairs.

Materialism is the philosophy that the universe consists exclusively of physical matter and processes. Since there is no proof of supernatural, mental, or spiritual explanations or phenomena, only material explanations are reasonable and valid, such that there is but one reality and it is material (i.e., biochemical).

Monotheism is the belief that one God presides over all things visible and invisible (included are Judaism, Christianity, and Islam).

Multiculturalism is a view that the ideal society is a blending of multiple cultures, all of which provide identity and enrichment to the collective unity, and therefore should be equally preserved (see also *Pluralism*).

Mysticism is the belief that one can join with a deity, nature, or an absolute and receive revelation through that connection. Connecting with one's inner being, soul, or spirit, or via altered states of consciousness.

Nationalism is a position or policy of desired independence from outside or international influence; also, patriotism and loyalism to one's native land.

Naturalism is a philosophy that human thoughts, intentions, and actions are determined by natural laws, desires, and processes; that there are no supernatural forces or descriptions that can account for these phenomena, only science and reasoning (see also *Humanism*).

Nihilism is a philosophy that rejects religious beliefs, holding that there is no true meaning or purpose to life, and that existence is not a reality and neither is truth.

Pantheism is a belief that the universe is God, or they are equal; that both God and the universe possess equivalent laws, forces, physics, and attributes.

Pluralism is a view that society consists of multiple entities of essential importance; that diversity, more than anything, improves society through the influence of ethnic, religious, cultural, and political inspiration mixed with tradition (see also *Multiculturalism*).

INTRODUCTION

Polytheism is the belief that multiple gods govern the universe, often of unequal power and differing purpose (includes Hinduism, Shintoism, and the mythology of ancient Egypt, Babylon, Greece, and Rome).

Populism involves supporting and promoting the common people over the elite (power to the people). Basically, the opposite of elitism where leaders are an exclusive assemblage of the affluent and powerful.

Postmodernism is a philosophy that endorses the redefinition of traditions, beliefs, rules, values, and justifications in order to reflect more modern or progressive thinking; a reworked understanding of society, culture, politics, law, and history.

Pragmatism involves establishing a practical application of inquiry to establish truth and causality for the purpose of developing theories, beliefs, constructs, or ideologies.

Progressivism involves advocacy for reforms that improve the conditions for society as a whole. Originally a movement for progress in the areas of technology, economic development, and education, progressivism itself has evolved, proceeding in a different direction with the aim to reorganize the classes, rewrite the laws, and redistribute wealth.

Rationalism (also *Intellectualism*) is the belief that knowledge is produced via reasoning alone; being devoted exclusively to the intellect at the expense of emotions.

Reductionism is a view that all processes can be explained using the laws of physics, biology, and chemistry whereby causal linkages can be established which regress from the complex to the simple, from the sophisticated to the basic. Explaining the physical mechanisms controlling or producing higher order operations, components, or organisms; tracking backwards to determine the cause or source.

Relativism is a view that knowledge, morality, and truth are constrained by the person or persons judging or defining them; that such assets can vary as a function of individuals and situational conditions and therefore are never absolute or universal.

Satanism is the belief that evil is good and vice-versa; being obsessed with Satan, sometimes involving devil worship.

Scientism is the belief that science, with its methods and discoveries, is the ultimate source of knowledge and outperforms all other means of investigation and understanding. There are no other reasonable means to enlightenment to include spiritual and supernatural.

Secularism is the belief that religion has no place in society, education, or government.

Socialism is an economic and political system promoting the collective, by allocating the authority for administering services and distributing goods to the state, such that there is no personal property, enterprise, or control. It is often characterized as the transition period between capitalism and communism (see also *Collectivism*).

Spiritualism is a belief that everyone is a spiritual being and can communicate with other spirits. It has been extended to include the use of mediums in attempt to connect with spirits of the dead or to channel familiar spirits.

Statism is a political system in a nation-state wielding consolidated and authoritative control over social and economic activity, industry, and policy.

Theism is a belief in God or gods; most commonly, a belief that there is a supreme creator of the universe who rules over all of nature and humanity.

Totalitarianism is a political system in which those in power control everything (see also *Fascism* and *Statism*).

Utilitarianism is a doctrine holding that optimal action is that which brings about the greatest benefit for the most people; unfortunately, the utility of decisions can be subject to opinion or debate, depending on who decides and who is impacted.

THE GREAT DEBATE

As with many issues debated by people of intellect, there are two diametrically opposing sides. And both sides typically use the same talking points but from a position which appears controversial to the other side. So, what is the great debate all about? It is primarily concerned with whether or not the Holy Bible is true. If the Holy Bible is true, then Christianity is true and God is real. Some of the most hotly disputed topics of our day are being argued by believers of the Holy Bible and unbelievers, and by believers in God and unbelievers. The controversy often pits scientific beliefs against religious beliefs, as if you don't need faith and facts for both.

I will introduce the fundamental areas of contention and give both sides of the argument. Keep in mind that evidence supporting one position does not necessarily refute the other position. Evidence points to truth regardless of which side of an issue you support. You can decide which point of view is the more reasonable or verifiable. To begin, I will briefly elaborate my personal perspective.

I contest allegations that the Holy Bible is full of errors, or has internal inconsistencies, or has changed over time, or is completely allegorical, or might be partially true, or is purely a work of fiction. These arguments can be rebuffed, seeing how the Bible is an accurate compilation of historical events and people. It was assembled by men of God who either were eyewitnesses or obtained their information from eyewitnesses; they were living the miracles and interventions of God, eager to be a witness and record the wisdom being imparted to them by the Lord of the universe. Regardless of whether you believe that the writers of the Bible were inspired by God or not, this does not detract from its accuracy. If you disagree, perhaps you will find a reason to rethink that, as long as you are patient and contemplate thoughtfully the research. With my obvious predilection aside, I feel strongly that my Christian position is supported by the evidence. But I yield to the reader to resolve this for yourself.

The Bible provides profound and detailed prophecy which can be traced in terms of authorship and origin; and those prophecies have come true years, even centuries after they were written. The Bible has been authenticated by dedicated scholars, investigators, and historians and has held up to intense scrutiny, even among those who sought to disprove the Bible but stumbled upon its truth. The Bible has been preserved over centuries, and retranslated in numerous languages, yet it continues to remain consistent in its presentation of God's plan, his truth, the mysteries of spirituality, the foundation of morality, and the principles of Christianity. The Bible continues to be the most widely distributed and frequently read book of all time.

There are four areas of validity that I often ascribe to the Bible: History, Authenticity, Reliability, and Prophecy (keyword *HARP*). The history has been corroborated extensively, the text has been authenticated repeatedly by experts, the teaching is reliable and consistent, and the prophecy comes to pass to the finest detail. In addition, the Old and New Testaments validate each other, though separated by hundreds if not thousands of years (Barber, 2020; Geisler and Turek, 2004).

The most valuable gifts that God has given us are life, love, and truth. These are attributes that God also possesses; to be sure, he is the epitome of them. For God is Love, he is Truth, and he is Spirit. The eternal Spirit gives life; and our life resides from the spirit within us. God emanates only love and he speaks only truth. Like God, we think and we feel; and we live. But unlike God, our emotions and our reasoning are not always in agreement. We know what is right but we don't always feel like doing it. We know what is true but we don't always want to think about it. When life, love, and truth come together in purity, it is very powerful indeed. The more we seek God, learn his ways, and speak his words, the more we can feel him and love him. And this pleases God very much, to the extent that we can abide forever in that blessed state if we so choose. In unfolding the facts, I am positive that this is what I long for.

Proof

The lack of proof argument is commonly held by certain historians and scientists that reject the Christian worldview outright, to include dismissing the Holy Bible as a source of truth. Closed-minded individuals are not interested in the truth; and they will reject credible evidence without reviewing it. Often, they will not listen; some will remove themselves from situations where intelligent people are discussing this topic. Interestingly, there is actually more proof for the existence of God than against. This same proof adds to the validation of the Bible being true. And that evidence is largely gleaned from the archives of history and science.

The events in the Bible are real; they have been documented in countless external sources from various cultures to include Egyptian, Assyrian, Babylonian, Persian, Roman, Chinese, and Indian. The scriptures were shared, copied, and quoted among the early church leaders, and handed over to students of the Christian faith. To this day, the Bible has not changed in content or meaning, despite the millennia that have transpired since its origin. In particular, the number of dated New Testament manuscripts and portions is astounding and can be traced from the first century to the present; no work of antiquity has anywhere near the documentation. Many historical accounts are corroborated in the writings of historians antagonistic to Christianity such as Thallus (Greek), Josephus (Hebrew), and Tacitus (Roman), to name but a few. Additional confirmation has been gleaned from archaeological findings. Much can be learned from the Bible about ancient lifestyles, politics, customs, practices, cultures, nations, timelines, and events.

Let us appraise the available historical evidence first, and then we will appraise the scientific evidence second. The Bible has been established as an accurate record of history. In particular, the Old Testament is an excellent account of people, places, and times—more accurate than ancient Greek, Egyptian, and Mesopotamian historicity combined (Keller, 1956). I believe that a fair examination of the historical evidence will totally negate the argument that the Bible is a fairy tale and God is an invention of imaginative people.

Review for a moment the examples listed below and see if you agree. Is the Bible supported by a reasonable consideration of the archaeological and historical data? Research these findings on your own if you believe them to be fallacious and you will discover convincing exposés. An Internet search will yield multiple sources providing corroboration. You will likely find even more compelling evidence if you continue studying biblical archaeology (see *www.biblicalarchaeology.org*). While the dates provided below are approximate, they follow closely the chronology of the Bible. Look up the Bible passages to see how they interlace with external historical versions. Take note that no archaeological discovery has directly contradicted or rebutted the testimony of the Holy Bible.

The Bible as an Authority on History

- Laminated petrified wood from a buried ship the exact dimensions of the ark of Noah (GEN 7:1–24), embedded in the mountains proximate to Ararat (GEN 8:4–5); petrified animal dung, cat hair, antler, and metallic rivets also found. Could this be the remains of Noah's ark? Also, the Ararat anomaly, thought to be the ark, was photographed from USAF reconnaissance aircraft in 1949; the photos were declassified in 1995 and can be viewed on the worldwide web.
- Traces from a deluge of water that covered the Black Sea shoreline (once a fresh water lake), dated to be of the time period of Noah (circa 3000–4000 BC).
- A colossal layer of clay was formed (circa 2500 BC) suggesting a gigantic flood once receded along the Tigris-Euphrates valley, dividing two eras of anthropologic and geologic history.
- Ancient cities of Babel and Nineveh were among those founded by King Nimrod and family (circa 2400 BC); he was the great grandson of Noah (GEN 10:8–11). Note that some scholars believe Nimrod could be the legendary Gilgamesh.
- Clay tablet from the ruins of Nineveh (circa 2300 BC) describes the epochal reign of King Gilgamesh, also recounting a great flood.
- Stele of king of Accad (GEN 10:10), another city built by Nimrod in the land of Shinar (Mesopotamia), where the Tower of Babel was erected (GEN 11:1–9). The Tower of Babel has been referred to as the House of Nimrod (Jewish rabbinic teaching).
- The ziggurat at Ur of the Chaldees (circa 2100 BC) is a structure not unlike the envisaged Tower of Babel (GEN 11:1–10). Ur was the homeland of Abraham (GEN 11:31) the premier patriarch of Judaism, Christianity, and Islam. Historians have proposed that Abraham and Nimrod were rivals.
- Sodom and Gomorrah razed to the ground (GEN 19:1–29). Ruins buried in brimstone (sulfur) and ash have been discovered alongside the Dead Sea and the banks of the Jordan River (circa 1900 BC).
- Code of King Hammurabi engraved on Babylonian stele (circa 1750 BC) detailing laws not dissimilar to the codex of Ur-Nammu (circa 2050 BC), Eshnunna (circa 1930 BC), and Lipit-Ishtar (circa 1860 BC). Laws of Hammurabi also were similar to Mosaic laws (EXO, LEV) established 250 years later (circa 1500 BC), the major difference being the polytheistic versus monotheistic references, respectively.

THE GREAT DEBATE

- Intact Egyptian chariot wheels (circa 1500 BC) covered with coral in the depths of the Red Sea, from the time of Moses and the exodus of the Hebrews (EXO 14:21–26).
- Ruins of outer walls of Jericho (circa 1450 BC) during the time of Joshua, indicating complete collapse (JOS 6:1–21).
- Stele portraying Canaanite god Baal (circa 1350 BC) during the time period of Judge Othniel, who waged war with the Canaanites to eliminate idolatry in Israel (JDG 3:5–10).
- Papyrus (circa 1275 BC) detailing a period of Egyptian history, and describing a series of plagues and the evacuation of the Hebrews (EXO 7—13).
- Palace of Rameses II (circa 1260 BC), descendent of Rameses (GEN 47:11; EXO 1:11; EXO 12:37). Discovery of a treaty between Rameses II and ancient Hittites (EXO 3:8).
- Egyptian stele of Merneptah, son of Rameses II, declaring victory over Israel (circa 1225 BC); this is perhaps the earliest mention of Israel in secular archives.
- Ruins of Hittite capital city (circa 1200 BC) unearthed complete with informative cuneiform tablets, fully debunking a once held notion that Hittites never existed and the writers of the Old Testament invented them.
- King Saul's palace (circa 1025 BC) found at Gibeah (1 SA 10:26); Saul was the first king of Israel (1 SA 9:15—1 SA 10:1).
- Egyptian relief (circa 925 BC) commemorating Shishak's victory over Rehoboam (1 KI 14:25–26), and the ransacking of riches from the temple built by his father, King Solomon.
- Black obelisk of Shalmaneser III (circa 860 BC) records the Assyrian conquest of Israel and portrays kings Jehu and Omri paying homage (1 KI 19:15–19). Historians date the arrival of Jonah into the capital city of Nineveh some thirty years later (JON 3:1–10), after the conquering king had died (circa 825 BC) and the prince had assumed rule; a peace was established that lasted two generations.
- King Ahab's palace (circa 850 BC) found in Samaria (1 KI 16:29–30). Kurkh stele referencing King Ahab and his formidable army (1 KI 22:35–39).
- Moabite basalt stele (circa 840 BC) documenting the wars waged by King Mesha against Omri and Ahab of Israel (2 KI 3:4).

- Assyrian stele (circa 820 BC) commemorating King Jehoash handing over the riches of Israel to Hazael, king of Syria (2 KI 12:18).
- Tel Dan stele from Aram (dated approximately 775 BC) with Aramaic inscription, *House of David* (2 SA 3:1). A rare find as there are few ancient references to King David.
- Jasper seal of Amos (circa 740 BC), a prophet and scribe (AMO 1—9).
- Cuneiform record of Assyrian king Tiglath-Pileser III (circa 725 BC) mentioning military engagements in the land of Naphtali (2 KI 15:29–30) during the reign of Hoshea (2 KI 17:1–2).
- Royal seal with the names King Hezekiah and his father Ahaz (2 KI 16:20).
- Sennacherib prism, a clay obelisk found among the ruins of his palace in Nineveh (circa 710 BC), documents the Assyrian king's siege on Lachish (and other fortified cities) during the reign of Hezekiah, king of Judah (2 KI 18:13–36). It declares that Hezekiah was confined inside the walls of Jerusalem; in the biblical account, Sennacherib did not attack Jerusalem because his army was decimated by the angel of the Lord. This is the same timeframe when Hezekiah's chief prophet Isaiah foretold the coming of Messiah, his birth, ministry, assassination, and resurrection (ISA 7:14; ISA 9:6; ISA 35:5–6; ISA 50:6; ISA 53:1–12; ISA 60:6).
- Capital city of Nineveh unearthed in 1840s revealing dynasties of Tiglath-Pileser (2 KI 16:10), Sennacherib (2 KI 19:15–36), and Sargon (ISA 20:1).
- Siloam tunnel (circa 700 BC) brought water from the Gihon Spring into Jerusalem (2 CH 32:30). Inscription in Hebrew chronicles Hezekiah who commissioned the project (2 KI 20:20). Jesus healed a man blind from birth by instructing him to wash the mud from his eyes in the pool of Siloam (JOH 9:1–7).
- Babylonian clay receipts (circa 600 BC) for tribute payments made by King Jehoiachim to King Nebuchadnezzar (2 KI 24:1,10–17).
- Seals used by Baruch (circa 585) the scribe of the prophet Jeremiah (JER 36:4,32; JER 39:1; JER 45:1). Seal with the impressions of the names Jerucal, and his father Shelemiah (JER 38:1) from the same time period.
- Ishtar Gate (circa 575 BC), reconstructed in Germany from ruins of city built by King Nebuchadnezzar. The prophet Daniel interpreted the king's dream about the future demise of Babylon and the subsequent empires to follow: Media-Persia, Greece, and Rome (DAN 2; DAN 4:30–31).

- Babylonian clay cylinders (circa 550 BC) mentioning King Nabonidus, and his son Belshazzar, descendants of Nebuchadnezzar. Also, stele of Nabonidus worshipping the moon god. Daniel interpreted the writing on the wall for Belshazzar, declaring that the fall of Babylon to the Medes and Persians was looming; the king was slain that same night and the kingdom changed hands (DAN 5:1–31).
- Clay cylinder found among the ruins of Babylon (circa 540 BC), noting Persian King Cyrus permitting the return of exiles to Jerusalem (2 CH 36:22–23; EZR 1:1–2). Isaiah prophesied the return of the exiles and the restoration of the temple, mentioning Cyrus by name almost two centuries in advance of that event (ISA 44:28—45:1).
- Artifacts documenting Cyrus's conquest of Babylon and defeat of Nabonidus; also, Cyrus's mausoleum (circa 530 BC) located in Iran.
- Palace of King Xerxes (aka Ahasuerus) at Persepolis (circa 500 BC), one of the capitals of Persia. His favored queen was Esther (EST 1—2). Relief discovered among the ruins depicting Darius the Great and his son Xerxes.
- The tomb of Esther and Mordecai (EST 1—10) is a popular shrine in Susa (aka Shushan), Iran (Persia). This city was the location of Xerxes's main capital (EST 1:1–5). Tomb of Daniel (attributed) also located in Susa.
- Palace of Artaxerxes (circa 375 BC), son of Xerxes (EZR 4:7–11).
- Pool of Bethesda where Jesus healed a lame man (JOH 5:2–9), described to have five porches and twin pools (circa third century BC). It is still a popular tourist attraction in Jerusalem.
- Dead Sea Scrolls (circa 250 BC to AD 70) preserved in clay jars (see 2 CO 4:5–12) found during 1940s and onward, containing almost the entire Old Testament, plus additional documents written in Hebrew. Includes the oldest intact copy of the book of Isaiah (99 percent identical to current Hebrew version and dated to 125 BC).
- Aqueduct and Port built by King Herod the Great (MAT 2:1) in Caesarea (circa 35 BC); Citadel of Herodion, a fortress and palace built by Herod in Judean desert south of Jerusalem (circa 25 BC).
- Ruins of the city Tiberias (circa 15 BC) along the coast of the Sea of Galilee (JOH 6:1,23), built by Herod Antipas (aka Herod the tetrarch) (MAT 14:1–6; MAR 6:14–22). Coins bearing the names of Herod, his son Herod Antipas, and his grandson Herod Agrippa I (ACT 25—26).

- The names "Tiberius" [emperor of Rome], and [Pontius] "Pilate Prefect of Judea" (MAT 27:1–2) carved in rock (circa AD 30), found among the ruins of Caesarea (MAR 8:27–28).
- First century fishing boat that emerged from mud along the banks of a receding Sea of Galilee (MAT 3:18–20).
- Bone evidence of crucified victim from first century Jerusalem complete with nail still embedded in the heel (PSA 22:16–18; JOH 20:19–30).
- Blood evidence on Shroud of Turin of a crucified victim bearing Christ-like wounds on the hands, feet, side, head, and back. Sudarium of Oviedo is a head cloth with blood stains matching the wounds on the shroud (JOH 20:6–7).
- Ossuary (circa AD 50) of Caiaphas the high priest (MAT 26:3) discovered in Israel in 1990. Along with his bones were Roman nails of the type used for crucifixion (possibly from Jesus's crucifixion).
- Stone inscription naming "Proconsul Sergius Paulus," who was mentored by the likes of Paul, Barnabas, and Mark and who maintained his faith despite being coerced by a sorcerer to recant (ACT 13:6–12).
- Coins bearing the name of Roman governor Felix (circa AD 54) to whom St. Paul presented his witness and defense (ACT 23:14—ACT 24:27).
- Stone nameplate bearing the inscription "Erastus Commissioner of Public Works," who became an associate of Paul while visiting Corinth (ACT 19:22; ROM 16:23; 2 TI 4:20).
- First century ossuary discovered in Israel with the Aramaic inscription "James, son of Joseph, brother of Jesus" (MAT 13:53–56), authenticated in 2002. James became the leader of the Christian church in Jerusalem (ACT 21:17–18; 1 CO 15:1–8; GAL 1:18–19); he was martyred around AD 62, an event document by Josephus a few decades later.
- Ruins of Miletus, near Ephesus where Paul preached (ACT 20:15–17).
- Ruins of the ancient cities of Ephesus, Pergamos, Smyrna, Thyatira, Sardis, Philadelphia, and Laodicea. St. John sent to each church an original copy of the book of Revelation (REV 2—3).
- Demolition of the temple in Jerusalem in the year AD 70, during the sacking of Jerusalem by Roman emperor Titus; Jesus predicted this event almost forty years earlier (MAR 13:1–2; LUK 21:5–6,24). The event is commemorated with the Arch of Titus in Rome, and mourned in Israel every summer at the Wailing Wall which is all that remains of that temple.

The most credible evidence one can find to certify the accuracy of history is eyewitness testimony. St. Luke diligently set out to identify and interview primary sources to ensure his research was truthful, reliable, verifiable, and precise (LUK 1:1–4). Luke was able to establish many facts not reported in other New Testament books; he reported numerous names, places, and incidents enabling cross-referencing with internal and external sources. Scholars regard Luke as a topnotch historian for accuracy and thoroughness (Marshall, 1982; Ramsay, 1915; Greenleaf, 1874). Luke identified the following officials to establish the exact timeframe of important occurrences; this adds further credibility to the Bible's historical accuracy as these men and their lofty posts in government have been attested.

➤ Jesus's birth (LUK 2:1–2): Caesar Augustus emperor of Rome, and Cyrenius (aka Quirinius) governor of Syria.
➤ Jesus's ministry (LUK 3:1–2): Tiberius Caesar; Pontius Pilate governor of Judea; Herod tetrarch of Galilee, Philip tetrarch of Ituraea, Lysanias tetrarch of Abilene; Annas and Caiaphas high priests in Jerusalem.

The historical evidence is overwhelming, not just about the worship of God but also the coming of Jesus Christ the Messiah. In fact, no credible historian denies that Jesus lived, was crucified, died, and was buried. They might dispute the resurrection, but even that event has a great deal of testimony and documentation to confirm that it happened. Try as they will, numerous atheists, scientists, and outside religious leaders downplay the resurrection, by advancing laws of physics or divergent historical accounts. Those who denounce Christ do so despite the dominance of facts to the contrary; their positions have been sufficiently discredited but they cannot let go. So, they propose wild theories that contradict the evidence; in particular, it wasn't Jesus, he didn't die, the whole event was faked, or the body was stolen. Details on this matter will be presented in The Resurrection section.

In conclusion, a plethora of historically validated facts exist concerning Jesus life, as well as countless other events recorded in the Old and New Testaments (Geisler and Turek, 2004; Habermas, 1993). The best proof of all is the resurrection of Jesus Christ (ACT 17:31). Without that, Christians have no religion; it all hinges on Jesus's victory over sin and death. Substantiation for the resurrection of Christ and the circumstances accompanying that holiest of weeks include the historical fact of Jesus's birth, ministry, arrest, crucifixion, and entombment; the stone being removed and the tomb found empty, but for the burial cloths which were separated and folded; the Roman guards abandoning their posts, and the fact that doubters never produced a body, while government and priestly officials conspired to conceal the incident by bribing the guards; the multitude of eyewitnesses that saw Jesus alive, many of whom related their experience which was passed along, to the degree that this communication is still available today; the numerous non-Christian accounts of the event; the fact that many people went to their deaths proclaiming Jesus's resurrection and still do; the canonization of scripture and adoption of Catholicism under the auspices of the Roman empire; the change in people's lives then and now, and the fact that there are more Christians than any other religion; and the proof that the rest of the Bible, Old and New Testaments alike, is historically accurate and reliable. Incidentally, many prominent Jews, Romans, and Greeks converted to Christianity because they became convinced of Jesus's majesty; a few of these narratives are cited below.

- Pharisees: Nicodemus and Joseph of Arimathea, who buried Jesus in a newly cut tomb (JOH 19:38–42).
- Paul: formerly Saul, a Pharisee trained by the renowned Gamaliel (ACT 5:34; ACT 22:3). Paul persecuted and murdered Christians (ACT 7:58–60; ACT 9:1–8) before being personally called by Christ (ROM 1:1); Paul authored most of the New Testament (NT) epistles.
- Half-brothers of Jesus: James and Judah both of whom wrote epistles in the NT (MAT 13:53–57; MAR 3:31–35; MAR 6:3; JAM 1:1–4; JDE 1:1–2).
- Roman centurions, one whose servant was healed, another who witnessed the crucifixion of Christ, and a third who had a vision that Peter would come to his home and preach the Gospel (MAT 8:5–13; MAT 27:50–54; ACT 10:1–48).
- Dionysius who was a Greek judge (ACT 17:16–34).

The Bible as an Authority on Science

Scientists have been unable to repudiate the Bible in spite of concerted efforts to do just that. Although they have submitted themes of contention, the Bible has prevailed. Dedicated scientists seek truth, and will not fudge the data, spin the evidence, or alter the facts, as their primary objective is to discover facts and uncover trends. Consequently, many scientists have adopted a deistic or theistic approach precisely because the preponderance of the evidence implies intelligent design in the universe and in all lifeforms. And while some continue to search for a theory of everything, many concede that God is the best explanation for everything. Moreover, there is an inherent limitation of science for explaining nonmaterial or metaphysical phenomena, to include conscious awareness, morality, logic, spirituality, and the supernatural. But while scientists are ill equipped to explain God, Christianity, faith, and religion, the Bible is often quite adept in explaining science. To illustrate, many descriptions in the Bible are remarkably in agreement with the following scientific disciplines, theories, and findings.

- Archaeology (see the preceding section on Bible history).
- Astronomy: Celestial bodies, the composition of space, and astronomical phenomena are revealed in the Bible to include configurations of constellations, arrangement of planets, reason for seasons, and vastness of the heavens (GEN 1:14–15). Review more on this topic in the Physics and Cosmology bullet below. Noteworthy scientists and astronomers also were highlighted in the Bible as follows.
  - Daniel, Shadrach, Meshach, and Abednego were men of knowledge and science (DAN 1:1–21), selected by King Nebuchadnezzar of Babylon to learn, teach, and advise.
  - The three wise men (magi) were astronomers, magicians, and historians who were fascinated by the Star of Bethlehem (MAT 2:1–12). It is possible the star was produced via successive alignments of Saturn and Jupiter: spring 7 BC; winter 7 BC; spring 6 BC; autumn 6 BC. Another reasonable suggestion from the second century was a comet, large and rare with a long tail, may have been present during the same timeframe. A supernova also has been suggested (5 BC). Of course, God could have produced supernatural events that will never happen again. Either way, the Persian magi were drawn to Jerusalem as a result of an unusual astronomical phenomenon believed to be a portent in fulfillment of prophecy, with which they were well-acquainted (NUM 24:10–19; DAN 2:36–48; DAN 9:24–27).
- Geology and hydrology are evident in the precise descriptions of terrain and topography, concomitant with the travels of the patriarchs and prophets. Further, there is considerable explanation of the forces of water, air, earth, and fire.
  - Catastrophes have been recorded throughout history like the great flood, solar eclipses, and various earthquakes, some of which occurred simultaneously with significant events in the Bible: Israelites crossing the Jordan River on dry land (JOS 4:5–10); fall of Jericho (JOS 6); and rolling away of Jesus's tombstone (MAT 28:2).

Both an earthquake and an eclipse may have occurred during the crucifixion of Christ (MAT 27:54) as reported by Josephus.
- The fossil record from the Cambrian explosion indicates a multitude of unique lifeforms bursting forward, impugning the theory of macroevolution. Massive numbers of lifeforms emerged possessing seed and DNA able to reproduce only within kinds (GEN 1:11–12,20–25).
- Wind cycles, sea currents, and shipping channels are described (PSA 8:8; PSA 18:15; PSA 77:16–19; ECC 1:6–7).
- Sequences, states, and movements of water (vapor, liquid, solid; evaporation, rain, freezing) are explained (JOB 26:5–12; JOB 28:22–27; JOB 36:26–30; JOB 37:9–11; PSA 135:6–7; JER 10:13); plus, the dividing of waters during Earth's adolescence, and the connection between lightning and thunder (JOB 38:25–28).
- Air has weight (JOB 28:24–25).
- Springs of water underground; fountains beneath the seas are recognized (GEN 7:11; JOB 38:4–16). Water covered the earth before the mountains emerged and the land and oceans shaped the boundaries (PSA 104:5–9).

➢ Geography is broadly introduced in the Bible, such as the lay of the land, bodies of water, cities, cultures, and societies throughout the Middle East and beyond, enabling mapping and navigation. Here is a sampling.
- Dawn of civilization in the valley between the Tigris (aka Hiddekel) and Euphrates rivers, where the Garden of Eden was situated (GEN 2:10–15).
- Fertile Crescent which Abraham passed through on his way from Ur to Egypt (GEN 12:1–10).
- Israelites crossing the Red Sea and into the Sinai desert (EXO 12–16), prior to fording the Jordan River, defeating Canaanite peoples and destroying their fortified cities.
- The travels of St. Paul were extensive and well documented, as were the fates of Christ's apostles who took the Gospel to the far reaches of the earth (MAT 28:18–20). Their journeys and demise are outlined in worldly historical collections.
- Israel and the Holy Land mapped with precision.
- The Mediterranean and surrounding territories historically verified.

➢ Biology and Medicine: Most people are unaware of the wealth of information provided in the Bible on these subjects.

- Flora, fauna, and phyla are comprehensively described in order of appearance, with humans arriving last; four classifications of phyla are acknowledged: men, beasts, birds, and fish (1 CO 15:39). Pasteur's law of biogenesis established, whereby living things come from other living things via reproduction, which contradicts Darwin's theory of the origin of the species but agrees with the Bible (see GEN 1 and following).
- The sun makes plants grow and turn green via photosynthesis and chlorophyll (JOB 8:16).
- Irreducible complexity (JOB 10:9–12; PSA 139:14; PRO 20:12) is found in all lifeforms, particularly evident in DNA; case in point is the single-celled bacterial flagellum, a machine resembling an outboard motor. Such intricacy cannot occur from incremental changes in an organism because the apparatus will not function with any part missing (Behe, 2006). Systems do not evolve part by part; they are complete assemblies. Complexity of design is evident in the cosmos, solar system, earth, and within even the most rudimentary lifeforms (Dembsky, 1998). Consider the human brain, consisting of billions of neurons and hundreds of billions of interconnections, with a computing capacity of two million bits per second (Carson, 2014). This advanced complexity has been apparent since humans arrived on the scene and is proof that we are exceptional among God's creations above all lifeforms found on Earth (GEN 1:28; ECC 2:13).
- Medical knowledge was quite advanced: sanitation, blood-borne pathogens, parasites, quarantine, contagious diseases (LEV 13:45–46; LEV 17:11–15; LEV 23:12–13; NUM 19:22).
- Man was formed from dust/stardust (GEN 2:7; GEN 3:19; ECC 3:20; ISA 40:12). For example, exploding stars emit necessary heavy elements found in your daily multivitamins.

➢ Sociology is evident in discussions of industry, commodities, trade, currency, communities, civilizations, governments, laws, politics, and rulers. Some interesting political facts surrounding the birth and death of Christ have been verified as stated in the four Gospels.
- Provincial census and tax collection in Judea (circa 6 BC).
- King Herod's obituary (circa 4 BC).
- Pontius Pilate, governor of Judea in office (circa AD 26–36).
- Caiaphas, Jewish high priest in office (circa AD 18–37).

- Physics and Cosmology: This category is perhaps the most surprising insofar as many relatively recent scientific discoveries were understood millennia ago by some of the writers of the Bible.
  - The universe began in an instant (big bang theory): the beginning of time, space, energy, and matter. It has been proven repeatedly that the universe is not steady-state or eternal, and it is still expanding (Hubble, 1929). These facts were predicted by Einstein in his theory and equation of general relativity (first published in 1915), in the discovery of cosmic microwave background radiation (Penzias and Wilson, 1965), in the laws of thermodynamics, and in the Bible (GEN 1:1; MAR 10:6–8; JOH 1:1–3; TIT 1:1–3; 2 PE 3:4). Because the universe began to exist, an external cause is necessary, since the cause for the universe cannot be the universe itself; even multiverse theorists suggest an external cause, like an unlimited universe generator, since they accept that our universe had a starting point. God could be a universe generator could he not?
  - Layers of atmosphere are depicted (GEN 1:6–10; DEU 10:14; PSA 148:4–5; AMO 9:6).
  - Forming of the earth and heavens consistent with scientific theory (GEN 1:6–10; PRO 8:22–30; ISA 51:13; JER 51:15–16; ZEC 12:1).
  - Innumerable stars of varying magnitude exist, more than the eye can see (GEN 15:5; JER 33:22; 1 CO 15:41). The current estimate by cosmologists is that there are approximately 200–300 billion stars in the Milky Way galaxy (GEN 22:17) and there are approximately 200–300 billion galaxies in the universe (PSA 19:1; ISA 40:26); one can infer an estimated 40–90 septillion possible stars (add 21 more zeroes). And each star is unique from all others (1 CO 15:40–41).
  - An empty place at due north is relatively absent of stars (JOB 26:7), enabling humans to view outer space.
  - Circular shape of the earth and horizon were obvious to many ancients; no true scholar would have supposed the earth to be flat (JOB 26:10; ISA 40:21–26). [Note that the book of Job just referenced is deemed by many biblical scholars to be the oldest OT book.]
  - Gravity, mutual attractions between heavenly bodies, magnetism, and the fixed movements of celestial bodies in concert with one another are surmised (JOB 38:18–38; ISA 48:13; JER 31:35).

- The universe is expanding, indicating the unlimited capacity for space (JOB 9:4–9; JOB 37:18; ISA 40:12; ISA 42:5; ISA 45:12; JER 10:12–13).
- Entropy and heat death (eventual passing away of heaven and earth) is explained (PSA 102:25–27; PSA 104:1–3; ISA 13:10; ISA 34:4–5; ISA 51:6; JER 4:23–28; MAT 24:35; ROM 8:22; HEB 1:10–11) as well as the ultimate demise of the earth by fire (2 PE 3:10–16).
- Light can be refracted into components or wavelengths (JOB 38:24).
- Fine tuning and precision in universal formations are revealed and the applied physics fixed (JER 33:25–26). The anthropic principle is represented; that is, the universe was designed for life, especially ours (GEN 1:26–30; GEN 2:19; PSA 8:4–8; ISA 46:9–11). The probability that the known constants and factors, over 140 (see Ross, 2001, 2008), would be perfectly calibrated in such a way as to support human life is infinitesimally small (1 over 10 followed by hundreds of zeroes).
- The universe was made from and is comprised of things that cannot be directly observed (perhaps particles, quantum strings and fields, gravity, strong and weak forces, dark energy and dark matter); in other words, things visible and invisible (ISA 43:7; ROM 1:20–21; 1 CO 1:19–31; 2 CO 4:18; COL 1:13–17; HEB 11:3).
- The universe and everything in it are extremely complex, synergistic, inter-reliant, directed, and purposeful, insinuating intelligent design (PSA 148:5; JOH 1:3; ACT 14:15; ACT 17:24; REV 4:11; REV 10:5–6).

➢ Paleontology: The Bible does not mention the word dinosaur, but it describes them. First, there is the behemoth, a gigantic vegetarian with a tail the size of a tree trunk (JOB 40:15–18). Then there is leviathan, a titanic marine animal that cannot be hooked or speared due to its thick scaly hide (JOB 41:1–7; ISA 27:1). The Bible also speaks of dragons in numerous passages (PSA 74:13; JER 51:34; MAL 1:3) which live in the wilds and the waters; one dragon described by Job appears to be fire-breathing (JOB 41:19–31).

Most people are amazed when shown the degree of conformity concerning scientific findings and biblical accounts. The progression of creation days, for instance, portrays a process not unlike the way astrophysicists describe the development of the universe and how celestial bodies melded together. And the Genesis account of the progression of lifeforms emerging on planet Earth follow the same sequence found in fossils, bones, phyla, and DNA.

The laws of physics, mathematics, biology, and chemistry coincide with our observations of the orderliness of nature, and can be discovered and comprehended in the consciousness of an inquisitive mind, all of which can be stored in a brain that weighs but a few pounds. How can anyone not be enchanted by this complexity, coordination, synchronization, symbiosis, fine tuning, and specification? It is even more of a marvel that we can actually understand and explain these phenomena.

The law of cause and effect, one of the most fundamental in the field of science in general and physics in particular, favors there being a superior intelligence behind creation. The concept of causality rests on the fact that something that begins to exist must have an associated cause. The cosmological argument holds that the universe had a beginning; so, it could not have come from nothingness because a causal agent is required. The teleological argument poses that, if the universe was caused, it must have been designed that way, probably to support life. The ontological argument upholds the idea of life coming from life, as opposed to springing out of some primordial soup and evolving, or rather leaping into beings of superior intelligence. The epistemological argument would follow that advanced intelligence, discernment, reasoning, understanding, and knowledge cannot be accounted for by nature alone, as humans arrived on the scene already possessing these capabilities.

The universe must have a living executor, as it did not cause itself; and that includes all lifeforms abiding herein. The way we know that we know is through God and his Word. Consequently, heavenly bodies, laws and constants, energy, time, matter, and living creatures came into existence by the will of a being far more excellent than we are. And that creator bestowed upon us intelligence, morality, and freedom proving we are special to God; and he wants us to seek him and connect with him in spirit, truth, and love.

Summary: I have reviewed at length some historical and scientific data. Interestingly, the arguments for God match up with the arguments against God. Which position is most in line with the facts just presented? Clearly, the evidence makes a splendid case for the Bible being true. Collectively, the data appear to defeat the counterargument. That is, there is more proof to confirm God's existence than to refute it. But the critics often concentrate on missing data; that is, while there is an abundance of confirmatory evidence, archaeologists have yet to find proof of every single person, place, and event recorded in the Bible. This is their case. Is that reasonable? No, it is not. You may have heard the statement, "absence of evidence does not point to evidence of absence." So have the doubters. Lack of evidence does not prove or suggest that evidence does not exist. When historians and scientists uncover pieces of evidence from the past, they are exactly that: pieces. Seldom is it possible to retrieve the full exhibit; and rarely are all the components recovered to complete the picture, edifice, skeleton, or artifact. But sometimes there are enough pieces to the puzzle to make a case, as might be presented in a court proceeding, enough to surpass reasonable doubt.

Further, it is understood in archaeological communities that many empires, dynasties, and monarchs (Egyptian and Assyrian especially) purposefully destroyed records of defeats in battle, removed things built by predecessors, and otherwise spun the data to look favorably upon themselves. Yes, even back then, those in power deliberately obfuscated evidence, disseminated propaganda, obstructed justice, and advanced false narratives. It stands to reason that there will be gaps in the archives; it is expected. But a great deal of the evidence has survived, thanks to God. Someday, there will be proof of every word God has spoken; for the scoffers it will be too late.

Causality

What caused God? Believe it or not, this is actually one of the reservations that atheists submit, as if they had an inkling who God really is. Besides, if they didn't believe in God why would they ask that question in the first place? The objective of such narrowminded idiocy is to belittle God, by ascribing to him attributes that could not possibly apply to God or any reasonable conception of a supreme being.

During causal assessment, the analyst attempts to systematically trace effects back to causes and continually reduces the data to determine where the chain started. But the only logical conclusion of reductionism is there must necessarily be an original cause or a beginning. It is conceptually illegitimate to assume one can discover preceding causes ad infinitum; there would never be a resolution. It would be more logical to assume a first cause than an infinite number of causes; but the first cause must be an entity unto itself. The reductionists look for a root cause in the existence of things. But the unavoidable finale is that there needs to be an uncaused first cause when it comes to a Creator God.

Materialists lean exclusively on observable effects from the physical world, totally neglecting the fact that much of what we observe may have an immaterial cause. Naturalists dismiss the supernatural as not real and not a cause. The postmodernists assert that there are no absolutes, and therefore, no cause or meaning other than personally ascribed. All these camps would disallow the spiritual domain precisely because it cannot be measured, reduced, defined, or observed with the five senses. There are two possibilities: it is either an infinite state of time, matter, and energy or an infinite God behind it all. But astrophysicists have proven that time and matter had a beginning; our universe is finite. Therefore, the latter must be true, that God does exist.

Scientists cannot explain a great many phenomena in the universe. For example, they are unable to define energy, light, or gravity succinctly, much less trace their origin or composition; they only can describe the observed effects or properties. Such is the spiritual domain of God, and we can see the effects of his creative prowess; the simplest conclusion to the Christian is God did it. But the scientific theory still used to explain away God is evolution, though that theory has long been abandoned, particularly due to a lack of fossil evidence which was Darwin's dilemma from the start (Sunderland, 1988). The fossil record unveils an explosion of lifeforms, during which an estimated 75 percent of the phyla extant on our planet emerged quite quickly, geologically speaking (Meyer, 2013). This evidence actually supports the biblical narrative (GEN 1:20–26). It also bolsters Darwin's greatest fear that scientists would never uncover fossils to back his theory of sequential, progressive evolution over a very long period.

Proof that the universe has not been around forever is clear to all modern cosmologists. Things that begin must have a cause, which could be natural or intelligent. But since nature cannot cause itself the cause must be intelligent or supernatural, or both. Since time cannot start time, it assumes a timeless timekeeper. Because life is required to create life, there had to be intelligent life to begin with. Such intelligence must be extraordinarily advanced, greater than any known to exist on Earth. There is only one explanation: God is the uncaused first cause, who exists outside of time, nature, and space.

One God can explain everything, and the cause for everything, such that what we see did not emerge from nothing, but from someone greater who we cannot see. And we can recognize and also get to know this God. Even the physicists will grant that the world is built from features we can't see like electrons, photons, waves, dark matter, energy, etc. But what caused those things? Did they launch forward from nothing? Try to define nothing. One would have to believe in miracles to think that everything came from nothing. Oh, but naturalists, materialists, reductionists, and postmodernists deny miracles. But then, they violate another fundamental principle of logic and physics which is the law of noncontradiction. Essentially, atheist-scientists are a contradiction unto themselves; the phrase itself is an oxymoron. To believe that everything is the product of mindless, unguided processes is to espouse a position that such theories are equally mindless and unguided. It stands to reason that one cannot take an atheistic scientist seriously, nor can they take themselves seriously. They are engaging in what C.S. Lewis (1946) tagged, "intellectual dishonesty" which is a betrayal of science. Take the words of Isaac Newton, "Atheism is so senseless and odious to mankind that it never had many professors."

How are we to conceptualize the intricacy inherent in the universe? It is beyond our comprehension. Only acumen beyond the composite of humanity can invent one; we scarcely have begun to understand it. Science is in its infancy in terms of identifying the various laws and constructs that permit the universe to occur and be sustained. It wasn't long ago when scientists first described the complexity of life illustrated in our DNA, the sophisticated double helix. The information database in the human genome consists of roughly 3.1 billion base-pairs. How do you get that much information to merge in the right order via unguided processes? Hoyle (1983) calculated the probability of 2000 proteins comprising 200 amino acids being randomly arranged into a living entity to be $p < 10^{-40,000}$. It would be more likely that a tornado sweeping through a junkyard could produce a jet airliner, he jested.

All of creation, particularly life, speaks of intelligent design (Meyer, 2009). Even many scientists are getting on board with that notion; they just don't want to speak the "God" word for fear of embarrassment or retaliation (notwithstanding the so-called Higgs-boson, nicknamed the "God particle" which unlike other subatomic particles gives mass to matter). The fine tuning of the whole shebang intimates that the universe was designed precisely to support life (Davies, 2007; Hawking, 1996). This is the basic premise of the anthropic principle (Carter, 1974): it is all intended for people (ISA 45:18). And the lack of apparent change, or uniformity, is so that it doesn't vary this way or that, which could mean death to us all. It is so beautiful, synchronous, specialized, elaborate, contiguous, calibrated, and enduring that it is inexplicable without a causal agent.

Things Not Seen

Why would anybody believe in a God that hides himself? So say unbelievers. They refuse to accept God because they cannot prove that he exists; or if he does exist, he doesn't seem to want to have anything to do with us. These people are either agnostic or deist; they follow the previous weak argument concerning lack of proof. They make assumptions about God that are not true, such as he doesn't reveal himself, he can't be bothered, he is just observing, he will not or cannot intervene, or humans are unable to have a relationship with him. The opposite is true for all these propositions because God has revealed himself in his creation (PSA 78:32; ROM 1:17–20), in the Bible (EXO 3:14; HEB 1:1–2: 2 PE 1:21), and through his Son Jesus Christ (ISA 9:6; JOH 1:14; 1 CO 2:10; COL 1:15–17). God wants all people to come to him and be saved (EZE 18:27–32; 1 TI 2:3–4; 2 PE 3:9). God is invested in us and he is involved in our lives (JER 29:11; JOH 1:12; 1 PE 3:18). God wants to fellowship with us and establish an intimate bond that lasts forever (JOH 15:5; ACT 17:27; PHP 2:13–15; 1 JO 4:10; REV 3:20).

God placed eternity into the hearts of everybody (ECC 3:11). The earth is filled with the knowledge of him (HAB 2:14). The problem with people who suppose God is hidden is they haven't made a serious attempt to look for him (MAT 7:7–8). If you believe in your heart that there is no God, without checking it out, you are foolish (PSA 14:1). God asks that we love him with all our heart, mind, and soul (DEU 6:9; MAT 22:37). Those who do not think in their minds that God exists have turned away from him (JER 17:5). They'd prefer that God didn't exist; that way they won't have to feel obliged to him (Nagel, 1997). What an imposition, to have to report to God. That is one of the main reasons people reject God; they do not want to be held accountable to God or anyone, not even their own conscience. They don't want God, they don't need God, and if they did believe in God, they wouldn't like him or want to be with him. They would just as soon God stayed hidden, if indeed he does exist. But it is they who mask God from themselves (2 CO 4:3–4).

Another argument along these lines is there are many who will never be told or learn about God because they live in remote areas of the world. It is not fair for God to be available to some people but not others. God should not condemn someone to hell just for being ignorant. To make such statements, a person would themselves have been told or informed. So how did they find out about God? And how do they know that people in remote areas of the globe never have and never will learn about God or find him (JER 29:13; MAT 24:14)? If God is as great as he says he is, can't he find them (ACT 8:26–40; ACT 10:1–48)? If they seek God, and truly want to know him, they will find evidence of him everywhere (ROM 1:20; HEB 11:6). One can see evidence just by looking into the mirror (GEN 1:26; PSA 8:4–6). It isn't rocket science to gaze into the heavens and be awestruck; and it isn't a great a leap of faith to wonder if there is a creator behind it all. And it takes very little effort to speak to God or ask him questions; and it is not a stretch to assume that such a powerful being as God can hear prayers and respond to them in accordance with his will. And if your prayers, wishes, or dreams come true that surely would amplify your faith, and possibly stimulate more prayers. Before you know it, you could actually develop a relationship with the Almighty by talking to him, and listening to him through his Word, and his answers to your prayers; and by worshipping with fellow believers in a solid evangelical church, receiving instruction from people trained in biblical theology.

Anybody can figure this out on his or her own (TIT 2:11). But if they did not have the capacity, do you think God would condemn people simply because they were mentally impaired, too young, or otherwise innocent (JOB 4:7; ISA 7:14–16; LUK 18:15–17)? Seeking God and loving God are choices available to anyone who can seek and love. If an intelligent person prefers to disregard God, or do it their own way and not be concerned about God's way, that is their prerogative. Given that all people have a brain, a conscience, the ability to reason and love, and a full array of sensory-perceptual faculties, it follows that those who ignore God or dismiss him are fully aware they have made their choice. They do not want God, or to know God, or to find him at all, much less live with him for eternity. And God will honor these choices.

What do you tell someone who thinks God is hidden? Well, consider the spread of Christianity throughout the world. It started with Jesus who appointed his twelve apostles and then Paul; they preached the Gospel to the world, speaking the native language of the populace where they were called (MAT 28:18–20; MAR 16:17). That could count as a miracle I should think. They went to their graves proclaiming Christ, as do all Christians; but the grave will not keep them. Even in countries known to persecute Christians, the faith has spread. It is now the fastest growing religion in places like China, India, and a few Muslim countries. The notion that remote localities inhibit the ability to discover God is a tenuous one, given that it was in a remote place where Christianity originally gained traction. Besides, people in cities, suburbs, remote countries, the boondocks, and even tribal recluses in the middle of nowhere are human enough to observe, reason, and wonder. God has a way of getting his Word out and using people of God to do it. Like the apostles, you can find missionaries in the most distant locales on the globe. As a result, many primitive tribes have come to believe and worship.

Yes, a lot of people reject the good news, and some are spiteful toward Christians who are being persecuted, banished, and butchered all over the place. But they persevere and continue to outnumber other religions (between a quarter and a third of the world's population). All a witness can do is try to illuminate others, and if not accepted, simply move on (MAT 10:14–16). Have you ever met an atheist that would travel to remote areas of the world in order to proselytize people into their belief system? Would they risk death defending their faith? Well, they do anyway, whether they know it or not.

Why shouldn't God keep his distance? We know he watches us, but does he have to be visibly present all the time? It would be like a parent that hovers over his or her child to the degree that the child would constantly be nervous and reluctant to say or do anything for fear of being reprimanded. I used to do research for the government and noticed that military personnel performed a lot better when their commanders were not scrutinizing their every move. While being monitored by evaluators, operators concentrated on preventing any errors; and although their accuracy was fair, their responses or decisions were not timely. It's like when someone is watching me use a keyboard; I try to type at the same speed but I make considerably more typographic errors, and both speed and accuracy decline. Constant supervision may be effective to instill discipline, like when I was in the army and the drill sergeants hovered over us like vultures. But who would be able to love God or their parents if they were never given any freedom, responsibility, respect, or trust? Did you ever have a parent, employer, or spouse that constantly kept you under surveillance? That situation only harbors suspicion and rebellion. Yes, God keeps tabs on us, but he is very discreet about it. Like a loving parent, God allows us to explore, try things on our own, and learn things the hard way; he disciplines us only when we have crossed the line or strayed too far. He is not exclusively authoritarian or overly permissive; and he accepts us and loves us without fail, without condition, and without end.

THE GREAT DEBATE

It is resolved that God cannot hide, because he is omnipresent. Actually, the contention of hiddenness seems more applicable to the staunch scientist who believes that science and religion are somehow incompatible or mutually exclusive. Yet their theories propose a great number of objects that are hidden if not invisible such as quantum particles, exotic matter, black holes, dark energy, and nuclear forces. They believe in things not seen more vehemently than many Christians. You can see God in the man Jesus Christ. You can appreciate the character of God revealed in his Word. You can see the results of his love for life in his creation. The physicist may counter with the claim that you can see the effects of quantum mechanics or forces weak and strong. Then how is it so difficult for them to notice the effects of God?

The most bizarre explanations for immaterial entities like the mind, consciousness, and self-awareness have been tendered, the favorite being unguided chemical processes. Really? Species reconstitute their DNA in order to jump into a completely different lifeform, without the intervention of any intelligence at all, okay? What is hidden from these imbeciles is not God, it is the truth which they have distorted beyond recognition. Proponents have to take the data and chop out the part they don't like and jam something else into the void that doesn't quite fit, producing a pseudo truth that looks like a confabulated heap of missing pieces. They cannot distinguish mind from brain; the brain is a computer with no programmer, you see. I guess the brain is controlling them with its biochemical processing, and they have no choice concerning what they think. That makes sense. Maybe that's why they run like the devil when you try to present an absolute to them. Conclusive spiritual truth is irritating to their eyes and ears, for it dissolves their reasoning into complete entropy.

Allow me a few words about the mind versus the brain. First of all, they are separate because the former is mental and nonmaterial, and the latter is physical and material. The brain is part of the body. You can hook electrodes to my head, observe and examine brain activity, but you cannot tell me what I am thinking. My mind is the programmer and my brain the processor. The body can sense; and in my brain, I perceive. But with my mind I interpret and decide; and that decision invokes neural events in my brain and body in order to execute a selected response. All of this information is stored on my hard drive and can be retrieved at will using my mind. The mind can create brain patterns, and the patterns can elicit feelings in the body. Unfortunately, when the brain is damaged it disrupts my ability to process, program, and compute; but the psyche, or soul, is not damaged. This phenomenon is evident in dementia (like Alzheimer's) where the sufferer will try but cannot execute, because the wiring is ruined. When a person dies, the body (including the brain) is gone; but not the spirit or the soul. Presence of mind is not physiological, it is cognitive; so, it stands to reason there may be a capability to think outside of the body. In the words of Descartes, "I think, therefore I am." What if the body and the soul are destroyed? The converse would be true: you can't think therefore you are not.

It must be frustrating when theorists are faced with concepts such as mind, awareness, eternity, and infinity. These issues mess with theoretical models concerning the origins of the universe, life, and knowledge. Scientists concoct infinite universes to avoid the idea of an infinite God as the explanation for ours; or assume that life emerged from benign matter, totally defying all physical laws; or propose that an immense amount of time can produce advanced lifeforms from mutations, knowing full well that a mutation mostly produces a defective product; or conclude that thoughts are nothing more than a disturbance among atoms; or suppose that aliens brought life to our planet since the evolution thing bombed, as if they didn't have to explain where the aliens came from; or propose that our universe was the lucky one among trillions, and it had nothing to do with fine tuning or the anthropic principle. Do any of these arguments coincide with the laws of cause-effect and noncontradiction? I think the uncertainty principle fits these points of view, for those believing in such theories do not appear to be certain about anything, much less the source of the universe, or life, or thought. That is to say, uncertainty by definition is nondeterministic, meaning some events simply cannot be predicted or explained. Determinists assert that God was invented to fill in the gaps. But this is absurd, because believers in God maintain that he is responsible for everything, not just the things we cannot explain.

The lack of definition of God is another dispute raised by skeptics, particularly agnostics that believe it impossible to prove or disprove God. There are so many views about God that no two religions define God in the same manner. One must audit the holy books of religions to see how God is described among their followers; often the picture is hazy. But such ambiguity is not found in the Holy Bible where the attributes of God are plainly enumerated with respect to his character and his works. Whereas man tends to define God in terms of human traits, the Bible defines the traits of God to be totally different than those of man, and instead reveals how man has some of God's traits (*Imago Dei*). Hence, the lack of definition argument is not applicable to Christendom. In fact, most anybody, whether deist, theist, or atheist, can list attributes most commonly ascribed to God, the Creator, the Almighty, and the one supreme being, to include omniscience, omnipotence, omnipresence, benevolence, and infiniteness.

Remember the atheist asking, "Who created God?" Obviously, he didn't consider how ridiculous that sounds. Such shallowness illustrates a lack of understanding based on a personal definition of a god that atheists claim does not exist. Nobody with common sense believes the distorted reasoning that an all-powerful Creator needs a creator. Maybe they know, but they don't want to believe, so they attempt to demoralize God, or joke about him, or refuse to take evangelicals seriously, simply to rationalize or to avert their own cognitive dissonance, or otherwise keep God hidden away.

Morality

How can a supreme being allow suffering and evil? This stance deems a compassionate God could never permit such things, and only a vindictive God would condemn people to hell. If you ask atheists who is most responsible for evil, what can they say? Will they concede that it has to be humankind? They can't blame God since they don't believe he is real. Instead, they will try to explain away evil as a consequence of mindless biochemical processes. Or they will argue that morality itself is relative and inconsistent, and likely the invention of people to endorse communalism. They fall back upon the evolution foundation, suggesting how the conscience evolved as a result of the development of civilized societies.

If all thought and subsequent actions were the result of uncontrolled processes, then nothing could be verified as true, including their confounded intellectualizing that all is relative. It is a self-defeating statement to say that absolutes regarding truth and right do not exist. For example, I doubt if they would be okay with me stealing their dog, claiming it was a moral act in my book. The evolution argument is groundless and so is the naturalist position; because you don't see immorality or evil occurring naturally, and you don't see other species acting deliberately sinful. Sin was found in humanity from the start; it is a result of our human nature. Why don't animals have a moral compass? They've had more time to evolve than humans; and they live communally among their own kind. Discernment of right and wrong, and the free will to choose between them, are exclusive to humans. No other physical being on this planet exhibits these capacities.

Then there is the argument that animals suffer naturally, and so do humans, and that would be true. But an animal does not suffer because animals are sinful; they are subject to suffering due to the sinfulness of humans, however. Sin causes most human sufferings. But natural disasters, disease, and death cause suffering also; and the reason they do is because of love. Even animals know how to love; and just like us, animals grieve and feel pain at the loss of a loved one. So does God (JDG 10:15–16; EPH 4:30–32). But only humans originate disasters, pain, and suffering that are unnatural, like pollution, genocide, mass destruction, sexual deviancy, discrimination, and terrorism. To repeat, the problem with sin is that it is only found among humans; it is part of our nature but not found in nature.

Without good there is no way to define evil. Therefore, we must have a standard of goodness and perfection from which to judge what is not good and otherwise imperfect or evil; that standard is God. Thus, the proof of evil favors the existence of God. Since we can choose between good and evil, we know when we are doing wrong and we do it anyway, realizing that negative consequences are likely. We can just as easily choose the good, if we let go and let God.

Let's get back to the problem of suffering and evil, which is more of a problem for the atheist to get around than the theist. The foundation of morality is endless love; all laws and legal systems are based on that absolute. Since we are imperfect beings, we are unequipped to establish a standard of perfection; only a flawless being is capable of that. And since we are the only species on the planet possessing a moral compass, it must be for a reason. Yes, God gave us this knowledge so we would learn to choose the good (namely God). But for us to choose at all we had to be given free will as well. We have the freedom to do it our way or to choose God's way. Either way, it is a conscious and deliberate choice based on one's personal preference. Thus, nobody should be surprised at the outcome, as we learn at an early age via knowledge of results whether something is good or bad; because the outcomes line up with our thoughts, words, and behaviors whether good or bad.

Would the cynics reject law and order also? They believe in the physical laws. How about the moral ones? Both physical and moral laws imply a lawgiver. Humans establish laws, and governments enact legislation. Social laws require a lawmaker or governing body, don't they? Without laws, responsibility, accountability, and punishment the whole of humanity would derail. The argument that morality is relative is typically made by someone who shuns justice and judgment, chooses to do whatever they want regardless of the consequences, or denies faith regarding it a shortcoming reserved for morons. But they have a faith that is based on zippo evidence, which is the definition of blind faith. As for me, I prefer to base my beliefs on real evidence; it helps to remove the doubt.

The central aspect of morality is the intrinsic value of humanity; particularly in God's mind as we are made in his image to be his children. We have been given dominion over God's creation (PSA 8:4–6); that requires we behave responsibly, for we are superior to the other creatures. And there is one superior to us all—God; and we have the privilege of becoming members of his household. We are very important to God and so loved by him that he became one of us precisely to redeem us. How precious can we be to him that he would suffer and die for us? Evil and suffering fell upon Jesus Christ, God's only Son, so it is nonsensical to assert that God ignores evil and suffering. Yes, you are unique, special, called, purposeful, and loved. And because of this, God will destroy sin and suffering, and invite those who adore his Son to live forever in peace (ISA 26:3).

We are thereby commanded to love God first, with all our heart, mind, soul and strength, for his love is perfect with which he loves us unconditionally. We are likewise commanded to love everyone, including ourselves, with the same kind of love God shows to us (MAT 22:35–40). Obviously, we cannot love unconditionally the way God does; otherwise we could fulfill all the laws and do the right thing. If that be the case, we would not require a savior and we would not be subject to judgment (ROM 13:8–10; GAL 5:14). But we are compelled to love and obey; and God will judge us accordingly. God's justice is fair and he will not condemn the innocent, and he will not coerce anyone to obey his commands, and he will not constrain a person to spend eternity with him in heaven. By the way, God does not condemn people because they are sinners; sin causes death for which we all are guilty and must die (EZE 18:20; ROM 6:23). Heaven is for sinners who confess and repent their sins and trust Christ for forgiveness (PRO 28:13; LUK 13:3; ROM 10:9; 1 JO 1:8–9). They enter into heaven blameless (COL 1:20–22), having received the righteousness of Christ in exchange for their sins (2 CO 5:21). Those who go to the other place won't accept this payment so they will pay their own way; call that justice. I will address the dilemma of evil more thoroughly in the next chapter.

Miracles

I have considered the premise that miracles do not occur. Apparently, they do. The argument that there is no such thing as miracles because they cannot be explained in terms of physical or natural processes lacks merit; supposedly, miracles would violate the laws of physics and nature because they cannot be predicted or reproduced. Are there miracles that defy physics? Are there miracles that do not defy physics? I would argue there are miracles that defy the laws of physics and nature, there are miracles that challenge realistic probability, and there are miracles that adhere to nature but are still so awesome they can be considered miraculous. God performs wonders, sometimes people do wondrous things, and sometimes things that cannot be explained happen on rare occasions and may never happen again. One aspect which seems to be common among all these occurrences, is you usually don't know when a miracle is occurring, but possibly afterwards.

Some events adhere to the natural sphere and still can be considered miracles. We can agree that the conception, gestation, and birth of a child is quite amazing. I mean, how is it possible for one sperm cell from a man and one egg cell from a woman to merge together and become one zygote—a marrying of chromosomes defining a unique person? Then it reproduces the configuration countless times, with every new cell containing the exact genetic blueprint, collectively forming into a fully functioning human being. Through the process of meiosis, genetic data are translated into each and every cell as they congregate into organs, limbs, brains, and other parts embodying a matchless living, thriving, and growing child. Trillions of microscopic cells in your body have that sole DNA sequence comprising enough information to fill a library. Okay, this will pass for a miracle. Incidentally, I have just provided a scientific explanation for why I am here. But there is another explanation equally valid that does not contradict the scientific explanation—agency. You see, another reason I am here is because my parents had sex. This implies that life was here before I was.

The universe, nature, living organisms, and basically everything which subsists could be deemed miracles. Artlessly, the atheist would maintain that this is the work of random processes evolving; a combination of time, matter, energy, mutation, and natural selection, none of which can direct anything. Humans appear to be endowed with self-awareness, a moral conscience, the ability to induce and deduce complex issues and solve multifaceted problems, the freedom to choose a future, as well as the knack to figure out how the universe is configured, how the body operates, and how attendant mechanisms function. If such sophisticated machinations and computations were the product of uncontrolled, unguided vehicles there would be no need for meaning or understanding, much less any application for science. Nobody could learn this material; we'd be senseless and disoriented organisms subject to the quirks of nature with no forethought, hope, or purposefulness. So how do the tenacious naturalists, humanists, and materialists explain these phenomena? They don't. And then there are postmodernists determining that all is meaningless, and there is no purpose much less a requisite for one; conclusions like these are truly meaningless, thoughtless, and purposeless.

What about miracles operating outside the laws of nature? Critics would say there is no such thing. They reject Christianity because they have no fondness for Jesus Christ; they cannot demean themselves by believing in God, much less anybody who walks on water, turns water into wine, heals people crippled from birth, or returns alive after being tortured to death (JOH 7:19–23; ACT 2:22–24). But if God is all powerful; he can intercede anytime, anywhere since this is his creation and without him it wouldn't even be here or continue to hold together. The scientists will retort that it is held together by gravity. But they cannot see gravity, explain it, or define it; they can only observe and measure its effects. But they are sure it is there despite the fact that it is not fully understood how it operates. Likewise, I can only understand the power of prayer from the effects; and sometimes the results are miraculous. The only explanation I can muster is God.

Did you know that scientific experiments have replicated over and again the positive results of faith and prayer in healing, including physical, mental, and spiritual? Since this process cannot be observed, I wonder how an atheist would explain that. There is an inherent dilemma, because a miracle cannot be reproduced in a laboratory, and it cannot be inspected scientifically, historically, or forensically. Have you ever experienced a miracle in your life, like someone surviving a disease, accident, or calamity? I have, more than once. In some cases, the miracle may have a deterministic flavor, as in the case of prophecy coming true or healing occurring overnight. But how can one trace preexisting conditions that would account for water instantaneously being turned into wine? There is no way to duplicate that event without the power of God.

If an obstinate atheist, hedonist, or psychopath converts to Christianity, could that indicate a miracle? Can the bad become good? I deem my conversion a miracle, given the number of times I've fallen and Christ has picked me up and dusted me off. Do you never wonder what is out there? Can't there be more than we actually perceive? Is there a greater reality than this one? Does nothing compel you to search and find out what's up (see Metaxas, 2015)?

Then there is quantum theory, where all things seen come from the unseen, which can neither be observed, measured, nor fully explained. Where subatomic little boogers can be in more than one place at one time, and they can be both a wave and a particle, and it is uncertain where they are going, and you cannot locate one and know its movement, or vice-versa. Okay, that sounds like an explanation that necessitates faith in a controller or cause. This would make the quantum physicist religious by his or her own definition, as the tenets are actually less provable than God's existence. If the universe really does function at the quantum level, with particles, fields, strings, singularities, and eleven dimensions of space and time, that would surely be a miracle as these conditions do not adhere to the same physical laws as the rest of the universe. The scientific explanation of the big bang also sounds like a miracle; the universe and everything in it sprang from nothing all by itself, or maybe from some obscure quantum vacuum fluctuation; however, this suggests that a quantum vacuum is something, not nothing. It takes a great deal of faith to believe such contrivances; probably more than it does to trust God. But they shun faith as a weakness, how ironic.

Let us turn our attention to the phenomenon dubbed *singularity* for a moment. Depending on how the term is applied it could be construed many ways. But in all cases, whether we are talking physics, mathematics, or technology, it is a unique event or outcome, not replicable, and about as probable as one chance out of an infinite number. Take for example the singularity of the big bang, which defies one of the laws for which it is responsible, the first law of thermodynamics which states matter and energy cannot be destroyed or created. Yet they were both created at once. If God created them, he surely has the ability to infuse matter and energy into the system whenever he wishes. And that would be the substance of a miracle, something so rare, so far from the realm of possibility, so outside of space-time, so not in accord with the laws of physics, that the only normal human reaction would be awestruck. Miracles are unprecedented events, like passing through the event horizon of a black hole (also a singularity). Not that God cannot repeat an intervention, such as healing a person, forgiving sinful mortals, or appointing everyone a guardian angel. But to be a truly singular, miraculous event, you typically will find no explanation other than God. Though the miracle may defy the laws of physics and nature, it might likewise adhere to them. Although God came to Earth as a man, that man adhered to the natural insofar as he bled; but he proved he also came from the supernatural insofar as he performed miracles including his own resurrection. In fact, his birth and his resurrection can be considered singularities. Who else can claim immaculate conception, or who can prove they raised themselves from the dead?

It is a lot more logical to presume there was something before the big bang, scientists just don't know what. Some assume nothing, a notion which contests every universal law. Sounds like a miracle to me, which implies the supernatural, a word that is excluded from many scientists' vocabulary. It is not natural for universes, lifeforms, and intelligence to spring into being without an agent. There is nothing within this universe to explain our universe in general or miracles in particular (Lewis, 1947). Therefore, the inventor must not be confined to our realm. A being who is powerful enough to design a universe certainly can make miracles happen. Being at a loss for any physical or natural explanations, is it not foolish to disown God when nothing inside the universe can explain these phenomena, much less the existence of God?

There are countless miracles recorded in the Old Testament (OT) and New Testament (NT) of the Bible. Their importance cannot be dismissed; clearly, they were pivotal in the lives of those who reported them. Some examples of OT miracles are listed below. Notice how momentous they were, how lives were permanently changed, and how destinies were evermore altered. And notice how God often empowered humans to exact his purpose among the people via miracles, as well as using the forces and laws of the universe to perform them. Note also the fulfillment of OT prophecies relating to future NT events, such as Christ's coming; such predictions could be considered miracles as they defied the laws of probability.

- Immediate and complete obliteration of Sodom and Gomorrah (GEN 19).
- Moses parting the Red Sea, ensuring safe departure of the Israelites from Egypt (EXO 14).
- Manna sent from heaven to feed the hungry Israelites (EXO 16).
- Aaron's rod budded, blossomed, and produced almonds (NUM 17).
- Balaam's donkey spoke and admonished him (NUM 22).
- Time stood still (JOS 10).

- Samson killed one thousand Philistines with the jawbone of a donkey (JDG 15:15).
- The prophets of Baal were exterminated by Elijah, after calling fire from heaven to destroy their altar (1 KI 18).
- Elijah raised a boy from the dead (2 KI 4).
- Elisha caused an axe-head to float (2 KI 6).
- The angel of the Lord slew 185,000 Assyrians overnight (2 KI 19).
- The sundial reversed ten degrees (2 KI 20).
- Jonah survived the whale and fulfilled God's mission (JON 2).
- Shadrach, Meshach, and Abednego survived the fiery furnace (DAN 3).
- Daniel survived the lions' den (DAN 6).

Here is but a sampling of the many NT miracles that Jesus performed in addition to his own resurrection.

- Changed water into wine (JOH 2:1–11).
- Healed a man paralyzed from palsy (MAR 2:1–12).
- Cast out a legion of demons from one possessed man (MAR 5:1–13).
- Raised a young girl from the dead (MAR 5:35–43).
- Fed over five thousand with a boy's lunch (JOH 6:1–13).
- Gave sight to a man born blind (JOH 9:1–41).
- Calmed the storm (MAT 8:23–27).
- Walked on water (MAT 14:23–33).
- Obtained money to pay taxes from a fish (MAT 17:24–27).
- Cleansed ten lepers (LUK 17:12–19).
- Restored the sight of two blind men (LUK 18:35–43).
- Raised Lazarus who was dead four days (JOH 11:1–45).
- Reattached a man's severed ear (LUK 22:47–51).
- Predicted two huge catches of fish (LUK 5:1–10; JOH 21:1–11).
- Ascended into heaven (ACT 1:9–11).

Everything concerning Jesus Christ is a miracle, a fusing of the natural and the supernatural, the physical with the spiritual; a connection between humans and God, the visible with the invisible; a pathway to relevancy and to everlasting life; a quantum phenomenon that defies physics, challenges science, and precludes neutrality. His birth was a miracle, his life was a miracle; his death, resurrection, and ascension were miracles. He made the blind to see, the deaf to hear, the dumb to speak, the lame to walk, and the dead to come alive. He freed the lost, beaten down, abused, demon possessed, imprisoned, sinful and depraved. He was addressed by others as

God and Lord and proclaimed himself God and Messiah (JOH 14:1–14; JOH 20:26–28). He was feared and cursed for being independent in his thinking, humble in his demeanor, compassionate in his actions, and resolute in his convictions (MAR 5:1–15; LUK 8:35). He was foretold in over three hundred passages in the Old Testament, all of which would be confirmed in the New Testament recording his first and second comings. He saved everyone that ever lived, though many will reject the salvation he offers for whatever reason. There has never been anyone like Jesus Christ, and that is a certified historical fact that no one can deny.

Exclusivity

Have you heard: religions are exclusive? Well, this would actually be a valid point, because all religions are different; and Christianity is perhaps the most exclusive as it is the only one that puts Jesus Christ at the center of one's deliverance. That is, nobody can earn redemption without faith in the atonement of Christ. It is solely by God's grace that anyone can be saved (JOH 1:14,17). No other religion relies exclusively on faith in Jesus; other so-called paths to God or heaven generally depend on actions. For instance, in Islam your good deeds must outweigh or outnumber your bad deeds in order to be saved (Surah 11:114; 17:9; 53:39–41). The same is true for Hinduism, where one must graduate to a statelier class after each reincarnation until he or she achieves moksha (called "nirvana" in Buddhism). But it is the blood of Christ that redeems, saves, and pays the price of admission into heaven. In that regard, Christianity is as exclusive as it gets. Without Christ, nobody would be saved, since an accumulation of good deeds won't expunge a single bad one (ISA 64:6; JAM 2:10). It is not what you do but what you believe that leads to salvation, and this doctrine is exclusively Christian.

That Christians claim exclusive rights to the kingdom is not an argument against God, or against the Bible; because, the Bible is God's Word and that is what it teaches (JOH 14:6). Religions denying the deity of Christ have rejected the Bible (JOH 14:9; PHP 2:5–8; TIT 2:13–14) or altered its meaning in order to reflect an alternate worldview. So, those who disavow Christ as their Savior, consider him to be merely human, or make him out to be a subservient god, actually have excluded themselves from Christianity. If you do not love Christ, and you do not follow and worship him, you are not a Christian.

As to the uniqueness of Christianity, it is the only system which acknowledges all of the aforementioned facts about the resurrection, with the added assurance that Jesus is actually God in human form (JOH 10:24–33; JOH 20:28; PHP 2:6). In order for the debt of sin to be paid, someone has to die because the payment is death. In order for someone to die for others and return to life after being dead for days, that someone must be without sin, otherwise he would be guilty and unable to pay anybody's debt. The only human being without sin is Jesus Christ. Further, with respect to miracles, the creation of the universe (to include us), the immaculate conception of Jesus Christ, and his resurrection are the three greatest miracles that ever happened (for humans). The next most significant miracle will be the resurrection of all humankind when Christ returns in judgment to bring his people home; he will apportion the rest to die a second death (REV 20:14–15). His second coming will be followed by another outstanding miracle: God's creation of a new universe with a wholly different heaven and earth in which his saints will dwell (ISA 65:17: REV 21:5).

Let's get back to the argument of exclusiveness. If there is any system that is ultra-exclusive it is the atheist worldview. They shun all religion as nonsense; or worse, ridicule people of faith as being stupid, superstitious, bigoted, egocentric, fanatical, and dangerous (sounds like those who worship at the throne of atheism fancy themselves exempt from these attributes). It's like you cannot be a believer and a scholar at the same time. This is especially the case with secular news outlets in general, and Hollywood or television productions in particular, where Christians are portrayed as lunatics, ignoramuses, and sociopaths. This nonsense is not only about excluding Christians from membership to society, it is denigrating them as subhuman; singling them out to assassinate their character; refusing them to participate, be recognized, or be served; or finding ways of destroying their position and livelihood. In any case, it is one thing to disagree with someone, but it is entirely unnecessary to be hostile, antisocial, and violent about it.

You will not witness a dedicated Christian habitually putting people down, denying their civil rights, attacking or insulting their character, questioning their patriotism, or excluding them from life, liberty and pursuit of happiness (to include atheists). Devout evangelicals are not mean-spirited since they have the Holy Spirit; they actually tend to be loving and merciful, as God prefers (ROM 12:9–21). I would think typical Christians will be the most inclusive of people. After all, God does not exclude anyone from being heirs to his kingdom. Every human receives the same invitation (JOH 3:16);

it doesn't matter your ethnicity or any other demographic. That's why the Bible is the most translated book in history, it is for everyone who seeks God. A better example of exclusionism is Islam, which purports that one cannot adequately understand the Koran unless they can read Arabic; this is their argument to counter those who have read the Koran and found contradictions or are otherwise uncomfortable with its teachings. It is not that Christianity is exclusive, but non-Christians exclude Christianity. You can decide to attend the banquet of Christ or not; but you must RSVP if you intend to partake.

I have pondered why people hated Christ and his disciples or hate Christians today. These people will expound the countless outrages committed in the name of religion. They identify Christians with the Crusades, the Inquisition, abortion clinic bombers, or sexually deviant clergy. Unfortunately, all walks of life have their worst sides, to include religions. But a person of intellect knows that crazy and criminal people will say and do anything however untruthful or immoral. That excludes them from being a representative or spokesperson for any religion or group of people, except for lunatics and criminals perhaps. This is an extreme fallacy of logic—stereotyping, or worse, bigotry; purporting that a few bad apples are representative of the entire grove.

If you want to point a finger, consider the hatefulness of atheism, most notably as the foundation of a group, religion, or government. Have you noticed the way their spokespersons often behave in public? They are loud, rude, prejudiced, unfriendly, aggressive, arrogant, and spoiled. Or, check out the history of atheism. Do you think Hitler was a Christian, doing God a favor by eradicating every Jew his henchmen could get their hands on, and twisting the cross of Christ into a swastika? How about the communist slaughter of millions at the orders of Stalin, Pol Pot, and Mao Zedong? Collectively, these atheists liquidated more innocent people than all of history. Talk about exclusionary and intolerant; those serial killers were demented, reckless, evil, obsessive, and anti-Christian. They'll pay the ultimate price; justice awaits them. Do you blame God for people like that? Personally, I think they ought to be excluded from the living; but indeed, they probably will be when judgment befalls them. Nietzsche wrote that without a solid moral reference (if indeed "God is dead") the world would become uncivilized and violent; and this would lead to mass death and destruction. That's awfully prophetic for a man who proclaimed himself an atheist. By the way, it may interest you to know that, in America, the theists far outnumber the atheists. About 75 percent of Americans identify themselves as theists, meaning they believe in God, with Judeo-Christian accounting for about 70 percent. On the other hand, less than 10 percent identify specifically as agnostic or atheist; the remaining 15 percent are undecided (Pew Research Center, 2015). So which position reflects the positive aspects of our development as a democratic republic? One could say this country has been exclusively a monotheistic nation from the start.

Excluding people for whatever reason is intolerance; but some behavior and some people should not be tolerated. Intolerance is not always a bad thing, even though tolerance can be regarded as a virtue, because true tolerance is shown in love (EPH 4:1–2). Contrast the following: terrorism should not be tolerated; religious freedom should be tolerated. Tolerance is inconsistent with relativism. We do not have to sanction everything to be tolerant or reasonable. Some scientists and historians cannot tolerate God as an explanation for anything; they cannot even tolerate the idea. Instead of debating the topic, or reviewing the evidence, they will dismiss it out of hand. That is exclusionary, unreasonable, and intolerant in my mind. I will concede that not all atheists, scientists, and religious people are mean and spiteful. Please have the courtesy of extending to me the same consideration, regardless of my religion, ethnicity, worldview, or lifestyle.

But tolerance is being redefined by the relativists to imply you can engage in disorderly behavior and everyone has to be okay with that. True tolerance is basically accepting something or someone that you don't particularly like or agree with. Being tolerant is not the same as being judgmental, which is closer to intolerant. Anyone judging another based on his or her culture, beliefs, drives, or penchants are not being tolerant or reasonable. While everyone has preferences, there are some fascinations we do not choose for ourselves but we tolerate in others. Violations of the law or one's constitutional rights should not be tolerated. To assume that a person who is against something is hateful or intolerant is baseless; people that are intolerant are not necessarily hateful, for you can be against something and still be tolerant, even caring. Tolerance and hatefulness are actually irreconcilable, for people that are hateful are very intolerant, exclusionary, and judgmental. Disapproval is not intolerance. Let's say a belief that homosexuality is wrong does not make the believer a homophobe; and it does not make the person intolerant of homosexuals either. It means these persons simply cannot allow themselves to engage in that behavior; but they can care about, even befriend people who do without condoning the behavior and without condemning the person. I believe that homosexuality is a sin, still I have had many friends who were homosexuals; they accepted me and I accepted them. I am not about to judge them for their sin, because I am every bit a sinful as they, perhaps not in the same ways. Those who accuse others of being intolerant simply because they do not agree with their behavior or lifestyle, that signifies intolerant and judgmental. People who are unceasingly screaming intolerance are usually a flashing example of it.

We are taught in the Holy Bible to love everybody just as God does. But God commands us not to judge others; judgment belongs to him alone (ROM 2:1–3; JAM 4:12). However, we are to judge what people say and do, whether right or wrong (MAT 7:1–2; 2 CO 10:12–18; 1 JO 2:15–18). Christians consider certain crazes to be sinful, but tolerate others that do those things, and love them just the same. It is possible to tolerate people with other opinions and not judge them, even when compelled to instruct them. Intolerance and hatefulness seem most applicable to those who despise Christendom in general and Christians in particular; because they judge, they hate, and they refuse to listen or accept. People like that are inclined to persecute Christians simply for their beliefs; they will never tolerate, or listen, or communicate with Christians because they can't stand them. Some will resort to heinous acts to avoid or eliminate Christians. How intolerant, hateful, and judgmental can you get? Some will murder Christians imagining they are commissioned by God to do so (JOH 16:2).

Christians are among the most tolerant people in the world, and possibly the least judgmental; and they are every bit as capable as anybody else in making sound judgments, possibly more so. But Christians are becoming a people least tolerated, as if they are deliberately annoying to non-Christians. Christians are not the type to get in your face and yell at you; but that is behavior we must tolerate in others who exclude Christians. Forget about being allowed to speak your mind, voice an opinion, or participate in peaceful protest. So, who is intolerant and exclusionary? Remember, we should not judge a person, only the behavior; and that judgment should start with our own behavior. Does it match up with what is correct and proper?

Comfort

Unbelievers propose that believers just want to be justified or pacified, and that's why they would prefer to have a God. It makes them feel better. Relativists, atheists, and naturalists prefer not to have a god. They usually side with Freud (*The Future of an Illusion*, 1928): religion is an invention of man to cope with frustration due to the prohibitions imposed by society. It's funny how these same deniers will rationalize that morality is relative, in order to cope with frustration due to the prohibitions imposed by society. They would prefer there not be consequences or judgment for sin. That way they would be able to do anything they want and not feel guilty or accountable, or be tried and condemned. But this is a choice they make to appease their own psychological comfort, which fades rapidly when they encounter the grim actuality that there are penalties for carefree, foolhardy, and shameful behavior. But they do not want to be held responsible and they do not want to be punished. Remember, neither truth nor morality can be absolute to those claiming that such concepts are subject to interpretation and are not universal. They view these tenets as devised by society or the result of evolution, holding that ethics developed over time in order for civilized people to live together in harmony.

What is being invented here *is* an illusion, because they don't care to recognize a God that will judge or sentence them. And that illusion has no future. Thus, disbelief is for personal comfort by feeling okay about being one's own god; answering to nobody but oneself. Yes, faith in God does provide comfort, real comfort not imagined. For God will forgive us and accept us the way we are if we believe; we act on that belief by behaving in a responsible manner and caring about everybody. We have comfort in the knowledge of being found not guilty, in spite of our sinful nature, simply by placing our faith in Jesus the Redeemer. The antagonists find comfort in the deception that there will not be eternal judgment, so when they die that's it. Those refusing to adhere to rules depend on nobody but themselves; they can't be bothered worrying about others. But without the love of God they would be unable to care about anybody, ever.

Ask a person who converted from any position or worldview to Christianity and they will tell you it was life-changing; and that change was very heartening and strengthening. Those people feel more complete, happy, and hopeful; they become successful, they are respected and admired, and they are healthier in mind, body, and spirit. That's what it means to be born again (JOH 3:1–17); everything becomes new (2 CO 5:17). It enables followers of Christ to appreciate features and details, the beauty, goodness, opportunities, and blessings. It influences them to be concerned, to be nicer to people, and bring out the best in them. It inspires them to learn, from every experience and every person; to be tolerant and look for the positive attributes rather than focus on the negative aspects or qualities one dislikes. This rebirth can change the person from the inside out into a better human being, not to mention being renewed by the Holy Spirit continuously.

Plus, converts become increasingly more aware of spiritual phenomena (1 CO 2:9–16; 2 CO 4:18), such as the Holy Spirit working in their lives and in the universe. It brings great comfort knowing that God is with you in spirit and guiding you along the right path; in fact, he is the Great Comforter (JOH 14:16–17,26). The Holy Spirit provides strength, courage, wisdom, and resolve in your pursuit of truth; as well as the boldness to share that truth at every opportunity, for the Holy Spirit is the truth (JOH 4:24; 1 JO 5:5–6). Thus, the argument about personal comfort is definitely one of the reasons people who become Christians ordinarily remain so. Comfort is not invented or feigned like the cynics assert; it is authentic and powerful (2 CO 1:3–8). You are assured of provision, protection, and prosperity; and God will deliver unto you the longings of your heart (PSA 37:4–5; PSA 145:13–21).

When you are in the spirit you are keenly tuned into God and you can perceive spiritual and supernatural phenomena of which you were previously unaware. In particular, you begin to understand the impetus of God's Word and how to apply it to your life. Those who believe in God also are keener to the presence of evil spirits working in the world to convict, discourage, and dissuade people (EPH 6:12–13). God's Spirit gives us the power to reject, rebuke, and expel them (MAR 3:9–15; JAM 4:7; 1 JO 4:4).

Upon accepting Christ, a wealth of spiritual gifts become yours; gifts such as love, faith, hope, joy, peace, patience, kindness, and self-control (GAL 5:22–25; PHP 4:8). These are very formidable because they can defeat complications that bring us down, or tempt us, or confuse us, or distract us such as fear, doubt, despair, anxiety, anger, greed, pride, and self-indulgence. Spiritual gifts give us the will, the right, the authority, and the aptitude to teach, to lead, to minister, to comfort, even to perform, or at least experience, miracles (1 CO 12:1–11; HEB 11:33–34). Above all, the Holy Spirit strengthens us in our faith giving us the guarantee of salvation and eternal life (HEB 11:1–3). You bet that gives me comfort, knowing that this life is nothing compared to the comfort awaiting me in heaven (JOH 14:1–4). I'll wager that the misguided faith of disbelievers and atheists never provided this degree of comfort, ability, might, and confidence.

And let's not forget the power of petitioning the Lord to bring healing, direction, empowerment, and success (JOH 14:12–14; JAM 5:16). Prayer is a direct connection between your thoughts and God. And in reading God's Word he is able to communicate his thoughts to your mind. The relationship builds into an intimate friendship as real and stimulating as any relationship you will ever have. I will finish this paragraph with the words of C.S. Lewis (1952): "If you look for truth you may find comfort in the end; if you look for comfort you will not get either comfort or truth…"

Prophecy

Probably the most compelling evidence that the Holy Bible is true is found in profoundly precise prophecies, sometimes proclaimed centuries earlier, in which every specified element is confirmed. There is no other truly prophetic literary work, period. To argue that there are prophets such as Nostradamus is a very shaky position as there is no comparison; one needs only look at the particulars to see how vague predictions do not constitute prophecy. Some people are pretty good at guessing the future from past events or via trend analysis; actually, everyone's brain has this capacity. But nobody can predict the future consistently with any reliability, not even the weatherman. Conversely, a bona fide prophet of God speaks on behalf of God, and therefore, always gets it right. The only argument left to the unbeliever is there is no such thing as prophecy, which is an even more precarious position. True prophecy is a miracle, which is probably why they will not assent. The Bible has uncanny exactitude since it is God that provides the information. Prophets are people instructed by God about what will happen; they are not people who think they have it figured out by themselves. You can see for yourself by examining the prophecy discussed in this section that there is something supernatural about it; and it should not be ignored or disregarded.

Elijah was one of the great prophets. Consider the curse he levied upon King Ahab and wife Jezebel. They conspired to have a nobleman named Naboth murdered to confiscate his vineyard (1 KI 21). As prophesied, King Ahab's blood was spilled on the very tract of land where Naboth was slain; and dogs licked the blood from Ahab's corpse just as they did when Naboth died. Queen Jezebel perished in Jezreel after being thrown from a balcony; then her body was ripped apart, eaten, and scattered by dogs, as prophesied. Now how many people have died in this manner? Elijah further told the evil pair that their heirs would be annihilated because God intended to erase their family line. And so, it was (1 KI 22; 2 KI 9).

Daniel is my favorite OT prophet. God empowered him to interpret dreams. Take the extraordinary dream of King Nebuchadnezzar in which a progression of kingdoms destined to crash was revealed centuries in advance: Babylon, Media-Persia, Greece, and Rome. Distinct pieces to the puzzle were provided, not the least of which outlined how Babylon would break into two factions (Media-Persia), to be melded into one led by a great conqueror (Alexander); and how his kingdom would split into four, to be rejoined into a terrible empire that would become Rome (DAN 2 and 8; REV 13:1–2). That's pretty amazing prophecy, considering those future empires didn't exist yet. Another astonishing prophecy from Daniel concerns the seventy weeks of years (DAN 9:24–27); I recommend that you investigate this on the Internet as it is beyond the scope of this book to give it due diligence.

The OT presents incredible detail with respect to the coming of Messiah. Hundreds of prophecies were fulfilled in Jesus Christ as presented in the NT. Messiah was proclaimed to be born of a virgin (ISA 7:14) in the small town of Bethlehem (MIC 5:2) and worshipped by kings (ISA 49:7). He would minister throughout Galilee (ISA 9:1–2), healing the lame, blind, and brokenhearted (ISA 35:5–6). He would speak in parables (PSA 78:2) and perform miracles (ISA 35:5–6), blessing some and angering others (ISA 66:4–6). He would be betrayed by a friend for thirty pieces of silver, which would be used to buy a field for a pauper's graveyard (ZEC 11:12–13). He would be tortured to death, an innocent man, for the sins of the world (ISA 30:6; ISA 53:4–7). They would pierce his body and gamble for his clothes (PSA 22:16–18), but never a bone in his body would be broken (PSA 34:20; JOH 19:32–36). He would be counted with the criminals but buried in a rich man's tomb (ISA 53:8–9). He would rise from the dead after three days (HOS 6:2: JON 1:17; PSA 61:6–7; ISA 53:10); and that event would be proclaimed throughout the world until the end of the age (ISA 42:6; ZEC 3:9; MAL 1:11). Incidentally, there is ample prophecy about his return, so you might want to look into that because it is right around the corner (REV 22).

Jesus Christ was a most amazing prophet. He prophesied his own betrayal, crucifixion, and resurrection (MAT 20:17–19; MAT 27:57–66; MAR 8:31). He prophesied forty years before, the destruction of the temple in Jerusalem which occurred in AD 70. He predicted the scenario of the end times, some of which has already happened, is occurring at this time, or has yet to be completed (MAT 24:3–51; LUK 21:7–33; REV 1:1–20). Actually, the book of Revelation was dictated to St. John by Jesus, long after his resurrection and ascension (REV 1:1).

Conclusions

I reviewed common arguments for and against God, including collections of history and science. I find nothing to explain away God or the Holy Bible. Quite the opposite, the preponderance of the evidence was supportive and conclusive that God exists and the Bible is true. The usual disputes about the Christian faith were presented: causality, unseen forces, morality, miracles, exclusivity, comfort, and prophecy. It would appear that these considerations actually confound the reasoning of those unreceptive to Christianity.

Certainly, there is a Christian slant to my analysis, but it is more objective than the naysayers, as they don't take the time to examine both sides. I have presented two worldviews and their relative merit because, like many other people, I require convincing. Even so, in addition to being religious in my private life I am a scientist by profession. I imagine I could defend the unwavering scientists' position better than they could defend my unwavering Christian position. But I am totally content knowing that I base my belief in Christ on facts. With enough of them, one can approximate if not validate truth. The Holy Bible is the most reliable resource for truth and wisdom, since it is the Word of God (*Logos*). Logos refers to the thoughts and words of the Almighty (GEN 1:3; HEB 1:1–2), whereas the universe was spoken into existence, just as the Bible came from the breath of God.

Does that mean I discount the truth found in nature? Absolutely not! There are many facts revealed in nature, which also come from God (PSA 19:1–9; ROM 1:20); that is, the creation itself provides evidence (Wallace, 2015). One can apply science to understand that which is revealed in the physical universe. As a research scientist, I employed sound scientific methods to investigate, observe, analyze, and predict human behavior. Both my religious and my scientific foundations have pointed me towards the truth; they complement each other. God has made himself known to us via the natural and the supernatural, via the physical and the spiritual. Thus, both domains stimulate and educate the mind, leading to truth, knowledge, understanding, and certainty.

My conclusion is that God most certainly exists. I believe he is the Creator, the Comforter, the Sustainer, the Redeemer, and he is my Lord. I believe the Holy Bible to be the true Word of God. I believe that the study of nature supports these propositions. I believe the profusion of the evidence confirms God's supremacy. How about you? Well, read on and you will be presented with more evidence from which to draw your own conclusions.

THE PROBLEM OF EVIL

What is evil? The dictionary defines evil simply as wickedness or immorality; but it is more than that. Evil, from the biblical standpoint, is the absence of God (PSA 14:1–5; EPH 2:12–18). We have here a dichotomy, for goodness must be known in order to discern evil; thus, evil represents the absence of goodness. Similarly, darkness is understood as the absence of light. And light can overcome darkness the same way goodness overcomes evil (JOH 1:1–5; ROM 12:21); the more the light, the less the darkness and the more the goodness the less the evil. Since God is totally good, there can be no darkness in him, and evil cannot persist in his presence. Holiness negates the need for change, for God cannot deny who he is, perfect in righteousness (2 TI 2:11–13).

Evil exists; that is obvious. Evil is unpleasant, or worse. There is nothing good about it. Evil is ascribed mostly to humans. It is observable using our sensory-perceptual faculties, making it easy to identify. Most people are repulsed when they witness or commit an utterly evil act; it looks, sounds, and feels awful. Unfortunately, everybody thinks bad things, says bad things, and does bad things; maybe not all the time but enough to know that we're all to blame. What we say and do are tied to the way we think (PRO 23:7; PRO 27:19); that means we can sin just by thinking something evil (MAT 5:28; JAM 1:15; 1 JO 3:15).

Evil doesn't seem natural. I mean, the animals don't appear to act in methodically evil ways, unless a human trains them. Therefore, evil is largely our fault; and it appears to be associated with superior intelligence. How is that possible? The most advanced species on this planet is the only one that purposefully commits wicked acts. If it were solely biochemistry, the animals would too. Since God set humans apart, why would he allow us to be evil since he is holy? The ultimate question to ask concerning the problem of evil is how does God fit in? Either he exists or he doesn't. Does evil exist because of God, because there is no God, or in spite of God?

The Greek philosopher Epicurus (341–270 BC) speculated about this dilemma. He pondered the possibility of a loving God permitting evil to occur. He asked himself, what if God wanted to prevent evil but was unable? That would suggest that God is not omnipotent. Or, what if God was able to prevent evil but was not willing? That would make him a malevolent not a benevolent God. Then Epicurus thought perhaps God was both able and willing to stop evil, but if true, evil shouldn't exist; but since it does exist, then the origin of evil would be unknown and God would not be omniscient. The fourth consideration was that God was neither willing nor able to prevent evil; but that would imply God possesses none of the properties commonly ascribed to deity. The logic of Epicurus is flawed, however; because God can be willing and able, but maybe he is not ready.

These same premises are advanced by atheists and other nonbelievers to presume there is no god, no creator, and no judgment. Evil is simply an inconvenience. Morality, many conclude, is nothing more than a product of human evolution for the protection afforded by community. Laws are promulgated simply to prevent people from acting in accordance with their primitive wants. The citizenry must adhere to the prohibitions of society or else. But who gets to decide what is permissible? And what standard do they use to measure it? There must be more to evil than personal preferences to truly care, right?

C.S. Lewis struggled with this quandary during his conversion to Christianity. Lewis contemplated two opposing arguments, one from the Christian and one from the atheist viewpoints. In his book *Mere Christianity* (1952), he wrote the following (paraphrased).

> My argument against God was that the universe seemed cruel and unjust. But how did I get the idea of just and unjust? A man does not call a line crooked unless he has some idea of a straight line. What was I comparing the universe to when I deemed it unjust? If the whole show was bad and senseless from A to Z, so to speak, why did I, who was part of the show, find myself in such violent reaction against it?... Of course, I could have given up my idea about justice by saying it was nothing but a personal preference. But if I did that, my argument against God also would collapse. The argument depended on the world actually being unjust, not simply because it did not please my private fancies. Thus, in the very act of trying to prove that God did not exist—in other words, that the whole of reality was senseless—I was forced to assume that one part of reality—namely my idea of justice—made perfect sense.

> Consequently, atheism turned out to be too simplistic [it was insufficient to explain injustice or cruelty].

Lewis's conclusion was that the world really is a cruel and unjust place. He could tell by comparing it to what is righteous and just. He is not the only one to arrive at this distinction; in fact, everyone does in a way. It doesn't matter one's religion, culture, history, geography, or nationality. Cruelty, lawlessness, and sin occur in every society; and there are consequences for such behavior. While laws, rules, and morality may vary somewhat from nation to nation, or state to state, or person to person there is a general consensus on what is acceptable behavior and what is not. In particular, everybody knows that the senseless destroying of a human life is categorically insupportable. Now, one might justify killing as the consequence of war, enforcement of the law, or to preserve innocent life; but mindless homicide is unconscionable, and it usually invites dire penalties regardless of culture or religion. To be sure, religion alone is not a reason to kill anyone; neither are euthanasia and abortion. All lives matter. Moral law is not established in any hard field of science, but it is philosophically relevant and absolutely true.

War is, overall, bad; but is it ever good? You may have heard of the "just war" hypothesis, suggesting that it is acceptable to wage war to eradicate evil or prevent atrocities such as "ethnic cleansing." Can there be such a thing as a righteous war? Actually, yes there can. Unfortunately, the criteria might vary depending on what different people, religions, or governments define as appropriate. Sometimes, nations agree on certain rules of war, like with the Geneva Convention. However, the USA tries to abide by them though our enemies do not. In war, there are no referees, unlike a boxing match where a rule violation can cost a contender the bout. But we can find common ground. If a crazed terrorist begins blasting innocent schoolchildren, is it not a virtuous act to eliminate that threat? But war should never be a means to an end, except maybe justice.

The sixth commandment God gave to the Israelites refers to homicide. Anyone of sound mind and clear conscience knows that there is a difference between killing and murder. It is not difficult to discriminate when killing is just or unjust. Dissent against the government or its laws should not foster assassinating police officers or ambushing military personnel. Disagreements on religious grounds is not a reason to massacre innocents. Is it immoral to put to death a murderer under any circumstances? I submit it is magnitudes more immoral to let a homicidal maniac walk, or be allowed to plead guilty to a lesser charge so he or she can spend little or no time in prison.

Capital punishment is found in both the Old and New Testaments of the Bible; it is legal in most US states, as well as federally for certain crimes. However, we find in the Bible occurrences when innocent people were executed, such as Christ, John the Baptist, and St. Stephen; these innocuous men were slain simply for telling the truth. They committed no crime but merely exercised their God-given rights to think independently and speak their minds. Like the Jewish zealots and the Roman leaders of Jesus's time, communist leaders and Islamist zealots of our time religiously eradicate people who tell the truth. Perhaps they are afraid of the truth. Pontius Pilate declared he'd seen nothing in Christ to warrant a death sentence ("I find no fault in him"), but ordered him to be crucified anyway (MAT 27:1–25; LUK 23:4; JOH 19:4). He symbolically washed his hands of the affair as if that exonerated him. I wonder how people like that sleep at night; probably some of them don't. Or maybe evil comes easy to them; I would imagine it gets easier over time the more one embraces it. In attempting to do good, one realizes the inherent evil within; but when motivated by evil one becomes less aware of it (*ibid*).

The knowledge of right and wrong, the ability to discern good and evil, and the moral compass of the conscience is inherent in humanity. And that knowledge is reinforced every time a person says or does something wrong, as it will bring negative reactions from society, from other people, and even within one's own heart. There will be judgment and punishment, not only under the rules of civilized society, but also in accordance with God's law, his punishment being death (ROM 6:23). Thus, knowledge of results is itself a motivator to do the right thing, especially if you seek a positive outcome such as happiness or success. Any person that continuously behaves in an uncivilized manner will eventually have to pay the piper, and they know it. Indeed, with people like Pilate, knowing and caring are not always synchronized. Humankind has been endowed with basic discernment, but there is considerable variability among persons in terms of how much they genuinely care.

If all people are endowed with a conscience it must be an intrinsic feature. We are born with it; but it is not found in the DNA or in nature. Morality develops to the degree that people become accountable for themselves as they mature; and it becomes stronger with age and experience

THE PROBLEM OF EVIL

(PRO 20:11; ISA 7:14–16). Virtually all cultures or societies have a sacred rite to represent passage into adulthood and the duty to answer for oneself. We also are answerable to one another, not to mention being wards of the planet and its inhabitants, and are therefore answerable to God. This is what morality is all about, responsibility and answerability. God has appointed us to take care of his creation, especially each other (GEN 1:26–27).

Science does not attempt to explain morality or conscience, as these attributes cannot be quantified, qualified, or replicated empirically. I have determined that morality and discernment are unnatural, insofar as no other species on this planet possesses these characteristics, though they have had more time to evolve than humans. If not of this world or inherent in nature, then morality must be out of this world, or supernatural. Simply put, morality transcends humanity. We are superior to other species on the planet in terms of conscious awareness, moral forethought, and intellectual reasoning. But humans have always held that distinction; other earthly creatures and organisms never have exhibited these advanced capabilities. So where did this preeminence come from? It didn't evolve, it wasn't invented, and it doesn't go away or fade, unless due to dementia or another organic malady. And how can we possibly know what is imperfect or substandard if we can in no way be perfect or achieve that standard ourselves? It follows that there is one supreme standard, one lawgiver, a flawless being that is the model, who exists outside of this world, is superior to humans and angels, and is all knowing, all powerful, unchanging, and incapable of error and wrongdoing. Who else could this be but God? In fact, these attributes are generally ascribed to God regardless of religion, culture, or worldview, even among those who choose to deny God's existence. God has made us in his image (GEN 1:26–27), proof that we are special to him and have been given authority over his creation.

St. Augustine (AD 354–430) expounded on the truth that evil is not an entity unto itself. Evil must necessarily exist, however, if there is such a thing as good. Each extreme assumes the other. God is perfectly good (LUK 18:19); and his is the definition of perfect love. Unconditional love is the standard upon which morality, goodness, law, and justice are founded. It is about doing no wrong, loving your neighbor as yourself; doing unto others as you would have them do unto you. In other words, love is the fulfillment of the law (ROM 13:10), God's law and all other laws. Violation of the law, whether God's law, man's law, or the laws of nature, results in unpleasant repercussions.

Anything short of perfect is imperfect; any act that is not good is at least somewhat bad. One thing cannot be good and evil, or right and wrong, or moral and immoral at the same time; that would violate the law of noncontradiction. You cannot have evil without goodness, you cannot have injustice without justice, and you cannot have cruelty without kindness. But in all these cases, the latter can overcome the former.

Clearly, in order for us to do what is right, we must know the difference between good and evil. We are sinful by nature (ISA 64:6); we think, speak, and act evil (ECC 7:20). That's why God gave us his law, to realize our sin; for where there is no law there is no sin (ROM 3:20; ROM 4:15; ROM 7:7). Whoever violates God's law commits sin (1 JO 3:4; 1 JO 5:17). Thus, an evil act is when we do wrong, defined as sin or disobedience to God. It is pointless for God to give us the gift of discernment about these matters if we are not empowered to choose rightly. It would make no difference whether or not we knew right from wrong if we had no free will to choose one over the other. In short, you cannot have morality without liberty, and vice-versa.

God allows evil to exist (ISA 45:7); but that doesn't insinuate he likes it (PSA 97:10; AMO 5:15; ROM 6:23). However, God has not programmed us to do only good; he prefers that we choose goodness willingly. He wants us to seek him, choose him, and become like him: righteous. Therefore, every sin is voluntarily. God does not sin, nor does he tempt us to sin (JAM 1:13). In fact, God is incapable of sin (HAB 1:13); and Jesus Christ, though he possessed the human nature, also could not sin because he likewise possessed the divine nature (1 PE 2:22; 1 JO 3:5). Humans and angels can sin, but not God or Christ. Those who accuse God of being evil for allowing evil to exist are self-defeating in their logic. Atheists would ascribe evil to God if they believed in him. God is not the one who is guilty of sin, we are (JOB 19:28–29). God is not the cause of evil but the cure, for he is blameless.

Evil was not in the world when God first created it (read GEN 3). Evil came with the rebellion of Lucifer, followed by a host of angels, and subsequently humankind (ISA 14:12–15; 1 JO 3:8). We are the guilty ones, not God. But this world is temporary. God intends to destroy this world, and sin will be destroyed along with it (1 JO 2:2; 1 JO 3:8). Being omniscient, God knew that sin would enter into the world and he already had a solution for that problem (PRO 8:20–23; 1 PE 1:15–20). That solution has always been to destroy sin (HEB 9:26–28) and death (1 CO 15:26), which is what Christ accomplished with his death and resurrection, respectively.

THE PROBLEM OF EVIL

God will fashion a new universe in which suffering, pain, sorrow, and evil will never again exist (REV 21:1,4). And people who have been redeemed of sin by faith in the salvation of Christ will live with him in that new universe, free of sin, because we will receive glorified bodies like his that are incorruptible (1 CO 15:42–44; PHP 3:20–21); no more cruelty and injustice, forevermore. So then, sin is not a permanent condition; it has come and it will go (ROM 8:18). To think that an eternal God can himself be sinful is irrational given that sin itself is not eternal. Since God never changes (MAL 3:6; JAM 1:17), he will remain perfect for eternity (DEU 32:4; ISA 25:1; MAT 5:48). When Christ returns, believers will live forever with the Lord in a place where evil cannot enter. There can be no sin in God's kingdom (GEN 3:22–24); evil is destroyed in God's glorious presence just like light destroys darkness. In Christ, there is no darkness (1 JO 1:5). God is not only willing and able to do away with sin, evil, and suffering—he is going to do exactly that any day now. Too bad for Epicurus if he never reconsidered this proposition.

God is the example of perfect love; he is love. He loves us unconditionally for we are extremely valuable to him, and therefore, to one another. All life is precious, and that is the ultimate ethic founded on God's blessed love. When we act in love, we please God; when we do not, we suffer and other people suffer. And make no mistake, God suffers too. If you do not think so, consider the suffering and death of God's only Son Jesus Christ. He paid the price of evil, redeemed us from our sin, and ransomed us from the grave. Just invite him, that's all he asks. God wants a relationship; he wants us to follow his example and love him and love everyone (MAR 12:30–31). He has shown us the way which is Christ (JOH 14:6). Those who choose him will shine and thrive in his royal, magnificent, and hallowed presence for all eternity (ISA 59:1–2; 2 TH 1:7–10). Those who choose not also will get their wish. Such is the power and gift of free will and the essence of the problem of evil. But that problem has been resolved.

Atheists posit that a good God would not create a world where evil thrives; but they do not grant that God himself will create another world without evil. He must first weed out those who disregard him (MAT 3:11–17; MAT 13:24–30). God could do one of three things: he could save everybody, but that would render sin inconsequential; he could save nobody, but that would render goodness inconsequential. Or, he could save some people, because they got the message. Love is the answer, God's grace is the remedy, and our faith is the power to become children of God (JOH 1:12–13;

ROM 8:14–19; GAL 3:26). The new heaven and earth are for the third group that gets this message.

The universe God created reveals quite a number of dichotomies that provide profound meaning and understanding. They often seem in direct opposition but they differ in power. There are humans and animals; humans are grander in knowledge, intrinsic value, and ability. There is goodness and evil; goodness is greater as it defeats evil. There is matter and mind; mind is superior because it can manipulate matter. There is God and there is the universe; God is omnipotent because he created the universe and everything in it, including us. We can discern these matters though we are innately evil, while God is incapable of evil. Why would God make us that way? Why would he let us be so stupid? Could it be to ascertain the price of evil versus the prize of goodness; to seize upon the greater power of the two, thereby conquering the evil? And what would be the origin of that power? It is God's unconditional, unending, supernatural love!

God can ensure good experiences happen despite our attempts to sabotage this through disobedience (ROM 8:27–28). It is futile to second-guess God; his plan is so elaborate there is no way we can comprehend the vastness of it. We try to do it our way, but God's way works better. He has eternal life planned for those who believe so he can change us (ISA 64:4); one of those changes is to purge us of our sinful nature. But without knowledge of the recompense for sin we would not be sufficiently motivated to do the right thing (JOH 3:19–21; EPH 5:17). And this teaches us what not to do, for our conscience convicts us making us feel ashamed. But the shame and guilt fade when we discontinue the bad behavior, and when we make an earnest effort to fix the damage we have caused. The guilt disappears completely when we place our undivided trust in Jesus. His forgiveness erases the sin and along with it the guilt, if one repents with penitence. So, I guess it is not that farfetched to see how evil can be used to work towards our good by inspiring us to change for the better. Little by little we become more like Christ, in preparation for a heavenly reward and a new beginning, when God creates all things anew including us (2 CO 5:1; 1 JO 3:2; REV 21:5).

Temptation

Evil is what tempts us to sin; it takes on many forms, enticing us with earthly amusements. Our sinful disposition compels us to succumb though we know in advance it is not good for us. And no matter how hard we fight it, sometimes we give in and that is why everybody is culpable (ROM 7:14–25). The sinful flesh is common to human beings; unfortunately, seductions of the flesh are forceful and deadly. We have the ability to resist, but that requires considerable willpower (PSA 1:1; JAM 1:12–15). With Christ living in us we have the power to be victorious over any and all temptations (1 JO 4:4).

God gave us the rules and everyone knows what not to do (ROM 7:7); but Satan tempts us to do it because he likes it when we defy God. When we sin, it makes us evil like Satan (JOB 15:16; 1 JO 3:8), and it moves us farther away from God (ISA 59:2). It started in the Garden of Eden when Satan persuaded Adam and Eve with his crafty lies to disobey God (GEN 3:1–6); Eve (and Adam who was with her) saw that the forbidden fruit was good for food (the lust of the flesh), pleasing to the eyes (the greed of our covetous eyes), and desirable to make one wise (the pride of man). They were not the only ones to fall for such temptations, because we all have acquired the same weaknesses (PSA 51:5; MAR 7:23); everybody has allowed Satan to dupe them into doing his will (ROM 3:23; JAM 1:13–14). Lust, greed, and pride—the big three provocations (MAR 7:21–23; 1 JO 2:15–16); correspondingly, sex, money, and power are among the most common enticements into crime (Wallace, 2013). Satan even tried the big three on Christ (LUK 4:1–13), who was tempted just like everybody else (HEB 4:14-16). But Satan should have known better; no way was he going to beguile Christ in whom dwells the Holy Spirit (ISA 11:2; MAR 1:10–11). As cunning and canny as he is, Satan is quite the numbskull. He tried to oppose God and still does, as if he had any chance in hell to outwit God; consequently, hell is where he will find himself, and he would love for you to join him.

Take a moment to appraise the methods of Satan based on the scriptures referenced above; then apply them to your own life experience. First, ponder the lusts of the flesh. Satan tempted Adam and Eve with the forbidden fruit; they perceived it looked delicious, possibly better than the rest of the fruit in the orchard simply because it was prohibited. Satan undertook the same ruse with Jesus in an attempt to convince him that he was so hungry he should convert stones into bread to satisfy his want. That's what lust is all about: hunger. I want to feel good, satisfied, pleasured. In my generation, Satan showed us all the sex and drugs we could handle; I indulged my flesh figuring everybody else was doing it so what's the harm. Can you relate? Haven't you overindulged in things of the physical realm: sex, food, alcohol, drugs, whatever; and then tried to justify it in your mind?

Second, let's examine the lust of the eyes. We want just about everything we cast our eyes upon: the palatial home, the yacht, the prestigious job, celebrity status, and all the beautiful things displayed on television, the Internet, and elsewhere. Too bad we can't afford them. What did Adam and Eve want? They were tempted by Satan to possess the knowledge of God; they wanted to know what he knows. And they quickly learned that the shamefulness of sin wasn't what they'd bargained for. Prior to that momentous event they were naked yet unashamed and unafraid; subsequent to it they were fearful, ashamed, and tried to hide from God (GEN 3:7–11). Lucifer told Jesus that he could obtain all the kingdoms on Earth if he would worship him, as if they belonged to the fallen angel and he had the ability to bestow them. But Jesus commanded Satan that one should worship God alone. I had a friend who wanted to get rich quick, so he started selling drugs. But he wasn't gathering wealth fast enough and decided to play with the big boys. He was set up by the FBI and ended up doing five years in a federal penitentiary. He was lucky the feds caught him before the mob did. I lost touch with him after that. Deep down, we all know that possessions are accumulated by devoted labor; there is no legitimate way that is easy or free. Even those who are born into luxury will not get to keep it if they refuse to work hard and walk straight (2 TH 3:10–12). Have you ever wanted something so bad that you would do just about anything to have it? Was it worth it in the end?

Third, consider the pride of man. We want to be credited, superior, adored, admired, and important. Have you told a lie, or stole something, or backstabbed someone to impress another? In high school, there was a guy who wanted so bad to be part of our clique that he would tell tall tales of his exploits and fortunes to impress us; all he succeeded in doing was repulsing us. Like Satan, Adam and Eve wanted to be their own gods. They didn't want to report to God their Father. They were grownups; they preferred to do it their way. After straying from God, they felt lost and hopeless, as if they were totally on their own. Satan took Jesus to the pinnacle of the temple high atop the city, and suggested he jump. "Your angels will protect you," Satan urged. Imagine, if everybody saw Jesus jump and the angels caught him and he landed softly on his feet. That would be impressive. Who else could do that; wouldn't that prove how important and special Jesus was? Jesus shunned Satan saying he was way out of line trying to tempt God. Jesus was soon to perform far greater miracles than those, after dismissing Satan and commencing his ministry.

THE PROBLEM OF EVIL

It is interesting how Satan would quote the Bible to Jesus, taking passages out of context to convince him; and Jesus would come right back with a passage from the Bible that proved Satan's interpretation wrong. But Satan is always wrong for he is the most notorious liar ever. And the cost of what he presents is never what you'd expect. Yes, there always is a cost that outweighs the purported benefit. Pleasures of the world are available to everyone, in moderation, if used in accordance with God's will and not for the purpose of indulging the flesh. Worldly things themselves are not evil, but the love, worship, or craving of them, that is the root of all evil (1 TI 6:10).

Satan is the quintessential con artist. He pretends to offer you things that you otherwise cannot gain, unless you act unlawfully and unfaithfully. But he cannot give you anything that you are unable to achieve yourself in an honest manner. Truthfully, all things are possible with Christ (PHP 4:13). The only thing that Satan will bring is certain death though he has no power over that either. Anything on this planet is available to you, and God is happy to give it to you if you utilize it in accordance with his instructions. He didn't put desire into your heart or allow you the experiences of pleasure to serve some nefarious purpose. God opens the door of experience to establish an ultimate yearning for him and his love. C.S. Lewis (1952) nailed it when he wrote the following.

> If I find in myself a desire which no experience in this world can satisfy, the most probable explanation is that I was made for another world. If none of my earthly pleasures satisfy it, that does not prove that the universe is a fraud. Probably earthly pleasures were never meant to satisfy it, but only to arouse it, to suggest the real thing. If that is so, I must take care, on the one hand, never to despise, or to be unthankful for, these earthly blessings, and on the other, never to mistake them for something else of which they are only a kind of copy, or echo, or mirage. I must keep alive in myself the desire for my true country, which I shall not find until after death…

If you experience a void in your life and you cannot find anything in this world that fills that emptiness to the brim, then you are searching in the wrong place. Your wants and needs must be for God; I recommend you try seeking outside of this world for real and complete satisfaction. In the meantime, the Lord will satisfy all your earthly needs, and lead you home in due time. God wants you to enjoy life but you must not overdo it or employ his gifts outside of the purpose for which they were intended. For example, he directed Adam and Eve to be fruitful and multiply, not to go fornicating with anybody and everybody. He wanted them and all people to produce godly offspring within the sanctity of marriage and family (GEN 2:24; MAL 2:15–16). Therefore, our passions can be appeased without transgressing, and with a custom that actually pleases God (1 CO 7:9). Satan and others will influence you to chase prohibited hungers and pacify your selfishness in a depraved manner; do not give in to them (PRO 1:10; 1 CO 5:11). You might have heard the famous story about a guy who sold his soul to the devil for worldly pleasures and wisdom (*Faust* by Goethe). It is largely based on the same tale the serpent told Adam and Eve. The awareness of sin made them ashamed of themselves, and for good reason; for what you lose in the end is your life if not your soul (PRO 8:36).

Fortunately, God figured in the beginning how to bring us out of the grave, free of the sin that put us there. And he will take you to paradise if you believe. Why would anyone think that Satan can offer something better than what God offers? Who in their right mind believes fascinations of this world are more desirable or valuable than found in God's realm? If you long for success, amusement, companionship, peace, fame, or glory you can acquire these treasures sensibly, as long as you employ them for Christ's sake (MAT 28:18–20; 1 CO 10:31). Besides, when you are ushered into his kingdom, you will share also in God's glory (ROM 8:17). I really don't think you want any share of Satan's legacy. When Satan tempts you with possessions that do not belong to him, they will not bring gratification, only misery. Satan relishes in your misery because he despises you for being immensely precious to God. He enjoyed watching Christ suffer on the cross; he didn't believe Christ would come alive again (at least that was his hope). When Jesus arose victorious it was the worst day of Satan's life. And all it did is make him hate Jesus, and humanity, all the more.

If you want to be happy stay on the right path; exit that path and you will not find happiness there, for Satan will be lurking in the shadows. Everything you want and need happen to be available on the path of righteousness and are assurances of God. He will give you everything and more. There is no reason to be in a hurry, or forfeit your integrity, or barter with the devil. All Satan wants is for you to lose your soul and your life. Does that mean he wins your soul? No, he wins nothing, he loses everything, and his reward is death. So, you can select the inheritance of Christ or the inheritance of Satan.

The Conscience

Resolved: the only creature indigenous to planet Earth that possesses a conscience is the human. The conscience is very unique; it is a repository of our knowledge of right and wrong. I have argued that we are born with this faculty, insofar as it was endowed by God; this is one of the ways in which we have been created in his image (GEN 1:26–27). In the Garden of Eden, God gave Adam and Eve the knowledge of right and wrong; thus, humans possessed this knowledge from the start. He permitted them to eat of any tree in the garden except one, the Tree of Knowledge (GEN 2:16–17). But they disregarded God and ate, though they knew it was wrong even before they partook. And after they did, they immediately knew they had sinned against God and tried to conceal it (GEN 3). The devil tricked them into thinking they would acquire the knowledge of God, and in their greed and pride they ate. But it only gave them the knowledge of sin; and they became sinful like Satan, who wanted to be God and persuaded Adam and Eve to want that too. This is the great deception, that you can become a god or be your own god, as if you don't need God Almighty.

Essentially, a principal attribute we can ascribe to the conscience is that it convicts us of our sin. We know there are recriminations for doing wrong which is counterproductive to our becoming; and we know that doing right usually yields beneficial outcomes. And even if we figure we can get away with a wrongdoing, we do not really, because our conscience punishes us (ACT 23:1; ACT 24:16; ROM 2:14–15; HEB 13:18). We are found out by our own conscience which bombards us with guilt; and we are found out by God who knows all things. Isn't it interesting how Adam blamed Eve and she blamed the serpent, hoping they could escape the wrath of God, or play dumb, or rationalize their guilt by explaining it away (GEN 3:9–13; JOH 8:3–11)? We only succeed in digging our graves a bit deeper each time we open our mouths to justify misbehavior.

People learn from their thoughts, words, and actions when they produce positive or negative results which are usually immediate. There is no excuse for failing to do the right thing; if you don't know what that is, you are not listening to your conscience (JAM 4:17) or paying attention to the results. All laws are based upon an absolute standard, which is God's unconditional love. That standard is faultlessness; anything less than perfect righteousness is unrighteousness, the opposite of God. And when one violates the law, they can expect penalties, whether a violation of God's laws, nature's laws, or the laws of the land. Nobody is ignorant of the law, because every culture has rules. You have heard the cliché, don't do the crime if you can't do the time. Society will punish you your conscience will punish you and God will punish you; sometimes, nature punishes you. The best advice is to behave in a godly manner and try not to go against your better judgment (ROM 7:19–20; 1 CO 8:12; 2 CO 1:12). But that necessitates stopping to think seriously about what you are about to say or do.

The conscience is a reminder, showing us the right way to go, and redirecting our path when we have gone astray. Generally, the feeling of guilt may linger because we love the Lord; but he now owns the sin so we needn't dwell on the guilt. But the sin and shame will not diminish until one allows the blood of Christ to cleanse him or her of unrighteousness (PSA 51:1–3; 1 JO 1:9). Otherwise, the person will die in their sin, because that is the judgment imposed by God (ROM 6:23; 2 CO 4:1–2). The true Christian knows full well, only Jesus can redeem them and bring them into God's heavenly presence, free from the impurity of sin (HEB 9:8–14; HEB 10:1–14). To reiterate, Christ has removed from us our sin and taken it upon himself, while bestowing upon us his righteousness. Only by trusting in him can we hope to appear holy before God (PSA 32:2; ISA 46:12–13; ROM 8:1–4; 2; CO 5:19–21). Our response to this eternal reward, the greatest gift known to man, is to keep raising the bar, to continuously recalibrate that yardstick of our conscience and align it with the will of God and the obedience of Christ.

Love is clearly the standard, as commanded by Christ to love God first and everyone else next, including yourself. Love is your higher power; love is the highest power. Let your conscience be your guide, follow your heart, listen to your higher power (1 TI 1:5–7,15–19). It all means the same thing, to heed the Golden Rule (LUK 6:31). People who blatantly rebuff what is right, it is not that their consciences are misplaced, it is that they do not care having deliberately vacated all scruples (1 TI 4:1–2). They refuse to listen and they refuse to love. They do not fear judgment, because they will not assent to the retributions; the only outcome acceptable to them is getting what they want when they want it. Their philosophy is anything goes and at any price. They give no importance to the common good, because everything they do is to benefit them alone. This is a devastating way to live, leading only to oblivion. It is the way of those who want to be their own god.

There is more often a positive outcome if you do what is good and right, and more often a negative outcome if you do the opposite. Unfortunately, it doesn't always work that way does it? In a corrupt society or with faulty leadership, sometimes people get rewarded when they do wrong, and some are punished when they do right. But there is a greater reward for those who are persecuted and tormented for doing what God demands, at least in his court of law (2 TH 1:5; 1 PE 2:19–21; 1 PE 3:15–17). So, no matter what society does or the government proclaims to be lawful, we always must adhere to God's commands to the best of our ability. That is, God's law supersedes all other laws. And if you are forced to choose between God and man, heaven and earth, righteousness and unrighteousness, choose God. You will be choosing life over death (DEU 30:15–20).

Who Am I to Judge?

There is nothing in the Bible suggesting that we are to judge others (LUK 6:37; ROM 14:10–14; 1 CO 4:3–5). In fact, Jesus said if we judge others, we will be judged by the same standards that we exact upon them (MAT 7:1–5). We must be careful when we pass judgment and ensure we are not accusing our neighbors for things we ourselves are guilty. While it is acceptable to judge what people say and do (LUK 12:57; 1 CO 2:15), it is unwise to be judgmental of another person's heart, because when we judge them, we judge ourselves (JOB 9:20; JAM 4:11–12). We are guilty of sin, we will be judged, and we will face the music; but God is the ultimate umpire. However, God also appoints and allows us to elect arbiters to represent society and adjudicate matters in civil and criminal cases (DEU 25:1). Every system of government has laws, and all are based on regarding others' rights and refraining from harming them. Enforcement of just laws ensures justice.

I think we can agree that there are obvious consequences for doing the wrong thing versus doing the right thing, and these corollaries are generally negative and positive, respectively. And though God instills in us the knowledge of morality, we gain immediate knowledge of results by observing the aftereffects of our words and deeds, as well as the words and deeds of others. Everybody has this capability and everybody knows, both in advance and after the fact, when they have behaved in accordance with the moral, natural, and civil laws, or not (GEN 2:16–17). Logically, God's law trumps them all as he is the perfect standard, the divine lawgiver, and the just judge (HEB 10:30–31; JDE 1:14–15; 2 TH 1:5).

Appropriately, the best way of obtaining serenity, conciliation, and victory is to do right by others. That way you don't have to worry about being caught, getting arrested, or going to jail. The good life consists of bearing fruits of the spirit: love, joy, peace, patience, kindness, humbleness, goodness, self-control, etc. (PHP 4:8). St. Paul taught that there is no law against these things (GAL 5:22–23). Like I said, sometimes there are penalties for doing the right thing; in particular, followers of Christ can expect ridicule, torment, or worse (LUK 21:12,26–27; 1 PE 4:16–19). Actually, God holds his people to a higher standard anyway, especially those who hold the office of prophet, priest, church leader, or teacher of the faith. We are to present ourselves as an example of Christ, to walk in righteousness, to call out evil and injustice when we see it, to grow as a disciple, to make sacrifices for one another, and to be a witness of the truth. It will be very bad for those who adulterate religion and extort followers, confusing their faith, leading them astray, or gratuitously fleecing them of their money. The worst kind of ill-gotten gain is using a guise of religiosity for self-aggrandizement (PRO 1: 18–19; PRO 10:2). This is an atrocity to the Lord (PRO 10:2; JAM 3:1), and offenders will receive the greater damnation (MAT 23:12–33).

Who am I to judge? It is not who, but what. I have a conscience same as everybody. It is not difficult to distinguish right from wrong. People make judgment calls countless times each day, particularly with respect to their standards of conduct. If something is wrong, say so; if you are wrong, confess and repent (MAT 3:1–2; MAT 4:17; 2 CO 7:10). If someone does the right thing, praise God and give thanks. But do not judge the person for we all bear the sinful nature and are prone to succumbing to temptation. God calls everyone to himself and has given his Son as an example of compliance with God's law. In Christ, we see the proper way so we can judge what we observe with a righteous judgment (JOH 7:24).

Clearly, God provides guidelines; he has from the start. His laws have been passed down from generation to generation (PSA 9:16). Even those who were not privy to the words of the prophets and patriarchs still have the law written in their hearts (JER 31:33). Nobody is excused from living a life of evil as if they don't know any better (ROM 1:32—ROM 2:16). But God also gave us free will, and we have a choice to believe him and to obey him, or not; to follow the rules, or not (PRO 10:2; PRO 11:4). Those who choose wickedness will face the wrath of God; for his judgment is sure and it is permanent (PRO 10:16; PRO 11:19–21). If you deny him and recklessly ignore his warnings, you will be judged guilty and pay the price, having your transgressions counted against you. For if a person disregards God's law, he or she will be judged by it, and reap the ultimate penalty (MAT 12:36–37; 2 PE 2:9).

The fallacy with many is they think that they can be justified by obedience to the law. But there are no paths to freedom through works of the law (ROM 3:20–28; GAL 2:16; GAL 3:11,24); because all have fallen short and departed from the path. We cannot make up for our sins by doing good because a single sin will condemn us all over again (JAM 2:10). And we cannot quit sinning no matter how hard we try (ROM 7:14–25). However, we can put our trust in God's plan, because he knew all along that we would fail. That plan is salvation, undeserved and freely given to those who will believe and receive God's grace (PRO 28:5).

Grace is receiving something undeserved, such as the proverbial wakeup call beckoning you to return to the path and follow Christ; to abandon your evil ways and to secure the gifts of salvation and eternal life that God offers (ROM 5:18–21; EPH 2:4–9). Mercy is not receiving something you deserve, such as a death sentence (JAM 2:12–13). Given the harshness of the punishment, and the impossibility of anyone living up to the ideals of God exhibited by his Son Jesus Christ, we have only one way out—Jesus himself. Therefore, you have two choices, accept Christ as your personal Savior and be judged by the righteousness of Christ, or opt out and be judged by the Book of the Law, which has recorded all of your deeds, and misdeeds (REV 20:12).

Hence, you can be judged by the Law of God or by the Word of God. Keep in mind that God's Word, which is represented in Christ, is true; and it saves. God's Law, which has been consummated on our behalf by Christ, is also true; and it condemns. Both are wisdom, and both came from the pronouncement of God. They teach us the way of the Lord that leads to redemption, and the way of the world that leads to destruction. But how can Christ save anybody, much less everybody? One can declare this only by faith. Jesus Christ has taken your sins upon himself, exchanging them for his righteousness, if you believe (PSA 32:1–2; JOH 16:7–11); he has traded your imperfection for his perfection. He has purified and preserved you for entrance into the kingdom of heaven where sin cannot exist due to the holiness of God; and it is that holiness with which he has covered the sins of believers, for those sins no longer exist. With his sacrifice Jesus paid your penalty; and with his resurrection he will bring you to your heavenly home, blameless, pure, and worthy (ROM 4:7–8; 1 CO 1:4–9; 1 CO 6:9–11; GAL 2:20; 1 TH 5:21–24). That is why Christians wait earnestly for his return, for we will be given a new life (PSA 116:8–9; JOH 5:34; 1 JO 3:14).

It is proper and fitting that Christ will be the one to judge humankind, as he is the only one who can (JOH 5:22–30; JOH 8:15–16; JOH 12:47–50; 2 CO 5:10; 2 TI 4:1). That is, he took the burden of sin upon himself as charged by God the Father. He paid the price for the iniquities of us all, so they belong to him. He knows who has worshipped and praised him for this and who has not. He is the advocate (1 JO 2:1), the counselor (ISA 9:6), and the mediator (1 TI 2:5) between us and God; because, he possesses both the nature of God and the nature of man. He has chosen his sheep out of this world to be members of God's flock. The rest will be judged accordingly, those who rejected Jesus outright and didn't want to believe in him, or know him, or live with him in his kingdom (DAN 7:10; 1 CO 11:31–32; HEB 9:27–28). It's not as if the lost cannot know; the reason they don't is they have no affinity for a redeemer. God's justice is impartial because he will never press anyone to love him; and he will allow people to go their own way rather than his. I for one am leaving this evil world behind. Goodbye to everyone who prefers to die with it.

Thus, evil is not a problem anymore; it has been answered and the matter is closed. Well, except for those who reject God's solution; unfortunately, those folks will never solve the problem themselves. And that mistake will lead to their undoing.

Justice

Governments assume responsibility for administering justice. Obey the laws and you usually can avoid getting into trouble. That requires you also avoid others who deliberately violate the law, else you get entangled in their affairs. Different crimes result in different penalties; generally, the worse the infraction the greater the punishment. There may be rewards for doing good, but not necessarily commensurate with degrees of goodness.

Actually, we should be doing good deeds without expecting a reward. Some people do good just to get the reward; in that case, they make it known to everyone how wonderful they have been. Therefore, they do so for the wrong reason (MAT 6:1–4). Believe me, if you are a doer of good deeds, people will notice without you having to mention it or advertise it. The same is true if you go around doing bad deeds; you'll eventually be found out no matter how hard you try to bury it. I suppose that's the origin of the cliché, "What goes around comes around" or as the Hindus put it, karma.

The Old Testament of the Bible is, among other things, a great discourse in law. It spells out a great many things that are okay to do, or not; that are healthy or unhealthy; that are unadvised, perilous, and lethal. Let us begin with the Ten Commandments. Do you know them? Did you know that they are displayed in several locations at our Supreme Court building and at the Library of Congress? Well, until some fools sue to have them removed. Anyway, here they are in a nutshell (EXO 20:1–17): 1 – Place God first in your life; 2 – Do not engage in idolatry; 3 – Do not use God's name in vain; 4 – Keep the Sabbath Day holy; 5 – Honor and obey your parents; 6 – Do not murder anyone; 7 – Do not commit adultery; 8 – Do not steal; 9 – Do not lie; 10 – Do not crave what others have. The Ten Commandments imply a hierarchy. Evidently, murder is more heinous than lying; either way, a violation of any commandment makes you a sinner. As I said, you are guilty if you even think about disobeying a commandment of God. Accordingly, God's system of justice is quite different than any established by societies. God is intolerant of evil, and those who commit evil against anyone is doing it against God, and they will be reproved unless they prefer to be condemned.

Morality and liberty cannot operate without justice; there must be a price to pay for sin and evil in order to discourage people from violating the law. Since all people are blameworthy, everyone on the planet will suffer as a result. However, there will be no suffering in heaven, where sin, death, and every source of evil has already been eliminated; where there is no injustice, immorality, or inequality. God will not countenance any imperfections in his kingdom. Who can be saved if everybody is guilty? The answer is, everybody; that is, everybody who relies exclusively on the grace of God the Father and the mercy shown to us through his Son Christ Jesus (TIT 3:7).

You see, death is a fair price to pay for sin. Such is the justice of God, for he is a reasonable and righteous God (ZEC 9:9); but he demands submission. However, salvation cannot be gained from good works, unless those works are perfect in entirety (GAL 2:16). Only Christ can claim absolute obedience to the Father as he alone is without sin. Only Christ can make payment for another, because those who are found to be in sin must pay with their lives. Christ paid the price for us with his life, but the grave could not hold him because he was innocent in entirety.

Disbelievers maintain that God is unjust because he condemns people for sin; well so do we. But the fact of the matter is, God himself has paid the price for sin (GEN 22:8). Believe this and you will receive a pardon. Doubters are free to choose like anybody else; and they have the option of changing their mind, choosing God's way, and being forgiven. In response, believers are obliged to confess and repent of their sins, and trust absolutely in Jesus Christ who has taken their place in death (1 JO 1:9). He has borne the sins of humankind for all time, thereby paying the ultimate penalty (HEB 2:9). You can elect either to keep your sins or to keep your soul (LUK 21:19).

God knew humans would fail and fall; he accounted for sin in advance of creating humans. That plan is clearly seen in the essential doctrine of Substitution. Throughout the Bible, Old and New Testaments alike, this tenet has been spelled out again and again. Christ is our substitute. He suffered and died in our place. And since he was guiltless, death could not hold him (ACT 2:24). He gave his life and took it back again, so that we too could receive new life (JOH 10:15–18; ROM 6:4). Anyone believing this can be saved.

In accordance with God's law, atonement for sin has always required a blood offering; that is, the punishment demands blood (HEB 9:18–28). Death is the penalty, and all must pay. Under the Mosaic law, blood sacrifices were offered regularly. But sacrifices offered upon the altar never were sufficient to absolve a penitent believer of his or her sin (MIC 6:6–7; HEB 10:1); because nobody could cease sinning. So, they were required to continue the sacrifices periodically. But it is easy to see how such offerings would be inefficient to absolve sin; they were a precursor that pointed to a sacrifice God would make since the sacrifices of men were incomplete. God permitted evil in order to teach us the law, so we could understand and acknowledge our need for a savior (GAL 3:23–26). The Father knew all along that there needed to be one final, unspoiled, and decisive blood offering, and that would require he surrender his only begotten Son (HEB 10:10–19).

Substitution is abundantly clear in the Sacrificial Lamb. The story of Abraham, who was commanded by God to sacrifice his dear son Isaac, is a wonderful illustration of God's mercy. Isaac was spared and a ram was offered instead (GEN 22:6–13). The story of Moses presented the Passover lamb, another type of Christ, whereby the nation of Israel was spared the loss of their first born, and a lamb was offered as a substitute (EXO 12:1–14). We see the sacrifice of God's first born and only Son, the Lamb of God (JOH

1:29–37) as the propitiation of God's promise to the prophets and patriarchs. Their testimony trained our eyes to the cross of Christ. He became our substitute in death as the payment for sin, not just yours and mine but the sin of the whole world (JOH 1:29).

We remember with humility and awe the sacrifice of Jesus whenever we partake of the Lord's Supper (LUK 22:19–20; 1 CO 10:16–17; 1 CO 11:26–32). During Holy Communion, we are joined with Christ in a solemn and sacred sacrament, whereby the consecrated bread and wine become a substitute for his very body and blood, broken and shed for us for the remission of our sins. As we live in him, we invite him to live in us, and to nurture our bodies, minds, and spirits.

Another fine example of replacement is the scapegoat; the modern definition refers to someone enduring the blame for somebody else. The term literally originated from the Levitical law whereby the sins of Israel could be removed symbolically (LEV 16:7–10). Two goats were selected, one to be sacrificed and one to be set free and escape into the wilderness never to be seen again, or bear any burden, or be slain by man. Christ became the scapegoat for God's chosen people; he was sacrificed and we are set free, our burden is lifted and our transgressions forgotten. We see this illustrated in the fortune of a man named Barabbas, who was set free while Christ was crucified in his stead (MAT 27:15–26). There is only one mention of this shady character in the Bible, a criminal of ill repute who was scheduled for execution. But the riotous mob pleaded for Jesus to be executed and Barabbas to be released. Did Barabbas repent and change his evil ways? The Bible does not say, but then the fate of the Old Testament scapegoat always remained uncertain.

The greatest comfort available is to place all your burdens upon the Lord Jesus (PSA 55:22; ISA 58:6). After all, he requests that you do, so he can carry your heavy load and give you rest and peace in return (MAT 11:28). He will provide everything you need from now until eternity (ROM 8:32). You have attained the keys to heaven if you have been justified, that is to say, if you have been found not guilty. Jesus Christ himself will proclaim that verdict if you have bathed in his blood (ROM 4:7–8), being sanctified by the Holy Spirit (1 CO 6:9–12) and conformed into the image of Christ (ROM 8:29). You must respond by sacrificing yourself to him just like he did for you (ACT 13:37–39; ROM 12:1). How do you know if you are saved? The answer is, anyone can be justified by faith in Christ (ROM 3:20–28). Through sincere faith, the Holy Spirit gives assurance in the midst of doubt.

The greatest mystery ever revealed is unraveled in the crucifixion of Christ. In particular, contemplate upon the words of Jesus at the brink of death which says it all (PSA 22:1; MAT 27:45–46), "My God, why have you forsaken me?" You may wonder "why" as well; and you may wonder how God can forsake Jesus if they are one. But what people do not reckon is that it is our sin which God separates from himself, and at that moment Christ bore the entire sin of humanity. And since Jesus was human, he felt alone, though God was always with him. At the very same time, his righteousness was conferred upon humanity, to those who would receive it by faith. For those that have received it, God will never forsake them (DEU 31:6,8; HEB 13:5). Can you imagine how it must have felt for Christ, who was fully human, to be willing to give up his kingship for us and take on all that pain and suffering in our place? And then feel what it really means to be disconnected from God and buried alone (JOH 12:23-28, LUK 22:42)? On a single point along the continuum of eternity, Christ experienced this emptiness and darkness; it must have seemed like an eternity. But that will be the fate of those who reject Christ, for they will die in their sin and they will be condemned, forever separated from God. But it is they who have departed from God, as they are ungodly and possess not the Spirit (JDE 1:18–19). I cannot begin to fathom the burden of carrying my sin forever, much less feel the burden of the compilation of every sin committed in the course of history. If you refuse God's grace given in Christ, you are unwise. Why? That is the ultimate question; and Christ is the answer. Why, indeed, would anyone choose otherwise?

I ask you, is God just and fair, or is he a dictator and an executioner? Well, his justice is true and clear. Compare that to the justice of society, which is wrought with corruption, treachery, and deceit. Yes, there are costs for wrongdoing, no matter who passes the laws. But God's justice is measured impartially, administered equally, and implemented precisely. He makes no mistakes; the innocent will be set free and the guilty incarcerated. And the way God classifies the two is simply by identifying those shining the light of Christ, versus those who are filled with darkness, void of God's love. Those who follow Christ have had their penalty paid in full; those who do not have selected their own path. Everyone has equal opportunity to be saved and live with God for the rest of eternity. How can God be more judicious?

Government

Governments are installed mostly for preserving law and order, the principal objectives to protect and defend the citizenry. Remember, morality doesn't work without justice; there must be retribution or there is no deterrent to crime. People acting on an evil intent to harm or abuse another can expect repercussions when they are found out (1 PE 2:13–14). However, to maintain civility, punishment for violating the law is relegated to government instead of individuals. The Bible teaches how authorities are instituted by God to perform these functions (ZEC 12:5–6; ROM 13:1–5; 1 CO 12:28); they are justified in collecting taxes to support those who protect us, enforce the law, and govern the people (ROM 13:6–7). Unfortunately, our administrators seem to have gone overboard collecting taxes for things that are not within the purview of government; or invoking harsh recriminations that are not evenly distributed, are not commensurate with the infraction, or deflect their own malfeasance.

There are different types of governments, and they are not equivalent in purpose or effectiveness. Three basic styles identified by John Locke were democracy, oligarchy, and monarchy. Governance by one man (monarch) or by a small group (oligarch) were specious, he reasoned, because the right to rule should never be inherited due to lineage or privilege. Locke promoted the democratic formula, whereby elected leaders exemplifying honor, integrity, and trustworthiness should rule (as long as they retained those attributes). For the same reason, our founders advocated decentralized government over centralized. This particularly made sense given the nation's growth potential and the far-reaching vastness of subsumed territory that would make it impossible to govern exclusively from one corner of the nation.

Would you rather be nominating your leaders, or have some autocrat, court, or dictator making all the decisions? Do you think it feasible to consolidate rule in a single place like Washington DC? Or is it more reasonable to have federal, state, local, familial, and individual components that are self-governing? Empires fall because emperors are flawed, possibly more than the average individual. Is a despot interested in what you want or need? Such a ruler neither knows nor cares. Do you want a voice in who makes the laws and calls the shots, especially within the confines of your own home? Would anyone pick one person or a small group of persons to interfere, control, dominate, or micromanage every aspect of his or her life?

How can outsiders possibly know what is best for each state, or city, or family? Potentates tend to assume the general population consists of a bunch of bunglers that cannot make informed decisions for themselves or their families. These are reasons why republics choose self-government, because we the people are not stupid but instructed, we are not inept but sophisticated. The new progressives would move us away from our self-governing roots (Levin, 2017). Beware the intellectual trickery of the likes of Rousseau, Hegel, and Marx, and behold the wisdom of Locke, Montesquieu, and Madison. The latter group imparted keen insight into the benefits, workings, and principles of an egalitarian government under which the populous flourishes; the former group of ideologues favored inadvisable alternatives benefitting only the elites (*ibid*).

Now consider the prospect of a one world rule; that notion scares the daylights out of me. I cannot begin to fathom the scope of corruption and exploitation of the foreseeable global command. But it is inescapable, according to the Bible (DAN 7:23–25; REV 17:9–14); and it will be the worst of times (LUK 17:26–33). It is a result of free will gone berserk. Why would God let that happen? God will let it transpire since it has been prophesied, but the dominion will not endure for long (REV 17:12); because there can never be an accord, much like the outcome associated with the Tower of Babel (GEN 11:1–9). With many vying for standing, their greed will trigger a cave-in, the fate of every other global empire that sought to rule the world (REV 18).

Rich businessmen and investors, secret societies, bought-off politicians, unscrupulous educators, and other intruders plan and execute destabilization, takeovers, and self-promotions to establish consolidated elite governments in pursuit of global power; in the process they amass mammoth quantities of treasuries, antiquities, currencies, properties, technologies, intelligence, and assorted resources. This was the case in the early stages of twentieth century Europe and Asia, resulting in the Third Reich (Marrs, 2008), as well as preceding empires bent on world domination. Not as wise in their subterfuge as the instigators had assumed, there persisted a blatant miscalculation of the antipathy, both from within and without the conglomerate.

But changing regimes have exhibited enough foresight to plot their escape just in case, complete with a substantial booty chest. Not to mention leaving behind insider connections, deep state holdovers, secret agents, infiltrators and insurgents, and the skeletal remains to reformulate the body politic in the event the political climate changes. These tactics were evident in previous presidential elections and motivated the drive of the current administration to pluck them out. Globalists install a shadow government to maintain influence when elections result in a changing of the guard; by the way, both Democrats and Republicans engage in this. The sinister motive is to connect insiders from every angle for disruption, takeover, and rule.

Another deep state conspiracy is underway to denude the three branches of government and replace them with a fourth that keeps growing in influence (Corsi, 2018); it is comprised largely of unelected insiders whose objective is to hamper and delay any agenda other than their own. The way they fund it is with big money from the private sector which equates to big power, especially from tycoons, kingpins, Wall Street moguls, "K-street" contributors, and ideologues in the DC area (Lofgren, 2016). The instigators employ financial institutions, credit unions and banks, large corporations, international partners, government and military contractors, high technology firms, law enforcement and intelligence gathering mechanisms, assorted media outlets and the worldwide web. Ironically, schemes are unsound and counterproductive, engaging in groupthink, denial, deceit, unaccountability, obfuscation, permissiveness, self-preservation, lawlessness, false accusation, influence peddling, spying and surveillance, and uneven dealing (namely, trades, treaties, loans).

Clearly, globalists come from all walks of life, but have infiltrated America from everywhere. The balance of power will shift again in due course when self-motivated, independent, and committed patriots have been sufficiently silenced. There will be nobody left to speak up, band together, object, or get involved; meanwhile the numbers of those who are unqualified, ill-informed, and uninvolved will multiply. At that point we may experience a Fourth Reich, ostensibly starting with the USA (*ibid*). This scenario is not altogether unfeasible given the number of billionaires, power brokers, foreign entities, and magnates in our midst straining to sway elections and to undermine candidacies, officeholders, leaders and lawmakers, often illegally, clandestinely, and seditiously. If they can coax a powerhouse like the USA to lead the charge it will be easier to suck in our allies, beginning with Europe. The economic powermongers in the USA intend to take over the world, but they'll have to get in line behind the Islamic jihadists and the Chinese imperialists. Lord knows it won't be their first attempt, as it has happened here more than a few times, primarily when one party wielded control.

Nowadays the ringleaders comprise the establishment, regardless of partisan leanings. This creates incoherence regarding party lines and respective voting practices to the extent that the distinctions are blurred. They vote for a bill when they know it won't pass and then decline to vote for the same bill when it has a chance for passage; and all the while the populous would have supported that legislation had it become law. Legislators are losing the support of the people for they do not act on our account. Do the Republicans want the Democrats to win and vice-versa? Intuitively they could be in cahoots. Suffice it to say that both factions stimulate the standoff whereby things will not change, not the least of which are their positions of power. Unfortunately, there is no agenda and nothing gets accomplished, for their objective is to prolong the existing state of affairs. One can only ask, what are the platforms that the caucuses endorse? It really doesn't matter, because the policies for which they are elected usually disappear once they assume office.

To be fair and effective, administrators should follow the qualifications set forth in the Bible: be honest, just, truthful, transparent, and impartial, bearing in mind all authorities are subject to the authority of Christ who is the embodiment of these traits. Governments are subordinate to God's governorship for he is the ultimate authority in heaven and on earth (PSA 67:3–4). When administrations turn evil and corrupt, they should be subject to an ominous aftershock, as they are commissioned to comply with the will of God and the people, not subvert it. Stated another way, leaders are to report to their constituents and to God, not to donors, lobbyists, and elitists. We find many examples in the Bible how those in power were brought down hard and fast due to suppressive rule, excessive corruption, and self-aggrandizement (JOB 34:17–18). So, while your government "does not carry a sword in vain" neither does the angel of the Lord (2 KI 19:35).

Remember, all authorities in the earthly and heavenly realms are under the supremacy of Christ (MAT 28:18); the ultimate right to govern rests upon his shoulders (ISA 9:6–7). He is the ruler over humanity and he will return to judge the living and the dead (2 TI 4:1; 1 PE 4:1–6). And his judgment will be righteous and true (JOH 8:14–16). Are you guilty or not guilty? Well, everyone is guilty; but you will be found not guilty if your trust in Christ remains true. Otherwise, the punishment for sin will be levied upon you and anyone else who refuses Christ, and it will not be lenient, but it will be permanent. I sincerely hope you have weighed your options with respect to who you should trust with your life. I hope it is not the government.

The final accounting will occur at the white throne judgment seat. Your reward (good or bad) will depend on whether or not your name is listed in the Book of Life; if not, you will be judged according to the Book of Law. Jesus appeased the law on your behalf; if you believe this, he will be your advocate (1 JO 2:1–2). If not, it is within your rights to stand alone and defend yourself. One thing is for sure, everybody will have equal representation under God's law, but if they choose to represent themselves, they are doomed.

Once God's judgment is concluded on Earth, there will be no requirement for laws. The jurisdiction of heaven will require no government since justice will have been served and the law satisfied. Additional punishment for sin will not be necessary, as sin itself will have been obliterated from the record. Being made pure in Christ, we won't even think of evil; for we will be serving God in "everlasting innocence, righteousness, and blessedness" (*Luther's Small Catechism*, 1943). We will report directly to God our Father for direction, assistance, and instruction. This is a paternal relationship not gubernatorial. As adopted sons and daughters we will be given the same privileges, glory, authority, and blessings as the Prince of Peace (DAN 7:26–27), but not his status or his title as God (ROM 8:17–18). We can never come close to the completeness, power, intelligence, and majesty of God; instead, our potential for growth, understanding, and becoming will be endless. Freedom itself will be absolute, for never again will we be willing to violate the will of God. I can live with that, forevermore.

Accountability

For justice to work, people must be held accountable. But in a free society, we have to depend on one another to act responsibly; regrettably, the trend is in the other direction. Libertarianism becomes a weak position when it partners with relativism, and therefore cannot be sustained because of the absence of individual liability. When it comes to government, there is a serious lacking in that regard. It's as if the bureaucrats believe themselves to be above the law or immune from prosecution. Many of them get away with heinous acts, criminal enterprises, obstruction of justice, and even espionage which would land any other citizen in prison or worse. It appears the populace is beginning to become disgruntled about these atrocities. Bravo, let's keep it up. But we must first exemplify what we expect in them.

This message came through loud and clear in recent national elections, where a christened candidate got walloped by the electoral college. But the diehard supporters couldn't believe it; they engaged in every form of denial possible, blaming everyone and everything. This is a basic ego defense mechanism, to render excuses or submit rationalizations; what they refused to do is admit being feckless, misguided, or plain wrong. They never asked themselves what they could have done better. They screamed about cheating, foreign intrusion, manipulation of the media, and hate-mongering, for which they themselves were guilty (MAT 12:36). This is another classic ego defense mechanism known as projection.

The news media backed up their innuendo and put it out as front-page headlines; and all the while they were reporting about an emerging epidemic concerning "fake news." What they would not sanction is that the candidate was flawed, the ideas were objectionable, and the campaign was ineffectual. It was not just the candidate that was corrupt, unethical, and lackadaisical; for the bulk of the protestors and the press were too. Rioters went out and destroyed property, assaulted opponents, and terrorized people with threats and abuse to include electors, voters, and the victor; meanwhile, they were accusing the other side of malpractice. However, before, during, and after the election, it was they who were performing loathsome acts. Has anyone been held to account for any of this? No; not the rioters, or the looters, or the hostile campaigners, or the slanted media, or the crooked nominee, or the officials that perpetrated and covered up the madness. Lack of character is the main reason the nominee was unsuccessful in the first place, though that was the only aspect these dimwits never considered.

How arrogant can you get, to think everyone else is supposed to act responsibly except you? If these kooks truly believe they are better than others, shouldn't they hold themselves to a higher standard and not a lower one? One can only speculate why the justice system also acts underhandedly. Are they in collusion with these boneheads? Why do they get a walk and others get the book thrown at them? It depends largely on your political point of view, apparently. It also depends on your religion; if you are a Christian you will be held to the highest standard. That's okay because we hold ourselves to a higher standard. But it is not Christians who are gallivanting about the globe gushing with hate speech, beating up innocent people, mowing down pedestrians with trucks, shooting cops, desecrating the flag, or demoralizing the military. Oh, some may claim to be people of faith; they typically hide behind a vale of religion, though this is a fraud.

It will be a sad day for this nation when upright citizens get tired and give up (PRO 11:11). For who will take a stand then? Christians came out in droves during the aforementioned election and soundly defeated the status quo. Their voice was crystal clear, but many didn't hear a thing because they blocked it out. If they were ever to get the message, they would have to assume responsibility. That is precisely what they have been avoiding; but they'll never apologize. To affirm any blame would be devastating to their egos. It is impossible for them to admit any shortcomings, lest their self-image drops to where they place others; so, they accuse others for everything they don't like, or agree with, or have done themselves. When famous people act irresponsibly and get away with it, this is not a reason to give into them.

Yes, you can expect persecution when you uphold freedom, rights, and justice; especially when the rivals are pushing to alter these principles or revoke your privileges. They are loud, obnoxious, and hostile; eventually, they will outnumber the rest of us. Still, we are obliged to remain virtuous. Don't expect to be rewarded for that in this world, but God will know your heart and this is what really matters. It is not that we can quit caring about those who forsake the ways of righteousness, but we needn't worry about them either. When they escape the justice of society, they think they have nothing to fear; but they will encounter the wrath of God (ROM 14:12; HEB 4:13), and his penalty will be worse. Make sure you don't fall into that trap (GAL 6:1–5).

Many of our youth have been conditioned, confounding their sense of decency. They have been barraged with graphic presentations of wickedness, making it interesting to them, so they dig into it, getting hooked by the deterministic underpinnings of the hype. Is it possible they don't know any better? I mean, they aren't provided many role models, and are taught only the wrongdoings of past ones. Research has shown that moral education is the foremost deterrent to criminal behavior (Wikstrom et al., 2012). The problem is, young people are not getting much of an education, neither in the home nor in the schools; society is sending mixed messages as well. Teens and young adults tend to divide into two groups, crime prone versus crime resistant; the factor that distinguishes the two is character (*ibid*). While environmental influences will contribute to their proclivity to engage in criminal behavior or abstain, it is still the individual who determines whether to succumb to the pressure.

With liability removed and impediments to justice introduced, morality is softened. Fledgling youngsters are easily confused, distracted, and influenced. They are at an age where risk-taking is deemed admirable, doing anything on a dare. They might experience a cheap thrill getting away with something scandalous. What should we expect? If parents, teachers, ministers, and educational systems around the country do not return to implementing lawfulness as a lesson, instilling discipline as a requirement, and invoking punishment as a deterrent, our children will grow up to be narcissistic, rebellious, self-gratifying, and amoral, if not psychopathic.

Research also indicates that the problem of broken families is the greatest social issue facing this nation, as well as worldwide. Broken families equate to broken communities, which equate to broken societies. The disintegration of marriages, families, and communities and the connection of these disruptions to crime and violence has been well-established (Fagan, 1995). This is exacerbated by the consequences of poverty, dropping out, unemployment, juvenile delinquency, incarceration, substance abuse, and mental health issues among children (Amato, 2005). The long-term effects on individuals and societies include spiritual deterioration and moral decay.

It seems matrimony has ceased to be acknowledged as a union between one man and one woman as plainly defined by Christ (MAT 19:3–6). And because of the sexual revolution encompassing the last five decades, extramarital sex (adultery) has become the norm. Despite the overabundance of contraceptives readily available nowadays, upwards of 50 percent of births are out of wedlock. Abortion has become a preferred option, negating countless other potential births to unwed mothers. Single women will find it harder to raise children without male support and many throw away the child for that reason.

Families without fathers is the principal concern. Without two parents, children often are underprivileged, disadvantaged, and reside in poor and rundown neighborhoods. They lack sufficient guidance and discipline, so they are predisposed to being influenced more by peers than parents. In the absence of responsible role models, kids will not develop adequate character. Not that a single working mother is a poor role model; but there will be less supervision when there is but one parent in the home, especially if he or she is constantly laboring to make ends meet.

The reason statistics indicate a race component with respect to crime and violence is because the fatherless children problem is more prevalent in ghettos and among minorities. But let me be clear, this is not a race issue as much as it is a broken family issue; and it is fast becoming pervasive among all races. The biblical construct of a wedded mother and father is without exception the most wholesome and nurturing environment in which to raise kids; those kids are more likely to have higher education, good paying jobs, and emotional stability. The family constellation promotes growth and development, plus moral fiber. This should be reinforced by the community; but when those communities are likewise deprived and degraded, developmental disorders become more prevalent. The primary objective for kids growing up in those communities is to find any possible way out.

Certainly, local governments need to get on board with improving living conditions and ensuring adequate education for these subcultures and for inner city residents. Their schools are dilapidated and neglected, resources are limited, and many teachers are incompetent. The media gurus are contributing to the problem; they do not represent the moral high ground though they allude to moral and intellectual superiority. All too often the press aims for reports that are provocative, pushing issues or statistics that are irrelevant or erroneous, and spinning the facts until the reportage is indistinct if not downright false. Furthermore, decadence, crime, and promiscuity are glamorized in news, music, videos, and literature, while traditional values like marriage, family, unity, and faith are shunned. Two absolutes that anyone can benefit from are truth and love; these are the avenues to building character. Unfortunately, the propaganda being disseminated diverges from these important foundations.

What are we to do? We could vote out politicians that relativize ethics; boycott media markets that distribute phony stories; and disband boards of education that look the other way when encountering a moral dilemma. We could standardize education of the basics, and offer coursework in ethics, homemaking, personal finances, and parenting as in years long past.

Every institution of learning from kindergarten to graduate school is indoctrinating students into the new world disorder. That pursuit also is perpetuated by some media outlets and in many political circles. They want things to break down, they want to relax the laws, they want to be more permissive and less restrictive. What they don't want is to be held accountable. Morality and truth must be diluted if not banned for the globalists to seize and maintain power. How else can they commandeer the masses, unless they throw out the rule book? And the Bible is the quintessential rule book.

Legacy of Corruption

The problem is, rebellion is inescapable due to the nature of man. A fresh resistance movement against God has emerged which is gaining momentum and actuating moral decline. It seems to be enveloping our country and already has overtaken countries abroad. We used to be the light on a hill, but that light is dimming and darkness is creeping in. This degradation of civilization is nothing new; it has happened countless times before. It got so bad in olden days that God had to personally smother it. At the time of the worldwide flood, Noah was the only righteous man left; he alone could hear the voice of God (GEN 6—8). The world was perverse to its core, what with the proliferation of wickedness, demonology, fallen angels, and all manner of depravity. Some of those demons were so evil, God locked them up in the bottomless pit (2 PE 2:2–5). God scorched the scourge in Sodom and Gomorrah for the same reason (GEN 18—19). God spared Noah and his family from the deluge of water, and Lot and his kids from the deluge of fire; the rest were taken out. Insurrection will multiply again according to Jesus's own prophecy of the last times, where he tells us it will be like the days of Noah and Lot, only worse (LUK 17:26–30).

Will God raze the cities again? Probably not, for the earth is destined to burn with fire, and that hellhole could be on us (2 PE 3:10). Prior to becoming president, Abe Lincoln warned about the only foe that would ever beat us: the terror within. Lincoln (1838) orated, "Shall we expect some transatlantic military giant to step the ocean, and crush us at a blow? Never!... If it ever reach us it must spring up amongst us; it cannot come from abroad. If destruction be our lot, we must ourselves be its author and finisher. As a nation of freemen we must live through all time or die by suicide." Well there it is, as foretelling as any prophecy found in the Bible.

God will burn the hellions in the lake of fire as soon as judgment has been pronounced (REV 20). Knowing the end is near, the insurgents hurry into the flames, not to rescue anyone but to abandon everyone. This is the dominion of Lucifer, for he is gathering up his brood of hatemongers. He knows the final act is playing out and he desperately wants you to burn with him. He rebelled against God and it got him kicked out of heaven along with a third of the angels who had joined him in mutiny (ISA 14:12–15: REV

12:1–9). During the end times, a third of humankind will die by the sword, plagues, famine, and wild or evil beasts and people (EZE 5:2–17; EZE 14:21; REV 9:15–21); these four judgments will be levied upon agitators of malevolence and animosity.

The great upheaval is imminent. Anger, hate, rage, abuse, and savagery are the strategies of this enemy. You can see barbarians everywhere on television; and they show up publicly in hordes looting, burning, assaulting, and destroying. They possess a mob mentality, whereby the group is magnitudes more dangerous than individuals who join. Engaging in groupthink and group polarization, members consequently lose their individuality, yielding to vacuous ruffians and thugs. It is easy to purchase a ready-made mob, especially if the motive is to silence conservatives and Christians. They pillage, attack, ransack, and plunder under a guise of fairness, justice, and protest as if wild and reckless behavior is protected by the Constitution. They are comprised of professional rioters and militant demonstrators posing as a "peaceful" march which is about as peaceful as conventional warfare. Wise up, you guys. What you are doing is in direct violation of the very rights you claim to value. But let's face it, this is the sham, and anybody that is paying attention knows it. Who are they trying to fool, if not themselves? They are the fools and they have been fooled by the great deceiver, Satan (REV 9:4; REV 13:16–18; REV 14:9–11). They will receive his mark while Christ already has marked his chosen for the final exodus (JOH 6:27; EPH 1:12–14; REV 7:3; REV 14:12). Walk towards Jesus; or run to your demise.

So, what can we expect during the final episode of Earth? Terrible times, that's what (2 TI 3:1–9). Let me break it down for you.

- ➢ People will care principally about self ("lovers of themselves"). The prime objectives will be gratification, extravagance, and exaltation of self. It will not matter to them how others are affected, in particular God, because these people are impure and ungrateful, unforgiving and unrepentant, disobedient to God and unconcerned about natural laws and civilized rules.
- ➢ People will be lovers of money and haters of goodness. They will crave power, glory, fame, praise, pleasure, and the means to overindulge in their worldly desires and nefarious pursuits. They will lie, cheat, steal, and slander; they will deal in treachery, treason, and torment; they will be out of control but will not admit or realize any fault.

- People will pretend to be honorable but will deceive themselves with their self-righteousness. They will deny the true power of a cleansed heart, and the source thereof which is Jesus Christ. And they will use their trickery and piety to sneak into homes, businesses, and governments to take advantage. Men will seduce weak-minded women to appease misogynous and deviant imaginations.
- People will shun the truth, knowing full well they are rejecting it; and justify their cheating and reprobate ways by operating under an invented faith that is based on a hedonistic worldview. They will openly display their arrogance and error, cloaked by the guise of liberty and political correctness. But they will be brought down because of their folly.

Is this not the trend today with certain governments and among power brokers who sponsor globalism? They use their wealth to persuade the feeble-minded who also love the money and want the delight it buys. Meanwhile, peeking from behind the curtain, the conceited manipulators relish in the viciousness they are sponsoring. They are mistaken in supposing they have sufficiently removed themselves from the hideous acts they are backing, for they cannot hide from God. Besides, they have been exposed already but the populous doesn't seem to care, except those who favor cleanliness of thought and heart and find rest for their souls by abiding in the Lord.

The following list is but a smattering of the insanity going on in our government and around the globe in the past decade. Decisions are being made by leaders which are idiotic at best and insane at worst. I think anyone condoning such behaviors should have their heads examined. How about you, do you rate the following episodes reprehensible or do you approve?

- Playing the race card at every opportunity to incite division or to smear an honest person's reputation. Race baiting is despicable; especially unsubstantiated accusations of bigotry or abuse levied in order to gain personal advantage or to defame a rival. It figures, the ones constantly yelling racism are usually the ones who are prejudiced or ethnocentric. And it is not just race bating, this includes false accusations of sexual misconduct, impropriety, or criminal behavior requiring the accused to either defend themselves indefinitely or give up the fight and bow out.
- Confiscating guns from law abiding citizens in high crime areas through imbalanced laws that preclude defending one's self, home and family, ensuring only criminals have access to weapons.

- Opening the floodgates at the border by endorsing unchecked migration, causing influx of innumerous, unwelcome derelicts. Providing welfare to illegals paid with taxpayer dollars and allowing them to vote. Turning known alien felons loose on society who are tagged for deportation.
- Delivering firearms into the hands of Mexican drug cartels, leading to catastrophic situations like the murder of a federal agent.
- Exchanging five enemy combatant generals for a US Army deserter.
- Abandoning an ambassador in enemy territory with no security or shield, only to be assassinated along with many of his staff and those coming to his aid.
- Giving $1.7 billion in cool cash to a state sponsor of terrorism that hates the USA.
- Permitting violence feigned as protected speech and prohibiting police and prosecutors from intervening.
- Relinquishing control of one-fifth of our uranium to a Russian operation.
- Using a concocted dossier funded by a political campaign to persuade a federal judge to issue a warrant allowing surveillance of the opposition solely to fish for dirt on a presidential candidate and his personnel.
- Congress wasting months and millions of taxpayer dollars pursuing false narratives, investigations, and accusations rather than doing their jobs by investigating real crimes, enacting legislation that will benefit the nation, and upholding the Constitution they swore to defend. Not to mention using unallocated money from an unauthorized slush fund to pay off victims of malfeasance and misconduct by congressional officeholders.
- Weaponizing federal intelligence and law enforcement to spy on private citizens and political opponents without probable cause, in search of a reason to harass or charge them. Then unmaking those secretly surveilled to throw suspicion upon innocent people. Mutineers from the deep state along with past executives planned and executed a coup-d'état against a duly elected president, which is sedition if not treason.
- Dropping legitimate investigations where criminal intent was clearly evident. Espionage was being committed to gain a partisan advantage; perpetrators have avoided culpability and justice, but not embarrassment.

Sexual Confusion

Possibly, the greatest atrocity responsible for the advancing deterioration of society is sexual promiscuity and confusion. It has multiplied across the globe and is spreading like wildfire in the USA. This has caused the dismantling of empires, the downfall of nations, the breakdown of families, the perversion of the institution of marriage, the demolition of reputations, and the twisting of minds. The real abomination is that such instability is being endorsed if not sponsored by the media, the arts, the entertainment industry, political pundits, and religious fanatics. It is contaminating our citizenry and damaging the brains of our children at every stage of their development. It's as if the instigators want future generations to be perpetually unsure, convincing youth to question their identity especially their sexuality. But this appeases only those who would defile little ones, and exploit the lost, weak, uncertain, brokenhearted, and disadvantaged.

As a graduate student, I studied developmental psychology (among other things) and was particularly impressed with Erikson's psychosocial model. He postulated phases in human development, each presenting an internal conflict to resolve. During adolescence, the primary personal struggle is identity versus role confusion (Erikson, 1968). These days, teens are especially unsure of their identity and confused about their sexuality because they are inundated with scenarios and images portraying all manner of deviant carnal behavior. And this drags them into a world of pornography, sensual acting out, and very high-risk behavior. Kids are being deprived of puberty completely, introduced to sex progressively earlier in life. For prepubescent minors declared unprepared, they prescribe hormone treatments (e.g., puberty blockers). Such sexual disruptions distort the psyche of children by interfering with normal maturity, thereby causing psychological problems that can pervade their thoughts throughout adulthood. Many victims attempt to relive the childhood they lost, only to carry on this abhorrent cycle.

There is a period of childhood when sexual desire is supposed to lie dormant until the hormones catch up, but the world does not allow it to remain latent. Sexual eccentricities are being disclosed to younger children who should be protected from such exposure. Without strict parental guidance kids are left defenseless. I imagine this is the intention, to make sex a free-for-all instead of a conscious act; to make it exclusively physical and eliminate the spiritual aspect altogether; to make it legal in any fashion or form, and to justify detestable sexual deviancy such as pedophilia.

Sexual confusion is becoming quite common, and it can result in dire consequences with regards to development, peace of mind, and behavioral regularity. The Diagnostic and Statistical Manual (DSM) has a diagnosis called gender dysphoria. This is when an apparent incongruence exists between one's gender identity or desire and his or her biological sex, causing the sufferer great distress and dissatisfaction. I have treated many patients with this problem and they are very uncomfortable in their own skin. They are unsure who they really want to be and are very much influenced by others' opinions about who they should be or who they should want to be. They do not realize that they can become anybody they desire, and they need assurance that the decision is theirs' to make; especially, they need reinforcement when their pursuits are honorable and upright.

The Bible teaches that God created all animals, including humans, to be male and female (GEN 1:27; GEN 6:19). Evolutionists teach that humans and other lifeforms erupted from slime. Either way, it is indisputable that all mammals started out as two sexes, male and female. So where did these other gender identities come from? Did they evolve or were they invented? You know, most anybody can stand naked in front of the mirror and identify their sex. So why the confusion? How do people come to believe they are not as they appear? Well, some rascal had to otherwise show them or teach them. People are born with a sex, but not with a gender identity issue. There was a slogan back in the 1960s that went like this: if it feels good do it. That's how the identity sneaks in; you see it, you do it, you feel it, maybe you like it, even though it doesn't seem right. Enter the confusion.

The abovementioned DSM is the handbook used by mental health professionals, providers, and payers. In 1973 the American Psychological Association (APA) reclassified homosexuality naming it sexual orientation disturbance (DSM II). To be politically correct, this sexual peculiarity was suddenly deemed normal, though statistically this was not the case. In 1984 it was redefined again (DSM III), before being removed completely in the 1987 revision, and in 1994 (DSM IV) and subsequent versions. Now we are up to the DSM 5 (in 2013 they changed to Arabic numerals). Sexual abnormalities listed in the DSM 5 are sadism/masochism, pedophilia, and paraphilic disorder (misleadingly, while a paraphilia such as fetishism or transvestitism is regarded to be a necessary criterion, its presence doesn't imply that a person has paraphilic disorder or needs treatment). Such DSM alterations have had very little to do with frequency distributions and standard deviations and more to do with politics, pressure, and profits. Sexual intercourse is a behavior, not a lifestyle. The only genetic predispositions in humanity are found in the chromosomal makeup; anything beyond that design is learned, not preprogrammed.

There is a zealous movement (LGBTQ) that periodically adds new sexual categories to the "normal" list. The purpose is to make it socially proper to sanction without reservation any and all sexual orientations and proclivities. You can be heterosexual, homosexual, bisexual, transsexual, questionable, pansexual, and all possible combinations. In time, it will be okay to engage in incest, adultery, bestiality, necrophilia, pedophilia, rape, sadomasochism, and every other variety of perversion and paraphilia. Such things used to be unlawful in this country; they still are according to God's law. People are having sex with anyone and anything, alive or dead, animate or inanimate, real or unreal. Is this what they mean by sexual freedom? This is not inborn it is an aberration! But it is not unprecedented according to biblical prophecy and history.

Should I dislike these people or judge them for who they are? Of course not! I will treat them the same way I treat everyone else, as a fellow human who is God's child. In my psychotherapy practice, I have treated many members of the LGBTQ community and I have attended their seminars. And I have no problem relating to them. They experience the same issues as anyone else to include depression, anxiety, psychosis, and low self-esteem. My job is to help them love themselves, and care, and to elevate their self-esteem; to teach them coping skills and assist them in facing reality with confidence. I have no intention of trying to change them, but to encourage them to become all they can be. Let it be known, however, that they have a much higher rate of suicide and mental illness than the general population for several reasons (Chakraborty et al., 2011; Bagley and Tremblay, 2000; Proctor and Groze, 1994). Whether their mental condition or emotional instability was instilled before or after their transformation depends on the person; though in my experience most have been abused or traumatized. I cannot conclude that they were born into this lifestyle because it is a preference not a predisposition. Possibly, a majority of those seeking counseling have identity problems but do not believe their behavior is the reason. I am obliged to help them change their beliefs if that is their goal; but I place the impetus on them to establish behavioral goals and have a vision of hope. Like I do with all my patients, I intend to work within their belief system, not impose mine. Thus, I make it a point to find out exactly what they believe and why.

My belief is that all breathing genera on the planet were created male or female to propagate a particular species. They were never intended to crossbreed; indeed, they cannot. Remember, evolutionary processes occur only within kinds. But what will become of the human race if sex is merely a way to appease one's lust and live out one's private, peculiar fantasies? I mean, you can marry your cousin, your career, your car, your computer, or your cat. Old-fashioned, traditional nuptials is out of vogue, while devout heterosexual monogamy could thwart many societal woes to include deadbeat parents, delinquent children, addiction, broken homes, and crime. Could humanity die out someday due to zero population growth? Well yes, but for the approaching apocalypse. You can chop your body up into all manner of disfigurations, though it will not change your DNA; but it might make you sterile.

It is generally unknown to those engaging in unnatural sexual behaviors that such activity eventually ceases to satisfy. That's why many of these people turn to increasingly more divergent practices simply to become sexually aroused; these persons behave kinkier in order to derive pleasure from sex, until they become completely impotent. In other words, deviant sex and sex addiction frequently leads to sexual dysfunction. It is next to impossible for those people to adopt a healthy, monogamous heterosexual lifestyle, as it will no longer be alluring. However, people have been known to change their lifestyles when spirituality is reintroduced in the context of intensive and extensive psychotherapy (Barber, 2016; Spitzer, 2003; Yarwood, 1998). But again, that must be their choice in accordance with their goals. Those wishing to alter their beliefs usually can change their behavior; indeed, without a change in thinking, behavior will never change.

The Greeks have several words for love. The most commonly understood is physical love (*eros*); originally identified with passion, it primarily connotes lust. This is the kind of love the world cares about, for it is not discriminatory and nothing is prohibited. Then there is self-love, playful love, and the ups and downs of romantic love. These are mostly physical in nature. Moving towards the mental side of love, we have the selection process associated with mating, followed by brotherly love (*philia*), and familial love (*storge*). Love is not just a feeling or a behavior however, it is a thought; and thoughts can become desires and vice-versa. While thoughtful kinds of love are more powerful than merely physical, they are not perfect. At the top of the hierarchy is God's perfect and unrestricted love (*agape*); it is spiritual and supernatural (not of this world). God loves us unconditionally and commands us to love him the same; we also are to love all people. We approach *agape* love with our inner circle (kids, spouses, dearest friends); though extremely powerful, our love is seldom without conditions. That is, humans can experience spiritual love and can express it, but are incapable of maintaining it. Animals cannot fathom such flawless and absolute love; but people can if they are able to see it in the man Jesus Christ.

The world would eliminate all types of love except the erotic kind. The world would disallow morality, if possible, as it is restrictive to the animalistic and egoistic passions of the flesh. Psychoanalytically speaking, the strategy is to deflate the superego, and let the ego watch, thereby enabling expression of the id. Passion, intimacy, and desire are overridden by hunger, craving, and aggression; and this is becoming the fad. The world would subordinate God's plan for love and his prescription for sexuality in favor of man's. It is a no-holds-barred approach to narcissism, sexual exploitation, and self-indulgence. It is not based on equality, but actually degrades others, their feelings, and their worth. It moves individuals to view themselves as a god to the degree that only their wants are important; there is no motivation to achieve any other purpose. And this is precisely Satan's solution, scheme, and thinking. The late Malcolm Muggeridge once stated, "If God is dead, somebody is going to have to take his place. It will be megalomania or erotomania, the drive for power or the drive for pleasure..." Personally, I rather expect it will be both.

Will you enable society to indoctrinate your kids, and teach them from preschool through graduate school that they are nothing but sexual objects and their reason for living is to gratify the flesh? Try to imagine how it will end if this be the case; it will truly be a hell on Earth. Study the triptych painting by Hieronymus Bosch entitled *The Garden of Earthly Delights* (Museo del Prado, Madrid Spain) and it will give you a visual impression of where this road ends. It's a dead end.

It is not God's will for us to stray in this way, but he permits us to pick our paths. He did not plan your sin, but he has a plan for your sin. If you turn to him you will be acquitted; if not you will be convicted. But you know this, because your own conscience can realize it without formal instruction. You were given this knowledge by God himself (JER 31:33–34; ROM 2:14–15); I suggest you listen to your conscience and follow it. Otherwise, God will permit you to follow these wayward philosophies, paths, and pathologies (ROM 1:21–32), which will sear your conscience like a hot iron (1 TI 4:1–3). And when you do you will know beforehand it is wrong and that the consequences will be calamitous if not damning (2 PE 3:3–8).

Do not be caught up in the ways of the world. (MAT 7:13; ROM 2:12; COL 2:8), which is redefining truth, decency, sexuality, and love. Admit Christ into your heart and he will show you what love is all about. Will it be a smoother ride? Probably not; in fact, it likely will be tougher and crueler (2 TI 2:3–4). The world will hate you because you claim Christ (JOH 15:18–21), but Christ has overcome the world on your behalf (JOH 16:33). God uses these challenges to make you a better person, and to move you in another, safer direction (ROM 8:28). And he will unstiffen your heart if you face misfortune with him and not blame him for it. God weaves a variety of twists and turns into your life, but the result is a lovely heart (Zacharias, 2007); for God's love is tender. And with his spirit living in concert with yours, you can build others up, even as Satan is trying to drag the world down. Everyone can use a generous helping of tender loving care, and that approximates *agape* love. TLC will strengthen every relationship in your life; it is particularly necessary for successful marriages and effective parenting. TLC will fulfill better than other kinds of love, for it reflects God (1 JO 4:5–21). But the current craze is to love worldly things, especially power over others; surely, love has nothing to do with that.

This Is War

There is a perpetual war between good and evil; this war began before humans arrived on the scene. It actually started in heaven when Lucifer (Satan) and his minions turned against God. They were wishing to set up a supreme kingdom of their own (ISA 14:12–15; EZE 28:14–19; REV 12:7–12); but instead got tossed out of God's kingdom. The war has trickled down to Earth because the fallen angels (including Lucifer) landed here. And the combat continues, because Satan's earthly quest has been to recruit human followers to join him in the fight and the fall (REV 16:14–16). Anyone opposing God is on the wrong side of the Law and the Gospel.

Allow me to include the current pandemic of Islamic terrorism as an application of this global war and an extension of the battle between good and evil. The war is real and we are fighting once again for our freedoms, loved ones, and livelihood. Are we no longer the land of the free and the home of the brave? The USA cannot be a spectator in this campaign; indeed, we must lead. Which is the nobler cause, love or fear, good or evil, truth or dare? I will dig further into the nuts and bolts of spiritual warfare in the next chapter, but for now we will explore worldly conflicts and what we ought to do about it.

I have proffered a strategy on how we can prevail in our struggle against terrorism. It is based on extensive research, as well as expertise in the areas of tactics, doctrine, and joint military operations (my experience ranges from active duty in a combat unit to two decades as a defense analyst). I also will be referencing *The Art of War*. It is one of the greatest treatises on warfare, written about 7500 years ago in ancient China by Sun Tzu (see Sun, 2017). The tenets outlined in his treatise still apply to this day.

Like prior global wars, the enemy's goal is to rule the world. Islamic jihadists strive for a worldwide theocracy where all inhabitants acquiesce to their fanatical creed. How do they propose to accomplish this totalitarian regime? By eradicating the planet of everyone who does not believe as they, which includes Christians and Jews, and well as Muslims that do not embrace their extremist ideals. They also intend to undermine united, independent, and neutral world leaders and their countries, and murder anyone they label an infidel including associates, friends, families, and offspring. Islamist tactics involve invading every sovereign land by posing as refugees, taking advantage of open borders, obtaining visas, recruitment and enticement, coercion, brainwashing of youth, traveling incognito with assumed names and forged documents, blending in, controlling the narrative, undermining institutions (political, educational, media), and all manner of deception and insurrection. Sound familiar? These are the same tactics used by most globalist movements, to include those of communist Russia and China, as well as anarchists in our own country.

The chief strategic errors of radical Islamists in particular and terrorists in general are they do not adhere to the leadership guidelines and preemptive principles advanced by Sun Tzu. Virtually all globalists violate these tenets. First of all, their leaders lack integrity, sincerity, morality, courage, and conviction. Indeed, they are the opposite; they are reckless, cowardly, quick-tempered, dishonorable, and glory-seeking. Furthermore, they are morally in the wrong. The foremost preemptive principle is to seize the moral high ground, which requires the cause to be reputable. A second principle is to study and know your adversary. Terrorists are neither in the right, nor do they understand who they are fighting against. Islamists proclaim Allah when they attack, shoot, or bomb harmless bystanders, but such atrocities are against Almighty God and he is against those malefactors. The godly have God on their side when facing extreme danger. Although we have no choice but to fight or die (JOE 3:9–14), God will fight with us if we take a stand against evil (1 SA 74:27), for the battle belongs to him (1 SA 17:41–47; 2

CH 20:15). A third principle is to refrain from killing when you are not threatened. But terrorists will kill anyone, even babies; they appear to enjoy it. A fourth preemptive principle is to refrain from waging war if you won't succeed. I can assure you they cannot defy God and succeed.

We can win this war if we adhere to our codes: liberty, morality, equality, accountability, truth, and justice. These virtues will sell themselves because they are highly valued, especially among peoples who are not allotted them. Terrorists will not sanction such virtues but seek to liquidate them and everyone who advocates for them. This is where they lose any semblance of religious or moral superiority. Jihadists are resolute in initiating World War III as if their destiny is to rule; but their destiny is to die.

We certainly are at war with terrorism, especially with respect to Islamic jihadism (Gorka, 2016), as well as homegrown fanaticism and related violence. The politicization of this issue has enabled the indoctrination of naive liberals to despise America, making them susceptible to radicalization. Unfortunately, they act out on their hate with no knowledge of the end game much less the eternal consequences. Terrorists are not victims; and retaliating against them is not aggression it is self-defense. Leftwing pundits have suggested that America is the aggressor, almost justifying jihadism and extremism (Horowitz, 2014). Whose side are they on anyway? If they are really against what this country stands for why can't they proffer one thing that they are not against (other than raising taxes)?

We can take a look back and evaluate this war or that war, and how we could've done things differently. But who can reasonably argue that we needn't foil efforts of nation-states, terrorist groups, and radicalized hostiles who have declared openly how badly they want us dead? Are we to stand idly by to see if they make good on their reproaches before reacting? We can be proactive without making preemptive strikes or killing innocent people; such are the tactics of the enemy and the reason this is a just war for us. The bottom line: we must pursue these evildoers and eliminate them wherever they hide. The following is but an abridged exposé on the ways we could and should weed out the scoundrels among us and thwart their efforts abroad.

1. Don't make deals with the devil. I start with the premise that diplomacy will be useless against jihadists, terrorists, and extremists. If you try to parlay, they will take everything they can get and return nothing but grief. Case in point, the recently revoked Iran nuclear deal where Iran gets weapons of mass destruction and we get a target on our backs. Iran has proven to be the primary sponsor of terrorism in the Middle East so why forge any deals with them? How about past dealings with North Korea? Has any negotiation or United Nations (UN) resolution ever changed their behavior one whit? They have never been a team player, except for being China's delinquent little brother; it is a relationship of convenience. But it is a house of horrors for the North Korean people. And China has consistently been an insincere dealmaker, infiltrating democracies to fleece them of capital, stealing intellectual property, devaluing currency, and creating trade imbalances; oh, and committing acts of war against the USA and Europe while pretending to be an honest broker. They are trying to scale the fiscal ladder and beef up their military so they can sustain their communistic autocracy and compete globally, while their citizenry remains largely underprivileged. Meanwhile, everybody seems leery of the Russians who are not in a position to hold the winning hand economically or militarily, though their leader maintains a good poker face and bluffs a lot. Russia wants to be a world player again, but I doubt they will accomplish this by allying with Syria. And what is the point of supposed peace talks between Palestinians and Israelis? There can be no agreement given that the Palestinians will never accede to being neighborly with Israel. They refuse to compromise, or live in harmony, because they hate Jews and everything about them; they will never be satisfied until every last Jew is dead and they occupy the land forever.

We can pretend to be diplomatic and speak with these losers when there is intelligence to be gained; but we should never commit to anything. Lord knows they are not to be trusted. But amongst their lies and demands one may infer motives and intent. We can maintain a dialogue, even trade with them, while keeping them at arm's length as well as in the crosshairs. If there is opportunity to verify that they are upholding their end, only then can we proceed; for example, if a rogue nation agrees to nuclear disarmament, our inspectors must be allowed to inspect anything, anytime, anywhere. Thus far, this has never happened.

2. Establish meaningful alliances. Let's converse with Muslims that do not submit to the uncompromising fanatics but are willing to wrangle with extremists of their faith. We can abet those taking up the fight by supplying weapons, training, and planning; but we mustn't fight their battles for them. We're fighting the culprits beside our partners and in our homeland presently. Let's aid any citizenry poised to overthrow an oppressive regime and help them stymie their oppressors. Disseminate information over the airwaves and via printed material to gain converts. Counterpropaganda should be distributed and broadcast to isolated peoples, victims, and the involuntary members of nations which subsidize and export terrorism.

A coalition based on an honorable position will attract a lot more support than one based on murder, rape, and plunder. And with the stakes being life and death, people are inclined to choose life and freedom over death and enslavement. We mustn't trust legates just because they seem earnest or throw us a bone; we can feign candor and toss them a live grenade though. We can ask those who pledged to support us to put up or shut up; or, using the words of General Patton, "lead, follow, or get out of the way."

3. Develop human intelligence. Intel can be enormously valuable in fighting this type of conflict, and the more the merrier. The various agencies gathering data should be working in concert, consolidating, concatenating, and securing consistent and reliable information. Merge databases from the various intelligence agencies in a way that accelerates cross-referencing, analysis, profiling, and reporting. Improve the gathering, sharing, selecting, and judicious circulating of intelligence to allies, military, police, and civilians. Most acts of terrorism on American soil could have been prevented. It's not like there was an absence of warning signs; the perpetrators were on the radar screens of different intelligence organizations, had an Internet presence, and a history of mental illness or aggression.

We should be infiltrating enemy countries, mosques, and terror cells; upsetting hostile governments and institutions; installing agents and insurgents; and taking out their leadership. Identify associations, networks, and so-called places of worship sponsoring clandestine operations, streaming subversive rhetoric or declarations, and affirming treasonous or treacherous plans and directives, and shut them down permanently.

4. Keep people informed. The general population needs to know everything there is to know about the hooligans and their unrighteous itinerary. Education should start here in America, where the conventional wisdom is to leave them be and allow them to practice their religion freely. You've got to be kidding me. Jihadism is not a religion it is a con game. Like General Sun instructed, you need to know your enemy as much as you know yourself. And most people haven't a clue what these people are up to and the wickedness and duplicity that resides in their minds. Spread the truth. They want to dominate the world and subjugate everyone deemed an infidel.

Disseminate training materials to everyone in the USA so citizens can be vigilant and expose potential threats. Perform regular public announcements and updates about developments and dangers. Establish procedures for observing and reporting suspicious activity and provide contact information for anonymously relaying any considerations deemed pertinent. Provide classes/trainings and distribute material about how to be an observant spectator and proactive neighbor. Encourage regional watches and related social networks that connect to our intel apparatus.

Boost cognizance of warning signs like someone shouting "Allah u Akbar" in a public arena, or wearing a thick vest or heavy overcoat in the summertime, or dropping a backpack or package and walking away at the terminal, or frequently casing a place where large groups of people gather, or transferring suspicious items into their garage, or tooling with explosives, chemicals, or containers in their basement. Each American needs to be familiar with the appearance, dress, behavior, and mannerisms of terrorists.

5. Provide advanced training. Being informed is one thing, being prepared to act is another. Train the military, police, our allies, and responsible men and women willing to get involved who can become a force multiplier by recognizing terrorists, suspicious activities, and likely cells, reporting them to the authorities, and possibly neutralizing them.

Pass stricter laws and beef up law enforcement to counter any crimes in which terror or hate are applied. Rotating task forces should be on call around the clock as first responders. Escalate penalties accordingly, by making it a class A felony to engage in, promote, assist, or plan violence against Americans. Rigorize the enforcement and punishment of those planning, organizing, and committing acts of terrorism or sedition. Provide a clear and immediate deterrent for those contemplating such involvement.

Lessen the requirements for accosting, questioning, arresting, and incarcerating terrorists to include redefining rules of search, establishing criteria for probable cause, and reducing the burden of proof necessary for prosecution. Loosen the rules of engagement so that our deployed military can engage enemy combatants, and empower local law enforcement to profile, question, and detain suspicious characters. Place enemy combatants, terrorists, and jihadists in military prisons; make their lives miserable and interrogate the bejesus out of them. This is not to imply that we should employ ancient torture devices on them; but there are ways of being persuasive without invoking excruciating pain or dismembering their bodies.

6. Be more deliberate. General George Washington effectively utilized guerila tactics, conducted surgical strikes, established intelligence and counterintelligence networks, and specifically targeted redcoat officers. It worked.

Disclose and confiscate financial assets, disrupt and destroy money stores and flows, and manipulate their sponsors into expending gobs of money fruitlessly. Confuse their communications, purge Internet accounts, and employ top computer nerds to engage the enemy with the most devastating cyber and electronic warfare they have ever seen (after all, this is what the enemy does). Hang up their operations, businesses, and money via inflexible and incessant legal proceedings, seizures, and lawsuits.

Terrorists love to terrorize, but they are not very fond of being terrorized. We must be more ruthless and treacherous than they, without being hateful, depraved, or evil. We are charged by God to love our enemies (MAT 5:43–45), but that doesn't mean we have to let them get away with homicide. The quickest and most formidable approach is to unleash a firestorm on them whenever and wherever they are gathering or maneuvering. That means we need eyes everywhere, and interdiction teams at the ready.

7. Act clandestinely and resolutely. We must be sneaky about our resolve. We must never let on about the mission, end game, tactics and doctrine, communications, intelligence, capabilities, and operations. Change the plays in midstream to conceal the objective and to display erroneous patterns and movements.

Submissions from General Sun include the following: tire the enemy; divide them; agitate, confuse, intimidate, bait, punish, block, and frustrate them. Dismantle their alliances, disrupt their plans, outmaneuver them, outsmart them, and keep them guessing. Entice leaders and zealots; bribe them, con them, and beguile them with lusts and debauchery. Turn the enemy's strengths into weaknesses, and our weaknesses into strengths. Develop sophisticated threat analyses to keep three steps ahead of them.

Feed news outlets an ample supply of compost for lunch, and let them plaster that all over the headlines, newsreels, and magazine covers. Sway the news media to deem the rubbish they publish to be leaks from trustworthy sources so they will assume the misinformation is credible and newsworthy. The enemy thinks Americans are shallow and stupid; let's guarantee they continue to presume this, by simulating ineptitude, uncertainty, and indifference. Lead them into thinking they are smarter and more cunning; well they already think that, all we have to do is exaggerate that belief. If the press is good at anything it is exaggeration and fake news.

8. Install preventive measures. We must protect the border and secure avenues of intrusion. Employ extreme vetting of foreigners wishing to enter this country, especially from nations with unstable governments, dilapidated economies, and undocumented inhabitants. While we open our doors to immigrants, they must obtain permission to enter the country legally through proper channels; and they should be able to demonstrate how they intend to contribute to our society, especially when they can fill a skill vacancy. They also should learn to speak English. Inspect travel documents of those wishing to return here after visiting certain foreign countries; screen those people requesting travel to and from these locations. Keep a database of all such travels and associated passports, and make it accessible at all ports of entry (air, land, sea).

Establish methods to identify and vanquish radicalization. Perform extensive background checks for anyone pursuing a license in aviation, applying for employment in transportation, seeking a government job dealing with classified material, or attempting to buy firearms or bomb building materials. In particular, have the capability to cross-reference databases on mentally unstable people, hardened criminals, repeat offenders, enemy combatants, and others who would be disqualified to engage in any of the above activities.

Monitor web traffic and social media using keyword triggers; require Internet providers to cooperate with government or face prosecution. Especially keep tabs on the associates and the conduct of known jihadists and militants, those who have travel restrictions, proven troublemakers, and assorted culprits, terrorists, and felons. If someone shows up on a list or a site identifying unruly or shady characters, keep them under surveillance. You can employ varying levels of eavesdropping without being obvious. Completely ignoring suspects who have stopped misbehaving is unadvised. Who wouldn't behave themselves if they knew they were being watched?

9. Define the mission. Sun Tzu was clear about the reasons to enter into war and the reasons not to. The sum and substance, be in it to win it. Our foes' intention is to kill with malice but without honor, plain and simple. They are not warriors, those who choose soft targets and run, assassinating civilians at the mall, church, school, business, or concert. Fringe journalists call them courageous martyrs when they blow themselves up for their cause; sorry to bust their bubble, but suicide bombers are unadulterated cowards.

The masked assassins parade around with a severed head in their grip, or dance on top of mass graves. If they are so satisfied with themselves, why hide? Fighters craving the power and glory of battle are in it for the wrong reasons. Warriors who enter a fight out of duty and honor but leave with hate and conceit have lost their humanity and the battle. We must do what we have to do to defeat the enemy without taking any pleasure in it; otherwise we forfeit moral superiority.

The best way to defeat terrorists is to kill them without hesitation or prejudice. Sometimes that includes spouses and children if they are complicit or they take up the fight when their patriarchs fall. You cannot deradicalize a man, woman, or child who is aiming a loaded AK47 at you. We must drastically increase the casualty count on their side and decrease the losses on ours. Risk analysis and reduction is essential; by the same token, we must drastically elevate the risk level for the enemy. All things considered, ensure the minimization of collateral damage and harm to innocents as priority one.

10. Take up arms. The more US citizens trained to conceal and safely discharge a weapon, the greater will be our success at home, because the bad guys are after good people who are exposed or vulnerable; that's why they frequent soft targets. Reinforce soft targets by emplacing plainclothes, armed security; increase entrance requirements to certain venues; and improve surveillance and reconnaissance in those areas. Advocate the right to bear arms and abolish gun free zones.

In conclusion, let me remind everyone that bad leaders are often the reason nations start wars. Take the second world war, where Hitler and Tojo decided to pick a fight forcing the USA to respond. We never had a beef with those countries until they jumped into the ring and started wreaking havoc. They were in the wrong, making it a just war on our part, so we prevailed. Great empires were ruled by warrior kings such as Alexander and Sennacherib; they were drunk with power and still were thirsty for more. Eventually they were waylaid and another greedy empire took over. Did their armies have any choice in the matter? Or the citizenry? This illustrates the importance of choosing the right people to lead your country. Congress has the power to declare war when another country starts it; the president also can deploy troops in an emergency. That's why it is imperative that we elect people who are themselves being led by God, or else there's no telling what kind of mess they could lead us into. If we attack for no good reason, it will not be a just war. But when God is on our side, how can we possibly lose?

SPIRITUAL WARFARE

Despite the many advances in science and its quest for ultimate truth, there is still conflict between those identifying exclusively with science and those identifying exclusively with religion. Well, not everybody ascribes to it, since some scientists are sincerely religious, and some people of faith employ the scientific method. Contrary to popular belief, science and religion are not incompatible, with possible exceptions being the religions of scientism and atheism which deny truth or deliberately mask it. It would seem atheist-scientists cannot separate mind from brain because only the material realm has meaning. If that were true then how would they be able to contemplate and theorize? It seems counterintuitive to be able to do science at all and be closed to the concept of God. Remember, many prominent scientists were God-fearing men: Copernicus, Bacon, Kepler, Galileo, Pascal, Boyle, Newton, Leibnitz, Faraday, Mendel, Kelvin, Pasteur, Maxwell, Planck and others. That list has grown tremendously in the modern past largely due to verification that the universe had a beginning, is still expanding, and was fine-tuned for life, further solidifying the intelligent design perspective.

I employ the word "religion" strictly to represent a system endorsing specific beliefs regarding the Almighty, for the purpose of establishing truth; in this context religion exercises the spirit. Many use the word religion loosely, purporting to love God and Jesus, while despising religion or at least that blasted word, notwithstanding those who are dedicated to the practice of "true" religion (JAM 1:26–27). I also am using the word "science" strictly to represent a system endorsing empirical study through scrupulous observation and measurement of the natural realm, for the purpose of establishing truth; in this context science exercises the mind. Similarly, many use the word science loosely to reflect approaches that are neither scientific nor practical, notwithstanding those who are dedicated to the practice of "true" science (1 TI 6:20). Both science and religion appeal to truth.

Yet the friction continues as if one way of seeking and discovering truth contradicts the other. Both science and religion can lead someone to the truth, because there is wisdom to be found in the book of nature, and there is wisdom to be found in the book of God; genuinely, God is the author of both books. Note that the creation is finite but God is infinite. God's Word gives us the foundation for figuring out the creation.

The science versus religion fiasco is just one of many in which the world attempts to suppress spirituality in general and Christianity in particular. I will discuss several ways that the world wages war against God. People of God are not beholding to this world as we have been chosen out of the world (JOH 15:19); thus, we have become a rival, particularly to those holding a materialistic worldview. But Christ already has conquered the world (JOH 16:33), so fighting him is futile and pointless.

As a Matter of Fact

Truth is a fact regardless of how it is argued, because truth must be absolute to always be true. To reiterate the law of noncontradiction, something cannot be true and false at the same time. However, the fact that something is false does not necessarily imply the opposite is true; but if something is true its opposite can never be. For example, if it is clear and sunny outside my front door right now, that fact will always be true, though this may not be the case one hour from now. That it is sunny outside my house proves it is not overcast at this moment; it also proves that it is not nighttime in my town. If it's not dark that doesn't imply it's bright, given the countless shades of gray. The point is, truth will always be so, for all people and for all time, within the confines of the reality in which it is derived. There also are truths that will remain so despite the conditions. Mathematically, two plus two equals four and that's a universal fact that will never change regardless of adaptations in reality. But something that is false, can it ever be true?

Let me put it this way: if you alter truth it immediately becomes untrue. But you can rework false until the cows come home and still it will be false. Untrue also can change with time, however. My closest buddy was not a father until his children were born; from that point on he will remain a father even though his kids are now parents; and he will be their father even if they precede him in death; now he will remain a grandfather as long as he lives. Truth is relatively unaffected by time, though time and circumstances can render something untrue that once was true, and vice-versa. But it is not truth that has changed, only reality. Reality is multifaceted and multivariant; there is no single way to measure, observe, interpret, conceptualize and predict it (Polkinghorne, 2005). Truth provides relevance to reality.

Truth is magnitudes more powerful than untruth; untrue usually remains so unless it is proven to be absolutely false. It makes me sigh when people claim that nothing is absolute, especially since they are absolutely sure of themselves. That God exists is absolutely true; atheism is absolutely false. Never can they both be true. However, I am aware of numerous atheists that have become Christians because they chose truth rather than living a lie. And sometimes it was the result of an encounter with reality if not God himself. I personally don't know any Christians that became atheists but I suppose it happens.

The thing about truth is, frequently it can be verified by a thorough check of reality under varying circumstances. A fact must be consistently true and in accordance with reality or it is not a fact. Everyone has the capacity to explain reality in a logical and rational way, as long as the definition of it is in agreement with the facts.

Partial facts do not equate to truth, and they do not provide definitive answers. Let's say I ask my pal Bob, "What's happening?" He replies, "Not much." That might be partially true but it sure doesn't answer my question. He could have answered, "life," or "death" and both of these replies would be true, at least in part, but neither of these responses would provide any information either. What if Bob says, "I'm fixing to head over to Bill's place." Now that is an acceptable answer, but is it true? I can verify this. Maybe I respond, "Mind if I tag along?" and Bob says "Okay," and we proceed together to Bill's house. I will have verified that not only did Bob sufficiently answer my question, but he also answered it with the truth. Truth enhances trust which forms the basis of real friendships, like the relationship I have with my pals Bob and Bill.

When we are not confident, we can do some research, get other opinions, maybe talk to experts. Information is power, isn't it? Enough of it can render something to be factual. If I assume that the burner on the oven is hot, I can test if that is true without getting burned. If every student in the classroom agrees about what they heard the instructor say, then it has been substantiated to be real for those present. If I am unsure about what I heard, I can ask the speaker to clarify what he or she said. It is a good idea to get and give feedback to ensure verbal communications are effective in both directions. It also is a good practice to engage in reality testing, sharing feedback, soliciting multiple opinions, and arriving at a consensus. You can appreciate that most people do not dispute absolute truth. Those that do might be deranged, impaired, deceitful, or ignorant. But they can be shown the truth, or discover it for themselves, by checking it out in light of known indisputable facts. Even a person who is psychotic can be trained to discriminate between real and unreal; it takes considerable practice. While truth itself is absolute, our knowledge of it is not; but God's is.

Humans have a unique ability for discovering truth through deduction; that is, we can derive facts from knowing other facts. In the Introduction, I defined a syllogism; to illustrate, if A=B and B=C, then A=C. But if A=1 and B=1 that doesn't prove that A=B, because A could be my child and B could be your child, and both were born exactly one year ago; however, they are different in most other respects. Before inferring facts from partial data, one must define specifically the components, conditions, and assumptions.

Another valuable faculty we possess is inductive reasoning; for example, if it is raining at my house it is very likely to be raining at my neighbor's house down the street. But I am not 100 percent certain, because I remember as a boy standing in the rain at the curb of my grandparents' house in Florida and crossing the street where it was not raining. So inductive reasoning helps to find truth, but it is not infallible; this is unlike deductive reasoning when I have completely verified my premises to be true before arriving at a conclusion. There is authority and muscle in truth, but before you declare something to be true, you'd better do your homework.

People (not just scientists) want answers to their questions, especially the crucial questions (LUK 2:47). We seek truth, remedies, success, solutions, and meaning; and when we find them, we are pleased and placated, if not captivated. Such experience serves to increase our fascination, imagination, curiosity, wonderment, productivity, and search (PSA 65:4; PSA 139:3–8). It's nice to figure out how something works or what caused it; but it is vastly more enlightening to find out why it exists or what it is made of. Unfortunately, science cannot be used to solve every dilemma, because there are simply some impasses in which science and technology are unavailing (at least for now). For example, scientists can explain how gravity causes things to fall to the ground, but they cannot tell you exactly what gravity is made of and why it exists.

Anyhow, aren't you interested in mysteries, and don't you muse about the unknown? Have you never been in awe of something amazing, or puzzling? For instance, are you not astonished at the intricacy, beauty, spectacle, and immensity of the universe, nature, and living organisms, not to mention your own body and mind (PSA 40:5)? These phenomena can be appreciated by people of all walks of life, religions, lifestyles, customs, disciplines, and worldviews. To find answers, reasons, and solutions one must make the effort; that is, seek and you will find (1 CH 28:9; JER 29:13; MAT 7:7–8).

Exploration and discovery typically lead to new ideas, innovations, and pursuits, as well as additional triumphs. Achievements make most people yearn for more. I am pleased when I gain greater knowledge and wisdom, better understand the grand design, or engage in dialogue with the artist, author, architect, or creator of an original work. How about you? Are you willing to make the effort to increase your knowledge and understanding? Certainly, to understand the truth of the Bible, to discover God's reasons for doing what he does, and to find answers to certain unnatural quandaries, it requires substantial vigor. Rarely does anyone grasp these concepts after a single reading of the Bible. But the more you study it the greater becomes your insight and wisdom.

Encounters in discovery can be life changing because they not only engage the mind but also stimulate the spirit. It follows that many explanations do not fall into the category of natural, causal, physical, or observable. Have you heard about this one? There is a growing religion these days called scientism, which rejects all explanations other than scientific. The notion of religion would be repulsive to followers of scientism as they deny faith of any kind. They are not representatives of true science, however, because they dismiss possibilities and they make presumptions without providing credible evidence. It is a form of blind faith, which is their handicap; yet they accuse people of religious conviction as being blind. Not only is the faith of scientism and atheism blind, but their followers also are blind regarding their unbelief. Therein rests the conflict, propagated by people who are limited, albeit blinded by their own prejudices. Mind you, there are people on all sides of an issue who engage in shallow reasoning, confabulation of proof, and cognitive conceit.

A large part of the disagreement can be found in several dichotomies, such as evolution versus creation, material versus spiritual, natural versus supernatural, visible versus invisible, physical versus mental, and emotional versus rational. However, none of these pairs are mutually exclusive, and each can exist in harmony with its counterpart; and they all contribute to the wonderment. It isn't either science or religion; but it does matter your foundation. One may ask, how did the universe get here? Did it come from nothing, from a multiverse, from a spontaneous explosion of matter and energy, from a singularity, from a quantum vacuum fluctuation, from an intelligent designer, or some combination of these (GEN 1:1)? When one proceeds from a particular vantage point, the findings might be constrained to comport with expectations; especially if the person is closed-minded, is ignorant of the evidence, or clings to a perceptual bias. But this limits knowledge and hides the truth. Consider Aristotle, who was unfamiliar with the Word of God but concluded that a divine intelligent being must exist given the complexity of the universe (Craig, 2010).

Humans communicate using a language that is very complex and rule-based; but it works quite well (ACT 2:1–12; EPH 4:29). Just like the universe, there is a mathematical complexion to language. One can infer intelligence when he or she hears people talking, regardless of the language; or sees foreign writing, computer code, hieroglyphics, or simple figures drawn in the sand. If you are reading this, you know that it was written by an intelligent being with a reasonable command of English. Persons might disagree about my intelligence, but they know this dissertation didn't simply fall together from an explosion of matter and energy; it came together via an eruption of thoughts. Considerably more complicated than this arrangement of letters, words, sentences, and paragraphs is the language of DNA. Would anyone propose with conviction that such a complicated and extensive configuration of information and instructions tumbled together by accident? There is no occurrence that has ever been observed throughout the history of humankind where information was found to exist in the absence of intelligence. No serious scientist believes that truth, meaning, and amazement arrive by way of unconscious biochemical processes in his or her brain. If he or she didn't seek it, attend to it, analyze it, or explain it then the meaning would be unverifiable, uninteresting, and unbelievable (i.e., immaterial).

What can science tell us? Not a thing. Science is a process, a discipline comprised of scientists who study, observe, experiment, manipulate, formulate, measure, interpret, and describe the universal realm and its inhabitants. Scientists postulate theoretical constructs based on causal and correlative relationships observed among variables. Experimentation is an attempt to prove or disprove hypotheses derived to test aspects of those theories. Sometimes findings are replicated to the extent that one can establish facts that holds up to scrutiny, thereby helping to define, explain, and predict. The scientific method is a very useful and effective procedure for determining truth, gaining acumen, establishing cause, and forecasting upcoming events (PSA 100:5; PSA 119:142; JOH 8:31–32; 1 JO 5:20).

Some scientific methods are more reliable than others, however. For example, operational science is the study of the here and now in a precise manner, so that one can repeat the conditions and replicate the findings, in order to detect trends, differences, and relationships. On the other hand, historical (also "forensic") science is the study of the present in order to draw inferences about the past or future. While the principle of uniformity would suggest that causal relationships from the present are representative of the past, or vice-versa, this is not always the case. The major problem with uniformity theory is that it is impossible to replicate all situational conditions or control all extraneous variables with precision; you cannot extrapolate a past using the present conditions if you cannot quantify with exactness past conditions. If I give my wife a kiss, I might get a different reaction than the last time because the situation might be different. I do not discount the use of operational research and historical research; they have unique applications. Certainly, forensic evidence helps considerably to establish a concrete case; but it has less predictive power than circumstantial evidence. If you have the perpetrator's DNA you can nail him for the assault, but it will not predict future assaults; a history of assault would be a better predictor. Yet, the generalizability of findings is limited in both illustrations.

At times, results may be contradictory, but facts will not. To illustrate, geologic columns were established via historical research using fossil evidence; these columns were proposed to extend over vast eras of time. But operational research has demonstrated that the process of fossilization can vary with environmental conditions and can occur in a very short period of time. Further, layers of sediment can be laid down quickly causing the same fossils to be found in multiple strata; they don't always follow the timeframe or pattern of geologic columns. Geologists formulated the columns using fossil evidence and dated the fossils according to which column they were associated. How's that for circular reasoning? This is not to say that workable models are not useful; but if they were proven they would no longer be models.

Much of the scientific evidence would insinuate that the universe is billions of years old. Well maybe it is, but a lot of experts disagree with that conclusion. All God has to do is speak and he can create or destroy universes in the twinkle of an eye. The assumption of uniformity precludes the possibility that some entities are not entirely constant, like the strength of gravity, the speed of light, and the rate of universal expansion. But a change in any of these factors could alter the postulated age of the universe. We will address this conundrum in an upcoming chapter.

Human egos often influence us into positions or suppositions that are not proven to be true. We are seldom 100 percent positive. Present your findings, debate them, and if they lead to sound conclusions publish them. When I conducted scientific research, the standard was usually the $p < .05$ level of significance (i.e., 95 percent confidence); this meant a finding meeting this standard had less than 5 percent likelihood of being coincidental. Such results do not establish truth but trends. Can things be proven scientifically? Yes, sometimes they can; but don't put them out as truth if they are not confirmed. When a breakthrough leads to a finding of truth, that is worth shouting about.

Columbus explored the prospect of an alternate trade route from Europe to India and discovered something far more amazing—America. And though he wasn't the first to stumble upon that truth, he was the first to bring the truth back to Europe and spread the word. Interestingly, that which he sought to prove was proven false, but what he found to be true was considerably more illuminating. Notice how some discoveries can change lives, or even the world, and have an impact for centuries to come. Everybody has the capacity to make such an impression, and it will bring glory to God.

The Power of Discovery

As previously mentioned, I have used scientific methods extensively; I had a prosperous career as a research psychologist, mostly for the government and military contractors. I have experience performing basic, clinical, and applied research. I have designed, conducted, and executed experiments; performed data reduction and analyses; authored and published scientific and technical reports; and coauthored a textbook on research and statistics (Barber et al., 2003). I have amassed extensive scientific knowledge because I am a psychologist, a doctor of philosophy with twenty years performing psychological research and twenty more years as a professor and psychotherapist. And all this experience made me even more convicted of my faith in Christianity (MAT 17:20; HEB 11:1). It did not lead me away from the Holy Bible but towards it, to the extent that I am certain the Bible is the true Word of God. There has been no conflict within my mind between my scientific and my religious pursuits; neither have I encountered any discrepancy between God's truth and scientific facts. Like Isaac Newton, considered to be the father of classical physics, my scientific journey has left me in greater admiration of our God and his creation. And I likewise view science as a gift from God to help humanity understand the universe, ourselves, and God. Still, I have questions, I seek knowledge, and I especially esteem wisdom and truth (ECC 7:15; JOH 18:32–38). To this day I continue to conduct research, read scientific periodicals and books, and study the Bible. I expect the learning will continue for eternity. Don't forget, there are many avenues to truth, including science and philosophy, but greater than these perhaps is spirituality.

The realization is evident that some things scientists can neither prove nor disprove. In particular, it is impossible to disprove the existence of God; and it is impossible to prove atheism. Scientists have yet to fully explain the cause of the universe, or detect and examine a cosmic string; they don't fully comprehend the sophistication and indestructability of light, and they haven't a clue what lies beyond the black hole. Science cannot be employed to discover the meaning of your life, cannot define God, cannot explain the origin of thought or love, cannot explain the aftermath of death, and cannot account for miracles (ACT 2:2–22; HEB 2:34). Thus, science is not the ultimate teacher, for it can only explore the natural.

What has been proven via science? Lots of things; for example, we know the universe began a finite period of time ago and that it has been fine-tuned to support life. The universe operates within certain physical laws; and humans operate within moral laws. God does not have to operate within those laws since he is the one that decreed them. God is the standard of morality and the legislator of universal regulations. Some things exist which are unseen; indeed, they cannot be perceived with any of the five senses. Invisible entities cannot be disproven to exist; in fact, we often can observe their effects, though we might not be able to pinpoint the exact purpose or mechanism (ROM 1:17–20).

It seems obvious to me that there are a great many phenomena that are explainable only in supernatural or spiritual terms, such as God, his attributes, and his works (COL 19). Matters that are discerned spiritually usually cannot be explained scientifically (1 CO 2:13–14). Take miracles; I bet everyone has experienced or witnessed one but we don't always know it. I propose that another very interesting field of study would be the spiritual essence of life, if one actually could develop a way to inspect and measure it. I suppose it may be possible, but to date I am unaware of anyone that has succeeded. Scientists have identified the effects of certain undetectable marvels like dark matter and dark energy, but cannot explain the cause or the reason, or the composition. Similarly, one cannot explain the spirit or its cause or composition, but we can observe its effects.

Let us appraise the effects of spirituality. Numerous studies have replicated the positive influence of faith, contemplative prayer, and an active spiritual life in the advancement of healing, to include physical and mental (see Byrd, 1997; Koenig, 2012; Larson et al., 1997). Although spirituality and the spirit are unobservable, their effects are quite astounding. In my work with psychiatric patients I have noticed considerably more positive growth and change, in a shorter timeframe, when spirituality was introduced as a therapeutic intervention. That is, people of faith respond quite well when the treatment plan includes spiritual goals, to include church attendance, silent prayer, Bible study, quality time with loved ones, and meditation. There is considerable research to suggest that methods incorporating spirituality are as effective if not better than traditional psychotherapy alone (Barber, 2016; Hodge, 2006; Hook et al., 2010; Oakes et. al., 2000; Propst et al., 1992).

The most widely accepted paradigm in the healthcare field is the holistic perspective. To be completely whole one needs to be healthy in body, mind, and spirit. Numerous organizations and institutions are adopting this philosophy; further most medical schools now provide spirituality training (Gunderson, 2000; Koenig, et al., 2010; Moore, 1996). I used to teach faith-based workshops to professionals wanting to add spiritual interventions into their therapeutic toolbox. Clearly, there are scientific disciplines with champions who acknowledge the influence and power of spirituality and faith. A number of physicians, physicists, biologists, geologists, and cosmologists are among those accepting this. Scientists who refuse to consider a higher power or a supreme being, or the fact that the spirit provides life and is the most dominant component of our being, they fall into the category of scientism and/or atheism. I don't really like the term scientism because numerous scientists do not share that perspective. In fact, many have concluded that science leads to God, and God has led people to science for that purpose; among them were the pioneers listed previously (see Mundt, 2007). Through scientific investigation and experimentation, the full potential of man is approached, thereby revealing the greatness of God through us, to the glory of his name (Haisch, 2006).

The staunch evolutionists endure without hope since the future of the universe is very bleak to them, and their lives a passing in the wind. They cannot fathom another universe that is flawless, in which we also can exist, a universe without end. Even the multiverse advocates cannot envision such a place, though they might contemplate how they could have done a better job if they had the power to modify this universe. They propose that our universe is poorly designed (what with entropy and all). Can they not ruminate on the alternative that it was designed to be suboptimal on purpose? Personally, I am expecting the new universe to be better by magnitudes than the current one.

Allow an analogy using the automotive industry. Engineers possessing exceptional intelligence are designing great cars and trucks, but the manufacturers incorporate cheap, nondurable materials, causing automobiles to wear out and break down faster. I suppose this may be intentional, perhaps to increase profits through sale of parts and costly maintenance and repairs. That doesn't indicate the design is flawed but that the manufacturers are ingenious. No doubt, they could produce vehicles that endure for decades. Just as God can manufacture a universe that never ends.

The very reason we can envision something that does not currently exist or that cannot be observed proves that everyone has the mental aptitude to imagine. Imagination is plainly a product of higher intelligence and not mere biochemistry. Imagination can lead to invention. The power of thought itself is like a surge of sheer energy. It feels very satisfying indeed when deep in contemplation or introspection, particularly when a light bulb goes off in your head and you proclaim "eureka." But it also can be draining when racking your brain mercilessly without nurturing your body. So, ensure that you get plenty of nourishment; and exercise physically, mentally, and spiritually to achieve holistic health.

Regrettably, the rivalry between science and religion has itself evolved into a fight between materialism and spiritualism. The secularization of society, the relativism of morality, the contamination of education, the denigration of religion, and the meaninglessness ascribed to just about everything—these are casualties of this devastating quarrel. It is waged by people who hate God; they call themselves atheists but this is a misnomer (Hitchens, 2010). Their position is untenable, irrational, meaningless, pointless, and unsupported; mostly it lacks imagination and truth. It is enormously more difficult to believe in the religion of atheism than Christianity (Geisler and Turek, 2004). If atheists opened their hearts and minds to Christ, they might discover truths significantly greater than any derived from science.

It's not that they cannot reckon an eternity of discovery and bliss with our Creator; it's that they refuse. The answers which they do not seek but desperately need are within their reach, but they cannot perceive them due to self-constraint. Even if God performed a miracle in their lives, they would call it a random event. Very narrowminded, wouldn't you agree? The religious scholars of Jesus's time were baffled by his wisdom (LUK 2:42–49); they especially grappled with the concept of being born again. But once you experience it, you will discover a reality and truth of which you were previously unaware (JOH 3:3–6; 1 PE 1:22–23). What exactly does that mean, being reborn? It means being regenerated in the Holy Spirit of the Lord, having been cleansed of sin by the blood of Christ. Once you experience this rebirth, your new life proceeds forever.

The payoff of exploration is discovery. The predominant outcome is encountering something much more profound than was the intended mission, adventure, or undertaking as was the case for Columbus. The more possibilities one investigates the more he or she finds the hidden potential within, followed by the countless destinations ahead. The compulsion of scientists is to understand the workings of the universe, so why would any scientist purport that exploration is prompted by unguided processes rather than objective search and analysis. It is the scientist who is motivated by his or her own curiosity, and the direction of focus is chosen by the will of the explorer in purposeful pursuit of knowledge and truth.

It is illogical to likewise dismiss the existence of God outright if one is open to possibilities. When a person discovers God, it is the most eye opening, mind expanding, and spiritually uplifting experience. Living with Christ in your heart and the promise of eternal life in your mind is very tempering. While finding facts and receiving answers brings joy, it is fleeting. What about a joy that lasts forever? What about a place where you never stop growing or discovering truth? Wouldn't that be great? What about never getting sick, tired, afraid, depressed, angry, bored, or upset? How about a place where there is no evil, suffering, pain, fighting, bondage, grief, or worry? What a wonderful world it would be—correction, it will be. If you want to go, follow Christ; he will lead you there (JOH 14:6). And you will encounter the most profound discovery of your entire life.

Show Me the Evidence

Does evidence equate to truth? No, it does not. Sometimes it adds up to truth if you have enough of it and it is trustworthy. I believe the preponderance of the evidence points to God. Evolutionists argue that the evidence points them in the other direction. But the evidence they use does not suggest evolution but adaptation. Adaptation, or microevolution, is a concept supported by sufficient proof that all species can adjust to environmental conditions, situations, experience, and maturation, from the most rudimentary organisms to human beings. Actually, Darwin's findings were precisely that; mainly, he observed bird beaks changed in size, the result of alternating weather and climate conditions. He overgeneralized the finding to suggest changing from one species into another could be possible given sufficient time. But he had reservations, because he knew that macroevolution theory would crumble if subsequent findings in the fossil record did not suggest transitional lifeforms. He so wanted to be right that he titled his book *On the Origin of Species by Natural Selection, or the Preservation of Favored Races in the Struggle for Life* (Darwin, 1859).

Well guess what? The fossil evidence does not support macroevolution over a long period; quite the contrary, none of the evidence supports it (Jeffrey, 2003; Meyer, 2013). The evidence actually supports the Bible in terms of the massive appearance of new species over a short period; paleontologists call this the Cambrian explosion. There has not been an emergence of new lifeforms since then. And though Darwin's theory has long been debunked, a position held by most dependable scientists, it is still taught to our children and included in school textbooks. But educators refuse to entertain or teach the theory of intelligent design even though it is scientifically sound, supported by rigorous enquiry, and experimentally testable and predictable (*ibid*). Why do you think that is? Are they trying to brainwash kids using false data to steer them away from God and the Bible? The reality is, much of the so-called evidence for macroevolution emerging since Darwin has been proven to be fabricated or fudged (Eldridge, 1988; Perloff, 2002). Further, evolutionists employ historical research assuming that one can extrapolate about the past by observing the present; but there is zero evidence of macroevolution happening now just as there is zero evidence of it happening ever.

To be precise, macroevolution, or the transformation of one lifeform into a completely different kind, has been discredited. Those evolutionary trees showing various animals springing from a single root is nothing but rubbish; and those pictures of an ape with progressive changes into a man are the creation of a wild if not warped imagination. Microevolution, on the other hand, is basic adaptation within a species or kind and has not only been verified to occur, but also agrees with the Bible (1 CO 9:16–23; 1 CO 10:33). The next time someone is talking about evolution, ask them how they are defining it.

It helps to investigate things before you take to heart what others proclaim to be factual. Especially, scrutinize carefully what scientists, attorneys, educators, commentators, newspapers, newscasters, elected officials, political candidates, and theologians say or write. Some of them misinterpret data, spout obscure statistics, contort facts that they heard or read, take statements out of context, and bolster unsupported opinions; some employ circular reasoning, equivocation, non-sequiturs, and other common fallacies of logic discussed in the Introduction. You can fact-check just about anything nowadays, given the flexibility of Internet search; but even then, you ought to appraise and verify sources and references. Better yet, research the phenomenon by spending some time in a university library (onsite or online). I also encourage everyone to become well-versed in the Holy Bible. These studies will equip you to challenge if not refute what is purported to be factual.

I for one am prone to researching and analyzing things to the utmost degree. I have done such a study of the Holy Bible and found it to be the most reliable source of truth (Barber, 2020). It is internally consistent, authenticated by scholars, corroborated by dependable external sources, and has not changed over thousands of years; it has withstood the tests of time and scrutiny. It is God's Word, spoken through the prophets and lived in the person Jesus Christ (JOH 1:14). Many religions and religious teachers claim the Bible as their authority or foundation but have amended it to suit their personal contrivances (COL 2:8,18; 2 TI 4:3–4; 2 PE 2:1–3). Therefore, such claims cannot be true because they have modified the truth, thereby rendering it unbelievable.

To base a belief system on a spin of the evidence is unreasonable. This is the great mistake of the evolutionists, postmodernists, secularists, politicians, and various religious crazes—inventing a lie and coming to believe it, to the extent that they attempt to force it upon others. If they are deliberately propagating lies, they are working against God because he is truth; Satan, on the other hand, is the father of lies (JOH 8:42–45; 1 JO 4:1–4; 1 JO 5:5–11). The sole reason I am a Christian is because I believe God; I cling to every word that proceeds from him which would include the words of Christ (MAT 4:1–11). I proclaim that the Holy Bible comprised of the Old and New Testaments is the Word of God, is inerrant, and is the final arbiter of truth. The Bible is the foundation of Christianity, Judaism, and Islam. Religions and religious works that have distorted the Bible, or contradict it in any way are, by definition, false. If you already have God's Word on it, why doubt it, change it, or reject it?

If you carefully dissect what is advanced as evidence, you might conclude as I have that theories of evolution, geologic columns, multiple universes, and quantum mechanics are far from irrefutable. That does not prevent me from studying such things, only believing them. When the proof surpasses reasonable doubt, I might reconsider. To this day I continue to stay abreast of the latest theories and studies, and I read profusely. I also continue to study the Bible diligently. I don't think either of these activities is making me stupider, especially when I experience the expansion in my knowledge. I greatly value the feeling which comes after learning something new.

Oddly, many world religions have branched off from the Bible such as Islam, Mormonism, Jehovah Witnesses, Baha'i, Kabbalah, and the countless cults (Scientology, Unification Church, Branch Davidians); all these systems are distortions of the Holy Bible or spinoffs from Christianity Actually, they are antichristian (ISA 8:20; 1 JO 2:22; 1 JO 4:2–3; 2 JO 1:7), because they have changed the words, concepts, and events in the Bible and produced their own sacred books and teachings rendering them antithetic to Christianity (PRO 30:5–6; JER 14:14–15; ROM 16:17). And they hold those works and words in higher esteem than the Holy Bible. In my mind, that means they cannot be true, primarily because their doctrines do not include exclusive dependency on Jesus Christ for salvation, and they do not acknowledge Jesus Christ to be God in the flesh. Routinely, the followers of these offshoot schemes appear more interested in earning salvation through their own good deeds or in accumulating worldly wealth through indoctrination.

While the Bible had many writers, whose words are complimentary and collectively provide a clear picture of God's plan of redemption, these other religions are based chiefly on the words of one person whose words are not consistent with God's and whose accounts, events, and prophecies have no external validation whatsoever (unless lifted verbatim from the Bible). In short, they lack validity and reliability, the mainstays of scientific research, and also the Bible. Note that there also are science-based cults that veer from the mainstream of attested scholarship, assuming facts not in evidence and professing theories unsubstantiated (like the stalwart Neo-Darwinists).

Do not forget, in order to demonstrate a finding as representative, reliable, and generalizable, it should be duplicable and verifiable; it should be encountered via methodologically sound investigation; and it should be reported by recognized sources (though even experts have been known to violate these basic parameters and posit unvalidated findings). To discover the truth, or check information for factuality, one must become a scientist of sorts. In a way, everybody is, since we learn how to obtain positive results using trial and error (i.e., through experimentation).

It takes considerable work to gather, weigh, analyze, and synthesize evidence. You must examine everything that has relevance, big or small; what is there and what is not there, the reputability of each source, and the overall power of the evidence itself. It is a good practice to perform a decision analysis by classifying relevant alternatives in light of the amount and weight of the evidence. But we get lazy, and jump to conclusions, or accept mere opinions without concerted effort to establish truthfulness, rendering us vulnerable to being wrong or duped. The upshot is obvious; truth in education, justice, religion, advertising, government, business, and the press have flown out the window. In short, you shouldn't trust findings that cannot be corroborated.

Have you ever tested the provocative sayings of some of the theological and historical programs on television or radio in light of what the Bible says (DEU 18:20–22; JER 23:15–26; JER 28:7–9; MAT 7:15–23)? Have you taken a look at the craziness being taught in the public schools, to include institutions of higher learning? Have you noticed some of the baloney taken either as evidence or the unwarranted endeavors to dismiss sound evidence in order to convict someone of a crime, or acquit them? Have you bought into the grandiose promises and plans of politicians who will say anything to get elected, but seldom follow through? Have you fallen for any of the bogus news being put out by the media? Have you watched actors make amazing claims about advertised products that have not been reasonably attested by any robust analysis? Maybe you have you heard this one: 75 percent of doctors recommend our elixir to solve your health problems. For all you know, that means they talked to four people who bought an online doctorate degree from a diploma mill, and three of them guessed the answer wrong. Nowadays, the evidence gets spun in so many ways it's difficult to glean anything truthful, especially what is being disseminated by the mass media, the worldwide web, and the plethora of compulsive liars on Capitol Hill.

The crux is, don't simply take another's word for it. Listen, smile, and then research it. This doesn't mean that everybody is a pathological liar. They may believe what they say, whether right or wrong, because they trusted the source. They may have done some research but not enough; or collected an insufficient or unrepresentative sample from which conclusions were drawn. They may be ignorant, uninformed, biased, brainwashed, or afraid to tell the truth; or they may be lying on purpose. Who knows? Well God does; and if you have God's Word on it, you need search no further.

Let's consider the contention that there is no God. Many who think so also believe this life will eventually end and that's it. If these things were true, what would be the purpose; what would be the reason to become, to persevere, or to succeed? Everything would be meaningless, with no incentive to do the right thing, or to do anything for that matter. There would be no difference between a righteous person and an evil person. But people want answers, they require meaning, they favor justice; they have needs, and they pursue goals—even people who purport that all is relative, and therefore, irrelevant. They are deceiving themselves thinking there is no God, though they definitely value their lives, they love their family, they pursue their dreams, and they consent to law, order, and morality. I don't think a true atheist or nihilist exists, with no values, doing whatever they please, inconsiderate about how it may affect others; sounds more like a sociopath to me. They would have nobody to love or care for, much less anyone to love and care about them. What a dismal, despairing life that would be. This leads us to the answer: love, the power of God from which all virtues proceed, the universal standard. It is the power to care, to be ethical, and to be happy.

Now let's cogitate the view that God does exist. What is that to me? Even if he lives, he's out there and I'm down here, right? How is it possible to relate to God? Well, he created you and still loves you; and he gives you knowledge of him, and of right and wrong, and the freedom of choice. He gives you purpose, direction, hope, worth, and meaning. He gives you his Son, his wisdom, and eternal life. Even famous atheists throughout history conceded that many explanations worked better with God; but they chose not to believe because they were above that. Or so they said, because many atheists also have proposed that they don't consider God because they want to be decadent, immoral, and self-indulgent without feeling remorse or facing judgment. In their hearts they know there is a God; they prefer to ignore him because they've decided to do everything their way. They presume that if he does exist, a real God wouldn't condemn anybody, especially them because they are superior to most people. Many of them know in the depths of their souls if they are damned, giving them license to do whatever they please. What more do they have to lose? That is their self-deception. They get a thrill from evil. What do you think, will there be payback, and for how long?

I haven't the time to list all the excuses people use to talk themselves out of loving God. But it really bewilders me when they rationalize relentlessly to protect their egos against the knowledge, guilt, and pain of their sin; because that should be the path to accepting God and clinging to his promises. But the proposition that baffles me most is the idea that it is impossible to have a relationship with God. How would they know since they don't want one? By the way, you can have a relationship with God if you accept Christ as your personal Savior.

Those opposing Christianity are often spiteful, arrogant, and mean-spirited. Sometimes, they insult, abuse, and/or murder Christians. Why are they so hateful? Do they feel threatened by Christianity or people of faith? To many, faith is a joke. Christians are deluded, the atheists propose; but it is they who have been deluded by their own false beliefs. That's what a delusion is, a false belief. They are apt to place their faith in unproven scientific theories, yet disclaim faith of any kind. They exhibit the attributes of the very people they accuse of being ignorant of, or blind to, the truth. They disregard, fabricate, and dismiss evidence if it does not coincide with their lies. And they spread those lies as if factual and persuade the masses to invest in them (EPH 4:14). The Bible speaks about such wayward thinking, and the false beliefs of the world (1 CO 18–31; 2 TH 2:10–12). Those lies being perpetuated are of the devil, who wants you to think that this world and this life is all there is. Satan wants you to invent your own god or to be your own god (ROM 1:21–23), because he knows you will lose God. God allows people to believe as they wish; he will not coerce anyone to believe in him, but everyone will when Christ returns. Those who do not believe in God's truth cannot get their brains out of the physical realm of reality, as the devil prefers. You would think that learned and scholarly persons would never delimit growth in knowledge and truth in this manner; you'd think they would be openminded and would study all possible explanations objectively. Many who finally search assiduously will encounter God and leave atheism or agnosticism, because the proof is quite overwhelming once assembled.

Follow the evidence where it leads you, not where you want it to go. Evidence paves the road to truth; ask any scientist, detective, or philosopher. And as you continue down that path, you'll locate more evidence and bear out more facts. If you go your own way it likely will be the wrong way. It makes complete sense to do it the right way, which is also the best way. The way of God is the way to life and peace, and Christ will show you the way if you let him, so you never will get lost. But if you don't stay on the right path you could get lost forever. It is a very easy choice my friends; don't make it so hard on yourselves.

Political Correctness Run Amok

I've heard it said, "You can't legislate morality." Well, yes you can; that's what laws are for. God has stipulated directives and these are incorporated into laws. Regrettably, you also can legislate immorality. The irreligious community has a movement to destroy our Judeo-Christian heritage by forcing people to adhere to imperatives that totally violate human rights or go against our religious mores; some of these ingrates are downright vile. Policymakers have managed to adulterate marriage, promote transsexuality, stigmatize people of faith, constrain free speech, prevent peaceful assembly, make guns available only to criminals, and so forth. They want to turn this nation around from a democratic republic to a socialistic oligarchy. And how do they intend to do it? By devaluing ethical behavior, legislating tolerance, diminishing spirituality, and redefining equality. The ultimate objective, it seems, is to slacken the law, relativize faith, destroy our sacred institutions, and temper justice (ISA 5:20; HAB 1:4).

It's a rigged game. Let's begin with the intervening in recent years of a liberal Supreme Court into affairs ascribed to Congress by legislating from the bench. They also have managed to usurp powers that belong to the states in order to change or produce laws and bypass the democratic process altogether, not to mention disregarding the will of the people. To illustrate, they have declared it a constitutional right for homosexuals to marry. Marriage, being established and defined by God and not the Constitution, was instituted for propagating the species, raising godly children, and enjoying sexual pleasure between one man and one woman without committing the sin of fornication. Any sex outside of this definition of marriage violates the seventh commandment: Do not commit adultery. All other means of sexual intercourse is forbidden. How is it possible for homosexuals or transsexuals to meet any of the above requirements for marriage? To make matters worse, the court has forced people to violate their own consciences and religious freedoms in order to serve or accommodate those who choose what people of faith consider an aberrant lifestyle.

And then there is the nuanced definition of family in which it is unnecessary to have a mother or a father. No doubt, women do not necessitate a husband to bear children and can be financed by the government, who becomes the breadwinner for the family, and the decision maker. You can have one parent, or two moms, or two dads, or extended families unrelated by blood. How is it possible for a child to grow up in such environments without being confused about sexual identity, matrimony, intimacy, and developing wholesome relationships and attachments? The government is being allocated the responsibility to determine what constitutes a marriage, family, and the proper way to rear children, whereas we already have the handbook for life and rearing children, the Holy Bible; and we already have the perfect example for parenting, God the Father. And we also have the perfect example of a child's obedience, Jesus Christ.

Your federal government has decided that the First Amendment freedom of religion does not count for much; it is being trumped by the individual freedoms of deviant persons, even though some states still have laws on the books prohibiting their behavior. Not only do you have to tolerate circumstances which go against your moral stance, you have to violate your principles to demonstrate that you are tolerant; that is, you are forced to sin against God to accommodate others who are sinning against God. If you do not comply you can expect stiff penalties including fines and even jail time. In order for one subculture to exercise their unalienable rights to life, liberty, and pursuit of happiness you must give up your unalienable rights to the same. This forces people of conscience to close their businesses, move to another town or state, or give up their possessions and livelihood. What comes next, allowing citizens to marry anybody, anything, anytime?

The other essential element of the First Amendment that is being hijacked concerns freedom of speech and the press. Inherently, there are reasonable limitations on freedom of expression; particularly, you can't yell "fire" in a theatre as a joke, you can't show pornography to a child, you can't attack someone simply because you disagree, and you can't maliciously slander or libel another person. Well, I presume you can now, because lamebrains do these things all the time and get away with it most of the time; or at least there is insufficient punishment to dissuade them. The newscasters selectively report on people and events, with a favoritism as obvious as red herring in a fishbowl. You really have to dig to find any truth coming from numerous news organizations. Making up lies and publishing them as truth is not protected speech. But if you peacefully protest for what is right and true, or you publish or voice Christian views without redactions, you can expect to be hounded, possibly arrested. A free person cannot voice an opinion that another person or group doesn't like without getting sued, fired, expelled, beaten up, or publicly disgraced.

However, riotous mobs parade violently for a cause that is contrary and nothing is done about it. This is even happening in our colleges and universities where activists are preventing people from speaking if they do not adhere to a radical platform. It used to be that an institution of higher learning was the one place you could rely on people to respect free speech. Why the double standard? If they can control information, they can control the way people think; ultimately, they aim to utterly control the people.

It is not only the judiciary, it is the executive branch acting unilaterally; dictating what laws will be enforced, invoking regulations, and instituting agreements with foreign nations, completely bypassing the authority of Congress. But what is the president to do if Congress refuses to act at all? So, both the executive and judicial branches end up doing whatever entertains them, and Congress does little to block, curb, or reverse their illegal, unconstitutional actions. But this is by design. Our so-called representatives have their own initiatives, complete with excesses of power, spending, and influence. Some will do nothing but interfere with the legislative process, to ensure the establishment continues to reign supreme, while their constituency is ignored and disenfranchised.

The government selectively applies the rules, or refuses to enforce the laws, or is unable to count votes accurately, or prejudices the courts. The framers would be rolling over in their graves if they had an inkling how federal overreach has reached epic proportions; especially the circumvention of states' rights in violation of the Tenth Amendment, and the virtual abandonment of due process at the federal level.

The instigators want control over everything; to achieve this they want everything to be out of control so they can step in and take charge. Why else would you suppose people in power intentionally create division? They are moles, purposefully generating conflict between the political parties, the sexes, the races, economic classes, husbands and wives, old and young, the labor force and business, the police and the criminals, and on and on. They want chaos so they can look like the good guys who restore order. They calculatingly manufacture culture wars and subculture wars to effect the changes they want and disguise it to look like the changes the people want. United we stand, divided we fall; disunion is what they want, for if we disintegrate as a nation, we can be assimilated into the new world order.

That is the aspiration of globalists, to rule the world. But a global society already has been tried and God disallowed it. Such was the case with the Tower of Babel, when God confused the languages in order to disperse people about the globe (GEN 11:1–9). Because, collectively they sought to exalt themselves, do anything they want, and answer to nobody. Beware of globalism as it seeks to subdue the people in defiance of God, resulting in subjugation, while simultaneously elevating those who intend to snatch the power and control.

These conspiracies are nothing new. You may want to familiarize yourselves with the works of Marx and Engels in their *Communist Manifesto* (1948). Through oppression, antagonism, and exploitation, redefinition of truth, rights, and morality, and affecting dissention and division they purposed to indoctrinate ignorant and unwitting residents. Proponents make promises of prosperity, jobs, freedom, and welfare to instate a centralized political apparatus with constraining laws, burdensome taxation, and severe penalties for noncompliance. By gaining advocates through deceit, slanting the truth, destabilization, slaughter, and sabotage, communists have striven to overthrow the middle class and thwart conservativism, procure political power and confiscate everything, then make the proletariat fully dependent upon the government. In such a society there will remain no personal property, no free trade; no focus on individuals, families, or country; no religion and no morals. Likewise, socialism is disguised as a system where the people are teased with rights, freedoms, and control, all of which are stolen in the end. The ultimate goal of all these approaches has been to destroy Christendom, which is the biggest obstacle in their way. In the USA they are whittling away at your freedoms, as if you haven't noticed already.

It starts with empty promises to improve living conditions, which are attractive to people who are frustrated, downtrodden, impoverished, unemployed, helpless, or hopeless. They persuade hard-working people and the poor to be resentful, angry, and invigorated, blaming misfortunes of the populace on the well-to-do. They feign sympathy for the underdog, explaining how they will support them and provide all manner of social services by charging the wealthy. They belittle, insult, harass, accuse, bully, and attack those who oppose their policies. They are constructing a radical move to the left in order to destroy capitalism entirely and replace it with socialism. Their promise of change is actually complete and total change (D'Souza, 2015; Levin, 2015; Starnes, 2014). For we the people it is a change for the worst: because the impending economic collapse will leave us with nothing (REV 6:6). They intend to take God's place in your life. If you don't believe this, take a gander at *Rules for Radicals* (Alinsky, 1971) a book which was dedicated to Lucifer in the preface; the author spells out these same basic tenets, strategies, and goals. Did you know that a certain USA president admired that man and his methods, and followed almost verbatim the strategy outlined in that book during his tenure in office? This also was true for a contemporary presidential candidate, who was fortunately rejected (see D'Souza, 2015).

Note the seven things that God hates, proposed by King Solomon in the book of Proverbs (PRO 6:16–19): 1 – Pride and Arrogance; 2 – Lying and Deceit; 3 – Shedding Innocent Blood; 4 – Wicked Imagination; 5 – Mischief Makers; 6 – False Witnesses; 7 – Sowing Discord. Do these examples ring a bell? Didn't the leadership pretend that you were stupid, as if you needed them to forge decrees about your healthcare? Didn't elected politicians promise excellent benefits like better medical insurance at less cost which turned out to be the opposite? Hasn't recent military action, or the lack thereof, ended with considerable needless bloodshed? Haven't those in power promised transparency and answerability, then done everything clandestinely, much of which violated the Constitution, and later attempted to cover it up? Can you even count the number of scandals in government, business, and Wall Street in modern times? Remember when the President said there was no wrongdoing, not a smidgeon, with the IRS debacle? If that was so why did the director take the fifth (she refused to testify due to fear of self-incrimination)? And why did thousands of pages of documents get shredded, hard-drives get bleached, and cellphones get hammered right after the federal government requested them? And who went on live television and blamed a militant attack on some obscure video after telling family members it was terrorism? And how is it they can assist felons sneaking into our country but prevent law abiding ones from immigrating? What happened to liberty, justice, peace, and rights; and why do they deny them to citizens but grant them to illegal aliens? I'll tell you why: ignorance and poverty keep people uninformed and dependent (PRO 14:15); they want to import more people like that. Information and education provide potency so they hold these things back and circulate propaganda instead. But accurate information and advanced education do not assume common sense, as demonstrated by the wheeling and dealing of unprincipled administrators.

Can you concede that class warfare is worsening? Wounds have been reopened that had long been healed between races. Do you see the gaps widening between political parties, worldviews, genders, the rich and poor, the young and old, the government and the people, and practically every demographic in this country? Now you can tell what is happening and it is not by coincidence. Are you going to sit there and let them get away with stealing your freedoms and equality? The fifty states and the populace should retake those rights that the politicians have been confiscating. If we don't, we will lose them forever. Federal power was deliberately limited via our Constitution and Bill of Rights precisely to prevent overreach and expansion of the government. At this point, it might take a Constitutional Convention (of states) to solidify the intended meaning, mandates, and morality of the framers (read Article V of the Constitution). Certainly, Congress doesn't appear inclined to act, but only to duck.

Attacks on Christianity

The idea of separation of church and state was promulgated initially in a letter written by Thomas Jefferson to a Baptist association in 1802 to underscore that the government cannot meddle in their religious affairs. It subsequently has been presupposed that religion has no place in government, though that verbiage does not appear in any founding documents or accompanying legislation. Under that guise the secularists and politicians have determined the First Amendment to the Constitution to be no longer valid. The initial rights of religion and speech were of utmost importance to the framers, which is why they were listed first in the Bill of Rights; but they have been superseded by gay rights, illegal immigrant rights, sharia rights, and censorship rights. Rights extended to gays are not presupposed from the Civil Rights Act of 1964, which outlawed discrimination on the basis of race, religion, sex, or nationality; apparently, homosexuality (among other things) is now a sex. So ruled the Supreme Court, which condoned gay weddings as if its purview was to define anything but what is explicitly written in the Constitution or Acts of Congress.

In violation of religious liberty, people of faith are emphatically being discriminated against. Jesus said, "You must worship and serve only the Lord your God" (LUK 4:8). Nowadays, you are not entitled to choose who you will serve. If you choose God, you will be removed from service, whether a baker, photographer, teacher, writer, preacher, ballplayer, or government official (Starnes, 2014). Religious persecution, especially against Christians, has reached astronomical proportions, banning prayer, Bibles, and crosses, and prohibiting the mention of Jesus, God, or Christmas in the public square, in educational settings (all levels), military gatherings, charity fundraisers, and food distribution centers including churches (*ibid*). You cannot even hold Bible study groups in the privacy of your own home if you are affiliated with a place of worship. A student cannot present anything in school mentioning God or Jesus. In the meantime, they have forced public school students to study Islam and sing praises to Allah. Now, that would be a prototypical violation of separation between church and state.

Speaking of political correctness, it appears to be accepted practices to desecrate a church, to verbally and physically abuse a teacher, and to aggressively prevent someone from voting. But it is grossly inappropriate to wish someone a Merry Christmas, to authorize students a moment of silent supplication, or to witness Christ on a college campus. Nowadays, freedom of religious expression applies to every other religion, to include atheism, scientism, and Islam; but it does not pertain to Christianity or Christians. How soon before Christians have no religious rights at all?

The scam is obviously working, the secular war on Christendom. It has infiltrated and brought down Europe in a big way and is now corrupting America. This country prospered when God was acknowledged as our strength and the Bible as our foundation. The same was true for the nation of Israel in the Old Testament; but when they strayed and were unfaithful to God, they experienced destruction and death. Isn't the same thing happening here? This is not déjà vu; it is a consequence of removing God from our heritage.

I have not seen such inhumanity, insanity, and unadulterated evil in my entire life as occurred in the last few decades. Neither have I encountered such decadence and decay in the chronicles of American history. Our founding fathers were men of faith, almost all of them believed in God, and the majority were Christians. Though some of the framers were deists, our founding documents were largely based on the Holy Bible. But leftists would like to abolish or alter them. I frequently hear pundits suggesting that the Declaration of Independence, the Constitution of the United States, and the Bill of Rights are living documents, inferring they ought to be reinterpreted as the culture evolves, as if our original culture was hollow. No, they oughtn't. Everything written in these documents still applies today; nothing needs to be updated. Now, if the people and our elected representatives agree to add or delete amendments, the Constitution allows for that. I can think of a few new amendments that might help, like forcing the government to spend within their means, limiting terms of office to prevent career politicians, overturning erroneous Supreme Court decisions, and tort, immigration, and regulation reform. Don't forget, the underlying goal of both anarchists and communists is to destroy Christian values and principles and adopt precepts that are directly opposed to what this nation used to stand for. Society is imploding from within, now that decadence, debauchery, hatefulness, and hedonism are becoming the norm.

Then there is the aforementioned jihad being waged upon Christianity by militant Islamic extremists. Here is found multiple contradictions in the Koran. In one verse it says to fight those who come against you, but not to instigate the fight (Surah 2:190), while another passage instructs to make peace with those who desist from hostility (Surah 4:90–91); elsewhere it commands the torment of unbelievers (Surah 3:151; 9:123) and declares war on them (Surah 8:39–40,59–60). Then there is the demand to kill infidels wherever they can be found unless they convert to Islam (Surah 9:1). It is easy to cherry-pick which posture to take, whether of peace or war; that's why there are peace-loving Muslims and those promoting genocide. The jihadists choose war as it makes them feel powerful and important. They terrorize, torture, and terminate Christians, Jews, even Muslims in the name of Allah; they maintain that their holy books demand it. Though to intentionally kill another Muslim is considered a deplorable sin (Surah 4:92–93). How the stealing of artifacts and obliteration of ancient architectural wonders comes into play is especially questionable. They'll sell treasures on the black market and destroy everything else so that others cannot enjoy them after they leave, to include irreplaceable shrines, relics, and edifices. Obviously, their motive is selfishness and their legacy, dishonor. Since they are the epitome of intolerance, I see no reason to tolerate them. If destruction is their mission, they must be destroyed. They want to impose their laws on everyone else. Aren't we obliged to enforce our laws on them if they want to live in the USA? Winston Churchill diagnosed the nefarious mission of Islamism and clarified it quite succinctly on numerous occasions; as early as 1899 he compared their treachery to that of a rabid dog (Hammond, 2010).

Many foreign peoples, and particularly governments, hate our guts. A few have spoken openly that they are at war with the United States. We know for the most part who our enemies are. Why don't we keep them at arm's length rather than embrace them? Yet we give mischievous nations billions of dollars in aid, which might be used to fund terrorism or buy weapons. How ridiculous is that? They may well end up bombing us or our allies. Why encourage residents of hostile or unstable countries to immigrate here if they cannot be properly vetted? If we can help them get back on their feet, let's do it there, not here. They have to show themselves worthy before being admitted into our country, meaning they exhibit skills, ambition, and commitment. Thus, the burden of proof is on them. When they actually produce documentation, it is next to impossible to verify authenticity.

Besides, many immigrants refuse to adapt and often espouse anti-Americanism. They'll attack our townspeople in the name of their beliefs, laws, or religion. Religious radicals calling themselves refugees seldom adopt the ideals, culture, laws, beliefs, or religion of their host nations. Multiculturalism and pluralism simply will not work; let us embrace our culture and welcome others to fit in and not the other way around. Assimilation, allegiance, and basic English should be requirements for immigration and citizenship. How about that for hope and change? That's the way it used to work, when it worked at all.

All religions are not alike. Those purporting that the god of Islam is the same as the Christian God are sorely mistaken. Yes, there are many commonalties, largely because the patriarchs and the prophecies are revered by both religions; but the disagreements are irreconcilable. In particular, there is a markedly different understanding of Jesus Christ and his resurrection. In the Bible, Jesus is God's Son; in the Koran he is mere man, even though the Koran proclaims the chastity of the Virgin Mary and her immaculate conception of Jesus (Surah 19:16–21). How do they square that, if Jesus is considered a lesser or equal prophet to Mohammed who wasn't a miracle baby? The Koran teaches that Jesus was not crucified but was translated by God into heaven (Surah 4:157–158). Mohammed was never raptured but died; wouldn't that render Jesus exceptional? It is often claimed by Muslims that someone else was crucified who resembled Jesus (Surah 4:157). Elsewhere, the Koran plainly states that Jesus died and rose again (Surah 3:54–55; 19:29–33); but Muslims deny it. This contradiction is very problematic, given the abundance of evidence substantiating the crucifixion and resurrection of Christ. Moreover, the Christian God is *agape* love, impeccable and unconditional; God loves all sinners, none are excluded (ROM 5:8). The God of Islam loves good people but despises sinners (Surah 3:57; 4:108); that is, evildoers are excluded from Allah's love, which includes basically everybody who has ever sinned. The god of radical Islam allows warmongers to operate under the auspices of fear and violence. Theirs' is not the same god at all, not even close; because the powers of love and fear are contrary. Don't forget that Adam and Eve first experienced fear and shame after their original sin. With fear as the motivator, the follower of Islamism cannot be working for God, but against him. But love is clearly the greater power as it defeats fear (1 JO 4:18); for love is the greatest power known to man, the very power of God. In addition, the heaven of the Bible is a place without sin; the heaven of the Koran is a place where sin gets a pass (Surah 37:39–48; 56:12–40).

The disgraces that Islamist extremists have committed in the name of their god are about as unhuman and insufferable as it gets. What father is so self-righteous that he murders his own child because he or she has not adopted dad's religion or has violated one of its edicts? How can they know their kids won't change their ways or their minds, anyhow? Are they not merely kids? Or what if they don't, are they not going to die just the same? Or how about beheading innocent Christians and putting the video on the Internet; is this how they bring praise to Allah (REV 20:4)? Or, burning a Muslim pilot alive for daring to oppose their fanatical position? Even so, they pretend to be God's appointees; but God is the judge and he exacts punishment. As stated in the Bible, it's never too late for a living soul to accept Christ and be saved. One thief crucified next to Jesus confessed Christ as Savior with his last words (LUK 23:39–43).

The disparities between Christianity and Islam are so distinct, they cannot both be true. Understand that radicalism in Islam is not supported by every Muslim. Clearly, one must not generalize the behavior of extremists to all others bearing the title of their faith. Further, there are striking disagreements between the Shia and Sunni factions, with hostilities that have continued since the death of Mohammed some 1400 years ago. Mohammed himself was quite the warmonger and jihadist, converting Mecca and other cities using military force.

Across the globe the Islamists have not met significant resistance, except from other Muslims and the Israelis. They are tolerated around the world, and often here at home; more than peace-loving Christians it appears. Terrorism has become a way of life in Europe, so they just accept it. Do you accept it? The USA has tried to employ diplomatic avenues to secure peace with terrorist nations. On occasion they have taken military action against them. But what is the point in jumping into a conflict or a negotiation if you are not determined to follow through? We get into the imperialistic venture of democracy building in countries that are incompatible with it, as dissimilar as the Bible and the Koran. We let them violate treaties yet we uphold our end. Get real; nobody in business does this, only our government.

Whether they take the form of homegrown radicals or Islamic jihadists, terrorists are enemy combatants (Clarke, 2017); we are at war against them and they against us. The enemy has no constitutional rights, nor do they qualify for having their case adjudicated in a civilian court of law. As an enemy of the state, they are subject to military justice. There are different rules when it comes to civil law and military law, and for good reason.

I ask you, what is wrong with taking out terrorists? They must be eradicated; it is not a sin to defend self or country. It is for the greater good. I say go ahead and remove the villains, then get out. If they can't fix their problems, that's their fault. If they threaten or attack us, eliminate them again and get out again. It is not for any nation to clean another's dirty laundry, impose a political regime upon them, or proselytize them. God sends missionaries, filled with the power of his Spirit and his love, to spread the Gospel. Leave those responsibilities to the people and you'll get better results. Depend on the government and they'll screw it up beyond all repair.

The jihadists are after the same objective as the other mischief makers: create chaos. They want to snatch control, subordinate the populace, and make them adhere to their rules and whims. They are the epitome of human rights violators, robbing people blind before murdering them and taking their land, despoiling women and children, and making slaves out of the rest. Again, their eventual purpose is to take God out of the picture and become their own gods. When that happens, who is really in control? It is Satan, the prince of darkness, the fallen cherub (ISA 14:12–15). He is known by many names: Lucifer, Beelzebub, Mephistopheles, the devil, the serpent, the dragon, and the beast (MAT 12:24–27; REV 12:9). He opposes God at every turn and influences people to do his dirty work. The crazy thing is, people do it believing they will reap rewards like dominion, pleasure, honor, power, and/or glory. But all these belong to God alone; neither Satan, nor any living creature, nor any evil kingdom can obtain them by extracting them from God. But if you are with God, he will give you those things for free (ROM 8:9–18).

Tyranny

The name of the game for all these devious movements trying to take by force your liberty, your money, your livelihood, and your beliefs is tyranny. Speech is repressed, maxims are redefined, laws are overturned, society is reengineered, and your entire life is upended. This is precisely the reason our forefathers proclaimed to the world that oppressive government violates the fundamental rights of the people; and it is the reason they chose to detach from Britain and form their own republic. While it should be self-evident to everyone that inalienable rights belong to everybody, these are often denied to all but the ruling party. When they rip away God-given blessings, people of conscience are driven to yank them back. Otherwise, you might just as well lie there and be violated. Did you know this was the very reason the Second Amendment was included in the first place, before the Constitution could be ratified by all thirteen colonies? Our right to bear arms has always been to protect, defend, and if necessary, rebel against tyranny just like the founders did.

Beware of activist community organizers and the progressives who follow them. They are pushing for a centralized government that steals the power, rights, and riches of the people. Their politics and policies are designed to accelerate fiscal failure, weaken the Constitution, and effect social upheaval. They intend to consolidate our three branches of government through weakening the boundaries erected among them by the framers. Separation of powers protects us from those who would consolidate the power for themselves. They will deplete our resources and treasures through redistribution and squandering. Look how careless the establishment has been with our money. Can you gauge the wealth that has been flushed down the toilet in recent years by elected and trusted leaders? It measures in the trillions of dollars. Take a look at some of the crazy things they have been doing; the full list would fill this entire book.

- The government grows by leaps and bounds, with enormous duplication of effort as well as extreme overstaffing. It is so compartmentalized and proliferous that the right hand has no idea what the left hand is doing, especially when it comes to money: gross misappropriations of funds and lack of accountability; irrational spending sprees like a trillion-dollar stimulus package in which nobody can trace where the dollars went.
- Ponzi schemes and other devices to redistribute wealth, taking it from one group and giving it to another; the overseers knew when they erected the pyramids that they would collapse someday into a mountain of debt.
- Aid, assistance, disability, and benefits payments extended to people who are ineligible, illegally in the country, or dead; what they seek is the eventual creation of a social welfare state where everybody is on the government till whether they belong here or not.
- Appropriations expended for buildings, systems, and programs that nobody wants or needs some of which never get completed, such as bridges to nowhere and useful land which is prohibited from use.
- Spurious taxes, subsidies, fines, seizures of property, and confiscation of assets; usually targeting certain citizens and groups without due process, cause, or constitutional mandate.
- Allocating millions of dollars to create a handful of jobs or to train a handful of foreign fighters.
- Forging pacts, deals, and coalitions in which Americans have to foot most of the bill, while other member countries take advantage (like the United Nations and the World Health Organization).
- Billions of dollars paid in cash to bribe foreign nations and operatives, often hostile to the USA; not to mention money paid for favors that benefit a few bureaucrats or that support an unofficial cause.
- Extravagant expense accounts and the reckless blowing of taxpayer money for trips and other private endeavors; also, using political donations for personal use with apparent immunity.
- Funding countless research proposals with exorbitant costs for the most ridiculous projects, yielding neither knowledge nor value to science, education, or health.

➢ Reparation imbursements to unharmed "victims" or their distant relatives.

Progressivism, once an ideal shared by those truly dedicated to the advancement of the nation, has been hijacked by a bunch of leftwing fascists who pretend to be advocates of progress, but who actually have globalist leanings. They assemble their organizers, agitators, and protestors to coerce, hustle, pilfer, loot, disrupt, attack, and incite; we're talking a gangster mentality not unlike that of organized crime (D'Souza, 2015). There is nothing progressive about racial goading, sexual exploitation of women, big government, socialism, or diminution of freedom. In fact, such repressive behavior, demeanor, and thought processes could be psychopathological in many cases. Being a licensed clinician, I can tell you authoritatively that leftwing neo-progressive activists exhibit some combination of the following mental ailments: major depression, acute anxiety, panic disorder; mania, phobia, hysteria, obsessive-compulsiveness, exhibitionism; antisocial, narcissistic, and borderline personality; and delusions (paranoid, grandiose, jealousy, and persecutory).

You cannot trust anything the radical left says. When they feign caring and compassion for fellow citizens, they act insubordinate, divisive, and advance only themselves. The fact is they are the least likely among political groups to be charitable and altruistic, though they can be overly generous with the money of other people. Maybe they fancy themselves modern-day robbing hoods. Indeed, religious conservatives are way more nurturing and giving. Interestingly, political liberals tend to possess more wealth than conservatives though they are far less likely to share it with those in need (Levin, 2015).

The new progressives intend to bombard our youth with their socialist philosophy, and this tactic has been largely successful. Today's youth enjoy the dispensation of wealth when it enriches them; or so they think, because the present generation has higher personal debt, poverty, and unemployment than those preceding it. They are less educated evidenced by failing schools, fewer graduates, and a fraction completing college. They are discontented, unmotivated, unproductive, and misdirected. Certainly, watching their elders and their government set the example of irresponsibility and unaccountability has contributed to that brainwashing. Yet they will inherit greater debt and destabilization than this country has ever known.

It seems our kids are being groomed to be tyrannical via radicalization and indoctrination, making them easy pickings for exploitation. Tyrants are spoiled; it's their way or the highway. You have to think as they do. You cannot voice an alternate opinion. The next generation is being steered towards gratuitous autonomy. They want to report to nobody, to be accountable for nothing, to do and say whatever they please, to abandon all rule of law and establish their own standards of behavior. But those who live by that ethic will not consent to you doing the same or to realize the privileges they relish. They can rape you but you can't touch them. You have to abide by the instructions dictated to you. There is no justice, no purpose, and no incentive. Does anyone really think that such a system will survive? Eventually, nobody will want to do anything because they won't care. They'll become numb, listless, and unimportant. The only emotion that will remain is desperation. If you aren't careful, the bleeding-heart liberals will program your kids to become wards of the "state."

What has been the outcome every time an unruly, domineering, and restricting scheme was imposed on the people? Well, you can still examine the remnants and devastation from the demise of Egypt, Assyria, Babylon, Media-Persia, Greece, Rome, the Third Reich, the Ottomans, the USSR, and others. Communism, socialism, totalitarianism, authoritarianism, despotism, statism, fascism, and anarchism—have any of these practices been successful ever in the annals of history? No, they have not. And why not? Because, there ultimately remains no equality, integrity, morality, liberty, faith, justice, or happiness.

Even theocracies are destined for failure, because the leaders make themselves out to be God's spokespersons; or proclaim themselves prophets, apostles, or deities. They become involved in politics, world governments, and foreign affairs; they make judgments about other leaders and religions; they dictate to everyone else the way to act. They think they are experts in everything, forgetting that they are supposed to be ministers of God and not play god. They are actually the devil's henchmen (and women). When they become great in their own eyes, they lose sight of the truth; this is the same message Jesus spoke to the Pharisees (MAT 23:13–39; LUK 11:37–54). Too many leaders try to take the place of God; but they condescend, they are arrogant, they are self-centered, and they are controlling. Make no mistake, common people try to play God too, like those who feel higher after putting someone else down. They want to be in charge, in control, worshipped, adored, and superior. They expect others to bow down to them, or kiss their ring, or place them on a pedestal, or engage in all manner of idolatry and sexual deviancy. Here is another effect of secular humanists attempting to define morality, excellence, and superiority.

Many early settlers came to America to escape religious persecution; the founders were especially keen to the value of being free to practice one's faith and worship God in their own way. Religious liberty in a democratic society allows people to unite under a flag of freedom and over a foundation of virtue, regardless of religious affiliation or denomination. Religious restrictions, where the church is the state, fosters vice; case in point, Rome. The depravity of man is unleashed because the avarice of power and domination become the tenets of justice in that system. The original theocracy established by God with his chosen Israel similarly crashed, for they did not maintain God as their king but insisted on selecting a king from among themselves (1 SA 8). Never again has such a system prevailed. Our founders recognized this and stipulated there be religious freedom, as long as the laws of virtue and accountability remained central. This precluded people from inventing any religion in violation of the law (like sharia) which enables individuals to administer judgment and enforce punishment, thus circumventing government and God.

The first of the Ten Commandments is to recognize no other gods than the Almighty. The second is to refrain from all forms of idolatry, where God is secondary to the world or worldly things. Satan wanted to be God, Adam wanted to be God, and we all want to be God sometimes, like when we insist on calling the shots and ignoring others that are affected. It's the perversion of selfishness, and sin, again. Some religions proclaim that you are above other people, you can become a god, or you are a god already. It is against God's law to act superior to anybody else; we are to love others as ourselves, not more, not less. We are to place God above all others including ourselves. Does that make God a tyrant? That is precisely what atheists suggest, though they purport not to believe in God. They accuse God of wiping out people he doesn't like, of ruling the world with an iron fist. But God loves everybody equally and unconditionally, and commands that we do the same. This is the basis of equality, that everyone is deserving of our love, to include you because you are somebody. Remember, love is the fulfilling of the law (ROM 13:10); love is the foundation of the law (1 JO 4:8). Tyrants do not love others as themselves, nor do they love God; but God loves them just the same. God will, however, wipe out those who do not love him, in order to set free those who do.

The new progressivist agenda is to gradually remove our liberties and move this nation further from soft tyranny into solid tyranny (Levin, 2009). The strategy is to dismantle and defeat conservatism, emplace statism, and ultimately replace God with government. Any society, religion, community, or society that exalts people or the state is in error since they commit idolatry. Leaders are to be supporting not controlling. They must serve the people, not be served. Even Jesus Christ came to serve, though he was God in the flesh (MAR 10:45). Christ is the example which God expects us to follow by serving, loving, and helping others. It is the aspiration and the error of Satan that we subordinate others by elevating ourselves, like when Satan tried to exalt himself above God (ISA 14:12–13). But Satan's true motive is to put you under him. And the progressives' motive is to put you under them. Therein lies the connection.

Abe Lincoln declared our government to be of, for, and by the people (*Gettysburg Address*). We must take our government back. We must stand against educators, politicians, and the media that would turn our children into brainless lemmings. We should convey, support, teach, and encourage students to embrace and exercise their rights to life, liberty, and pursuit of happiness. Isn't that the American Dream? Whatever became of it? The tyrants allude to happiness, but they will take it; in any case, you must pursue happiness yourself. Can you really depend on the government for everything, especially ensuring that you realize your dreams? The government has accumulated so much debt from their excess and wastefulness that the economy will soon collapse if they are not reigned in. If this continues, we all will be equal again very soon: equally despondent, lost, angry, and broke.

A system is innately corrupt which attempts to shove the minds of the people into a box. Those wresting control are themselves out of control. How can anybody control others if they cannot control themselves? Inspired by sin, they bulldoze their empires into ruins. Likewise, this entire world, its empires and its governments will pass away; but God's words will remain true forever (MAT 24:35; MAR 13:31; LUK 21:33).

Our republic was established precisely to facilitate all citizens in reaching their full potential, to exercise their inalienable rights, and to depend on others to behave accordingly, sharing individual responsibility and mutual respect. And our democracy thrived as long as we acknowledged from whom came our freedom, equality, and faith. God always will be the cause of the universe, the lawgiver, and the source of wisdom. When nations appoint God as the ruler and adhere to his words as highlighted in the Holy Bible, and elect people of faith to govern and enforce the laws—such a society can endure indefinitely (DEU 30:15–20). Anything short of that will eventually fail. And every nation that started out that way fell to ruins when they departed from the path.

Who do you think will benefit from that? Nobody, not even Satan, though this is what he strives for; he wants to be the tyrant of tyrants. But he must contend with the King of kings. Want to hazard a guess who will win that contest (ZEC 2:9–10)? Whose side are you on? Can anyone defeat the devil? Well, if you have Christ (JAM 4:7; 1 JO 4:4). A puppet of evil is coming with the power of Satan to change the laws and the times (DAN 7:23–27; REV 13:3–18). The new world order will be built upon disunion, disorder, and disaster. The Bible warns us of the perilous times to come (ROM 8:36). A whole new set of rules will apply, as your freedoms are jettisoned one by one, and this nation is dismantled brick by brick. When these events take place, get ready; and the best way of preparing is to seek the truth for yourself and listen to God when he speaks. You will know what to do at that point.

Strange Alliances

The Bible teaches about the end of times in both the OT and the NT. Preceding the return of Christ will be a troublesome time for the entire world. Jesus proclaimed that nations will rise up against nations and kingdoms against kingdoms; and there will be wars and conflict.

Nations represent societies, religions, races, peoples, and tongues. A war of theologies and ideologies is indicated, waged as a result of the blatant disregard and dislike for other philosophies, values, ethnicities, and cultures. Nazi Germany showed a prime example in its determination to exterminate Jews. This exact tactic was employed many times in the OT, when nations sought to subdue if not purge the nation of Israel from their neighborhood (see EXO 1; EST 3—8; DAN 1); the success of the hostile aggressors was varied because God spared Israel as long as they remained faithful. Aggression against Jews continues to this day.

Kingdoms represent countries. The implication is that global wars between sovereign states are eminent. Such was the quarrel between the republics of USA and USSR during the cold war; and the unprovoked campaign initiated by Japan against America at Pearl Harbor. Talk about strange bedfellows, consider that Japan and Germany are now our allies; as were the USA and the USSR during World War II. Remarkably, we became friends with countries with which we were previously at war, and enemies with former allies. Certainly, the United States and the United Kingdom have had their bitter quarrels costing many lives; yet our friendship has endured ever since. The UK has historically been our most trusted ally for two hundred years. Regarding Israel, another close ally, they are probably the only Mideastern nation with which we never have collided, militarily speaking; I would imagine most Israelis hold the USA to be a most trusted ally as well. This is no time to be turning our backs on our allies.

The goal of past fanatics, tyrants, and warmongers was to eradicate what they perceived to be an inferior or despicable race, nation, or people, with the misconception they were purifying the gene pool and the land; but it boiled down to unadulterated greed for power and arrogant pride. Modern militant Muslims have the same objective, to overpopulate the world with their people, to infiltrate and wreck all nations unbeholden to their beliefs and laws. In particular, they seek extinction of Jews and Christians. Again, it's about domination; but those coveting the power tend to be the least qualified to handle it.

Certainly, there has been an unremitting fight over the land of Canaan (aka Palestine) since time immemorial. Both the nation of Israel and their surrounding neighbors hold claim to that piece of real estate. The collision started between the first two sons of Abraham (Ishmael and Isaac) some four millennia ago and continuing to this day among their ancestors. In contemporary times, the principal contenders have been Iran, Egypt, and Syria. God promised that land to the Israelites and they possessed it, then they lost it, and now they possess it again; they will not leave without a fight, I can assure you that.

Ongoing competition also has prevailed between Shiite and Sunni Muslims, though many are unified in their disdain of Israel. A union of the two would constitute a strange alliance even though they both revere the Koran and the Hadiths as sacred; however, they have killed more of each other than of their mortal enemy, the Israelis. But there is no possibility for Islam to seize control if they do not join forces; and that would be a dangerous confederacy.

Ideological rivalries like this exist throughout the globe. While some have simmered down like the quarrel between Protestants and Catholics, many have flared like the adversarial relationship between socialists and capitalists. I see no resolution to the latter breakup.

The Bible speaks of an eventual siege upon Israel by Gog, the prince of Magog from the northern territories (EZE 38—39). Some theologians believe this coalition includes the nation of Turkey (Meshech and Tubal being identified in the passage); others point to Russia which is situated north of Israel and the Black Sea (the land of Magog), while still others point to Iran as a player (Scythians). An unholy alliance is indicated, which attempts to overtake Israel. It will not succeed because a mere one-sixth of their armies will escape annihilation (EZE 39:2). The preparation for this invasion will be a sign that the latter days are upon us (REV 20:7–9); it may have commenced already. Interestingly, Russia recently joined forces with Iran in Syria to gain influence in that unstable region. Talk about strange bedfellows. What could Shiites, Sunnis, and Russians have in common, other than desire for power?

A coalition of countries has been suggested as a precursor to the end, with at least one common purpose: driving out the Jews (see Barber, 2020). Some of the nation-states proposed to join this questionable league include Russia, Turkey, Syria, and Iran, followed by Iraq, Libya, Egypt, Sudan, and Ethiopia (e.g., Muslim nations at odds with Israel). This is the modus operandi of the Muslim Brotherhood, who are infiltrating lands throughout the Middle East. A previous president made it easier for them by deposing dictators in Libya and Egypt. But the Egyptians were having none of it and arrested the handpicked leader, and much to the president's consternation, installed a populous candidate.

The current jihad is not dissimilar in purpose to insurgencies of the past from Mohammed's conquests in Arabia (seventh century) to those of the Ottomans in Europe (twentieth century). In Saladin's heyday (twelfth century), himself a Muslim sultan and conqueror, the aim was to rule the holy land and claim Jerusalem as a capital, with eyes on the rest of the world. The objectives of the Crusades were to reverse that occupation and reclaim Jerusalem. While the crusaders were marginally effective in the early going, the territory revisited its turmoil after the departure of Richard the Lionheart. Those continuing the contest were wrought with corruption and the land changed hands countless times, while the Jews scattered about the nations as prophesied millennia in advance (DEU 4:26–28; DEU 28:63–66).

Instability continued until Israel reaffirmed their statehood in 1948, which was recognized by the United Nations. They have occupied that estate ever since, though lately the UN seems to support dismantling their country. These events also were prophesied to occur from days of old, that the scattering of Israel would be reversed, and they would return to their homeland (DEU 30:3–5; EZE 20:34; EZE 36:24–25; EZE 39:27–29); and their neighbors would come against them again in the end times (EZE 38; ZEC 12:2–3; ZEC 14:2–3). The Israelis have lived in constant alarm, especially nowadays as they are threatened frequently by the governments of Iran, Syria, and others who sponsor global terrorism. But God has vowed to protect Israel and will destroy those who drive against them (DEU 28:7; JOE 2:20; AMO 9:8–15; ZEC 12:8–9; ZEC 14:11–14). Is it déjà vu or are we witnessing the final uprising?

It is pointless to ally with anyone if that association goes against God. His is the only holy alliance. All others are bound for ruin. After the dust settles, the wrath of God will be poured out upon the wicked. This will be the consequence of any unholy war, expressly the final one. The conventional wisdom is that those redeemed by the Lamb will be raptured (i.e., saved) out of the tumult. It is beyond the scope of this discourse to debate scriptural references to the rapture, tribulation, and millennial reign. I beseech you to study such things. But be assured, when Christ comes for his elect, they will enter a land of peace and joy forever, where there will be an alliance as strange as possibly imaginable. Because, the wolf and the lamb will hang out and eat together (ISA 11:1–6; ISA 65:25). Similarly, people of all nations, kingdoms, races, languages, and political bents will no longer be divided, but united in Christ as brothers and sisters (ACT 10:34–35; GAL 3:28; REV 7:9–17). The community of saints, the church, the bride: we are the New Jerusalem (REV 21:2).

Imagine a bonding among Americans, Chinese, Russians, Iranians, Arabians, and all other ethnic groups, nations, tongues, and peoples identified previously as enemies. But Christians are not enemies with other people, though we are obliged to counter errant theologies. Our common foe is Satan, the archenemy of humankind. In Christ we possess the same core beliefs regardless of demographics; that bond is love and the ideology is faith. We can and we will defeat Satan and his armies, for with Christ we overcome the world (JOH 16:33).

Remember this: it matters not what you think about others but that you care about them. Back in the sixties, nonviolent demonstrators embraced the slogan "Make love not war." Most proponents were not considering the spiritual kind of love, however, but the physical; otherwise they would have been right. It was the initiation of a sexual revolution, not an embrace of spirituality; this only five years after the Supreme Court prohibited prayer in public schools. The entire philosophy conditioned naïve brains like mine to have a warped understanding of relationships; it took me two decades to decondition myself and really start loving properly. I implore that you care about everyone. All people are precious in the sight of God. The reason people can't get along is because they don't love one another, and therefore make no effort to know the people they spurn. Jesus loves all and knows all. This thought reminds me of a tune I sang as a child that goes, "Jesus loves the little children, all the children of the world. Red and yellow, black and white, they are precious in his sight. Jesus loves the little children of the world." With that kind of love there would be no wars.

Economic Disaster

This phenomenon has been suggested and needs to be elaborated. It is a worldwide condition that will precede the collapse of the global society and demise of its directors. Of all the prophecies indicating the latter days and the return of Christ, this is one that everyone alive will experience. There will be a broadening of the breach between the impoverished and the affluent such that a full day at work will earn barely enough to eat, for people less fortunate (REV 6:6). Meanwhile, those in power will relish in their wealth, but they will squander it; because they will refuse to heed the surging tsunami and will end up drowning in decadence. They'll be heaping up treasures for nothing and nobody (1 TI 6:17).

This will initiate the last phase, when cash becomes utterly useless, and the world transitions to exclusively electronic transactions. We are almost there now, for many people pay with plastic; it is too dangerous to carry a lot of money. Plus, you can use the "card" when you're out of money and rack up debt like the government does. Your finances will become more policed, via digital currency, enabling the tracking of your every purchase. And with biometrics they'll track your every move as well.

Speaking of debt, were you aware that the national debt is equal to if not greater than our gross domestic product (GDP)? I invite you to take a peek at the multiplying Unites States debt which is currently over 25 trillion dollars; that's 25 followed by 12 zeroes. Go to *www.usdebtclock.org* if you want to experience a major shock; as of this writing, the debt was increasing by about

$50,000 per second. Federal spending far exceeds the incoming revenue, thereby adding exponentially to the deficit. The government is unrestrained; imagine what would happen to your finances if you were disbursing your money that quickly. The politicians are not so wasteful with their own money, and all the while they are being careless with yours. They certainly ensure their families are well taken care of don't they, what with all the insurance, paid time off, and retirement benefits, not to mention nepotism and self-aggrandizement?

What does our government do to offset the imbalance between incoming and outgoing money? They just print more money and flood the market, which drives the value of the dollar incrementally lower and accelerates inflation ever higher (Friedman and Friedman, 1980). The Federal Reserve has far too much power; they can manipulate the economic environment by fiddling with interest rates, printing more money, and implementing crafty if not sneaky banking practices. It may surprise you to know that this institution is not part of the federal government, and the board of governors is not elected by the voters. They are beholding to nobody, though appointed by the president to stimulate our economy, regulate prices, and perform other activities in which they have no constitutional authority to meddle.

To make matters worse, our government has gotten into the habit of bailing out failing banks and other establishments, as if pet civilian enterprises should be immune from the consequences of bad fiscal policy. These bailouts ballooned into an economic crisis; well, that along with a pile of other debt racked up from risky loans which the government ordered banks to extend to people with zero credit. But do our leaders scale it back? No, they just keep spending more of our hard-earned dollars, with the last president spending more than all previous administrations combined. It is virtually impossible to squirm out of this mounting debt.

Eventually, all legal tender will become useless, which will pave the way for a new world order takeover, likely the motive of most spend-crazy, lying politicians. The globalists will confiscate all the wealth, direct education, government, and markets (*ibid*), and manipulate worldwide economics with a global reserve system, whereby a select group will be calling the shots for the world. They will trick people into thinking the cashless society will make everyone safer, will protect their privacy, and will be more convenient. But the opposite actually will be true, for they will have access to everything you possess, and know everything there is to know about you even your greatest secrets.

At that point, your name will become a number which coincides with your bank account. Some call it the mark of the beast, without which nobody will be able to perform any monetary transactions, period (REV 13:16–18). I prefer a spiritual mark, as God will mark and seal his own, without which you are susceptible to being marked or claimed by Satan. This scenario could occur during our lifetime; if it does, I would not be agreeing to an imprint, chip, or whatever being affixed to my forehead or wrist, nor pledge my allegiance to the global dominion. Oh, they will suck people in with their great promises and guarantees, but don't you fall for it, seeing how they cannot guarantee anything because their guarantees are horse manure.

This episode was spelled out eloquently by Jesus Christ to his apostle John. It is ushered in by the third horse of the apocalypse, black in color, with a rider carrying a pair of balances (REV 6:5). The scales will be knocked completely out of kilter and that's when the bottom will fall out. Ironic, since being "in the black" used to connote prosperity; in this case, it indicates poverty. The black horse follows two others; first a white horse representing false peace, and second a red horse representing war and bloodshed (REV 6:1–4). Take note that the last or fourth horse will be pale gray, bringing with it the grim reaper and mass death.

What kind of legacy are we leaving for our children and grandchildren? Can they fathom the dilapidated economy bequeathed to them? The upcoming generation knows not the value of things, nor have they been trained to be frugal with their finances or conservative with their investments. Given the example presented to them from previous generations, they have been conditioned not to guard their assets and funds; when they receive a windfall, they expend it just as fast. But this is not their fault as they continue in the pattern presented to them. They see the millions of residents receiving payments, handouts and all kinds of free stuff, and begin to view themselves as entitled as well. Those who work to earn such things will value them more than those who do not. People tend to spend money provided as a gift, but are more inclined to save money obtained through hard work. Youth of today are inundated with images of expensive playthings, beauty, and luxury, and want to obtain them overnight if not immediately. The majority of millennials and generations since will be ill prepared to work hard for what they receive, unless self-motivated. As they mature, they swiftly claim the privileges of adulthood before being able or willing to accept the responsibilities. They follow blindly the mavens, mainly because they don't know any better. If you do not want your kids to become ensnared you ought to keep them close and train them well, with gentleness, respect, love, and much repetition. They are unlikely to be educated in finances, personal responsibility, and exceptionalism at a public school.

The key to prosperity is doing the right thing. When people practice kindness and righteousness, God prospers them (PSA 35:27; ISA 26:2–3; ROM 2:10–11); and those who prosper in the Lord will live in peace (PSA 37:37–40; PSA 122:6–9) as well as health (3 JO 1:2). Those who are not at peace or are unhealthy, cannot enjoy their prosperity (LAM 3:17), because they are troubled in their minds; especially when they have been dishonest, acquiring status, wealth, and power in devious ways. Riches do not equate to peace and joy (PRO 12:20), particularly when gathered fraudulently (PRO 1:32–33); for those, there is no peace of mind but only the fear of losing all. Their sole purpose in life is to accumulate worldly possessions, seek pleasures, and relish in fame (ROM 8:5–6) in full disregard of the will of God (HEB 12:13–14). They are right in fearing they will lose it all, for this assuredly will come to pass (PRO 23:5). But those who are right with God need only to cling to his love and truth to obtain comfort, peace, joy, and prosperity (2 CO 13:11; EPH 4:1–3); and though trials and tribulations are unavoidable in this life, true tranquility lasts uninterrupted and forever in the next (JOH 14:27; JOH 16:33; 1 CO 14:33; PHP 4:6–9). Candidly, being people of God, we cannot sit idly by and let the world go to hell in a handbasket; because it will be the USA leading the way, whether up or down.

It will take a major turnaround to right this vessel; but if we don't it will plummet faster than the dollar has. This might require a revolution if not insurrection, in order to remove establishment politicians, deep state executives, classified communication leakers, corrupt businesspersons, embedded subversives, and the like. Leaders must shore back the spending, chop away at the bureaucracy, eliminate several entities and agencies, and reduce the federal government by at least one third. Our leaders will have to be fiscally adept and get out of the custom of telling people how to spend their money; and cease investing our money in corrupt or failing enterprises. Our government will have to discontinue initiatives best left to the private sector or the states, including healthcare, energy, technology, business, and manufacturing. Let the capitalists, entrepreneurs, visionaries, and free enterprisers manage the wealth and property; we the people are collectively more innovative, inventive, intelligent, creative, thrifty, and enterprising. The government does better when it concentrates on its primary duties, namely safety and security, defense and military, law and order, foreign relations and diplomacy. In 1791, Thomas Paine wrote that government is only useful in areas where society itself is less than competent (see Paine, 1979).

What happens if we don't get it together and the economy bottoms out completely? Well, that is what the globalists want, and they will eventually have it, because they own the media, they can buy most anybody, and they manipulate the markets. They have infiltrated all levels and nations and reside in their ivory towers. They are untouchable, like a secret society, illuminated in their own eyes and believing the commoners are incapable of making important decisions, like who should rule the world. Either way, they will have their way because that is the prophesied end which will occur sooner or later. I'm hoping for later, so that more people will see the real light and escape, if only in spirit.

Once the oppressors assume rule, the beast will step in, the son of perdition (2 TH 2:3–4), sometimes called the antichrist. But anyone who opposes Jesus Christ is an antichrist, so that label is a bit of a misnomer (1 JO 4:3). Regardless, an evil regime governed by Satan's scarecrow will result, and when that happens the apocalypse will be near, probably just years away. If you want to participate in that society you will have to receive their brand, but you will get burned if you do. Since nobody knows precisely when, it is best to keep a watchful eye and know the warning signs; and be ready to flee the incoming barrage of wickedness. Unless you are saved out of it, which will be a special blessing (JER 30:7; DAN 12:1).

The third world will be affected the most as they will not be able to compete. The only remaining alternative will be to fight. But they don't stand a chance against the superpowers, much less the global despots. The only recourse will be to band together, which may create a formidable force whereby things build up into a worldwide conflict (e.g., World War III). Some say it is preordained, the final faceoff. Well, I figure it depends on how you define it. Let us take a look at how the Bible defines it.

The Apocalypse

The eventual outcome of all this chaos will be total oblivion. It is all coming to a head in which the forces of good and evil will clash in a final battle called Armageddon (REV 16:16). The term means "Hill of Megiddo", which resides in the Jezreel Valley of Israel where many a skirmish has taken place. The area was described by Napoleon as the perfect battlefield in terms of terrain, at least for an army occupying the high ground overlooking the valley. Many theologians believe the final struggle will occur there. The forces of evil will be wiped out by the hand of God and the kingdom will be turned over to his Son Jesus Christ (REV 19:19–21; REV 22). And the former world will never again be remembered or exist (ISA 65:17).

A number of warning signs are given in the Bible suggesting the end of the age is near. Jesus himself provided a forecast in response to his disciples questioning him about this very topic; Jesus's reply is known as the Olivet Discourse as it was delivered on the Mount of Olives (MAT 24; MAR 13; LUK 21). Jesus spoke of calamities such as floods, famines, earthquakes, pestilence, and war. He told of a time of tribulation, persecution, false prophets, wickedness, and global fear. Some scholars argue that Jesus was referring to the times in which he lived on the earth; others believe that the reference is to the time of his second coming. Actually, both camps may be correct, because prophecy is occasionally fulfilled more than once; case in point, the Abomination of Desolation spoken of by Daniel (DAN 9:27; DAN 11:31; DAN 12:11) and again by Jesus (MAT 24:15–21). That prophecy likely pertains to the desecration of the first temple in Jerusalem by the Greek ruler Antiochus Epiphanes (167 BC); the destruction of the second temple by the Roman emperor Titus (AD 70); and the eventual desecration and destruction of a conceivable third temple in the end times by the eighth and last evil emperor (REV 17:10–11).

Regardless, if you have taken notice, humanity is experiencing an escalation of catastrophes across the globe, people dying of disease or starvation, and not just in third world countries; drought in one place and flooding in the next; wars and rumors of war constantly and everywhere, so that there is no peace anywhere; earthquakes, volcanoes, tornadoes and other violent storms often in places where they uncommonly occur; persecution of Christians worldwide, even in the USA; addiction, immorality, mass murder, and terrorism increasing exponentially. All of these disasters are raising the death toll. Jesus said it will be the worst of times prior to his return. How much worse can it get?

Occurrences throughout history resemble a collision of ideals, between the ways of the world and the ways of God. The world is Satan's domain (JOB 1:6–7; LUK 4:5–8; 2 CO 4:3–4; 1 JO 4:4). If the world is your first love then you belong to the world; if God is your first love then you belong to him. It is God's people on Earth and his church that must stand, unmoved like a rock (MAT 16:16–18), and that foundation is God's Word which is the high ground in this campaign. Moses took a stand against pharaoh and freed the Hebrews from Egyptian captivity (EXO 5—15). David rose up against the Philistines and slew their champion Goliath; and the Israelites scattered or killed the rest of their army (1 SA 17). Hezekiah held firm during a siege on Jerusalem, in which 185,000 Assyrians were massacred by the angel of the Lord (2 KI 19; ISA 37:36). Daniel refused to compromise his faith in God (DAN 6), and so did his friends Shadrach, Meshach, and Abednego (DAN 3), in defiance of monarchs from Babylon and Persia. And God saved them from certain death, which is what he does for everyone who takes their position next to him, since the reward is eternal life. Paul faced off with Rome and proclaimed the Gospel to a nation totally hostile to Christianity; and though he was executed in the process, his mission would eventually result in Rome adopting Christianity as the official religion. Dietrich Bonhoeffer, knowing that his life was in jeopardy, defied Hitler. He attempted to convince the Christian Church not to adopt the heretical positions of the Nazi party, but the church leaders caved to the pressure. Isn't it interesting that none of these evil regimes prevailed? And how could they, seeing how they opposed God and were antichrists in their own right?

If faced with the ruin of this country as well as humanity, how would you respond? What if they accost you and imprison you for your faith? Should we expect or anticipate torment and suffering for following Christ? Everyone will suffer for sin whether they believe in God or not, though persecution is a badge of honor that Christians often bear. But with Christ you will endure hardship better than you will without him.

We have seen immorality emerging in defiance of God ever since the creation of man. And though evil has been defeated permanently by the victory of Christ over sin, the warfare continues. But it will end someday, and that day might be very soon. Because, indecency and sheer madness have overtaken the world and people are afraid to get involved; even the church seems to be succumbing just as it did to Nazi Germany. This very scenario was advanced by St. John in great detail in the Revelation of Jesus Christ. John wrote of unfulfilled promises of peace, followed by global war, financial ruin, corruption in the church, and massive death. He described the final empire of evil, comparing it to all the other evil empires that previously fell, and naming it the new Babylon (REV 17—18). It will be the last kingdom and the most heinous. Look closely and listen carefully; and you will detect the numerous hoards, malevolent to the core. They are Satan's followers whether they identify as Islamists, secularists, communists, relativists, globalists, or progressivists. All are hellbent on running the world; but hell will run them into the ground.

Apocalypse is a Greek word meaning "to lift the veil." And who or what will be revealed or unveiled? It will be the resurrected Christ. The modern definition typically refers to a great cataclysm that is linked with the last days, and a corresponding evacuation of God's elect. These are the prevailing themes of Revelation and all other eschatological teachings from the Bible. Eschatology denotes the end to history; a final time for humankind on this orb. It is inferred in the words "the end of the age" mentioned by Jesus when he ascended into heaven (MAT 28:18–20); when time is up, he will return again in glory (ACT 1:1–11). It will be a day of retribution and judgment upon those who persisted in iniquity and allied with Satan, whether knowingly or unknowingly. Do you want to be an accessory to this hostile takeover given the eventual aftershock? Bear in mind that sitting by and doing nothing will make you an accomplice. Death is waiting at the door; but so is Jesus. Open the door when Jesus knocks and you will be saved out of it (REV 3:20–21). And he will mark you as his own, so that Satan can never touch you (REV 20:2).

Once the veil is lifted, history will be a done deal. Satan will have been cast out of the earth and sent down into the depths of hell (PRO 9:18; ISA 14:12–15; JOH 12:31–32). Truth will have prevailed, ushering in a new episode for those who acted upon their faith in truth. The exhibition will be over and the curtain will fall a final time for those choosing death. They will be shut out for sitting idly by as spectators, and watching everything unfold and collapse, as if unaffected. But they will not like how the drama ends, and they will have nothing to applaud. They will be prohibited from exiting the auditorium, while the chosen will be rejoicing endlessly in their new bodies and homes. So, it's really no big deal if you leave it all behind, because you can't take it with you and you won't really want to; not when you get a glimpse of what lies in store. It will either be fulfillment and bliss or emptiness and grief. Keep focused on that picture of heaven; we all get a preview, you know.

Christ is the only way to God; in him we see the glory of God. God wants all people to come to the knowledge of this truth (1 TI 2:1–6). We all have opportunity and potential, given that in us also can be seen the very image of God (GEN 1:26–27). Now you know why Christendom is the target of attack; this war is being instigated against God himself by his adversary the devil (REV 19:19–21). So, if you are among those who are inclined to abolish and destroy Christianity, guess whose side you are on (MAT 12:30). Well, if that be the case there is no way you can win, for when did anyone ever succeed in defeating the Almighty? The first time Lucifer tried it he was thrown out of heaven (EZE 28:14–17). Now he is down here trying to solicit company in the fall. But he will fail, and he will fall along with those who follow him (2 TI 3:1–7). You can choose to fall or to rise; I hope you choose wisely.

I wish to make a few more points about the fall; it applies to beings of conscience and not animals and other breathing creatures. This is because the animals do not commit sin or even think about it. The punishment for sin is death, and this relates to spiritual death. Yes, animals die too, every earthly creature does; but animals are not judged, nor are they condemned. But people are going to be judged. Judgment occurs after the resurrection of humankind but is decided prior to one's physical death. Condemnation applies to the second death, which is a spiritual death because the spirit of life is detached from the body and soul forever (MAT 10:28); thus, the second death also involves forfeiture of the soul. Adam and Eve sinned knowing full well the punishment was death; but they didn't die right then and there. However, death was forthcoming; and it will fall upon all people, after which comes the judgment (HEB 9:27). The quintessence of the fall will be damnation, for those whose sins have not been remitted. They will fall asleep permanently in a perpetual nightmare. Incidentally, the idea that there was no occurrence of biological death for any living thing prior to the fall of man is unsubstantiated in scripture. Death was the spiritual sentence levied only upon humans, with the sin and verdict of Adam being passed onto you and me (ROM 5:12,18). But Christ will reverse that, if you ask him nicely.

THE GOSPEL MAKES THE DIFFERENCE

It has been established that Christianity is set apart from all other religions and worldviews; and what sets it apart is the Gospel of Jesus Christ. Simply put, God's Messiah prophesied throughout the Old Testament (OT) and fulfilled in the New Testament (NT) is Jesus Christ. And that Messiah is our Immanuel, meaning "God with us" (ISA 7:14; ISA 43:10–11; ISA 47:4; ISA 48:16–17); in other words, Jesus is God in human form (JOH 10:30). The biblical patriarchs believed in the coming of the anointed one (*Christos*), as do other religions that hold the OT in high esteem; this would include Jews, Muslims and Christians. These three monotheistic religions claim Abraham as a patriarch and Jerusalem as a beloved city. What they don't acknowledge is the same Jesus Christ. Orthodox Jews reject Jesus Christ as Messiah, and orthodox Muslims reject Christ as God's Son. Though all three religions look forward to the coming of Messiah, Christians know him to be Jesus who already has come and will return again a second time in the flesh (ACT 1:10–11). Other religions have proposed that Jesus of Nazareth was a great guy, he helped people, he performed wondrous acts; maybe he was a prophet, a teacher, a preacher, a healer, but he wasn't God. The Christian answer to their viewpoint is that he most certainly was and is God (ISA 9:6; JOH 1:1,14). This fact is apparent in both testaments of the Holy Bible.

The Koran explicitly states that God would never have a son and that Jesus is not God, regarding such statements as blasphemous (Surah 4:171; 10:68–70; 17:111; 19:88–90; 23:91). The Koran further states that God has appointed no consort, meaning no queen or sexual partner (Surah 6:101); interestingly, Mary urgently said the same thing when the angel Gabriel told her that she was going to have a son though she had never lain with any man (LUK 1:34–35). Okay, God doesn't commit fornication or get married; mostly polytheists imagine gods doing this. It is a gross misinterpretation of the Bible to assume that God intended to have sex with a woman; such thinking may be ascribed to Greek mythology but not the Bible. The Holy Spirit is not a physical entity and does not procreate; God became a man named Jesus who never had sex with anybody either. How then was the Virgin Mary impregnated (ISA 7:14; MAT 1:18)? The Koran correctly asserts that Mary was revered above women, she was impregnated in the manner of the immaculate conception, and her child was named Jesus who would become a great prophet (Surah 3:35–37,42–47; 19:19–22; 57:27). Furthermore, the Koran accedes that Jesus's ministry was to proclaim the Gospel in fulfillment of the Torah (Surah 5:46–47). How can they reconcile that with a belief that God does not intercede in the lives of men? Did he not visit Adam, Abraham, and Moses? There appears to be inconsistency within Islam about this matter of Jesus. Despite the above citations, Muslims maintain that Jesus was not an extension or progeny of God or the Holy Spirit, much less the savior of humankind. While Muslims acknowledge the power of God to command something to happen, begin, or exist (Surah 19:35), they cannot conceive of the Holy Spirit entering anybody especially a virgin's womb, though it is declared in their holiest book.

The Almighty can easily interact with people. After all, is he not God? Christians believe we have a personal relationship with God; Muslims do not, though they purport that Mohammed did. How discomforting it must be to acknowledge God from a distance. As for me I interact with God as often as I think of him. Christians invite God's Spirit to inhabit us; the Holy Sacraments are such an invitation. It is written: our bodies are a temple for the Holy Spirit (1 CO 6:18–20). But Muslims believe God would never condescend to the level of communing with a human being; thus, Islam leans more toward deism. If God did not communicate with humans, we wouldn't have his Holy Word. Personally, I can hear his voice in the words; and I believe every bit of it. Regrettably, I've encountered many people that do not. Even those claiming to be Christians vary in the degree to which they embrace the Bible and its truth. While mainstream Christian denominations converge on many indispensable truths, the myriad of spinoffs generally do not.

As with most religions, there are different factions within Judaism. Some Jews revere only the Torah (first five OT books), some acknowledge the rest of the OT (all thirty-nine books), some add apocryphal works from the period between the OT and NT (history of the Maccabees and feast of Hanukah). Messianic Jews include the NT (all twenty-seven books); they believe in the deity of Christ and accept him as Savior and Redeemer. While they identify as Jews, they also are Christians by faith; and they likewise uphold the OT and the NT (all sixty-six books).

The OT is quite clear about the coming of Messiah, his lineage, birth, mission, ministry, betrayal, torture, burial, and resurrection (read PSA 22:16–18; PSA 34:20; 78:2; ISA 7:14; 9:1–6; ISA 35:5–6; ISA 42:6; ISA 49:7; ISA 53; ISA 60:6; MIC 5:2; ZEC 3:9; ZEC 9:9; ZEC 11:12–13; ZEC 13:6–7; MAL 3:1; MAL 4:2). The sacrifice of Christ is divulged through the ram sacrificed by Abraham in lieu of his son Isaac (GEN 22), the Passover lamb sacrificed to spare the first born of Israel from the angel of death (EXO 12), and the New Covenant proclaimed by Moses to the Israelites (EXO 18:15–19; EXO 24). God's Covenant with Israel, testified throughout the OT, was a premonition of the New Covenant of Jesus Christ testified in the NT. God's Law (OT) points us to God's Grace (NT). The epistles of Paul and the book of Hebrews explain this transition succinctly (read ROM 10:4–5; GAL 2:16; GAL 3:13–26; HEB 7:15–19; HEB 8:6–13; HEB 9:14–22). Thus, the OT and NT cross-validate each other; in fact, the OT intimates NT testimony several hundred times and the NT references OT testimony several hundred times. It makes me wonder how most of the Jews missed or misunderstood the OT prophecies about the prophesied Messiah, how he would suffer and die to take away the sins of the world, how it was God himself that would come among us to be the Sacrificial Lamb, and how Christ alone among men has the power to forgive sins, raise us on the last day, and restore us into righteousness. I've heard it said that we don't need the OT anymore, because the NT supersedes it. Obviously, this cannot be the case since Jesus and his apostles quoted it often. Similarly, the Koran allegedly supersedes the OT and NT though it also provides numerous references to the Holy Bible, while not adding anything relevant to it (DEU 4:2; PRO 30:5–6; REV 22:18).

The fatal flaw of theologies other than Christianity is they deny the truth of Jesus Christ, who he was, how he died, how he arose from the dead, how he liberated us, and the fact that he is the third person of the Godhead (ISA 44:6; JOH 20:28–31). This in a nutshell is the Gospel message, and those who believe it are actual Christians; those who do not believe it are not Christians. So yes, Christianity is an exclusionary religion; most religions are. Either your faith and trust are in, with, and on Jesus Christ or they are not. The NT is a compilation of the testimony of Christ and his followers, all of whom proclaimed this good news to the world. Most of them died a horrible death witnessing for Jesus, and with gladness. Sure, other religious people are willing to die for their faith or cause, but they are dying in vain if they are not dying for Christ who died for them. Their belief is that their death will save them; but only Christ's death can save anyone.

The Holy Bible has more supportive documentation and corroboration than any dated literary work, greater than all other religious works combined. A lot of that evidence is found in secular sources antagonistic to Christianity and the Holy Bible. Contemplate the exhaustive proof that the Bible is authentic, authoritative, and true; in particular the New Testament since it initiated Christendom and contains the Gospel of Jesus Christ. If you disagree with the evidence cited below, take time to check and study the sources; you will discover the testimony to be accurate, and you'll probably find additional reliable sources and pertinent truths in the process. It is obvious that God had a hand in the preservation of his Word so that all people of every tongue would have access to it.

- The NT encompasses the most manuscript evidence available (by far) than any work of antiquity. We are talking some 5600 complete copies in the original Greek, not to mention tens of thousands of partial copies, books, and fragments. Second place goes to Homer's Iliad with about 640 copies, followed by works of Sophocles falling below 200 (Geisler and Bocchino, 2001; McDowell and Wilson, 1993).
- NT manuscript evidence is closer in time to its origin (by far) than any ancient work. New Testament manuscript fragments date back to the first century AD; the complete NT was finalized about fifty years from Christ's death around AD 30 at the age of thirty-three. Complete copies originate from the early second century, less than fifty years after the death of St. John the apostle. Second place goes again to Homer with copies dating 500 years after his death. Sophocles falls out of the top ten with 1400 years separating his words from his passing (Comfort, 1993; Rhodes, 2016).
- There is sufficient manuscript confirmation from ageless scrolls (including the Dead Sea Scrolls) to reconstruct the entire NT. These were written in Greek, Hebrew, or Aramaic on papyrus, leather, and other durable materials (*ibid*). The original authors of the NT produced gospels and epistles in a timely fashion, so their testimony would not be contaminated. These documents were meticulously recopied; information was passed along orally as well due to the prevalence of illiteracy.
- There is sufficient literature containing biblical quotes from early church leaders to rebuild the NT (survey the references cited in this section). Accordingly, if all copies, scrolls, and fragments of the NT were lost, over 99 percent of the NT could be retrieved from these alternate source documents. The associated records date from the first century to the fifth

century AD. Research these names for more information about their writings and teachings: Ignatius, Papias, Polycarp, Clement of Rome, Justin Martyr, Irenaeus, Clement of Alexandria, Tertullian, Hippolytus of Rome, Origen, Cyprian, Athanasius, Eusebius, Ambrose, Epiphanius, Jerome, and Augustine (see Barber, 2020). Early church fathers obtained the NT message directly from the Gospel writers and other disciples of Christ, and handed them down to subsequent interns and successors, thereby preserving the message. The Holy Bible has continued to remain unaltered and intact to this day through a devoted and dependable chain of custody (Wallace, 2013; Greenleaf, 1874).

- Certification of the Holy Bible continued periodically during recurring ecumenical councils such as Laodicea, Hippo, Chalcedon, and Nicaea. These boards were convened to examine and validate the canon, or standard of scripture, and dispel false teachings, gospels, and theologies. The repeated canonization of scripture helped to ensure that the purity of NT testimony survived, and to elucidate vital Christian doctrines.
- The translation and interpretation of authenticated biblical manuscripts (OT and NT) discovered throughout history has never changed in content or application (Zuckerman, 2006). Recall the earlier mention of the book of Isaiah found among the Dead Sea Scrolls, virtually identical to the current Hebrew translation, predicting the birth, life, torture, death, burial, and resurrection of Messiah. The plentiful supply of manuscripts from different languages, times, formats, and regions rendered it impossible to remove the Bible from society, history, and the world, despite numerous concerted efforts to eliminate them by past secular, antichristian, and pagan governments and societies.
- The Holy Bible is the most translated work of literature in history. The current count is some 650 languages in which the complete Bible is available, with another 1450 NT translations, and about 1200 incomplete translations (Wycliffe Global Alliance, 2016). These numbers increase every year; they have, no doubt, escalated by now.
- Considerable outside corroboration exists for the NT in general and Jesus Christ in particular, from Jewish (Josephus, the Jewish Talmud, the Toledot Yeshu), Greek (Thallus, Celsus, Lucian), Roman (Tacitus, Suetonius, Lentulus, Pliny), Syrian (Lucius, Mara bar Serapion), Babylonian (the Babylonian Talmud), and other non-Christian historians and historical journalism (Wallace, 2013). And though their motivation was often to mock or discredit the Bible and the deity of Christ, these

writings serve to authenticate instead because they verify key events and personalities in the NT. Ever since the Bible was canonized, numerous scholars have performed rigorous research to expose its fallibility, but converted to Christianity instead (see Strobel, 1998). Most notably Greenleaf (1874), renowned jurist, legal expert, and Harvard Law founder, employed rules of evidence, court procedure, and cross-examination to interrogate the NT evangelists. Greenleaf declared the resurrection of Christ indisputable beyond reasonable doubt.

- Even the dozens of pseudo gospels and other distortions of Christianity, written long after Christ's passion and the deaths of eyewitnesses, provide elements of support to the NT. Actually, false teachings present enough partial truths to draw people into them. A good example is the Book of Mormon, which plagiarizes the Holy Bible, and is written in a manner and phraseology that simulates antiquity. Unfortunately, it contradicts the teachings of Christ like many gnostic counterfeits which ascribe attributes to God and Jesus that are erroneous, and which promote work-based or knowledge-based avenues to redemption. This is the tactic of Lucifer, who mixes truth with lies. It takes a keen understanding of doctrine and scripture to extract the untruths. Still, if one was to combine all such erroneous teachings and writings into an organized whole, it would undoubtedly reveal patterns of truth that could be extrapolated which would substantiate the Gospel. But imitations always add additional narrative that is false, intending to steer people away from the truth or otherwise introduce confusion, thereby rendering them untrustworthy. Only the Holy Bible is thoroughly trustworthy.
- Most reputable historians and theologians do not dispute the following facts concerning Jesus Christ. He was born around 4–6 BC (BCE), raised in Nazareth of Galilee, and baptized by a relative named John. He was a controversial figure that preached repentance and salvation, worked miracles among the people, and proclaimed prophecy that came true during his life and after his death. He was arrested by the Jewish leaders, tried and crucified by the Roman governor Pontius Pilate, and buried in a tomb donated by a Pharisee named Joseph. The tomb was found empty three days later and Jesus was seen alive by hundreds of people afterwards. His disciples went to their deaths proclaiming him to be the resurrected Messiah and the Savior of humankind, and the movement referred to as Christianity spread throughout the world unto this day (Craig, 2010; Habermas, 1993; Sanders, 1993).

Summary: The Book of John provides a wonderful synopsis of the Gospel message using Jesus's own words. The following is a compilation of direct quotes from Jesus Christ paraphrased from the Holy Bible (using the KJV, red letter edition).

I (Jesus) and the Father (God) are one (JOH 10:30). I bear witness of the Father and he bears witness of me (JOH 8:18–19,23). What the Father does, the Son does; and what the Son does so does the Father; in particular, raising the dead (JOH 5:19–21). I am the way, the truth, and the life; the only way to the Father is through me (JOH 14:6). Whatever you ask in my name I will give it to you in order to glorify my Father in heaven (JOH 14:13).

I am not of this world (JOH 8:23). I came down from heaven to do the will of my Father (JOH 6:38). I came so that you can have life and have it more abundantly (JOH 10:10). I am the light; follow me and you will not walk in darkness but will have the light of life (JOH 1:43; JOH 8:12). The words I speak are Spirit and life (JOH 6:13). If you keep my words you will not see death (JOH 8:51); and if you live in me you will never die (JOH 11:26).

God is Spirit and must be worshipped in Spirit and truth (JOH 4:24). Those who live in truth come to the light, and people will see their works and know that they are from God (JOH 3:21). If you continue in my words you will know the truth, and that truth will set you free (JOH 8:32). Those who hear my words and believe will pass from death into life, and in due time I will call them home (JOH 5:24–25); for I will raise them up on the last day (JOH 6:44).

Because God loved the world so much, he gave me to you, that if you would believe in me you would not die but receive eternal life (JOH 3:16). I laid down my life knowing I could take it back again; this direction I received from the Father (JOH 10:17–18). And because I live again, so will you (JOH 14:19); for I am the resurrection and the life (JOH 11:25). I am preparing a place for you in my Father's kingdom; and I will come back for you so that you can be with me forever (JOH 14:2–3).

I came from the Father and into the world; then I left the world and returned to the Father (JOH 16:28). But we have sent the Spirit of truth, who is the Comforter; and he will reside in you, and he will teach you so that you will not forget my words (JOH 14:16–17,26;

JOH 15:26). If you want to see the kingdom of God you must be born again, not just of water but of the Spirit (EZE 36:26–27; JOH 3:3–6). The world will not accept the Spirit of truth, because it cannot see him or know him; but believers know him, because he dwells within them (JOH 14:17).

I have told you these things so you can have joy to the fullest (JOH 15:11), and so you can have peace of mind (JOH 16:33). Keep in mind, however, if you love me the world will hate you (JOH 15:18; JOH 17:14). The world has hated me without cause (JOH 15:25); and those who hate me hate the Father (JOH 15:23). If you were of the world the world would love you; but you are not of the world because I have chosen you out of it, and that is why the world will hate you (JOH 15:19). You are not of the world, even as I am not of the world (JOH 17:16).

Those who reject me and my words will be judged by my words on the last day (JOH 12:48). They will have refused to come to me and receive the life I offer (JOH 5:40). I warned them that they would be condemned and die in their sins if they did not believe in me (JOH 3:17–18; JOH 8:24–27).

Entitlement

We live in an era of entitlement wherein a large segment of society wants a freebie. During the last decade, there have never been more people in this country on welfare, food stamps, disability, or other form of government handout since the Mayflower pilgrims landed at Plymouth Rock. All too often, those receiving such assistance have been incentivized to prolong it, even though they are able-bodied or otherwise rehabilitated. Welfare pays better than some jobs and requires less work. Laziness is becoming an epidemic. Our youth are growing spoiled and disrespectful to parents, conditioned to the handouts and the get-rich-quick schemes (PRO 30:8-16). Do you know someone who wishes to become an instant millionaire by winning the lottery or receiving a disproportionate legal settlement? The more a person ceases to be productive, the less motivated they become, to the point they quit caring and quit doing anything. This is a bleak prospect, as they also lose the will to carry on, and frequently end up addicted, mentally ill, possibly suicidal. What do they expect will be the eventual outcome of inaction? One wastes away in a cloud of hopelessness, helplessness, and worthlessness when he or she is perpetually idle (PRO 20:4; ECC 9:10–11).

I argue endlessly about how the globalists want to redistribute wealth and make everyone dependent on they who would wield control. The trend is a sliding away from free enterprise and towards collectivism. The reason why socialism will not work is it annuls any motive to excel, so the tendency is to do the bare minimum. The ultimate outcome will be living off the bare minimum. There is no glass ceiling to penetrate, no occasion to ascend or progress, no opportunity for entrepreneurship, no individualism or personal excellence required or pursued. Everything goes to the collective, and the power-mongers control that. If we the people do not act soon, our nation will slip away from us and we will accede to a mundane existence. If the USA goes down, it is likely the rest of the world will chase us; it's like a race to the bottom. What happens when the global economy takes a nose dive and the collapse bankrupts the world? It is a sign of the end (REV 6:5–6; REV 13:16–17).

The conclusion is that you have to get busy, to be productive, to realize your full potential. There are no benefits for sitting on your duff and watching the world careen into the primeval slime, which also will be the final destiny of the collective and its controllers if they have their way. Beware when the government promises to cover your expenses for college, healthcare, abortion, housing, food, lodging, and more. How will they pay for all this? They will confiscate the money from the worker bees. They will commandeer property too. And what do we profit in the end? Nothing, that's what; we end up destitute. And what will those in power do with the wealth? They will blow it all; this is obvious given their track record.

What does this have to do with Christianity? It is written that a faith without works is useless (JAM 2:14). If you believe an endeavor to be promising, you must act on that belief. You must pursue happiness; it will not fly into the window and land on your kitchen table. The bureaucrats are not going to accomplish your dream, only theirs. However, if you want the eternal reward of a heavenly inheritance, you will not earn it with your good deeds (EPH 2:8–9). Your works are an expression of your love and faith, not a substitute for them. Whereas Christianity is the only religion in which eternal life is granted for free if only you will believe that Christ earned it for you, many other religions presume that you can earn it yourself or receive it by default.

THE GOSPEL MAKES THE DIFFERENCE

Those figuring they are entitled to the kingdom because they have been good people have forgotten that they are equally bad. Nobody is without sin; and good deeds do not erase bad ones. It is impossible to maintain a balance, since all your goodness cannot neutralize any of your badness. Additionally, self-punishment cannot put a dent in your death sentence. If that were possible, nobody would need a savior to earn their passage into heaven.

The apostle Paul knew this all too well. He was a man zealous for the Lord but was misguided at the beginning of his ministry. Thinking he was doing God's work by eradicating Christians, it took Jesus Christ himself to snap him out of it. Once he saw the light, Paul regarded himself as the chief of sinners (1 TI 1:15). And like everyone else, he struggled trying to do the good he should and avoid the evil that he shouldn't (ROM 7:15–21). Paul concluded that we are incapable of righteousness; although we know what to do, we can't seem to accomplish it. He tutored anyone who would listen to trust in Christ alone and not to rely on their own understanding or works (PRO 3:5; EPH 2:8–9). Martin Luther struggled with these same dilemmas and entered a monastery, trying to merit salvation and punishing himself when he didn't measure up. Luther likewise concluded that we are justified by faith in Christ alone; there is no other path to salvation or to grace. Both of these evangelists snapped out of it after lightning threw them to the ground; talk about a wakeup call. Listen to their message and you too will see the light of Christ, who has secured your redemption.

Though Christ has purchased your admission into heaven, that doesn't indicate you are good to go and don't have to do anything. You still have to act on your faith; because a sincere faith is proven by your actions (HEB 11:17–40). We are indebted, and dedicate our lives to Christ because that's what he did for us (ROM 12:1). I'm not saying you have to quit your job and become a monk, missionary, evangelist, or priest; because you can glorify God and reflect his light in whatever vocation you have entered. You have free will, and you can affect your destiny. You can pursue pleasure in any way you choose as long as it is not in violation of the law. Especially, you want to be cognizant of God's law and what he expects from you; which although it is holiness, a standard you can never achieve (LEV 11:44; 1 PE 1:16), it is the example he wants you to follow which is God's only Son (1 CO 11:1). And Christ will cover your sins with his holiness if your faith is true (ROM 4:7–8; ROM 6:14–18). This is what entitles you to pass from death into life (JOH 5:24)—a heart for the Lord wherein dwells his Word, enabling you to think like Christ (1 CO 2:16).

There has been one and only one who was born of a woman that lived a life without sin: Jesus Christ (HEB 4:15). There can be only one to pay the price of sin for humanity, and he would be the one without sin (HEB 10:12–14). If Christ had sinned, he could have saved nobody, not even himself. Death had no power over him precisely because he was not guilty of any misconduct or offense. The rest of us are guilty as sin. So, what are sinners entitled to? We are entitled to everlasting life in heaven with Father God if we trust in him for forgiveness, atonement, and reconciliation. Otherwise, we are entitled to death. Nobody is excluded insofar as everybody gets to vote. Either you are for Christ or against him (MAT 12:30); to abstain is akin to being against him. That is, either you want Jesus to be Lord of your life or you want to be lord of your own life; but you cannot save yourself when your number comes up. Only Jesus can raise you from the dead and bring you home to be with God. How do we know this? Because Jesus raised himself from the dead (JOH 10:17–18), proving that he possessed the power of God (ROM 1:1–4). Those who do not choose Christ do not want to live eternally with God. Those who want to live with God but think they can buy their own ticket are equally lost; their way is not the correct one. You cannot pay your way into the glory land. It already has been paid.

A great many philosophers assert that you are entitled to an abundant life and/or eternal life; piety can earn this according to their misguided adherents. But they are in denial with respect to their sin which has convicted them. Which is it? Are you disgraced by your sin, exalted by your virtue, or is it both? I ask you, why would God send his Son to die if it was unnecessary? Was it simply to make a spectacle of himself? It would be unimpressive, that sacrifice, if done for show. What possible purpose could be achieved with Jesus's suffering and death if we already had the capacity to enter the pearly gates without an escort? The historical confirmation of this noble event has been carried along for generations. What are we to make of it? Do you regard it to be nothing but a random event which is equally meaningless as the boring interludes in your life? Is everything inconsequential? Are you wasting your time deliberating this matter? You might as well give up, right? Yes, that is what unearned entitlement leads to, not caring anymore. When you quit caring, you quit doing; when doing goes down, caring fades further. Engage your mind and you will find caring going up again, and your self-esteem too. Do it for God and there is no limit, not even the sky. Then you will be entitled to everything Christ earned for you.

Destiny

Life is the most significant aspect of this world is it not? Do you ever wonder why you arrived on the scene at this particular epoch of time? Are you here for a reason; is there a purpose for your life? I doubt if that purpose would be to commit suicide, to die of an overdose, or to live under a bridge in the cold rain and snow. I doubt if your purpose, if indeed you have one, is to live off a meager disability check and smoke medical marijuana the rest of your life. But you can pick that if you want. You see, the thing about destiny is that you have some control over it. Maybe you are familiar with the following quote by an anonymous author.

> Be careful of your thoughts for they become your words.
> Be careful of your words for they become your actions.
> Be careful of your actions for they become your habits.
> Be careful of your habits for they become your character.
> Be careful of your character for that becomes your destiny.

According to the author, your destiny is up to you. It all hinges on your thoughts. It is a difficult task indeed to maintain command of your thoughts; it demands substantial effort, for contentment and achievement never arrive without work. I would add one line to begin the above quote: Be careful of your desires for they become your thoughts. If you desire something, you can believe it possible. If you don't care, it matters not what you believe; because you cannot have a sincere faith without caring, which reflects love. If you really want or crave something, it will captivate your thoughts, which is just short of acting on it. Those thoughts can be positive or negative; if you dwell on something evil you could end up doing it, and you will reap the regrettable conclusion. To illustrate, if you enjoy pornography, spending hours viewing it, it is just a matter of time when you step out on your spouse or commit a promiscuous sexual act. And if that becomes a habit, the behavior will become progressively more deviant ending in something very bad, like disease, divorce, and/or death. But if the Lord is your desire you will receive everything you need here on Earth, and you will have reserved your spot in the Kingdom of Heaven (PSA 145:15–16; MAT 6:31–34).

Resolved: you can be the director and producer of your life story, which could have a happy ending or a dreadful one. In which case, I highly recommend that you reassess your thoughts and desires and determine if they are in alignment with your conscience. Better yet, are they in alignment with the will of God? It is not a difficult thing to discern what is right for your life;

it involves mindfulness, thoughtfulness, effort. Okay, that isn't exactly easy, to remain constantly mindful of what you are thinking, how you are behaving, and how it is affecting others. The key is this: don't just react, but reason. Emotions will get in the way of reasons, which is why you should keep a grip on your desires and let your higher power control your thoughts.

When it comes to destiny there is another important, albeit critical aspect to consider. Is death the final destination, or is there another destination after this life? Where do you go from here; do you just die and that's it—no more consciousness, sentience, hope, emotions, or desires? Do you remain in a state of suspended animation? Does your mind become a member of a collective soul? None of these prospects appeal to me, not in the least. I prefer the alternative of living again, in an unspoiled body that will never die because it will be without sin, pure and flawless like that of Jesus Christ (PHP 3:20–21). Visualize a world with no evil, suffering, pain, sorrow, worry, or conflict; this sounds like heaven to me. That's where I want to be; it will be my final destination. But it will be a destiny replete with new destinations. How can I be sure? Because God promised (JOH 3:16).

Maybe it's time to ask yourself these questions. Why am I here, do I have a purpose, can I make a difference, do I have control? And then the big one, is there life after death for me? To start, if you'd rather it be over after this life you can attain that result by doing nothing about it. Remember, it's your choice, life or death (DEU 30:19). If you opt for life, there is much you need to learn. Do your research; investigate the various philosophies about the end, which can actually be the beginning depending on which perspective you adopt. But be very careful, because many theologies advance promises that cannot be delivered, because those guarantees do not come from God. Be advised, your purpose is to seek God and love his Son, and your destiny will be God's heavenly realm. Unless you'd sooner not, then refuse it.

I have studied religion extensively; in fact, I used to teach college courses on world religions. My studies served to reinforce my Christian faith, which is the system in which I was raised. I was able to rule out logically, naturally, spiritually, and scientifically religions that are founded on deism, polytheism, pantheism, animism, legalism, atheism, and scientism (it is recommended that you study these paradigms if you are not sure what is presumed). I pretty much narrowed it down to monotheism. But I've already ruled out Islamism and Judaism because they deny the deity of Christ. Ultimately, it left me with Christianity, which explained everything via the

Holy Bible, to include law, science, spirituality, eschatology, redemption, salvation, resurrection, creation, and life after death.

If there is no afterlife, what is the meaning of this life? That is a false assumption because there is definitely meaning to this life, which is to prepare us for the next one. This is the Christian view, plainly outlined in God's Word. Unfortunately, people do not take the time to study the Bible assuming it cannot be true; or they are too lazy to find out so they take the easy way by taking someone else's word for it. When it comes to your destiny, I advise that you not place it in the hands of anyone else but Jesus Christ. This is something you should examine closely before determining what will be. Do you want to be set free from your sin or do you want to be buried with it?

One final thought about destiny. Though you can select your destiny, God who is all knowing is aware of what you will choose. He has planned in advance your ultimate destination because he knew you before you were even born (ROM 8:27–35; EPH 1:3–12). You were called, and if you heeded that call you were justified, and if that be the case you will be glorified. He chose you to be his own, to be an adopted child, and to be by his side. And if he is on your side, who can prevail against you (MAT 16:17–19)? God has given you these great gifts for free, and he already knows if you will accept them or reject them. This is the essence of the doctrine of predestination. But that does not preclude free will, and the time to act is now.

Freedom

According to Thomas Jefferson in the Declaration of Independence, it is a self-evident truth that God has endowed us with liberty. That gift is unalienable, insofar as it was not given to you by your government or by man. This country was built upon freedom, and to this day the USA remains the freest society on the planet. We have sung about freedom in our national hymns: "sweet land of liberty, let freedom ring" (*My Country Tis of Thee*); "land of the free and home of the brave" (*Star Spangled Banner*); "confirm thy soul in self-control, thy liberty in law" (*America the Beautiful*). We have sung about where that freedom derives, namely God: "God bless America, land that I love" (*God Bless America*); "glory, glory hallelujah, his truth is marching on" (*Battle Hymn of the Republic*); "America, America, God shed his grace on thee" (*America the Beautiful*). Would you voluntarily relinquish any of your freedoms, including those endowed by your Creator and those established in our Constitution and Bill of Rights?

The following are collections of rights and freedoms given by God or granted under our constitutional form of government. Both lists are supposed to be for all citizens and are enforceable in accordance with the laws of the land. God-given, immutable rights include life, liberty, prosperity, property, self-determination, opinions, safety and security, shared accountability, law and order, equality, religion, caring and not caring. Civil rights and freedoms awarded via our constitutional republic include voting, privacy, due process, presumption of innocence, speak, write, publish, assemble, free-enterprise, commerce, protection, bearing arms, states' rights, and separation of powers. These are the abridged lists. Our founders gleaned many of their ideas from John Locke who lived a century before them (see Locke, 2002). Locke wrote about the natural rights of man conferred by the Almighty such as free will, property, security, and protection which are preserved by governments via positive law, order, and enforcement. Locke stressed liberty over license, equality over privilege, accountability over immunity, self-defense over conquest, and labor over slavery (*ibid*).

Many of our fellow Americans have died to preserve these rights and freedoms, and many more will die; especially, if we acquiesce to rogue nations, demented marauders, corrupt politicians, and godless cults who deprive us of them. The saying, "freedom is not free" is therefore, true; or is it? After all, God gave it to us. And we have remained free precisely because our nation was founded on God's Word. I remember as a schoolboy frequently pledging my allegiance to this republic, "One nation, under God, indivisible, with freedom and justice for all." Countless kids these days have never heard that pledge. Actually, we seem to have lost pride in our heritage, commitment to equal rights and freedom, and genuine love for our country. Even our policymakers go about apologizing as if our nation is not great and blessed, or as if our nation is downright contemptuous. Well, not compared to a lot of other places, don't you think? I get the humility angle, that is a good thing; but placating terrorists, communists, jihadists, and dictators is beneath us. And why don't we reinstate our policy of arresting those making terroristic threats? Some have liberally threatened and promoted homicide, including against our President.

Obviously, freedom is a gift but it comes at a price; sometimes that price is blood, to include the blood of Christ. Our heroes fight, even die for freedom, because it is that precious. If you refuse to assert your rights someone may try to deprive you of them. When the enemy comes with guns, tanks, planes, and bombs you can opt for fight, flight, or freeze. If you freeze, you'll be extinguished. If you fight, be prepared to die. If you flee, you'll be on the run, and that freedom will last until they catch up to you. Then, you'll have to fight anyway to have a chance at freedom. The alternative is enslavement. Patrick Henry proclaimed that slavery is never a fair price to pay for peace. Except, you already are a slave, to sin (JOH 8:31–35). If you want to really be free, totally and completely, reach out to Jesus Christ because he fought and died for you. He frees you from sin and death (JOH 8:36); and that freedom lasts forever. And Jesus will be there with you, forever. Would you like to be free of sickness, pain, suffering, anxiety, temptation, fear, and fatigue forevermore? We are talking 100 percent healthy in mind, body, and spirit; living in unqualified peace, joy, and bliss with an unlimited and never-ending ability to learn, to achieve, and to become.

Being a Christian is like being a soldier. It is a fight for freedom and the enemy is pure evil. It is not the same as a clash with flesh and blood, because it is spiritual combat that is going on about you (2 CO 10:4; ROM 8:7). Flight and freeze are not viable options. However, it takes guts to fight for freedom, principles, faith, and decency. And the stakes are life and death; but in this case, the outcome is forever. So, there is enormous incentive to be on the right side. Followers of other religions, while many are eager to fight even against people that are no threat to them, are fighting for a lost cause. World domination is not a splendid benefit; neither is imposing an ideal or religion upon others. Objectives such as these violate freedom and free will.

Killing innocent bystanders is not a means to an end, except ending up in hell. Remember, it is not a war between one creed, color, country, or cause and another. We fight against rulers of darkness, evil spirits, and wickedness of colossal cunning and power (EPH 6:10–12). But we can stand firm for we are protected with the armor of God (EPH 6:10–18); and we have the best weapon ever, the Word of God that cuts into the very souls of men (HEB 4:12). If you believe in Christ you have the protection and power of the Holy Spirit. And when you die, whether by combat, illness, calamity, or old age, you will prevail against the enemy and be victorious (1 CO 15:55–57). A crown of life will be your prize (JAM 1:12; REV 2:10) for finishing the race without forfeiting your faith (2 TI 4:6–8). You finally will be set free from the bondage of sin and the clutches of death, as well as self-defeating messages and other cognitive interference. You will be free to discover answers, acquire knowledge, live under the umbrella of God's precious love, and appreciate and praise the magnificence of his presence for all eternity. This is a freedom that you cannot fathom because it exceeds by magnitudes your greatest worldly yearnings (ISA 64:4; 1 CO 2:9).

Free will is reserved for humans; that is, animals and other organisms, though they are born free, they are oblivious to free will. We humans are free to choose right from wrong, life or death, and God over the world. We get to decide in every case, regardless of the consequences; though, we usually know in advance the consequences. One must wonder, why do we choose unwisely so often? "Nobody is perfect," they say, well except Jesus; everyone else has sinned and fallen short of the kingdom and glory of God (ROM 3:23). But just because you have been set free doesn't mean you are now free to do whatever you please.

Don't forget, there is another war going on inside you, between the spirit and the flesh; being set free is to subdue the flesh and to live in the spirit. This is yet another restriction to freedom, because to live free is to trust in Christ. We cannot reach heaven on our own, which is the prevailing message of this exposition. Heaven is a place where liberty is never diminished; if you value liberty it is well worth the effort. Are you prepared to make the effort, even if it could result in conflict, injury, torture, or execution?

You are free to believe as you wish, but there are drawbacks for believing wrong. This is why it is critically important to know the Holy Bible. Immerse yourself into the Word and you will absorb the wisdom of God himself (JAM 3:17). Your increase in understanding, loving, and believing will be extraordinary. It is recommended that you contemplate the doctrine of the Holy Trinity; if you can experience that, the rest will come easy (1 TH 5:23). Find your way by coming to Jesus; join him on an everlasting journey (REV 21:17) and be set free forever (JOH 8:36).

Connecting

If you are interested in acquiring the above-mentioned endowments declared to be yours by God himself then connect with Christ through his Holy Spirit. That is, we connect to God by way of his Son, because Jesus is the go-between for us and the Father. Jesus is our advocate, pastor, teacher, leader, and Lord (MAR 10:43–45; JOH 13:13; 1 JO 2:1–2). He shows us the way, the truth, and the life (JOH 14:6). He is God who became a man so we could connect with the Holy Trinity (ISA 43:10–11; MAT 16:13–16). Jesus spoke for the Father to all people (JOH 12:48–50), and showed us the avenue to their kingdom via his resurrection. That resurrection will bring the dead back to life; and all will see God with their own eyes, face-to-face (JOB 19:25–27; 1 CO 13:12; 1 JO 3:2). You're going to want to meet Jesus before then, or it will be your last meeting with him.

This is what you can do to have that close encounter and commune with God's Spirit (JOH 4:23–24). Rejoice in the Lord, pray constantly, spend quiet time with God, and invoke the higher power within you to guide your thoughts (1 TH 5:15–19); you will recognize your spiritual connection to God and may be inclined to keep it. Delve into the Holy Bible (2 TI 3:15–17), read it often and jot down notes, find a church founded on that Word (Old and New Testaments); this is how God's Spirit connects to you. You easily can recognize a good church when you find one; the Gospel of Jesus Christ is preached, God's praises are sung, his Holy Spirit speaks to your heart through worship and teaching, and the people treat you like family (ROM 12:5; 1 CO 12:28–30; HEB 10:23–25). A supportive church comprised of members who are passionate about Christ is a good place to connect with other Christians. The church and the body of Christ are there to build you up in the faith as you also should support, edify, and serve them (1 CO 14:26; EPH 4:11–16; 1 TH 5:11). When you become equipped with knowledge, skills, and spiritual gifts you will begin to connect with others in your midst that are lost or unsure about the one true faith that saves.

We are joined to God via his Holy Spirit through the eternal covenant, wherein he enables us to be a part of him perpetually (ISA 56:6–7). This invitation was extended to all people and all nations (JER 50:5; ZEC 2:10–11). When you are joined with the Lord it is forever, just like the vow a husband makes to his wife to stay together forever (MAT 19:5–6). God considers our bond to be like marriage, with Christ being the groom and his church, the bride (EPH 5:30–33). In the fulfillment of time, God will join all things unto himself, whether in heaven or on the earth, except for those who have deliberately disconnected from him (EPH 1:10–12; JDE 1:19).

Likewise, members of the church are joined together in the spirit of love (ROM 8:35; 1 CO 6:17) making us of one mind (1 CO 1:10), not unlike the communion among the three persons of the Holy Trinity. The connectivity within the community of Christ is also similar to the way our body parts are joined together in harmony (EPH 4:16). In order to maintain that coherence, we are not to be joined with unbelievers or with people who pursue careless ambitions (EZR 9:14); otherwise we could become corrupted and tempted to follow them and not Christ. That doesn't mean we ignore those people or avoid any and all communications with them, but that we should not unite with them, get entangled with them, or marry them (2 CO 6:14).

Every connection joined by Christ is powerfully positive and supremely uplifting. It draws people near to you because you'll radiate his love and light; your countenance will glow, you'll have a twinkle in your eyes, and your demeanor and attitude will be endearing to most everyone. People will be intrigued by your graciousness, peace, and nurturing and will open themselves up to you, to be filled with the same Holy Spirit that indwells yours as you share the truth; for God will be speaking through you (LUK 21:13–15). If you plant a seed the Spirit will nurture it (ISA 55:10–11); and others will encounter the comfort, conviction, and entitlement allotted to everyone who reaches out to God through Christ. They will know what has been missing in their lives up until then, just as you did when you finally claimed Christ as Savior and welcomed him to be the protector of your soul.

Who wouldn't want to be connected to the Lord of the universe? We're talking Almighty God who is excellent, perfect, fearsome, and awesome. Why would anyone decline the opportunity to have him coach their team? How can you be defeated with God? You can have all honor, glory, and power backing you. You'd be a fool to cross God, to discard him, or to be on the wrong side of him (PSA 14:1–2). But many will; and I mourn for them. They think they are too smart to be falling for the Christianity myth. But God will destroy the wisdom of men who believe the cross of Christ is ridiculous; Christians know it to be the power and wisdom of God (1 CO 1:18–31). If only the wayward souls would entertain this truth even for a moment, it could save their lives.

What have you got to lose? Just ask yourself, what if God is right here right now (ACT 17:27)? Next, ask him to make himself known to you. Reach up to him and you will find he is reaching down to you. He will reveal himself to you in signs, wonders, and revelations. The greatest revelations of all are clearly seen in his creation and his words. Open your mind and heart and his love will fill you and surround you (JAM 4:8). Those who cannot see him, hear him, and feel him are putting up a wall; they are deliberately blocking him out (PSA 115:1–8; MAR 8:18).

Do you want to experience a personal relationship with God? Just pray this simple prayer: God, if you are there, I want to know you. If your Son is real, I want to meet him. I know I am not perfect but you are. I need to be forgiven for consciously choosing wrong, hurting others, and indulging myself. Because you are almighty, I know you have the power to forgive me and save me from myself. And I want that. I am truly sorry for sinning against you, others, and myself; and I ask that you would be merciful to me and change me from the inside out. Bring me into your presence and abide with me forever; and I will be yours. In the name of your Son Jesus Christ and my Savior, I submit my prayer before the throne of Your Grace. Amen.

Service

Ultimately, everybody has to make up his or her mind about whom they will serve. There are many available alternatives: God, self, idols, dictators, boss, parents, children, spouse, multiple gods, etc. Establish your priorities, starting with who is number one. Undoubtedly, you have served many masters, but which is at the top? God wants to be first in your life. If he is, whenever you serve anyone, including yourself, it will be for him. You see, everything you say or do is felt by God (MAT 25:31–46). If you put anything or anyone else before him, you have violated his first commandment (EXO 20:1–3; MAT 22:35–38). So those clerics claiming that you cannot have a relationship with God are misleading their followers. It is God that requests a relationship with us and invites us to be a part of him (REV 3:20). But we can serve anybody and everybody if we are doing it for God. In fact, everything we do or don't do should be for God (1 CO 10:20–33). If this be the case, you have your priorities straight.

Self-serving motivations are worldly and counterproductive, for they work against God. Those who serve their country, are they doing it for themselves? Those who serve others are they doing it for personal gain? I certainly hope and pray not. Whenever a person unselfishly serves another, they are serving God. If there are ulterior motives, it probably is not in accordance with God's will.

Our mortal strivings are not in conflict with the will of God if we acknowledge him in our earthly pursuits. If we give him our works, he will give us his thoughts (PSA 37:4–6; PRO 16:3). Though we live and thrive here on the earth, heaven is our home. Worldly goals, possessions, and riches are fleeting compared to what lies in store for us in God's domain.

Especially, we must not focus exclusively on material possessions like money (LUK 16:13–15). Besides, there is nothing in this world we need to bring when we depart; such items will have no value in heaven, with one exception, our love. And it was pure love with which Jesus Christ overcame the world (JOH 16:20–33). It was the same love God had for us when he created us; and he will continue to extend that love to his children always and forevermore. Is this not the reason we have children, to love and nurture our offspring hoping they will love us back? Like God, we love them so much we would sacrifice ourselves to save them from peril. God made us to be sons and daughters, in the likeness of his own Son, so it should come as no surprise that we reap great returns when we act like him and make sacrifices for others. And by doing so, we also glorify him.

Inviting God's Son into your life gives you the power to become a child of God (JOH 1:12). When you accept Christ, you begin to shine his light; and that light shines eternally. God will call you into service in whatever capacity he wills, empowering you with the knowledge and skills to be successful. You will perform incredible feats of faith that will amaze everyone, beginning with you. It will reinforce your knowledge, faith, and calling with the assurance that it is Christ who is working through you. And you will win the fight, the race, and the crown (1 CO 9:24–27). When you are laid to rest, you will immediately enter into the presence of the Lord (2 CO 5:8). And when Christ returns in judgment you will have been judged not guilty (ROM 3:28; ROM 5:1). Then will begin your new life of service, and you will be performing greater feats than you ever did here.

Doesn't that sound exciting? It does to me. Jesus said we will become like angels in a way (LUK 20:34–39). Angels are extremely powerful, and they have astounding capabilities (2 KI 19:35; PSA 103:20; 2 PE 2:11; REV 12:7–9), like darting this way and that as fast as lightning (EZE 1:13–14). Imagine, being able to move at the speed of light; actually, you will be able to move at the speed of time since, like Jesus, you will become a timeless being. That implies the capacity to be anywhere, anytime at the bidding of the Almighty. Not that we relinquish free will, because that was endowed upon us at the beginning. But we won't be choosing to sin ever again, you can be sure of that. It will be a fact that we can obey the will of God impeccably because we will be made perfect through Christ (HEB 10:14). Those who wish to maximize their full potential and become the ideal self, Christ can ensure you accomplish that here on the earth and again in heaven.

Serving is our response to God's grace which he has given us in response to our faith; and his response to our service is a treasure trove in heaven that surpasses the entirety of worldly wealth (MAT 6:19–21). The bonuses in heaven are unfathomable. It is not a sin to desire spiritual riches, because God wants to shower them upon us, just like any parent wants nothing but good things for his or her children. But to strive for earthly treasures is futile, as they cannot satisfy for long since the thirsts of the flesh are unquenchable. Further, although a person can become weary with physical pleasure, spiritual pleasures are exhilarating and everlasting. I daresay, the yen for earthly goods and sensations gets really tiresome; we think we want them so badly but the more of them we accumulate the more insignificant they become. And before you know it, you have so much junk you don't know what to do with it. When you move to a new home you scrap most of it anyway. But you can take spiritual valuables wherever you go as they are soulful and ethereal while always available. Just keep in mind that your service is not why you are being so generously blessed; your loving service is your dedicated reply to God's love (PHP 1:9–11; HEB 6:10–12). That, ladies and gentlemen, is a very beautiful thing.

So then, where do you want to be after this life ends? Did you know that even atheists and agnostics contemplate this question? In a survey of over 15,000 atheist and agnostic American adults eighteen to sixty years old, almost a third (32.2 percent) said they believed in an afterlife (Austin Institute, 2014). I wonder what they conceive to be their final destination. There are only two to my knowledge, heaven (REV 21:1–7) or lake of fire (REV 20:14–15); the ones that don't make it to heaven go to the other place. But to make it to heaven, you have to be anointed by Christ (JOH 6:37–40).

Additionally, it has been determined that the older a nonbeliever becomes, the more inclined he or she is to begin believing in God and the afterlife; this is because the shroud of death overshadows them, for they don't want it to be over. But it doesn't have to be over; simply believe in and serve Christ and your life will never end. For those who experience the second death (i.e., the lake of fire), it will be over. No matter how old you are, you must answer the ultimate question, because you cannot anticipate the moment of your death, and after that it will be too late to choose your next destination.

One more word about service—it is a form of giving. We are to freely give of our time, talents, and treasures to help those less fortunate (PRO 22:9;

PRO 28:27; ACT 20:35). Like Jesus said, when you throw a banquet, invite the poor, handicapped, and helpless; they would be the ones who cannot repay (LUK 6:38; LUK 14:12–13). Giving assumes it's free, so expect nothing in return. However, your return in heaven will be great (LUK 14:14). It is our duty to give to others in proportion to the degree that we have prospered (DEU 16:17; ROM 12:9–21). Another important part of your service is to become equipped with God's Word; it will prepare you to give testimony of the bounteous blessings God has rained upon you (2 TI 2:15–16; 1 PE 3:15), and it will give you the authority to publicly declare God's promise for the furtherance of his kingdom (MAT 28:18–20; 1 PE 4:9–14). This is your faithful service.

Most religions believe in some form of giving; but to truly be a gift it presumes that you are not doing it for yourself or expecting others to owe you. Altruism is an attitude, not an obligation; but it cannot erase sins, a misconception already put to rest. The major issue with the self-righteous is they do it for the reward or the recognition (MAT 23:1–28), not for the joy of serving God (GEN 4:1–8; 2 CO 9:7). Jesus often chastised Jewish legal scholars for being hypocrites, mainly because of their "holier-than-thou" attitude (LUK 18:9–14). Imagine that, thinking they were superior to others, including Jesus Christ the holiest man they ever encountered. In fact, holy is a term applicable only to the Lord. So be careful of teachers, evangelists, and theologians that point fingers at others who do not serve, pray, contribute, or donate enough, as if they themselves were the standard. God is the standard, and our service is towards him; and by serving others we serve him. But our service doesn't earn us anything because God already has given us everything (2 PE 1:2–4; 1 TI 6:17), including the keys to the kingdom (MAT 16:19; MAT 18:18).

It Is Personal

Why would God create us in his image and give us knowledge of him if he didn't want a relationship? God has said, "let us reason together" so you can prosper and serve (ISA 1:17–20). It baffles me that a person can profess to believe in God but assume it impossible to communicate with him, or experience his power in their lives, or be allowed to come to him with needs just like they would their own father. Didn't Adam, Abraham, Moses, Elijah, Paul, John, Jesus and others engage in intimate discourse with God? Actually, it is normal and acceptable to refer to our Almighty Father as "Dad" for that is who is he is (ROM 8:15); it is a term of endearment and love, and therefore pleasing to God. It also is acceptable to address Jesus Christ as our brother, for he is not ashamed to call us his brothers and sisters (HEB 2:11). Christians will be adopted into the household of God, with the same inheritance to the kingdom as his only Son (GAL 3:26–29; EPH 1:3–5); for God treats adopted sons and daughters as his own.

Having a place in God's household does not make us equal to Jesus Christ, however, for he is God. But the body of Christ is his family and we will be treated as such; not as a slave, or laborer, but as a prince and heir (LUK 15:11–32; JAM 2:5). In order to enjoy God's presence and power in paradise, we must request the same here on earth. Our mission is not to be good but to love and worship God; being good is not possible for us, because only the Holy Trinity is good (MAR 10:17–18). Intuitively, that will change in heaven where we can be good, we can think pure thoughts, and we will be made holy with the righteousness of Christ (2 CO 5:21). God obliges us to be holy but knows that only he can make us so (MAT 5:48; 1 PE 1:16); there is no other condition in which we can stand blameless before him (COL 1:21–22).

Simply put, it is personal, our relationship with God. How can anyone say God resides outside of this world if he is ever-present? He created this entire universe with us in mind. Why would he just dump us off and observe from his heavenly throne, only to watch us destroy the place? Heaven forbid it! He doesn't just sit there; he intervenes in our lives with revelations, wonders, wakeup calls, miracles, choices, and purposes. He gives us knowledge of his works and his ways via his Holy Word. He sent himself in the form of a man to reveal his message and promise and made a personal sacrifice solely to set us free. He offers himself to us and for us. How can it get more personal than the cross? If it is that personal for him, why shouldn't it be for us? I implore those who cannot fathom the Almighty stooping down to lift them up to reconsider. After all, isn't that precisely what his Son did on the cross? To receive God's Son is not a difficult thing and it is not a small thing. But it is the most important thing you will ever do.

The problem with the general public these days is that they are very impersonal. Forget trying to visit someone face-to-face; they would rather view your face on their phone or computer. That's because they don't want you to observe them in their natural state but a fabricated one. When you take time to visit your friends, do they spend more time messing with their iPhone than they spend with you? Nobody wants to go anywhere, because all they want to do is surf the Internet in the comfort of their own den wearing their pajamas, where they can shop, learn, receive counseling, email, blog, chat, and all kinds of things without getting close and personal. People are becoming inept at contemporaneous communication; they're forgetting how to do it. Kids are not leaning how to properly interact with others, unless it involves an electronic device. Relationships are crucial to life and happiness; and that includes relationships between people and with God. It is not healthy to isolate and withdraw from human contact; and it is deadly to withdraw from God.

Often, when people gathering together is televised, it's during a riot or after a shooting or bombing. If you want to see how impersonal the world is, take a look at the daily news. Hate is all around you; love seems to be absent. But violence gets better ratings, even if it is unfounded or untrue; unfortunately, togetherness is oppositional to the intended theme. When people join to help others in crisis, the news media spins it in the other direction trying to nullify the outpouring of love or minimize the suffering. Terrorism and activism dominate the news, with participating rogues exemplifying the epitome of soullessness. No wonder the instigators and architects of dissention deny Christ as Savior. Even if he offered them a personal invitation (which he has done) they would have an excuse not to come (MAT 22:1–14). Who are the ones saying that it is not personal? Those who themselves choose to remain anonymous, faceless, disconnected, and/or unattached (LUK 10:25–37). They wear masks to hide so they can commit crimes in public knowing that nobody will intervene.

There is a rare psychiatric condition called depersonalization disorder (now referred to as depersonalization/derealization disorder in the DSM 5). It is characterized by feelings or perceptions of living a dream, in a world that doesn't exist or doesn't include oneself. The person feels detached from self and/or the environment, like an outsider looking in. It is a way of dissociating from life and others, because the victim is dissatisfied, or unsure who they are, or unconvinced of their relative worth. Oftentimes, the person believes he or she is nothing but a contrivance with no purpose or will. These people are not necessarily delusional, but certainly disconnected. Anyone who truly believes that their life is meaningless, that they have no reason to be here, and there is no free will; that they are being controlled by random undirected processes and do not get to choose a direction—they are likely to be mentally ill. I am persuaded that the atheists, secular humanists, and evolution scientists are not mental cases; instead, I think they are deliberately aiming to deceive. I doubt if they actually trust this nonsense, not for a second. If they actually practiced what they preached, maybe they would be certified examples of depersonalization/derealization disorder. Because it would become evident in their inability to make decisions, perform science, assist others in need or in peril, or even fend for themselves.

Let us pursue this line of thinking further and relate it to the purposeful depersonalization of others. Whether atheists, extremists, nonconformists, leftists, secularists, or terrorists, there are those who treat classes of people and individuals in those classes as subhuman, deplorable, or undeserving of life, liberty, and happiness. If you disagree with them, you do not rate, and you are not worthy to enjoy the same rights as they. Anyone they disqualify will be hated, abused, attacked, bullied, vilified, and possibly murdered. Offenders justify this behavior by accusing their victims of the very things for which they are guilty, such as ignorance and fascism. They have warped morals, and they do not regard their fellow humans as equal. They are vicious, relentless, menacing, revolting, and ruthless. The only people they can tolerate are others in their clique. Who, then, are the subhuman ones in this circumstance? The amazing thing to me is that God loves them unconditionally same as everyone else. And he requests that we love them too (MAT 5:44; ROM 12:9–21). You see, the doctrine of equality is God's directive, and our framers embraced it. But a large segment of society has rejected it, while a great many are afraid to open their mouths and object or attempt rectification, for there could be retaliation.

To love your neighbor as yourself is a difficult assignment; which is why God alone can love perfectly and without conditions. But the outright disdain of another person is appalling, and it is turning into a ubiquitous anomaly. Though I honestly try to love those persons, I have no interest in being their friend or associate (PSA 101:3–5; 2 TH 3:16). But I also will never depersonalize them or hate them. Although I may deplore their methods and objectives, I must treat them with respect, and perchance that will influence them to reconsider their motives (PRO 16:7; ROM 12:20–21). But I am not required to befriend them or condone their behavior.

God wants to be your friend; this is made clear in both testaments of the Holy Bible. Abraham and God were friends (2 CH 20:5–9; ISA 41:8; JAM 2:23); they spoke frequently. God held Abraham in high esteem because he sought God with all his heart; and God listened, answered, and directed his path. The same is true for Moses; they were friends and they spoke often

(EXO 33:11; DEU 34:10). And we cannot forget Job who prayed to God throughout his ordeal, while his earthly friends continued to berate and chastise Job as if he was being reprimanded by God himself. Though he was boiling with resentment towards them, Job prayed for his friends (JOB 32:3); and God answered his prayer and rewarded Job for being faithful to his friends and towards God (JOB 42:10). One can see Christ in that friendship with Job. Same as God the Father, God the Son considered his followers to be friends and addressed them that way, even those who betrayed him (ZEC 13:6; MAT 26:48–50; JOH 15:4–15); and he prayed for them regularly, as should we.

Ponder friendship; a true friend is someone you can count on through thick and thin. Such a friend is a source of strength, encouragement, truth, and joy (PRO 7:17–18; PRO 18:24; PRO 27:6,9,17); he or she will be available to you anytime, anywhere. Jesus is that kind of friend; he is there to help you whenever you call (LUK 11:5–11). He will be the best friend you ever had. He would do anything for you, even die in your place (JOH 15:13–15); likewise, he will gladly save you from destruction (LUK 12:4–5). Do you have any friends that would do that? Would you die to save one of them? Would you be willing to fight and die for your country? Would you sacrifice your life for God, or for strangers (ROM 5:6–8; ROM 12:1)? Jesus did.

With God, you always have someone to talk to, turn to, confide in, and depend on. Growing up, I had a father who was gone a lot as his job required frequent travel. I would like to have developed a closer relationship with him but it wasn't easy. I felt totally alienated from him as a teen. I was well into my twenties when the communication began to improve and that's when my father died. My mother was always there for me, but there are things a boy cannot discuss with his mom. I resented not having an opportunity to bond with my father, until I came to accept that my Heavenly Father had been there for me all the while, and still was, and always would be. My father made us go to church every Sunday, and for that I am grateful. I don't hold a grudge towards my dad, he did the best he could, especially getting me into the house of my Heavenly Father. I decided I was going to be a hands-on dad if I ever was to have a son. By the grace of God, I was blessed with a son; and I assured him that I would try my best to always be there for him, and that he had a father in heaven that would absolutely be there for him now and forevermore. And I thank God that my son still cherishes God's grace and mercy in his life, now that he is a grown man.

Go ahead, ask God anything and he will give you everything you need, including his friendship, and even himself. But being friends with God denotes you will become an enemy of the world (JAM 4:4), for the world cares only about what you can do for it. The way of the world is to take, not to give. The way of the Lord is to give—everything. He gives his love, his Son, himself, whatever you require, and he forgives your sin. That is the example we should follow; observers may reciprocate with their love and kindness which will flourish and multiply. However, if the hatefulness continues, it too will be contagious, and become an infection (if it hasn't already). Jesus warned of a time when iniquity will abound and love will wax cold (MAT 24:12). Can you allow this to occur during your watch, or will you counter the cold-heartedness with the warmth of your love?

The Holy Trinity

The Holy Trinity is the most misunderstood and misrepresented doctrine in Christian dogmatism; yet it also is one of the most irrefutable. Why should God relate to us in three distinct personages? How is that even possible? Come on, if God is all powerful, then anything is possible. If you research this principle carefully, it makes perfect sense. But that requires one to become immersed into God's Word. Be advised, a creator God in multiple persons is inferred in the very first verse of the Holy Bible (GEN 1:1). The key Hebrew word used in that verse is *Elohim*, which always refers to Almighty God; this word happens to be in plural form: "In the beginning, Elohim…"

Let me unwrap the concept of Holy Trinity just a little. Well, for one, how is God to interact with us? Does it seem plausible that he would simply show up randomly as the eternal I AM, or would it be better to become one of us? I go with the latter scenario and I'll tell you why—sin. Sin fell upon us all and God knew that it would. When Adam was created, he had no earthly father; God was his only father. God communicated directly with Adam, and also with Eve the first woman, until they sinned and were banished from the garden. Adam's rebellion precluded him from entering God's throne room in his fallen condition. Nobody can linger in God's presence in that degenerative state, not until Judgment Day; well, as long as you have been regenerated (TIT 3:5–6; REV 21:27). With your sins removed you will be able to commune with God directly just as Adam did before the fall, and just as the disciples of Christ did when he was here among us.

God's face is seen in Jesus, who also appeared to Abraham in human form (GEN 18:1–3; JOH 8:56–59). How better for us to get to know God, experience him, and love him but through Jesus Christ, God incarnate, the physical essence of divinity? Christ was alive with the Holy Spirit, who is the lifeforce of God; that's right Jesus is alive and always has been, though he did experience a few days in the grave. In like manner, God breathed his lifeforce into our bodies and made us living souls (the concept of soul will be addressed in detail in the concluding chapter). Correspondingly, our spirit is what makes us alive (JOH 6:63); without it, the body dies. The spirit is as fundamental a component to our being as it is to God's. Unquestionably, the Holy Spirit is God, same as Jesus Christ is God, same as the Holy Spirit is Jesus Christ.

Jesus has been with God from the beginning, before us and before the universe (ISA 11:2; ISA 48:16; JOH 1:1–14; 1 JO 5:6–8; TIT 1:2). Together, the Godhead creates, sustains, and preserves (NEH 9:6). The Spirit instructs and edifies through the Word of truth; Christ taught and coached humanity via that same Spirit for he is the Word of life (LUK 23:46). The Holy Spirit impregnated the Virgin Mary who bore God's Son so he could live here among us (our Immanuel). When God sent Jesus to us, he was sending himself as a human being; he looked like us but he didn't act like anybody but God. And instead of us perishing in his holy presence due to our sin, Jesus was put to death in our presence due to our sin. But quickly he came to life again and thank God for that, for now you too can live again, or else you will perish in his holy presence due to your sin.

We are like God in a great many ways; we think, feel, choose, relate, live, and love. Like God, we have a spirit and we have a body. And like God, we have a soul, or mind. In substance, we both exist spiritually, mentally, and physically. But the three persons of God are eternally indivisible, which is not the case with respect to our body, mind, and spirit. To completely apprehend God's plan of salvation, it helps to study how the three persons of the Trinity interface and contribute to everything that was, is, and will be.

This is another aspect that distinguishes Christianity from all other religions, because no other religion explains, understands, or accepts the Triune God. All three persons play an integral role in our salvation. Some will argue incorrectly that the Bible mentions nothing about the Trinity. However, there are numerous Bible passages explicitly referencing the Holy Trinity. (To commence in this journey, read GEN 1:26, GEN 3:22; PSA 2:6–

7,11–12; ISA 44:6; ISA 45:11–13; MAT 3:16–17; LUK 4:1; JOH 8:19; JOH 14:6,9–11,26; JOH 15:26; ACT 4:12; ROM 10:12; 2 CO 13:14; PHP 2:5–11; EPH 2:18; COL 2:2,9; HEB 1:3; HEB 13:8; JAM 2:19; 1 PE 1:1–2; 1 JO 2:23; REV 1:8). You are encouraged to delve into this phenomenon more thoroughly by studying the above references and taking notes. This will provide a foundation. Listen with your heart and meditate with your mind; and pay attention when your spirit quakes within you. If your body, soul, and spirit are joined with God, you might get a glimpse of how the three personages of God unite and connect as one.

Consider the following excerpt from a poem by one of my favorite poets, John Donne (*To the Countess of Bedford*). "Reason is our soul's left hand, faith her right; by these we reach divinity..." This standard is a staple of many philosophers. Simply put, faith should be reasonable. For how do we come to believe things but with truth and understanding? And who but God is the source of all knowledge, truth, and understanding? Through these gifts, we are able to reason, deduce, engage, and explain. Such are the tools of science. With sufficient evidence, we may come to believe; but there is seldom an occasion when we are 100 percent sure, until something can be proven to be absolutely true. Only God can always be certain, so through faith in him we can be sure, because we know his words are true. God is incapable of lying. You might ask, how can God be all powerful if he can't even lie? This is a self-defeating statement. The easiest way to conquer deceit is with truth; so clearly, truth is greater in power. When God is rejected by the diehard scientist it is because he or she is operating with reason alone, discounting the importance of faith. The religious fanatic also reveals a reluctance to learn when he or she avoids science, preferring to operate within restricting beliefs. Neither one can hold onto the truth because it takes both hands to carry it.

It is with the mind that we seek God and it is with the spirit that we find him. Our pursuit is evident in our eagerness to learn his Word and commit it to memory (ROM 12:2; ACT 17:11–12). And God's Word gives us comfort, direction, and peace (Zacharias and Vitale, 2017). This ability to reason and comprehend is another attribute of God which makes us like him. Animals cannot reason; they don't need to. God didn't create them to be his children. In order to become his children, we humanoids have the opportunity to encounter God, know him, and communicate with him. And though I have his Word in my heart I still have uncertainty at times; but while I have doubts, I will not, indeed I cannot, stop believing. Because his Word is true.

This faith is the instrument of my expression, motivation, hope, and purpose. Similarly, Jesus Christ is the right hand of God; he is the instrument of God's will and his desire for us. Faith is my right hand, the dominant hand, the executor of my will; similarly, Christ is the right hand of God who performs the works of God (PSA 110:1; ACT 2:32–35; ROM 8:34; EPH 1:16–23; COL 3:1–4; HEB 1:1–4). With the left hand of reason and the right hand of faith I reach up to God to embrace him, for he is my loving Father and our relationship is filial (PSA 119:48; ROM 8:15; 1 TI 2:8: 2 PE 1:2–8).

We know God the Father who loved us so much he gave his only Son to die in our place, so that we might live through him. We follow the Son to get to the Father. You can understand these things and what to do about it because the Holy Spirit has revealed this wisdom. These truths can only be clutched by the spirit that lives within you; you will not make sense of them by relying solely on your cognitive ability (1 CO 2:13–14; 1 CO 12:3). With faith added to reason, you can unpack it.

It is particularly confounding to invoke moral reasoning in the absence of faith, because the sanctity of life is founded in the belief that there is intrinsic worth in humanity, to include dignity, equality, and liberty. Through faith, our forefathers knew this abundantly and founded our nation on such tenets. I mean, anyone can propose reasons, but to be reasonable there assumes a moral value to them; otherwise we would be selfish and uncompassionate continuously. In the higher order of thinking, ethics supersedes all other reasons. Without the Father there is no law, without Christ there is no moral standard, without the Holy Spirit there is no faith. In the absence of God there is no incentive to behave rationally or ethically, no motivation for accountability or justice, such that anything is fair game as long as it's okay with me. That is how people believe themselves gods, which is categorically unreasonable. If faith and reason are in conflict how can you be sure?

Satan decided to proclaim himself a god, and in opposition to the one true God he intends to confabulate an unholy trinity. When the global society takes hold, he will inhabit the emperor to seize control; this is his response to God's Son—the son of perdition (2 TH 2:3–4). While there may be many antichrists, this is the one proclaimed the Antichrist. His sidekick will be the spiritual and religious leader of Satanism—an unholy spirit called the false prophet. Then there is Satan, the beast, the dragon—he will compel the world to worship him who encompasses the evil empire. Too bad for Satan, since his last hurrah will be short-lived, before the lot of them are cast into the lake of fire (REV 19:19–20). Those belonging to God will be basking in his light and glory forever.

Holy Week

The significance of Holy Week cannot be overstated; every year it has been hallowed since the emancipation of the Israelites from Egypt. Obviously, is it not a coincidence that the holiest week of Judaism and of Christianity are equivalent. The Jewish feasts of Passover, Unleavened Bread, and First Fruits (LEV 23:1–14) occurred respectively when Christ entered into Jerusalem on Palm Sunday, established the Eucharist on Maundy Thursday, was in the grave on Good Friday, and was resurrected on Easter Sunday (MAT 26—28). Both Jews and Christians have incorporated these historically relevant and momentous occasions into their traditions and worship.

It was foretold from days of old that blood and grain offerings were insufficient to save one from their sins, and how God would provide a better sacrifice to last for the duration of the human race (ISA 53:10–12; MIC 6:6–7; HEB 9:28). The Passover lamb was a type and shadow of Christ, the anointed Messiah (EXO 12; ISA 61:1); Christ is that promised Lamb who was offered for humanity during the commemoration of Passover (LUK 4:16–21; 1 CO 11:24–29). Christ was represented in the feast of Unleavened Bread as well. Bread without yeast symbolizes the body without sin (EXO 23:15; GAL 5:91; 1 CO 5:8). Christ was without sin, and his body was broken on the cross for you and me, and his blood was spilled to replace blood sacrifices made upon the altar. The breaking of bread and the pouring of wine represent the body and blood of Christ, broken and poured out for you each time you participate in the Eucharist. Remember how the blood of the Passover lamb spared the firstborn of Israel; they dined on that lamb and ate the unleavened bread as commanded by God. This special bread was illustrated in the manna that sustained Moses and the Israelites in the wilderness, which also came from heaven (EXO 16; JOH 6:30–69; 1 CO 5:7). In fact, the significance of the bread and the blood is evident throughout the ministries of Moses (EXO 25:22; EXO 31:48) and Abraham (GEN 14:18–19).

Jesus's resurrection occurred in conjunction with the celebration of First Fruits, which traditionally culminated with the sacrifice of a lamb without blemish (LEV 23:12; 1 PE 1:19). Jesus has been referred to as the first fruits of God, the first to arise from the dead in his glorified state; who sits at the right hand of God forevermore (JOH 12:20–36; REV 1:5), with a name that is exalted above all other names (PHP 2:9–11). Those who believe in him will be transformed by him, becoming the first fruits of Christ when he returns. Then we will be reconciled with our Heavenly Father, having obtained glorified bodies, unblemished and without sin (1 CO 15:20–23; REV 14:1–4), to abide with him forevermore.

Can you see how everything comes together during Holy Week? There is an unbreakable link between the Old Covenant and the New Covenant; both are described in the Old and New Testaments of the Bible, which are correspondingly bound into one testimony. A covenant is a contract; when God enters into a contract with humankind you can bet that he will make good on his part of the bargain. Our pledge to God is basically this: we remain steadfast in our faith in God's promise of eternal life bought for us through his Messiah, and in return we receive that gift (HEB 3:14). This compact was presented to the Old Testament patriarchs, it is the foundation of the Christian faith, and it is available to all people, in all places, at all times (PSA 105:8; HAB 2:4; ROM 1:17).

Jesus, the Messiah, is the Lamb of God (JOH 1:15–36; 1 CO 15:16–58; 1 PE 1:19; REV 5:5–7; REV 7:9–14). He was explicitly present when Abraham was preparing to sacrifice Isaac, and the lad asked his father, "Where is the lamb for sacrifice," wherein Abraham replied, "God will provide himself a lamb" (GEN 22:8). This event will be elaborated in more depth in an upcoming section entitled The Real Jesus. Consider also the link between the Lord's Supper and the first communion, when Melchizedek shared bread and wine with Abraham. Melchizedek was the king of Salem meaning "peace" who also is associated with the Prince of Peace, namely Jesus Christ the only other priest of that ecclesiastical order (PSA 110:1–4; HEB 6:20). Abraham gave tithes of all to Melchizedek (GEN 14:18–20; ISA 9:6–7). This was long before Jerusalem (meaning "city of peace") was established; but Jerusalem would evolve into a major metropolis and become King David's capital.

Throughout the OT there is a thread that continues into the NT. It is God's way of communicating his purpose and his guarantee that we were made to be like his Son and to be his children, and we can appreciate and fulfill that distinction if we believe in him. All that you see around you, it is not some happenstance occurrence; it is for a reason, it is by design, and we humans are at the center of it. You can persuade yourself otherwise but not without considerable cognitive dissonance.

The period of Holy Week varies from year to year. It is determined using the ancient Jewish calendar which is based on lunar phases. It gets confusing due to the inexactness of using a lunar-based calendar, presenting a much shorter year than 365.25 days. The Jewish year originally began with the new crescent moon on the month of Nisan; the Passover season would commence in conjunction with the Paschal full moon some two weeks later. Traditionally, Holy Week celebrations coincide with the first full moon following the vernal equinox, which would be the beginning of Spring and the season of early harvest. Easter has been established to be the following Sunday, but this is merely a convention to celebrate Jesus's resurrection on that day of the week. This is why Christians generally worship on Sunday, in recognition of Christ's resurrection and the fourth commandment (honor the Sabbath), during which we likewise present our first fruits as an offering to the Lord. Moreover, the Christian way is to honor God every day of the week, not just on the day chosen for worship, since our time belongs to him (ROM 14:5–9).

The overlapping of Christ's passion with Passover, and the climax with the feast of First Fruits which Christians recognize on Easter Sunday, are significant. Remember, this period coincided with the first harvest, during which it was customary to present the best of the crop as a sacrifice (tithe) to God; this offering was called the "first fruits" (EXO 23:19; DEU 26:1–11; PRO 3:9). There are a number of historical events that also track with this timeframe. For example, Ruth and Naomi returned to Bethlehem during the early harvest (RUT 1:22). You may recall that Ruth became the wife of Boaz, an ancestor of King David, and later, Jesus (MAT 1:2–16; LUK 3:23–38). It also happened to be the timeframe when the Gibeonites executed the sons of King Saul (2 SA 21:3–13), after which David would officially become king. Remember, David's hometown was Bethlehem, where his great-grandparents Ruth and Boaz resided; and his capital was Jerusalem, the kingdom of Melchizedek, where Jesus was executed. Since Joseph and Mary were descendants of David, they had to travel to Bethlehem for the Roman census; that is where Jesus also was born, as prophesied (MIC 5:2). Note that Bethlehem means "house of bread" and Jesus is the bread of life (JOH 6:35). Other incidents that correspond with the first fruits of the harvest include the offering presented to God by Noah after disembarking the ark onto dry land (GEN 8:20–22), and the ram offered by Abraham in place of his son Isaac.

Certainly, location appears important here. Many solemn events occurred at a place called Mt. Moriah (GEN 22:2) where Abraham brought Isaac for sacrifice (GEN 22:2). Jacob later laid his head on the rock and dreamt of a ladder into heaven (GEN 28:10–17; JOH 1:51), yet another reference to Jesus. Solomon built a temple to the Lord on the site (2 CH 3:1), where it remained until Jerusalem was sacked and the temple was destroyed. Now the Dome of the Rock sits over the sacred stone, whereas Jews and Muslims both consider the place to be holy, and are divided as to who owns it.

With the USA acknowledging Jerusalem as the official capital of Israel, and moving our embassy there from Tel Aviv, it will, no doubt, stir up consternation among Muslim neighbors. That tension will escalate dramatically when Israel rebuilds their temple on the sacred site. Such are the dynamics that have led to wars and probably will again (see ZEC 1:12 – ZEC 2:13).

Evidently, there are particular times, places and episodes that are important if not special to God, and therefore should be to us. This is why they repeatedly surface to the forefront, so that the point is not overlooked. I could write an entire book about Holy Week, but God already has; hopefully you got the gist. The Hebrews looked forward to the time when Messiah would come; Christians look forward to the time when he will come again. Both systems have depended on a sincere faith in the promises of God. Muslims also look forward to the coming of Messiah, but they believe it will be his first coming not his second, as do many Jews who deny Jesus to be Christ, the anointed one. When Jesus does show up again, everyone will know he is Christ the Messiah; and that will be a holy day for sure, at least for the multitudes looking forward to his coming in the name of the Lord.

Watch and Wait

I'm sure you have heard about the end times prophecy and the Second Coming of Jesus Christ, even if you are not a Christian. People joke about it as if those looking forward to Christ's coming are a bunch of chumps (2 PE 3:2–3). Theorists and theologians purporting to explain this fateful occurrence with feigned certainty are a dime-a-dozen. Their schemas have portions in common while diverging in other areas. What are we to believe? Can anyone interpret with conviction, precision, and completion the prophecy about events preceding Jesus's return? Can anyone predict the timeline, or unravel the significance of circumstances leading to the end? Unfortunately, no. And why not? Answer: because we do not have a need to know (ECC 8:11). God reveals some things, he conceals some things; he explains some things with transparency and he does not explain some things on purpose.

In this book I entertain numerous concepts addressed in the Bible that are not spelled out conclusively, such as the age of the universe, details about heaven and hell, and models of eschatology. Why would God leave these things unexplained or ambiguous? Could it be because he doesn't want us to dwell on them, divide over them, or dispute them? The essential doctrines of Christianity are well established; it follows that obsessions about ancillary issues and their possible meanings are superfluous. Though they may be interesting to debate and are open to scrutiny, the various inferences that can be drawn will not save anybody.

What can be settled is why signs of the second advent are provided in the Bible; it is so we will remain aware, ready, and watchful (MAT 16:1–4). This is summed up in the last passage of the Bible in which Jesus proclaims, "Behold, I am coming soon," followed by St. John's reply, "Amen, come Lord Jesus" (REV 22:20). You do not require a checklist to keep tabs on every single sign regarding Jesus's return. You should prepare now. If we had an exact chronology, people would be waiting until the last minute to get their houses in order. Try as they do, sham messengers attempt to add it all up and proclaim that they know what, when, and/or where. When they present their data, do not believe them, because nobody has it down pat (MAT 24:23–27,36–38; MAR 13:32–37; LUK 12:37–40); and that's the way God intended it.

Why does God give us this sampling of signs, prophecies, and scenarios? Like I said, it is specifically so that we will keep watch like a watchman on the wall, ready to open the gate when the master approaches (HAB 2:1–4; HEB 10:35–39). There are plenty of reasons to suspect that the enemy is in the field and calamity is eminent; it is advantageous to get a head start if you want to stay abreast and afloat (ROM 13:11; REV 16:14–16). Do contestants sit idly by when the big game is at hand, or the deciding battle is about to be waged, or final exams are approaching? Are you apt to just see what happens and hope you have what it takes to prevail? Or do you train, study, practice, and prepare? Winners generally do the latter. They certainly don't assume the outcome in advance, but they can influence it if properly motivated.

The second you know what is coming, isn't it time to get yourself ready? Now is not a good time to take a nap, like the apostles did when Jesus implored that they stay alert and pray with him. They were blown away by what would happen next, as Jesus was accosted by the church elders accompanied by a riotous mob (MAT 26:36–47; MAR 14:32–43). What a missed opportunity that was for the apostles who could have comforted and supported Jesus in his time of agony and despair. He always was a true friend to them but not always the other way around, exhibited by them abandoning him. In a way, nonetheless, we are all chickens.

Throughout the Bible, the reader is warned not to loiter and not to be impatient, but to get busy. Those who tarry usually miss the opportunity and those who hurry usually miss the mark. God's timing is always right on, so we must be both patient and punctual; equipped and organized; instructed and dedicated; assertive and tactful; efficient and effective. The prophet Samuel told King Saul to wait for him seven days and he would return to offer sacrifices before God; if Saul had heeded that advice, he could have been victorious over the Philistines. But on the seventh day Saul got antsy and conducted the ceremony himself, though he was prohibited by God to do so. And who do you think arrived just as Saul had messed it up? That's right: Samuel, who declared it was the beginning of the end for the foolish king (1 SA 10:8; 1 SA 13:8–14).

Jesus tells us he will return and gives us an idea what to expect so that we will know that his coming is nigh. You do not want to be caught off guard (MAT 24:43–44). The parable of the ten virgins awaiting the arrival of the bridegroom illustrates this (MAT 25:1–13). Five brought extra oil for their lamps and five did not. The second group ran out of oil and had to go buy more, missing the arrival of the groom at midnight. Since the ceremony was already underway when they returned, they were not permitted to enter. If you are not ready for the groom to arrive, you will not be admitted to the wedding feast. The nuptials between the Lord and the Church is an event you should not take for granted or take lightly. He will be coming with a crown of righteousness and will give you that crown if you are among the invited guests who arrive on time (ISA 46:12–13; 2 TI 4:8).

Isn't that worth looking forward to, and waiting for? King David wrote about how he was waiting with baited breath (PSA 130:6). When Christ arrives, the game will be over; there will be no overtime. The clock will not only have run out, time itself will have expired (EPH 6:18; 1 PE 4:7). It is imperative that you remain vigilant, for it can happen in the next blink of your eye (1 TH 5:6; REV 3:3). Watch and wait; and "be prepared" like a dedicated boy scout. I will address this final pageant further at the conclusion of the book.

Regarding the demise of our nation, it is wise not to wait, but to take corrective action. When the world has reached the point of no return, however, there will be nothing more anyone can do but to get his or her own act together. Some people believe, after Jesus takes the elect home, there will be a grace period for those remaining. I wouldn't count on that if I were you. I urge you not to bide your time until you find out, but to plan now. Are you ready?

The Presence of the Lord

Would you like to live in the presence of the Lord? Actually, you already are for he is there at this very moment. How can he not be if he is omnipresent? The real question is, do you want to live in his presence forever? If the answer is yes you can begin that excursion immediately. Start by addressing a prayer to your Father in heaven and tell him you would like to sense his presence in your life, in the name of Jesus Christ. The more you ask, the more he will make himself known through his Holy Spirit. Staying in God's presence is to remain connected in spirit.

Remember, we connect by communicating; it is a two-way street with continuous incoming and outgoing messages between you and God. Church attendance is imperative, because worship, thanks, and praise offered in church are received by God where he is present; and he is delighted for these are expressions of our love toward him (PSA 95:1–6; PSA 100:1–5; 1 CO 1:29–31; 1 TH 2:19). The church consists of the body of Christ who is our head (COL 1:18); you can't get any more connected than that. What happens to the body if it loses its head, you know what I mean? Furthermore, your body is the temple of the Holy Spirit if you have received Christ, so God is never far from you (note the relevance in that statement to the Holy Trinity).

The patriarchs were well-connected to the Lord. In fact, they witnessed God's presence and received his guidance firsthand; and they gave praise and thanks to the Lord every day. Adam and Eve got to experience God's presence daily until they sinned and hid themselves from him (GEN 3:8). Have you ever tried to hide from God? Well, you can't; case in point, Jonah. But if you disregard God unreservedly, or reject his Son candidly, he eventually will banish you from his presence (GEN 4:16; ZEP 1:6–9). And that is a very lonely and despairing place (JER 4:24–27; NAH 1:2–15; 2 TH 1:7–9).

God made a covenant with Noah (GEN 6), Abraham (GEN 17), and Moses (EXO 19—20) on behalf of all people. Can you imagine how stirring those dialogues must have been? Would you like to have a close encounter with the most-high God? Those who met Jesus had such an encounter. Everyone will have that opportunity when he returns. Did you ever wish you could meet a favorite celebrity, maybe a movie star or a rock star? Well, God rocks, and his front man is Jesus; he would be my pick. I am abiding in his presence in spirit, and that will be my covenant, to remain forever in his presence. And when he brings me home, I will be allowed to touch him, and embrace him, and talk with him, and walk with him, and live perpetually in glory and honor (1 CH 16:27; HEB 9:24). Until then, I will dialogue with him in the manner described above, because it enables me to sense his presence and power. You can too, because he made that covenant with everyone who seeks him (ACT 3:18–21; JDE 1:20–25). In the meantime, he will provide direction, intervention, and intercession so you will not feel dismayed, lonely, or abandoned.

Guess what, you can put on Christ like you put on clothing (ROM 13:14; GAL 3:27). If you request his presence, he will cover you like a suit of armor (EPH 6:10–17). I explained this earlier but allow me to elaborate. On earth, Christians are in the middle of a spiritual war, with Christ on one side and Satan on the other. But anybody can defeat Satan with Christ living in them (1 JO 4:4). Not only will Christ abide in your heart but he will surround you like a force field. First, wrap the belt of truth around you, so you won't be persuaded by commentators merely pretending to know the truth. Then put on the breastplate of righteousness to protect your heart from desires of the flesh which war against your soul (1 PE 2:11). Put on the shoes of the Gospel of peace so you will be a peacemaker and not an antagonist. Don the helmet of salvation to protect your mind from intrusive, impure, and destructive thoughts. Carry the shield of faith to resist the temptations of the world and deflect the fiery arrows of Satan the prince of darkness. Not only do you have the ultimate defense system, you also have the most formidable weapon—the sword of the Spirit, that is the Holy Bible, which penetrates the defenses of God's enemies and cuts them in two.

You can enjoy the Lord's company anytime you like. Simply invite him to come. And he will invite you to come with him to his kingdom, where he already has prepared a mansion for you in which to dwell (JOH 14:2–3); where his glory illuminates the entire city and every dwelling forevermore (REV 21:23). Until then, you can allow his light to shine in you (MAT 5:14–16), and be a beacon of hope. Try this and experience the power (PHP 3:10); odds are you will want to keep it.

Which is greater, the power of God or the power of man? To the humanist, man is sovereign. Yes, people are capable of exceptional things, like destroying entire cities in the time it takes to wake up; eventually we may end up destroying the entire planet. This illustration alone should be enough to drop idolization of humans or self, for we are evil and can't fix ourselves. Perhaps you idolize Satan's power, whose evil purpose in life is to destroy life. God is life (GEN 2:7); Jesus is life (JOH 14:6). Satan wished he could destroy God, but he will settle for destroying you. Jesus wants to save you (LUK 19:10). Either way, Jesus will destroy Satan and all his works (HEB 2:14; 1 JO 3:8); accordingly, I'd place my trust in Jesus if I were you.

Whatever you choose to worship and adore, you should at least be able to trust in it. Who do you trust? I can't even trust myself to do the right thing, can you? But we need to fill the emptiness, the void within, so we search for fulfillment. To satisfy the emptiness, people will idolize anything or anyone, real or imagined, visible or invisible, past, present or future, if not themselves and their own accomplishments. When they cannot find an entity to adore, they might even invent or construct one (ROM 1:21–25). Things that bring satisfaction is where our focus settles; for where your treasure is, there also will be your heart (MAT 6:21). I believe life is our greatest treasure. For what can you pursue without it? Who is your life?

St. Paul found Athens to be replete with idols and idolatry. He addressed an assembly of Greek philosophers about an "unknown god" sedentary amongst the other idols. It had been identified in order to appease the one god who was missing in their lives (ACT 17:16–34). Maybe they were unable to find what they were looking for so they erected an altar to represent it. Paul was able to explain to them that the one true God is who they sought; in him alone would be found everything they were looking for. Paul understood that all other gods were material, in particular the Greek gods; that is, they were of this universe and thus had a worldly source as opposed to being otherworldly and the ultimate source of the universe. And many believed and were converted. If you are experiencing hollowness, you require the presence of the Holy Spirit, for he alone can satiate it. Once that occurs, the possibilities are limitless.

The ultimate reward will be to enjoy the presence of the Lord eternally, if you trusted in Christ (ROM 8:1). That will begin upon death of your body (LUK 23:39–43; ACT 7:59; 2 CO 5:6–9). Your spirit immediately will be escorted into heaven, which is basically God's domain; this is the current heaven (1 CO 15:44; 2 CO 12:1–6). You enter the new heaven when Christ returns in judgment, whereby you will have been declared justified (2 PE 3:13; REV 2:21). Then Christians will experience the presence of the Lord in spirit and flesh, with completely new bodies (PHP 3:21) in a completely new paradise.

Where does everybody else go? They go to a place of agony and hopelessness, far from the presence of the Lord. Their first stop is a place called Hades or hell (LUK 16:19–31), where their lifeforce will reside until the return of Christ, when they are reunited with their previously stained bodies. After that they will be judged guilty and receive the final sentence which is the second death, the lake of fire, the final hell if you will (REV 20:10–15); and their bodies and souls will be destroyed forever (MAT 10:28). I would strongly recommend being eternally united with the Lord over being eternally divorced from him.

How do you know if the Lord is with you? Again, I would refer the reader to the Gospel of John; he appeared to know the Lord better than most. The following are answers found in books written by St. John that would fill in the blank: God is _____.

> God comprises the Father, Son and Holy Spirit (1 JO 5:7–8). We connect to God through each person of the Trinity (JOH 13:13,20; JOH 15:5). Refer to the earlier section presenting an elucidation of The Holy Trinity.

> God is Light (JOH 1:4; JOH 3:19; JOH 5:35; JOH 8:12; JOH 9:5; JOH 10:11–14; JOH 12:35,46; 1 JO 1:5). His light illuminates your path and shows you the right way to go (JOH 10:7–9; JOH 14:6). You cannot commune with God if you abide in darkness or you pursue a path leading away from him.

> God is Life (JOH 1:4; JOH 11:25; JOH 10:10–14; JOH 12:50; JOH 14:6; JOH 15:13; 1 JO 3:16; 1 JO 5:11,20). He created life and he gave you your life. He offers you eternal life with him through his Son who is the

bread of life (JOH 6:35–51), which is yours if Christ is your desire (JOH 12:50). Plainly, you are his desire, since he gave himself for you.

➢ God is Truth (JOH 1:1,14; JOH 3:33; JOH 4:24; JOH 7:28; JOH 14:6; JOH 18:37–38; 1 JO 4:10). God only tells the truth, and his Word, the Holy Bible is the truth (JOH 8:47; JOH 17:17); so are the words of Christ the truth. Anyone, when he or she tells the truth, is a credible witness (JOH 8:18; JOH 18:37–38; 1 JO 4:10), for they reflect the Spirit of God who is God's witness (JOH 3:6; JOH 4:24; 1 JO 5:10,20).

➢ God is Love (JOH 13:34–35; 1 JO 2:5,15; 1 JO 4:8–21; 2 JO 1:6). His love is perfect, and he gives that love to all living creatures. When we share God's love it becomes perfected in us. Spiritual love is our connection to God and it is the means by which we connect with our loved ones.

To summarize, you are with God and he is with you in Spirit if you see the light, feel the love, know the truth, follow the path, and witness to others. If you see the light you will project it; if you feel the love you will share it; if you know the truth you will convey it; if your focus is Christ people will see him in you. You will become a conduit for all these attributes of God, like a conductor of electricity that electrifies others who will look, listen, and learn from your example. Your incentive will be abundant life in this world and the next. The thrill of an intimate relationship with Almighty God can begin now and last forevermore, if you so aspire.

YOU ARE SPECIAL

You are unique, important, precious, great, wonderful, talented, and beautiful (ECC 3:11). Nobody else is exactly like you, or has the same gifts, or can accomplish your purpose better than you. There is one thing in which everybody is exactly the same, however, and that is being very special to God. We are different from one another in every other respect; this is what makes life interesting. Imagine if we had the same abilities in the same areas; life would be quite boring. Nobody would watch basketball because no team could prevail; the score would probably be a perpetual tie in every matchup. You are the greatest at something and the worst at something else. But you can master anything, and turn your liabilities into assets; well, if you possess the necessary desire, exert sufficient effort, and exude ample determination. We must be reasonable though; positively, you won't see me at the tryouts for a position on a professional basketball team. But that doesn't prevent me from coaching high school sports and mentoring a future hall of famer.

Do not sell yourself short simply because you are inferior in some areas. Instead, explore the possibilities and discover your hidden potential; it may be the avenue to your purpose or calling. You will uncover interests and talents you never knew you had simply by attempting things you'd never imagined doing. I received a doctorate in psychology about a decade after taking an elective in the humanities on my way to achieving a bachelor degree in art. That course was Abnormal Psychology. I didn't sign up for the class because I was fascinated by psychology; I really didn't know anything about it. The class fit the schedule of my friend who also needed to complete a humanities requirement for his criminal justice degree. And when I decided to pursue graduate work in psychology, I discovered a knack for understanding statistics; ironic as I was intimidated by the negative hype from other grad students about how difficult the class would be, and how it was referred to as the make-or-break element in the curriculum. I had no idea what to expect because I knew nothing about statistics either; the last thing I expected was to excel at it, end up teaching it, and coauthor a book on it. It never dawned on me that I had interest in psychology or aptitude in statistics; it was sort of a fluke that I realized this about myself. I began to value education a lot more because I was realizing things about me that I never knew. Learning can be grueling or exciting depending on your perspective.

Funny how I understand research and statistics but I stink at accounting; I can't even balance my checkbook without a calculator, and then I often find myself recalculating until I get the same result more than once. I suppose I could improve upon my ability in accounting if I made the effort; but it would take more effort for me than for someone naturally gifted at accounting.

I hope you get the point here. You have interests, talents, and potential that you haven't discovered yet; and that goes for some of you old dogs out there (I can certify from personal experience that you can learn new tricks, ha ha). Everything that has happened is relevant because it teaches you: experience, education, skills, knowledge, training, challenges, setbacks, and successes. You are developing into the person you were meant to be; and the becoming does not have to end, depending on which path you take. God has projected for you to be who you are, with the aptitude required to achieve, the wherewithal to maximize your potential, and the knowhow to become like his Son Jesus Christ. He makes you special and proficient in things uncommon to ordinary men and women. Case in point, Christ's apostles who did extraordinary things to include healing the disabled, speaking foreign languages, and raising the dead.

You are very special and unique, a child of the living God capable of greatness and goodness, especially if you tap into the spiritual insight of God's Word. It is the handbook for life, a guide to righteousness, and God's revelation to all who study it diligently. The primary lesson is that you are loved, and you are called to be wonderful and perfect. Nobody is left out, but anybody can say no. You can stay on the freeway to freedom, or you can exit and end up in no man's land; you can stay on the path illuminated by the light or be lost in darkness; you can choose and reach your destiny or give up on it.

The Universe

If you do not think you are special, I am going to prove that you are. What does the universe have to do with it? Consider the aspects listed below which make the universe special, unique, breathtaking, and fantastic. I reviewed previously many fundamental principles, laws, and features of this universe we thrive in. Even those who reject God as the cause of our universe and prefer the multiverse explanation concede that our universe is special. They propose that among the infinite number of possible universes ours got lucky, with the innumerable, incalculable, and diverse phenomena merging together in such a way as to spawn homo sapiens. Let me break it down for you. Reviewing each factoid below, you will notice the increasing evidence of design and specialization.

1. Our universe had a beginning. The plethora of proof includes universal expansion, general relativity, and thermodynamics; uniformity of microwave background radiation, and scattering of matter and energy; dark matter and exotic matter; galaxy formation, density, and distribution; and the list goes on (see Wollack, 2012). This idea was first proposed almost one hundred years ago but was not widely accepted, until Hoyle, who didn't buy-in at the outset, sarcastically coined the term "big bang" and it stuck. Nowadays, there isn't a single cosmologist who denies that our universe comprising time, matter, space, physics, chemistry, and energy began at a single instant. But that beginning is not a point in space, since the entire universe began at once, as did time. Do you think this happened by itself, that our universe was the lucky one; or did an intelligent engineer initiate it? Take into account that existence necessitates a cause, according to the natural law of cause and effect. And since nothing causes nothing, well then...

2. Our universe is gigantic and growing. There are literally billions of stars in our host galaxy which we affectionately call the Milky Way (estimated 200–300 billion in number). There are literally hundreds of billions of galaxies and star clusters in the universe some bigger some smaller than the Milky Way, with billions more stars in each of those. And the universe continues to expand, with additional galaxies being formed and stars being birthed each day. The universe is expanding so rapidly that light cannot catch up with it (PSA 104:2); thus, the universe will continue to grow in size (as long as God says so). Telescopes are incapable of seeing how far the universe goes especially because it is going so fast. I reckon that's why we call it space, because there is plenty of it. The universe's size, mass, and age are necessary to produce and disperse the vital elements and diminish and restrict the dangerous elements in support of advanced lifeforms and to further their perpetuation (Ross, 2008).

3. Our universe is fine-tuned for life. There are countless factors, constants, and variables that have been tweaked to the nth degree in order for everything to hold together and for life to exist on our matchless celestial orb. The minutest alteration in any one of the hundreds of dynamics necessary to maintain our idyllic environment would mean extinction. Fortunately, vital aspects remain persistent and uniform. Does that mean they are being governed? This is why many scientists and philosophers suggest that intricacies, relationships, and regulations found in the physical universe are intended for life. Some of the constants include gravity, matter, energy, light, electromagnetism, strong and weak forces, entropy and expansion; some of the synchronizations are the relative distribution and movements of celestial bodies and the distances, masses, and rotations of such bodies; plus, there is comprehensive synergism from quantum particles to mega galaxies, from brown stars to supernovae, from bacilli to anthropoids. Without such organization, activity, and order we would be unable to derive the various laws of physics, chemistry, biology, geometry, and mathematics. Law and order strongly suggest that such calibration was incorporated prior to the beginning.

4. Our galaxy is isolated. It resides in one of the darkest areas of space which is relatively void of other galaxies. Our dispersed and comparatively insignificant cluster of galaxies is far removed from other clusters. We have only one galaxy that is visible with the naked eye which is Andromeda. It is the sister galaxy to ours, a couple of million light years away (not all that far, considering). If Earth was situated in a solar system within a larger cluster of galaxies, there would be no possibility for humans to abide. The fact that we are distant from the rest of the celestial activity is essential; we get just the right amount of energy, chemistry, and cosmic turbulence to sustain the planet, the natural laws, and us. Moreover, we would not be able to see very far into space without the darkness, because the ambient light would flood the sky just as ambient light from the city makes it impossible to see distant bodies like Andromeda at night, much less in the presence of sunlight during which you can't see any stars but the sun. This isolation enables us to survey the universe more closely. Accordingly, the separation of our galaxy, our solar system, and our terrestrial home from everything else is part of the fine-tuning, which includes lifeforms showing up at just the right place and at just the right time (*ibid*).

5. Our solar system is unique. Its position at the outer reaches between the spiraling arms of Sagittarius and Perseus, detached from other stars and celestial bodies to include the distance from our sister galaxy and the dwarf galaxies in our group, has been meticulously adjusted. The configuration of the planets, the sun, and the moon are necessary to protect inhabitants of

Earth. Outer planets including Neptune, Uranus, Saturn, and Jupiter are large and gaseous with enormous gravity; they suck wayward meteors and space debris into their grip. Most of the flying menaces that escape this protective zone are consumed by another, the asteroid belt between Mars and Jupiter. In the uncommon event that a meteorite approaches Earth, it is burned up by our atmosphere; pieces that make it to the surface are generally no larger than a pea; but if a big one was to hit or even come close, the damage would be catastrophic. The ozone layer shields us from deadly ultraviolet rays. Protection also appears to be the purpose of the encompassing Kuiper Belt lying far beyond the planets. It is expressly thought-provoking how the magnetic field of the earth deflects the deadly solar wind emitted from the sun, which in turn intercepts hazardous cosmic rays flying throughout space in our direction. Do you think all of this is by accident?

6. Our planet is marvelous. Earth's size, composition, and orbit, its distance from the sun and moon, its rotation and tilt, its distribution of air, land and bodies of water, and its proliferation of lifeforms is unlike any found elsewhere. With the projected number of galaxies and stars, an estimated 100 septillion (10^{22}) planets theoretically could occur throughout the universe. However, mathematically speaking, there is virtually no likelihood of even one planet having all of the fine-tuned components necessary for life as we know it ($p < 10^{-138}$), much less a second inhabitable planet (the likelihood of which would be infinitesimally smaller). When you throw in the human brainpower factor, the probability becomes incomprehensively trifling ($p < 10^{-1050}$) for any terrestrial abode to exist spawning intelligent beings like us (*ibid*). The denominator of that probability represents a quantity that is magnitudes greater than the sum of all the atoms in our vast universe.

7. Our species is amazing. All living creatures on this planet are exceptional and complex. Each phylum has a specific DNA composition making it impossible to cross-propagate with any but its own kind. And the ecological symbiosis among every organism ensures the cycle of life continues from generation to generation. But among the creatures on Earth, human beings are the most advanced. Our mental capabilities and aptitudes far exceed any other lifeform indigenous to this world. We are purposeful, ethical, creative, talented, flexible, and willful beings. While some animals have better sensitivity in sight, hearing, touch, and smell, we have the greatest sensitivity in terms of conscious awareness, reasoning, morality, and spirituality. Like all organisms, humans possess a self-preservation instinct; but it is a primitive aspect of our makeup. We are more inclined towards personal satisfaction (Polkinghorne, 2005). The only known beings possessing superior intelligence, power, and knowledge are angels and God, neither of which are native to this planet. Like us, these are spiritual beings; but unlike us they are not constrained by the physical. Of all the powers that be, whether living, cosmological, or natural, love is the greatest known to humankind. And we have access to that power, which comes from the most intelligent and superior of all living beings, God, in whose image we are created.

8. You are incomparable. Is there any other hominid that has lived or will live just like you? Not a chance. Well, we are alike in some respects (ACT 17:26). For example, we all come from the same original strain of mitochondrial DNA or single mother, and Y-chromosomal DNA or single father (Rana and Ross, 2005). In practically every other aspect we are different. Even if some lab produced a clone of you it wouldn't imitate you, because your spirit cannot be replicated; it is likely your physical appearance would be different also, as it is affected by developmental conditions, nurturing, and the environment. If you were cloned, it would produce a different person, because you would have dissimilar personality, abilities, memory, situations, and experience. Even identical twins are not really identical. Regardless, experiments with cloning have resulted in inferior replications, which either did not survive or lived a short life with serious health problems.

You might as well accept who you are because nobody else is like you and you are not like anybody else. And while you cannot repeat the life of another, much less be another person, you can become like Christ. You have free will, inalienable rights, and enormous possibility just like every human being that will ever live. You possess the competence to exercise these benefits to succeed and to prosper. Yeah, you will have setbacks, disabilities, and defects distinctive from the rest; but these are mere inconveniences compared to what you can achieve if you try. People with severe physical or mental disabilities have greatness as well, and many have become famous for their achievements; case in point, Helen Keller. So, is the obstacle blocking your path so daunting that you cannot surmount it and accomplish something fantastic? I think not.

Okay, now that you have proof, I hope you will start believing that you are special. Even if you do not feel special in your own mind, you do in God's; this alone is enough to admit how beautiful you are. And this universe in which we abide is outstanding. I believe that God has allowed universal attributes, constants, and measurements to be knowable in order to make himself known to us. Since every feature is so methodically designed with us in mind, the logical conclusion is that we are enormously important and valuable to God. He wants us to reach out to him as we seek answers, and not depend exclusively on the wisdom of humanity. Whose opinion do you value the most? I would go with God on that one. This is why God is special to me, and his Son who is my connection to the Father.

How Old Is the Universe?

Does it matter how old the universe is? It depends. Most unmistakably, it does not matter with regards to your salvation. If you are a scientist whose desire is to understand and explain the universe, well yes. Now there are old universe, old earth societies; and young universe, young earth societies; and those in-between. Personally, I don't bank on whether the earth is thousands or billions of years old, since I am looking forward and not backward. I don't think the age of the universe or the solar system can be ascertained with exactitude; except for God who probably doesn't care as he is not limited by space-time since he exists without it. Regardless, my faith does not hinge on any of the above stances. However, I still find these discussions intriguing, but I see no reason for it to divide people of faith. I'd say that any of the above camps can comprise dedicated Christians, similarly committed to the truth found in God's Word.

Let's look at the scriptures and the science and I'll let you decide. For starters, those believing the human race to be six to ten thousand years old base their findings on such things as OT genealogies and particular verbiage in the book of Genesis. Regarding genealogies, young earthers must assume that all generations are included in the list, that there are no gaps in the sequence; because they use longevities and timelines to estimate the age of man from Adam. But there very well could be gaps, because phraseology is ambiguous at times. Words like begotten, son, seed, or children can infer multiple generations. The Hebrew language has, by magnitudes, fewer words than English; accordingly, some words mean multiple things. If the Bible says "son of David" it could refer to his immediate offspring or a later ancestor such as Jesus Christ (MAT 1:1; MAT 15:22). Likewise, the expression "children of Abraham" could refer to followers of Christ (LUK 13:16; ROM 9:4–8; GAL 3:29) just as "seed of Abraham" often refers to Jesus (GEN 22:18; GAL 3:16). Son could mean great-grandson; or begotten could mean part of the named person's lineage. If there are gaps in the lineage, how is it possible to prove this one way or the other?

With respect to certain words, syntax, and context, let's consider the account in Genesis 1 and 2. The first two verses in the Bible are as follows (GEN 1:1–2), "In the beginning God created the heaven and the earth. And the earth was without form, and void; and darkness was upon the face of the deep. And the Spirit of God moved upon the water." Apparently, this beginning provided a context for the commencement of creation days (see GEN 2:4). As written in the Hebrew dialect perfect tense, the syntax of verses one and two would imply there was an indeterminate period of time prior to the next recorded event, "And God said, let there be light: and there was light" (GEN 1:3).

Not surprisingly, whenever God spoke something happened. Should we assume that the result was simultaneous, immediate, or procedural? Certainly, the six days of creation were sequential. The Bible says in six days God's work was completed (EXO 20:11); the text doesn't say "in the span of six days" or "within six days" but "in six days" leaving the interpretation open to discussion. Usually, the Bible is specific when it needs to be. For instance, the statement that Jesus is God's *only* begotten Son (JOH 1:14–15; JOH 3:16) ensures an explicit interpretation that God had only one human offspring; therefore, Jesus never could have sired a child either. Take note that when God's Son Jesus Christ spoke, miracles occurred; for example, he gave this direct order to the wind and the waves, "Peace, be still," and the storm instantly ceased and all was quiet (MAR 4:35–41). When God and Christ speak something happens, either immediately or eventually.

Noticeably, the interpretation of the word "day" not only connotes many things in Hebrew (*yôm*) but also in English. There is mention of day as the presence of daylight, denoting half a day, followed by the evening and the morning constituting one full day (GEN 1:4–5). To begin each creation day, God speaks; there is no clear indication that these are consecutive days but they certainly are sequential days. And after God speaks, his words become events. The evening starts the process and by morning's end it is finished. God creates heaven and earth, he creates matter and energy, and then he forms these into something more tangible such as a sphere with land, water, and living creatures. But how can one assume a literal evening and morning prior to having a sun and a moon (GEN 1:14–19)? Are we to take unequivocally that the preceding days were exactly twenty-four hours in duration (GEN 1:6–13)? Personally, I am unable to extract a pure timeline from Genesis Chapter One. Notice, you will find connections between creation days one and four, two and five, and three and six when you carefully study the text. I challenge you to read and discover them. There are many other mysteries in God's Word that are worth examining closely that are far beyond the scope of this text.

As an aside, I used to produce stoneware pottery. I would mix the clay and knead it; then I would form it into a vase or something. Next, I would bake it, apply the glaze, and bake it again. Perhaps this is the manner in which God formed people and planets (ISA 64:8; JER 18:6; ROM 9:19–23); that is, there implies a process. God allowed things to transpire, like permitting the waters to gather and the land to emerge (GEN 1:9–10); and letting the earth bring forth plant life before animal life (GEN 1:11–25). Does this suggest gaps between days or not? It doesn't really suggest either. Couldn't God create all of this in six seconds, six days, or six billion years just as easily?

The sixth day is the most important day for us, for that is when humans arrive on the scene, first Adam and next Eve. Once Adam showed up, he had a lot of work to do, like name the animals and cultivate the garden (GEN 2:20); but he was lonely because all the other animals had a mate and helper. So, God created Eve to be Adam's companion; I'm sure that elevated Adam's self-esteem. This episode also suggests a passage of time (GEN 1:26–31) prior to the seventh day when God called it a day and rested (GEN 2:1–3). Some will equate these seven days to one of our work weeks. Well, wouldn't it be something if we could get that much accomplished in one week? Of course, God could do it in a flash. But the Genesis week cannot be the same as our work week because the seventh day has not an evening or morning, inferring that it is ongoing. Surely, God doesn't take a day off from work each week. Often, this time period is associated with our Sabbath rest (1 CO 15:51–52; HEB 4:1–11), during which the saints who have passed await the resurrection (an indefinite period). Realistically, the Sabbath can be respected by worshipping God and reflecting on his works at least one day per week, if not every day. In closing, young earth creationists claim the Genesis text is unambiguous, though I don't presume this by looking at the actual wording; but neither do I profess them to be dead wrong in their explanation.

We will turn now to the scientific data which mostly conform to the old earth, old universe position. The current scholarship says approximately fourteen billion years of age for the universe and four to five billion for the earth. To arrive at those figures, science must adhere to assumptions such as the invariability of things like light, time, nuclear and electromagnetic forces; uniformity in the distribution of matter, microwave background radiation, and the speeds of moving and rotating bodies; gradualism in the accumulation of sediment, rock, water, and ice, and in the development and deterioration of living and nonliving things; accuracy in measuring the distance of heavenly bodies, the rate of expansion, and the size of the universe; validity of the experimental methods and the precise calibration of associated instrumentation.

Then there is unpredictability in tectonic activity, fluctuation in the magnitude of stars, periods of universal expansion versus inflation, limitations in the procedures applied, and unreliability of dating methods. For example, radiometric decay rates can vary due to environmental conditions and contamination of the sample over time. Plus, a great number of theories and findings are based upon extrapolation from things we can observe and measure today, as if the findings would agree with circumstances millennia ago; or conjectures about things we cannot observe and examine, such as the composition of dark matter, subatomic particles, singularities, and gravity. Another factor that can throw science off is when God intercedes via miracles and other interventions that breach the laws of physics, like when he fiddles with time (see JOS 10:12–14; 2 KI 20:8–11; ISA 8:7–8). Some scientific theories themselves defy the laws of physics, as in the case of the big bang, quantum mechanics, multiverse, and black holes.

Therefore, uncertainty is regularly present when pinpointing time frames via historical analysis and other methods. Unfortunately, science is all we have outside of God's Word to draw inferences about the universe's age, origin, structure, and configuration. And although there are inadequacies, it is not altogether fruitless or a waste of time. Scientists postulate theories, test them, validate them, and invalidate them. And from this we gain much knowledge; at other times, we become perplexed.

Take evolution theory; I think scientists have sufficiently renounced it. In fact, both the old universe and the young universe positions pretty much disagree with macroevolution being supported by the data. Amazingly, there are those who wish to integrate creation with evolution and call it theistic evolution, even though the theory of evolution is unsustainable. Does that make sense, to combine spinoffs from science and religion to produce a more convoluted system? Does it make sense to reject something that you know in your heart to be true? I think people may do this because they want to be more important to themselves than God is; it is a form of self-deception and self-adoration. This is what the Bible means by being double-minded (ROM 1:18–21; JAM 1:8); people can be divided within themselves though deep down they know the truth. The truth, when known, cannot be disputed by science or religion. But when science and the Bible are in agreement, it would be wise to take heed; if you are astute, you will find they usually are.

Okay, can we now put the issue of the age of the universe to rest? No, this analysis just adds more questions that we cannot strictly answer via a thorough reading of the Bible or via stringent scientific exploration; both camps provide educated guesses. I am not convinced. One reasonable conclusion is that the Bible is deliberately vague about how long the universe, the earth, and humans have been here. To me that signifies the question of age is irrelevant to the purpose and message of the Bible. This is not to say we shouldn't explore and study God's creation. Maybe he placed some ambiguity there to spark interest, so we would plunge into the workings of his creation, his reasons, and his will. I'm sure curiosity isn't there for us to fight about, or accuse those on the other side of an issue as being infidels or dullards. But it helps to seek wisdom and truth using both avenues to enlightenment, and the more we do the greater our understanding.

Like the Bible says, God conceals aspects of his creation, and people seek to uncover them (PRO 25:2). Do you not see the harmony in this? The more we experience God and our universe, the more everything makes sense. Our ability to observe and measure the universe has escalated rapidly over the last two centuries, such that astronomers can see far enough back in time to get a glimpse of how it began. Therefore, while the Bible may be deliberately vague about certain aspects of the universe, science brings us evermore closer to understanding them. Praise God for enabling us to advance in our learning, everlastingly.

Intelligent Design or Random Unguided Processes

Two explanations dominate the debate about how it all came to be. The way people bicker over it you would think it is a complicated matter. Well, it isn't. Random unguided processes cannot produce order, only chaos; and order cannot be a product of chaos either. This is testable and observable. Ask your child to place fifty lettered blocks into a box and sling them into the air at once; then see how many blocks fall together to spell words. Repeat that fifty times and you probably won't see three blocks come together to form a single word, much less a sentence. But if you come home from work and find three lettered blocks lined up on the floor that spell "cat" you probably will surmise it was the work of your intelligent child.

Our DNA sequence has a stream of data some three billion base-pairs long. The chances of randomization arranging that much information in the proper order is zero. To get a scope of this improbability, consider the chances of dealing all fifty-two cards from a shuffled deck in perfect order: ace through king of spades, hearts, clubs, and diamonds. There are fifty-two factorial possible combinations; you are betting on hitting just the one chance in 80658175170943878571660636856403766975289505440883277824000000000000.

The notion that intelligent design (ID) is inherent in the universe is nothing new. It gained traction over two centuries ago by noted clergyman William Paley (1802), not to mention Socrates. Being a man of the cloth, Paley attributed ID to a sovereign deity, a reasonable and logical conclusion regardless of worldview. Paley proposed the analogy of a gentleman finding a pocket-watch on the ground. What should the man think, that an intelligent designer created the watch, or blind unguided processes caused it? Some atheists would argue the latter option as a distinct possibility believe it or not (Dawkins, 1996). Paley applied this analogy to the complexity of lifeforms, which possess mechanics too sophisticated to assume that the conjoined components integrated together by happenstance.

Can anything design itself? I submit that artificial intelligence is an oxymoron since the smartest computers in the world were designed by humans. If you saw a robot, would you think it evolved? If your job is eliminated and a robot takes your place, be assured that someone planned it prior to discharging you. If robots, watches, computers, machines, and lifeforms require intelligence to occur, how can the universe, which is vastly more complicated, not?

Oddly, Darwinists and Neo-Darwinists are apt to take the blind watchmaker position. They chalk it up to mutation, natural selection, and other random, unguided processes (*ibid*). To their discredit, proponents never entertain or address the mechanisms underlying these theorized "natural" phenomena. Macroevolution relies on intermediate designs, common ancestry, mutual homology among lifeforms; spontaneous reconfiguration of DNA, RNA, proteins and amino acids; as well as missing links not apparent in the fossil record. None of these propositions have been substantiated at any time.

Alternate theories pose ideas like progressive explosions of transformed species, molecular clocks, mutating replicators, and genetic shifting or drifting; periodic, stepwise, transitional, and advantageous upgrades; real-time computing operations in the cell; preprogrammed, self-engineered, genomic renovations; and transmutable DNA. These propositions also have never been observed, tested, or verified, much less ascribed a cause or reason to occur.

But scientists rejecting ID outright are hooked on their desire for something else to be true, distorting reality like an addict on drugs. Why? Maybe because they think ID necessarily entails belief in God, since that would be the most viable explanation. Two foremost scientific observations support ID. One is irreducible complexity (Behe, 2006) seen in all DNA in general and the bacterial flagellum in particular. Another is specified complexity (Dembski, 2004), seen in programs, processes, and machines like the bacterial flagellum and the laptop computer. Combining irreducibility with specified complexity pretty much rules out everything but ID.

ID is, therefore, scientifically upheld. Further, it does not depend on, neither is it in conflict with, religious convictions or creationism. But while ID works without religion, it works best with God. The naysayers dismiss ID as not consistent with objective science, which is simply not the case (Meyer, 2009; 2013). But the naturalists cannot allow ID theory for it is contrary to the orthodoxy among scientific elitists; it's a temptation to them, as if a betrayal of their vows and their fidelity. How then, would they account for intelligence? Anyone can observe that a designed program, machine, or process can accommodate new information to enhance the capability; but a naturally occurring organism or process cannot accommodate the insertion of new information because functionality will be impaired if not halted.

Professionals holding any of the above positions will concede that the universe and associated life forms have an "appearance" of intelligent design, but will disallow the ID conclusion or theory as unscientific. Get serious! If it looks like a duck, walks like a duck, and quacks like a duck, must it be something else? The mainstream is in hot pursuit of a theory that is adequate to explain everything, ignoring ID as one defensible explanation. Note the following wonders that are unexplained via natural selection, random mutations, unguided processes, and other alternatives presented above—but can be explained in terms of ID.

- Nothing known to exist before the big bang.
- Fine tuning and sophistication of the universe, life, and mind.
- Cambrian explosion of multiple, unique lifeforms (phyla).
- No evidence of pre-Cambrian artifacts or advanced lifeforms.
- Lack of mass introductions before and after the Cambrian explosion.
- Common ancestry of humans; original mother/father DNA confirmation.
- The ton of organized information in DNA and body-type blueprints.
- Embryonic development; built-in sequencing and encoding mechanisms.
- Uniqueness evident in the universe, and in life, that cannot be duplicated.
- Biological, chemical, mechanical, genetic, and epigenetic processes.
- Specified, irreducible complexity in all lifeforms.
- Multifunctionality of advanced organisms (especially humans).
- Purposive behavior, goals, and dreams.
- Reasoning, emotion, morality, creativity, meaning, and choice.
- Consciousness, self-awareness, and abstract thought.
- Individual, collective, and universal determination.
- Beauty, art, music, aesthetics, spirituality.
- Scientific and experimental methodology; empirical research.
- Establishing cause-effect and relationships.
- Explanatory and predictive power of information.
- Intelligence…

Information is an effect, not a cause. Information itself necessitates intelligence. An exchange of information can instruct, by generating understanding thereby enhancing intelligence. However, when information is injected into a biogenetic process, it causes interference, because the new information is incompatible or asynchronous with the existing plans and structures. That is why organisms with inborn system capabilities cannot evolve into more advanced organisms with new systems. Take the dogged attempts to reengineer fruit flies. All they ever get is a fruit fly that is deformed, sterile, dead, or relatively normal; they certainly have not produced an advanced fruit fly, much less an alligator. Would it do any good to attach wings to your car? Without the accompanying mechanism it would never fly. Birds come fully equipped with functional wings and feathers; they did not evolve from giant lizards.

Information gleaned from educated guesses is unscientific and unreliable. Consider the noticeable uniform stratification seen in sedimentary deposits. Can that information be used to generalize age or epoch? Such visual information does not allow one to infer that it took millions of years, or thousands, or even days because of the wide range of climatic and geologic conditions that must either be controlled, qualified, or quantified. The ages attributed to strata in geologic columns, or layers of sediment, or layers of ice, or rings in a tree are therefore, imprecise. Cases in point include the intervals of fine and course layering resulting from the recent eruptions of Mt. St. Helens, or the fashioning of the Grand Canyon and the bending evident in the layers, or the geological remnants and strata laid from an apparent deluge known as Noah's flood. Though the layering in these sedimentary exhibits have similar attributes, the events are far removed in terms of timeframe and duration, whether recent and rapid versus ancient and slow.

The same fossils can be found in multiple strata in the Grand Canyon, implying relatively rapid settling of sediment. The receding of an immense waterway that once connected the Mediterranean Sea and the Caspian Sea (originally a fresh water body) reveals gradual and progressive layering. Interestingly, one global flood could explain both of these phenomena. It is very difficult to accurately timestamp natural events of the distant past, because we have to work backwards from the present by leaps and bounds and not along a uniformly regressing arrow of time. Results have been obtained from regulated laboratory settings controverting results extrapolated from historical research of geologic formations, fossils, and living species. Forming of fossils could have occurred ages ago, but under controlled conditions fossilization has occurred in a matter of weeks.

Obviously, information gathering must be precise if one is to draw informed conclusions. A coordinated assembly of information can lead to additional information. But a series of random events provides zero information because there is no pattern, cause, or trend. However, randomization can be useful when collecting samples precisely because it does not introduce bias or patterns that would skew the findings.

God employs a top-down process. He is at the top. All he has to do is speak and universes appear. Humans can create things too, but primarily by means of a bottom-up process. For instance, we start with a foundation, emplace a frame, attach a roof, enclose the structure, install plumbing and electricity, and voila, a house. Or your kid takes a box of lettered blocks and creates different configurations ranging from a house to intelligible words. Whether the creation process is top-down or bottom-up it still requires intelligence. Even if any of the alternative theories mentioned earlier were workable, they still would require a causal agent which points again to intelligence. The only question is, whose intelligence?

Experience

Since no two people have the same repertory of experience each individual will experience the same situation differently. People that live in the tropics have a substantially different understanding of rain than those living in the high desert, because rain is markedly dissimilar in duration, temperature, density, dispersion, and other factors. Situational, social, and environmental conditions are never the same for any two people. Experience adds up to the person you are and what you are to become; genetics plays only a minor role. Your experience is every bit as unique and important as everyone else sharing this dimension of space and time.

Our environment impacts us and we impact it, for better or worse. Everyone has the capacity to impact the world, time-space, and humanity. And although God never changes, we also can have an impression on him through our love and our behavior. Look at the impact ordinary men of God had on the world simply because they confessed Christ, whose effect has been greater than anybody in history. Do you ever wonder why that is? Such love needs no defense, or offense. Love stands on its own and empowers a person to take a stand and remain standing despite the avalanche of adversity. Love can change everything, even the world.

What you do affects others as much as it does you, and vice-versa. Every experience will influence everyone else involved, sometimes in a good way sometimes not so good. Look at the impact of trauma in your life as well as accomplishment; or the changes that occur daily in your life that shape you, intrigue you, sway you, invigorate you, hurt you, or disappoint you. Look at the impact of our heroes, and our villains. The impacts of people like Atilla the Hun and Mother Teresa have been remarkable. Whom would you prefer to follow or adopt as a role model?

How have you arranged your priorities? What were you taught? The way you were brought up matters as much as the way you rear your children, and the way they turn out will affect you enormously. Consider the effect of suicide on families and society. Definitely, our behavior influences others, their behavior influences us, and these effects can have lasting reverberations which can continue for a lifetime, or even eternity. I prefer to think carefully and take time to weigh the alternatives and their likely consequences before arriving at a decision. I might feel sure and still be wrong, but not as often.

We can shape and we can shake every sphere of influence in our environment from our inner circle, to our community, to society, to humanity, and to God himself. Like a ripple effect, what we say and do affects each existential layer, positive or negative, just like every encompassing layer of our existence affects us. And there is a similar ripple effect in the reverse direction, beginning with God and stopping at you. To attain the best results, your various connections to these domains of existence should be two-way streets of positive vibrations, because what you put out is going to be relatively proportional to, and have the same valence as, what returns to you. According to Newton, when two entities interact, they exert forces on one another: action-reaction. Similarly, your words and deeds result in corresponding reactions, which can be good or bad depending on whether you are thinking and acting appropriately. Regardless of the conflict or connection, the response should be loving and blessing (LUK 6:28; 1 PE 3:9). Jesus Christ loved and forgave the very ones who crucified him (LUK 23:33–34); this changed many hearts, including some of those who were a party to Jesus's assassination (MAT 27:54; MAR 15:39; LUK 23:39–43). Believe it or not, you also are a witness to this unseemly yet solemn event.

All experience has value because it teaches us. Irrespective of your upbringing, age, ethnicity, gender, location, and experience you can excel and succeed. You need not change any of these characteristics to actualize your ideal self, to be all you can be, to learn and master something really interesting, and to become God's own. If anybody can do it, you can. Remember, we are created equal and are seen that way in the eyes of God (ACT 10:34–35; ROM 2:11). But when it comes to your gifts and blessings, as well as your trials and tribulations, everybody is equally different (ROM 12:3–10,15). Thank God that we are. I sure am glad my wife is different than I; otherwise I probably wouldn't be able to live with her. But God made us different, man and woman, precisely to attract us toward one another (GEN 5:1–2; MAR 10:6–9) and to propagate the human race (GEN 1:27–28: GEN 9:7). Individual differences are essential for our exceptionalism to shine, and for establishing relationships with diverse walks of life.

If you are paying attention, you will find promise in each moment of your life. The possibilities are limitless because each situation offers opportunities. Be ready to seize the moment, take time to ascertain the point, and prepare to make a decision; because every burst of time can be life changing. And the action you execute can alter time and space; for every step you take leads somewhere else. While you can visualize a path and choose a direction, you might be surprised when you reach the destination. It may be miles farther than you anticipated; that is, it could tremendously exceed your expectations. But if you expect small increments of change you could constrain yourself and limit the journey. Sure, begin with baby steps; hopefully, they will increase into giant steps if you are resolute. The uncertainty does not mean you don't make plans, or take steps, or practice; or pursue education, or establish goals, or dream dreams. These activities are moving you towards your purpose and ultimate vocation. But arriving at a destination is not the end game, because there will be ample destinations once you get a taste of success. Each experience adds up to greater becoming, prepares you for more difficult challenges, and propels you farther and higher. As a result, you likely will be allocated more responsibility in the harvest of God's vineyard (ISA 6:8; MAT 9:37–38; MAT 20:1–16).

Understand that your every thought, word, and action is known unto God (PSA 139:1–4; HEB 4:12–14). He knows everything about you, even the number of hairs on your head (LUK 12:6–9). Since God is fully cognizant of what you are up to, it would be wise to consider that fact before you speak or act. If only we could be continuously mindful of the present moment, every moment, and God's presence in every moment. But, alas, it is not possible in this life. For this reason, we are urged to pray unceasingly and to stay in the spirit (EPH 6:18; 1 TH 5:17), remembering Jesus Christ in conjunction with every decision (PRO 3:6). Plead for God's Holy Spirit to sanctify you as you focus on Christ and follow his lead (HEB 2:11; HEB 10:10). That way you can be sure you are heading in the right direction and reaching the right destination regardless of the setbacks. The most crucial aspect of experience is what happens to you after you experience death; that can be affected by the direction you take today.

While the consequences of your choices can have varying extremes in the here and now, reflect a minute on how those choices might determine your afterlife. Or do you deny that possibility? If the answer is yes, what are you living for? If you are considering life after death, then contemplate the alternatives. You are able to ascertain with reasonable accuracy the outcome of your decisions before acting on them, assuming you are experienced, right? But even if you don't have much experience you can perform a thought experiment and imagine the near- and long-term rewards or penalties of available responses. Now, extend that process; weigh the possible rewards and penalties in the overarching picture, after your death and resurrection. Surely you can contemplate this even if you don't believe in the afterlife. But is it feasible to reject that prospect outright; and at what cost? It is written that the spirit gives life; and it is not extinguished when the body expires (ECC 8:8; ECC 12:7; ZEC 12:1; MAT 26:41; 2 CO 3:6). It also is written that there will be a resurrection of the body (REV 20:5–6), when the spirit and body are reunited and all flesh will be judged (ECC 12:14; ISA 66:16; EZE 7:3; DAN 12:2; MAT 12:36; ROM 2:6–10). What judgment will you receive? What judgment do you deserve?

Let us, therefore, privately judge our behavior pronto, before it's too late. There will be consequences now, and there will be consequences later. Your best bet is to stay in the spirit and be led by it; summon your lifeforce to control your thoughts, beliefs, and decisions (1 CO 2:10–12). This will be your connection to God. I recommend you stay connected to ensure you are raised into life eternal (ROM 8:11; 1 CO 15:42–44; GAL 6:8). Otherwise, you will die a second death and perish (EZE 18:4,20; JOH 3:16,36; REV 2:11). Ask yourself, will death be your final destination? Would you prefer to continue living or stop living? God is a God of the living (MAT 22:31–32). If you think you get to live free forever regardless of your faith or worldview you have not studied the evidence. The only proof on this matter is given by God himself in the Holy Bible. You'll not arrive at this answer scientifically, only spiritually.

For the most part, you get to choose your experience (read 2 SA 11–13). All too often we choose hastily and imprudently, especially in our youth. I made some pretty stupid decisions when I was wild and crazy, growing up as a baby boomer in the era of sex, drugs, and rock and roll. I let it influence me in the wrong direction; but I later rejected the nonsense (all but the rock and roll) and that led me in another direction. We are inclined to be considerably less careless as we age, apparently. Growing up taught me some valuable lessons, likely part of my grooming to be a mental health professional. Having firsthand experience often makes you a better helper because you learn things that are not taught in school or in books. Remember, everything works together for your good if you seek the righteousness of God (ROM 8:28).

I think we learn a lot more from our mistakes than from our successes. Either way, the experiences and choices we make prepare us for a greater calling that we consummate as we mature, while incrementally taking on more responsibility. If you can choose your experience you can ultimately choose your destiny, not just in this life but also the next. So, the degree to which you excel, succeed, reach your destiny, and make your dreams come true is mostly up to you. If in accordance with God's will (1 JO 5:14–15), he will help you make it happen. For it is God's will that you search for him, listen to his counsel, and become a member of his household; you will become more enriched and happier than even your wildest dreams when you submit to him. Stay on the right path and see what heaven is all about. It is an experience you will never forget.

Bias

Our experience shapes the way we view the world. Since that experience is limited, our view of the world is often biased. It takes discipline, exploration, and inquiry to be objective. But people tend to be lazy and reach for the most available information however relevant or accurate. If there is anything that science teaches us it is to be observant, inquisitive, unbiased, and thorough in our analysis. I was raised in a Christian home but that has not constrained my view of the world. I also studied to be a scientist, so I know how to be neutral and impartial when assessing the reliability and verifiability of information. But the average person tends to be somewhat ignorant of the truth, unscientific in their methodology, overconfident in their knowledge, and defiant in their positions. In psychology, we call this phenomenon cognitive conceit: jumping to conclusions, thinking we know it all, overgeneralizing, allowing only confirmatory evidence, blowing events out of proportion, having a one-track mind, acting superstitious, and so on. Okay let's face it; we all do these things, even scientists. But if you are cognizant of your logical fallacies and cognitive distortions, and not let them influence your assumptions, you'll be correct a lot more often.

When it comes to the choice between theism and atheism, positions are typically adopted without fully examining the evidence. There is inherent predilection to either have faith in God or trust in the world. In order to think independently it would behoove one to examine both sides. But even our institutions of higher learning are spewing out a false narrative based on a leftist, secular, and humanistic philosophy. It was bad enough when I was a student, but now leftwing progressivism and favoritism has pervaded most of our universities and colleges. It is an antichristian movement that postulates unscientific findings, skews the available data, and misrepresents facts and statistics. Much of the mass media is in collusion with this conspiracy, not to mention a great number of politicians and government entities. Yet they bury truth and hide its intentional degradation among the myriad of conspiracy theories bouncing about. Each individual should perform his or her systematic investigation and assessment before taking a self-proclaimed expert's word for it. When enough credible sources converge on the same result, you may be onto something.

Throughout this narrative I have deflated numerous arguments advanced by disbelievers and pseudoscientists if their thinking does not hold up to close scrutiny. When there are holes in their logic and emptiness in their evidence commentators look downright foolish. I'm sure the same accusation will be made by them towards me, but I have no predilection to obscure the facts or muddy the waters. Because my penchant is truth, and I have zero motivation to contrive it as it would place me in the same category as those I am calling out. But the reason they get away with it is because they realize that the vast majority of listeners will not take the time or do the work to validate or invalidate what they are hearing. They are fed the same rhetoric over and over again until it is assumed to be true; but that is the oldest trick in the book, to impel people to believe something simply by repeating it ad nauseam. This approach was employed devotedly by Goebbels, Hitler's minister of Nazi propaganda. And it is being employed to this day by others aiming to seize power. The purpose is to instill prejudgment among the populace; to create preconceived notions and opinions that are impermeable.

Bias can give a person tunnel vision. If you begin with a false premise you will never reach the right conclusion. While partiality is nearly impossible to avoid, given the saliency of one's experience and sporadic access to the facts, it can be subdued. Put your personal preference aside long enough to probe the matter. When in doubt, check it out. For example, do you believe unwaveringly in global warming? Thorough exploration will uncover a lot of flaky research and statistics, quasi experts, faulty experimental methods, and inaccurate computer models based on contrived data. But the proponents will generate their disinformation, intimating that all credible scientists hold to this assumption. Well, some do and some do not. Yeah, global warming will be a problem when the earth melts or is destroyed by fire (2 PE 3:11–12); this could infer a nuclear holocaust (ZEC 14:12). It would be very disheartening to experience that (MAT 24:35). As far as climate change, well maybe I can concur. After all, the climate and weather change in my hometown year after year, including temperature variations, inconsistent rainfall, unpredictable wind conditions, plate tectonics, and the rest. I don't see any trends to reject the concept of climate change; I also don't find anything mystifying about it. But there is insufficient evidence to claim that global warming is anything to worry about, or that it is worth throwing billions of dollars at. I believe this nation and this planet have far more important concerns than a possible increase in global temperature by half of one degree.

Unfortunately, you see slanting all the time in news media, institutions of higher learning, politics, the Internet, textbooks, technical research reports, and elsewhere. What is particularly troublesome is detecting preconception in supposedly rigorous scientific studies. I remember doing a research paper on investigator bias and experimenter bias incorporated during the conduct of empirical research. I found that it was a lot more prevalent than people think; it can occur consciously and intentionally, and it can occur unconsciously and unintentionally. Conceivably, the anticipated outcome might be inadvertently suggested to the test subjects, or errors introduced in the recording of the data, or mistakes made in interpreting the results. But the calculated fudging of data or misrepresentation of findings, well that is unconscionable. Some scientists betray their profession and their kind by stooping to such tactics just to be distinguished, to bolster a worldview, or to discredit or espouse another expert or finding. If you want to assess a sampling of debunked theories, findings, and scientists scrutinize the following.

- Mendel's work with pea plants (1860s) made genetic traits a popular phenomenon, though he fudged the data to concretize support for an otherwise valid hypothesis.
- Haeckel modified embryo diagrams (1874) to depict similarities in species, which remained in textbooks for almost one hundred years before the diagrams were proven to be refashioned.
- Dubois's Java man (1892) was a relative of the gibbon family, not a human.
- Dawson's Piltdown man (1912) was exposed forty years later to be a cranium from a modern human and the jawbone of an orangutan.
- Cook's Nebraska man (1917) turned out to be a tooth from an ape; however unintentional, it was a gross error in practical science.

- Peking man (1920s–1930s) was evidence of monkey skulls bashed in by humans to feast on their brains; the original bone samples were supposedly lost twenty years later.
- Protsch (1939) falsely dated Neanderthal man by a mere 18,000 years. By the way, neither Neanderthal man nor Cro-Magnon man were missing links; they were human remains.
- Fujimara's excavations (1970s) were of artifacts that he buried prior to "discovering" them there.
- Summerlin (1974) used a black marker to darken mice fur, then alleged a successful transplant.
- Fleischmann and Pons introduced their cold fusion project (1989) but quickly retracted their article from publication and refused to allow anyone to review their data and methods. There has never appeared any evidence before or since suggesting that cold fusion will work.
- Schoen (1998–2001) published numerous journal articles based on invented data before he was exposed as a fraud.
- The photograph of a fossil suggesting a link between birds and dinosaurs was published in National Geographic (1999) before it was determined to be a fabricated composite illegally imported from China.
- Moriguchi was fired from the University of Tokyo (2012) for faking the results of stem cell studies.
- Han was fired from Iowa State University (2013) after falsifying the results of his HIV vaccine and lying to the National Institutes of Health to secure more funding; he was criminally prosecuted.

Many forgeries and frauds of the past are connected with the theory of evolution. In their haste and insistence to validate the notion that humans evolved from apes, scientists concocted links and assembled bone fragments from unrelated samples to manufacture evidence of "homo erectus" in order to gain notoriety in the field. Instead, they eventually were unmasked and disgraced. Why do people risk their careers trying to devise truth rather than to search for and uncover it? I guess they want to believe the lie so bad that they will resort to drastic measures. What they really intend is to force evolution to be true and the Holy Bible to be false. They favor the lie and they want everyone else to join them; just like the "father of lies" (namely Satan) is going to hell and wants everyone else to join him. Yes, they actually hate the Bible and God that much. Such are the ways of the world which prefers to confuse the issue of God; whereas it is God's intention to disclose the truth about the world (1 CO 1:25–28).

Let's face it, there are counterfeits and there are mistakes. The former misrepresents the findings, the latter misinterprets the findings. It is the deliberate act to deceive that bothers me. When scientists purposefully fabricate proof, it begs the question why. Either they are afraid of the truth, or they can't handle the truth. What are they trying to hide or hide from? Is it not the truth that scientists seek to reveal? And the same is true for theology; isn't truth the ultimate objective? Then why change it or invent it? Such motives always reflect a disreputable undertaking. The focus is self and the method is indulgence. The one perpetrating a hoax knows it is false, so they obviously don't care about the truth. They have fallen back into deadly sin territory: lust (pleasure), greed (wealth), pride (conceit), sloth (laziness), envy (covetousness), and deceit (pretentiousness). Since God's objective is truth, he cannot be pleased with those who distort it on purpose which is Satan's way. The only thing God speaks is truth. The best way to eliminate subjectivity and doubt is with truth. The optimal approach is to listen to God.

What Is Truth?

Remember Pontius Pilate asking Jesus that question? Doubtless, the prefect hadn't a clue what the answer was, even though the source was standing right there in front of him. Apparently, Pilate didn't value truth much nor did he value justice; he washed his hands of both (MAT 27:24). Do you value truth? I do; I regard it as my most prized possession. Truth also connotes great power. Why else would scam artists go to such lengths to conceal it? Truth can collapse a stack of lies in a second. Besides, if you know the truth you won't forget it. If you deal in lies you will never be able to keep track of them. In a court of law, uncovering the truth trumps anything else presented as evidence; and if someone is caught in a lie, their entire testimony becomes suspect. At least, that's how it's supposed to work. Being the commodities that they are, truth and justice are being bought and sold all the time; funny because truth should be free and justice should be impartial. It certainly costs a lot more to buy a lie than the truth; and it is a lot cheaper to purchase your freedom than to pay for your defense.

Let us contrast two research hypotheses: seeking to prove something or seeking to disprove something (notwithstanding the null hypothesis). I submit that the former represents pursuit of the nobler cause and is perhaps the easier route as well. Plausibly, it is easier to prove that God exists than to disprove it; it is easier to prove intelligent design in the universe than to disprove it. In the USA a person is deemed innocent until proven guilty; that is a more reasonable and moral policy than to begin a criminal proceeding with the presupposition that a defendant is guilty until proven innocent. Governments that adopt the latter approach likely will convict more innocent people, while the former will acquit more guilty people. In the USA, we view punishment of innocent people as the worst mistake that our justice system can make, so we choose to err on the side of caution for the greater good. Wouldn't you protest vehemently if falsely accused and convicted of something for which you were innocent? Even the most moral people disdain injustice as much or more than they love justice.

There is a clear indication that morality and justice are not subjective or relative; they are proof of God. Morality certainly cannot be ascribed to humans. Who are we to concoct the moral high ground? Humans violate the moral laws, so how can we be responsible for instituting them? Why are we obliged to obey laws at all, except to avoid the consequences? And who gets to decide the consequences? People make and enforce laws, and levy penalties in accordance with the collective good, which implies they have agreed to that system of justice, however flawed. And such systems were in existence way before any of us appeared on the scene. Thus, truth and justice require a commitment, which is why people are swayed by relativism, naturalism, postmodernism and the like; they do not want to make the commitment. God is the only possible cause for moral laws. Thankfully, God never makes mistakes in judgment. A commitment to God is what is required of the moral law.

Regarding truth, it seems to be in low demand these days. You definitely cannot get the government to share it. Beware when the administration mandates transparency and clarity; you will get smoke and mirrors instead. I loathe leaders who make deals with hostile nations and withhold the details; or snub allies and embrace enemies; or pass thousands of pages of legislation before reading any of it; or bypass the process altogether and oblige people into obeying rules that are unconstitutional; or free terrorists and inmates so they can continue violating us; or exploit agencies established to serve the people in order to harass them instead; or alienate and vilify our police, military, and veterans; and countless other outrages, like promoting their lies to convince people they aren't liars. These are professional liars and darned good at it. Leaders are supposed to represent the will of the people but often betray the people. It is fruitless to try and sort out the lies, which outnumber the facts. Lies are their truth (ISA 5:20–21). This is the road to relativism and worthlessness, where nobody knows what to believe or what is true, so the populace stops valuing it. By brainwashing our youth, they sponsor ignorance, even in college coursework; they also foster repulsion for American traditions, reminding me of Nazi brainwashing of the Hitler youth.

Absolute truth is the only kind, because the Holy Spirit is the source of all truth and is perfect in every way. How can God not be perfect? He is the only living being that exists without being caused, and he is the cause of everything that does exist. Anything short of perfect truth is untrue, because truth has to be thoroughly consistent with reality to be factual. When a falsehood is offered as truth it violates God's ninth commandment. This is a serious matter to God. Who among men has never told a single lie? Only Jesus Christ, who was ready to share the truth with Pilate who wasn't inclined to receive it. God is the only absolute source for truth; the rest of us vary in the degree to how credible we are. But those who respect the truth earn the respect of others. I mean, who respects a compulsive liar? Thanks be to God who never lies.

God calls us by the power of his Holy Spirit to listen with our spirit and receive his wisdom, guidance, assurance, and truth. According to Martin Luther, the Gospel of Jesus Christ represents the Holy Spirit calling us (2 TI 1:9). But the Bible was written by men, right? Not exactly, since the writers were inspired by the Holy Spirit (1 TH 2:13; 2 PE 1:21) who proceeds from the Father and the Son; everything spoken by Jesus is equivalently true to the words spoken by Almighty God. In other words, *Logos* proceeds from the mouth of God (GEN 1:3; ISA 1:20; MAT 4:4; LUK 4:4) and from the mouth of Christ (JOH 1:1,14) via the Holy Spirit. God's Word, the Holy Bible, is therefore true. In order to believe this, one must receive the Holy Spirit who gives us the power of faith to know God, listen to him (ROM 10:17; HEB 11:6; 1 PE 1:5), and be saved (MAT 24:13; ROM 10:13). God doesn't want a single soul to give up the ghost; he wants everybody to find him and live (EZE 33:11; 1 TI 2:4; 2 PE 3:9). Those people who have willingly ignored God and resisted his Word have rejected the Holy Spirit, thereby committing the only unpardonable sin (MAT 12:31–32; MAR 3:28–29; LUK 12:9–10; 1 JO 1:10). You have to want and ask for forgiveness to receive it, but you won't ask if you don't believe. Without forgiveness there is no salvation.

Let me be clear, God is the only one who always tells the whole truth and nothing but. And he is the only one who can, because he alone knows everything. It is not so difficult to identify reliable sources for truth, however. Pinpointing people that are notoriously unreliable is even easier; you can spot them a mile away. When they open their mouths, they expose themselves (PRO 14:7–8; PRO 17:28). It is a major character flaw. Who wants to be pegged as a habitual liar? Even Satan would deny it. What a laugh, huh? He invented lying. Beware of false prophets who distort the Word of God (ISA 8:20); their lies lead people to their doom. Discover the truth for yourself, don't take their word for it when you have God's Word.

Who can you trust? Look at the world. It's getting harder to find an honest person when you need one. Some people are notorious for acting the pretender, like certain reporters, politicians, attorneys, scientists, professors, philosophers, evangelists, globalists, officeholders, diplomats, etc. Many of them tell lies for a living. That's why it is so important to know the truth, so you can test what you hear and read (1 TH 5:21–22). It was easy when I was a kid capable of a purer faith. I believed my parents, teachers, and pastors because I trusted them to be reliable sources of truth (although, they may have said things to hoodwink me or to shelter me). Maybe some of you didn't have dependable people in your lives; perhaps family members were untrustworthy because they were conniving, abusive, or worse. But you knew they were untrue, didn't you? And with all the corruption, excess, evil, and abuse in government, business, and society I suppose it is judicious to be a skeptic.

I trust God; he is my rock (2 SA 22:1–4). God is there for me anytime, anyplace; he is my shield, my counselor, and my deliverer. You can trust God too. Granted, he is not the only one in whom I place my trust because there are quite a number of people I can trust when the chips are down. Their standing has been demonstrated over the passage of many years. Though imperfect, they have a reputation for honesty, integrity, sincerity, generosity, and consistency. People like that reflect the love of God whether they know him or not. Unfortunately, there are bad people out there working for the dark side, who will defame honorable people, harm them, mock them, or bring them down. Those scoundrels will resort to character assassination; in their minds they elevate themselves when putting others down. They are doing the work of Satan (JOH 8:30–59), to destroy goodness, hide the truth, and indoctrinate others in order to control them. They behave as if possessed; but indeed, they are for Satan has claimed them. They have no idea the horrors waiting at the gate. Navigate clear of people like that, or their filth will wear off on you (PSA 1:1–2; PRO 13:20; 1 CO 15:33).

Have you encountered people who amble about claiming there is no God? Ask them to provide proof (PSA 10:1–7). Why would they bother to deny God if they don't believe in him in the first place? Even the devil and his hoard of demons believe in God (JAM 2:19). Like Pilate, brazen atheists wouldn't know God if he appeared before them in the flesh. They allege that there is nothing to worry about; that nobody is going to be damned to hell. They wish. They haven't read the Bible for all its worth, because it is worthless to them. They speak of things that they know nothing about (COL 2:8; JDE 1:10). When the words of God are spoken, they cringe. Satan will wrestle them away from the Bible because the truth is his greatest threat. Those who dismiss the Bible cannot diagnose the signs that Christ's second coming is nigh: famine and drought, pestilence and plagues, earthquakes and floods, wars and rumors of war, perversion and lawlessness, false messiahs (MAT 24:3–35; ROM 1:21–31). By the look of it, the return of Messiah is imminent. Do not be caught by surprise. Protect yourself, as if a tidal wave is closing in.

How is it possible to think all knowledge comes from your own intellectual prowess? The rationalists sure can be irrational sometimes. They simulate superiority in knowledge but are unable to know how they got here and what God has in store for them. They believe they have found the truth, and that they have a greater amount of it than most, yet they believe in things that cannot be explained. In that way, they betray their own religious fundamentals (e.g., rationalism, naturalism, relativism, secularism, hedonism, statism, nihilism, atheism, scientism). If intellectualism is the premier avenue for understanding truth, how can they purport things to be true that they can neither explain nor prove? When in doubt, people tend to invent a truth that is most appealing to them. Yet when the prevalence of the data point to one important truth, namely the resurrection of Christ, it won't be accepted because it cannot be fully absorbed with the mind; it requires the spirit, a notion that is grossly unattractive to nonbelievers.

It is imperative to know the truth; your life depends on it. Are you ready to hear it? Those blowhards that won't shut up are not being truthful. If they had an inkling of the truth, they wouldn't be so violently outspoken about it. Such emphasis is introduced to make a lie seem more plausible or important. They will denigrate others and smear their names to draw attention to themselves, so they can eject their malicious garbage. If the truth is spoken with gentleness and respect, people are more apt to listen (1 PE 3:15).

Scrutinize the delivery of the message and it might divulge an ulterior motive. Exposing a lie can result in illuminating the truth.

One of the faculties that make us special is our ability to discern many things, such as right from wrong, good from evil, real from unreal, rational from irrational, objective from subjective, positive from negative, true from untrue. There is nothing relative about it. Do you suppose these proficiencies evolved from lesser species? Or, did we receive them from God for a purpose? If we could not discern or reason, there would be neither science, philosophy, nor religion, much less discovery and invention. We are superior precisely because God wants us to enrich the planet and the animals. He wants us to gain knowledge of him and his creation, not just watch us grazing. He wants us to communicate with him and love him. God has communicated to us by cracking open the door of his mind, through which we get a glimpse of reality, truth, righteousness, and life. Without our advanced capabilities it would be impossible to approach God, much less apprehend his revelations or encounter this universe.

You cannot cheat truth and you cannot cheat death; for all will be revealed someday (LUK 8:17). And everyone will appear before God and give an account (ROM 14:12). Even if you think you can get away with it, you are found out in the end (NUM 32:23; PRO 13:6); because nobody is ever alone since God is there and he is aware. Ask yourself if God would approve of your private schemes and secrets. Better to be an open book than to have someone open it for you. Even when the truth hurts it won't last as long as the pain caused through lying and deceit.

I would like to make one final point about truth, which gets back to the issue of exclusivity. Truth is about as exclusive as it comes, insofar as it excludes everything else that contradicts. Truth is not subject to debate; if something is not true it is either false or unknown. Truth is known, it is verifiable, and it is absolute; no sensible argument can be made to debunk, disbelieve, or doubt truth. Those who deny truth are absolutely wrong.

Absolution

Absolution refers to absolving someone of sins; it literally means to be "set free." Absolution implies that your sins will never be counted against you. When Jesus Christ removes your sins, he removes every sin you will ever commit. A person may forgive another, but that does not absolve the wrongdoer of consequences. A criminal will have to face a judge or jury, whether the victim forgives the perpetrator or not. Even if a malefactor thinks he or she got away with a crime there still will be consequences, they just don't know what or when. But in the case of absolution, there is no more to be said about one's sins; for they have been extinguished permanently along with setting aside the eternal punishment.

In order to gain entrance into heaven, your sinful flesh must be cleansed by the blood of Jesus (1 PE 1:18–21). If you believe and trust in him your sins are absolutely forgotten (ISA 43:25; HEB 8:12). God will not impose any penalty or payment. Only Christ can absolve sins as he is the one who made payment for them. The Roman Catholic Church has a rite in which absolution is granted in lieu of penance. This is a nonbiblical concept. There is no compensation or punishment levied on those who trust that Christ has atoned for their sins. This does not mean that absolution cannot be pronounced in the name of the Father, Son and Holy Ghost, as long as the person receiving full forgiveness believes wholeheartedly in the salvation bought for them by Christ. But a priest, pastor, minister, layperson, or anybody else cannot acquit anyone of their sins. Only through Christ by the power of the Holy Spirit can anyone be set free.

Once again, I am stating an absolute. Either a person is absolutely free or they are not (JOH 8:38). There is no such thing as being partially saved. There is no such thing as being in-between heaven and hell, as if one could alter their destiny after death. When you die that's it; there is no further opportunity for absolution (PSA 6:4–5; ISA 38:18). You need to be purified, regenerated, and sanctified before you die. Are you absolutely sure that you are saved? If you are not sure, take a hard look at yourself. Once you accept Christ as your personal Savior, and depend upon him exclusively for your salvation, you are absolutely going to heaven. And eternal life is absolutely forevermore. Yes, we may doubt from time to time and that is normal (MAR 9:17–27). But when faced with the decision whether to confess the Gospel of Christ or not, you'd better be certain. In times of doubt we can turn again to God and ask for the Comforter (the Holy Spirit) to reassure us and strengthen us when we are down and out (JOH 14:16,26). You have the ability to submit yourself to God or to the world; the latter is to be condemned. If you cherish the Lord, he will lift you up in his loving arms where you will be safe and secure (PSA 23:1–6); but you have to want his blessing and respond accordingly to his lovingkindness with your love and commitment.

I have examined a number of absolutes in this text. The following are ascribed to God.

- Absolute love (*agape*) is the perfect, unselfish, pure, and unconditional love of God. It is never-ending and all powerful, and it is bestowed upon all living creatures. God's grace and mercy are revealed through his love, given freely to all who will receive it.
- Absolute truth represents unadulterated, complete, and all-encompassing facts that remain certain and true forever and for everyone. One could say it is the truth, the whole truth, and nothing but the truth, spoken through God's Holy Spirit (*logos*).
- Absolute power is the unrestricted, unlimited, incomparable, and incomprehensible omnipotence of God. It would take no less to create or erase a universe beaming with life much less an infinite number of universes.
- Absolute knowledge is the total understanding of all things visible and invisible, to include past, present and future, natural and supernatural. It is another characteristic of our omniscient God from whom all knowledge, wisdom, and understanding proceeds, bestowed upon us in accordance with his will.
- Absolute holiness reflects the righteousness, justice, sacredness, and beauty of the Lord our God. It can be seen in the man Jesus Christ who was excellent, pure, and faultless; and whose unyielding obedience to law, morality, and truth were demonstrated by the offering of himself on the cross as the perfect atoning sacrifice. How else could our sins have been absolved and forgotten if not by God himself (MAR 2:1–12)?
- Absolute sovereignty speaks to the eternal and supreme reign of God. In human terms he is the creator and sustainer of the universe and he is our Father. He is in total authority over everything to include dominions, powers, governments, and leaders (DAN 2:17–23; ROM 13:1–2), as well as the hosts of heaven and the inhabitants of earth. His will is done no matter what, and it is all for a reason which makes sense when he decides we are ready to understand (ISA 46:9–10; DAN 4:34–35). Whatever was, is, and will be is the way he has commanded it (EPH 1:11). It does no good to predict what he will do next because it all has been planned and synchronized in such an elaborate way that we will need eternity to figure it out (JOB 38:2–6; JOB 40:2; JOB 42:1–2). However, we can be absolutely sure that God will do what he says. If you want to know what he has to say, keep reading the Holy Bible.

➤ Absolute eternality reflects the infiniteness of God, his immutability, indivisibility, and perpetual actuality. He is a transcendent being in every respect, not the least of which is his perfection, which is why he cannot change. The Holy Trinity is real, pure, right, true, and alive. He is fully self-existing, timeless, and supernatural.

Being the only good, impeccable, unchanging, and holy being, God has established the moral law. Morality is based on his absolutely perfect love, a standard that humans cannot attain without absolution. Even so, everybody can discover what is true and what is right. Simply weigh each situation and decision in terms of what really matters the most. Which is more important, protecting your family or protecting yourself? Which is the greater good, being obedient to God or making charitable contributions (1 SA 15:22; MAT 23:23)? How do you conquer sin, by refining your thoughts or by modifying your behavior? Which is more powerful, hope or hopelessness? If you are thoughtful concerning these matters the answers will be abundantly clear.

The relativists and naturalists do not believe in absolutes. This is counterintuitive since the mere suggestion that "all is relative" indicates a one-track mind. Relativists hold that anything and everything can be subject to change, redefinition, or revision. There is no completely whole and perfect being or concept to them. But they are totally in error. If everything is relative, then nothing they say can be substantial to anyone, as it will be subject to the relative vantage point of everyone else. And since no two persons have the same experience, they could in no way see eye-to-eye with another person on a single matter if all was relative. That is, there would never be absolute agreement. But if everybody was absolutely dispersed in their thinking, there also would be no morality, justice, freedom, or faith. Without equality, which itself is an absolute concept, we would have no rights, laws, free will, aptitude, or promise. Though people cannot administer equality across the board due to our sinful nature, God (and only God) is willing and able. Therefore, his independence, justice, fairness, and impartiality are absolutely enforced equally on everyone (DEU 32:3–4).

While there are absolutes declared in the scientific realm, these are not necessarily invariant. For example, absolute zero (zero degrees Kelvin) is the temperature at which everything freezes; nothing moves, not even atoms. While this may be the coldest conceivable temperature to a physicist, that doesn't make it absolute to God. Even constants like light and gravity are subject to undetectable variations, as well as purposeful alterations by God

(JOS 10:12–14; ISA 38:7–8). Physicists admit that physics at the quantum level behave differently than in the classical sense. Furthermore, God is preparing or has formed a new universe (JOH 14:1–4); for all we know it will not adhere to the same physics and chemistry as the universe we live in now. Good luck trying to figure that one out. The limitations of our feeble minds prohibit approaching the wisdom of God (ISA 55:8–9; 1 CO 3:19). It follows that only God can be described in absolute terms as well as those things that proceed from him like absolute love, truth, and righteousness.

If you believe that you can soar through this world as a free spirit go ahead and try. You will find yourself as a bird trying to escape from a cathedral, eventually realizing you have no way out, your search is futile, and you are bruised and weary. But if you are absolved of sin, you will be able to soar through eternity with no restraints. Such is absolute freedom, something that will never be experienced down here for there are restrictions. On the earth, we are chained by sin and the penalty is death, neither of which will you find in heaven. But when Christ sets you free you will be free indeed (JOH 8:31–38; GAL 5:1). How I long for that kind of freedom.

Don't let anyone deceive you into thinking the Holy Bible is just a fairy tale. The God who possesses the attributes delineated above will make episodes happen that you cannot begin to gauge. But I encourage you to imagine the wonders of God nevertheless. Let your mind soar in deep contemplation, and let your light shine all the way to heaven. Feature God in your journey and you just might gather that he is not an invention of man but the other way around. He will steer you towards his Word, so that you can begin to accurately envision the wonders of his works and his thoughts. If that does not inspire you nothing will.

With absolution comes adoption. If you have chosen God to be your Father, he will choose you to be his son or daughter. And he will give you the same affection and inheritance of his only begotten Son because you bear his name (2 CO 1:21–22; EPH 1:13; REV 22:3–4). The chosen are connected to God in love for eternity. That same love connects us to one another. Do you not love your children unconditionally, your spouse, siblings, parents? Do you love your neighbor as yourself? Well I hope you will try; but alas, we are incapable of absolutely unconditional love, at least in this life. Not so in the next life. In heaven, we will be brothers and sisters with Christ and children of the Most High.

It is a lovely and rare event when an adopted child is treated as an equal to a biological child. Oftentimes there is preferential treatment that leaves the adopted child with an inferiority complex. In fact, a great number of these kids develop an adjustment problem due to perceived abandonment by their biological parents. This frequently continues into adulthood, such that it is very difficult for many to establish healthy attachments with others. Certainly, there are a number of mental health issues coupled with attachment disorders. But feelings of detachment disappear once a person has experienced the love and grace of God. One may not have earthly parents that loved and nurtured them, though their heavenly Father was always there, loving and caring. Once people recognize this, the loneliness disappears, a connection is forged between them and God, and they are able to love and connect with others, even strangers. In God we are made equal; and good or bad, we are equally loved by him.

Diversity and Division

Before I open this topic, I must define terms to avoid having them misconstrued through semantic gymnastics. Diversity represents variety, individual differences if you will. This is a good thing; like the saying goes, variety is the spice of life. When people of diverse backgrounds and experience come together in unity, you have university, the opportunity for growth and knowledge. Division represents separation, divergence; and it produces disunity. This is not a good thing. The former produces great power, strength of minds joined together. The latter fragments that power in an unbalanced distribution. We work best when we work together, as long as there is a common direction. The single, most devastating enemy of unity is sin because it separates us from one another and from God.

Our illustrious nation has been referred to as a melting pot with respect to the diversity of worldviews, ethnicities, religions, beliefs, and ideas. Actually, diversity is one of the attributes that has made America great. When you combine the extraordinary talent, distinction, and potential of each citizen, you reach levels of greatness in the whole that far exceeds that of individuals. In other words, the effect is multiplicative, not additive. Diversity truly unifies us; and we will prosper as a people if we bind with one another for the common good and not for selfish or ideological purposes. This requires mutual respect, understanding, and acceptance. It requires cooperation, collaboration, and sharing of viewpoints and philosophies. Remove any of the above-mentioned qualities and we will lose sight of the goodness, growth, destiny, and supremacy that enabled this country to reach its pinnacle of success, prosperity, parity, and fortune.

Why then, should we bend to those striving for division, dissention, and disunion? We cannot endorse individuals and groups that deny the rights and freedoms of other individuals and groups. Why doesn't the government or law enforcement mediate, given that human rights are supposed to be sacred in this country? And to top it off, divisive behavior is being funded, inspired, and emboldened by the affluent, influential, powerful, commanding, and controlling entities seeking to dismantle our republic, our charter, and our egalitarian way of life. Under the guise of diversity, tolerance, and respect for rights, these virtues are being deprived in a most underhanded manner. Diversity is treasured when combined with unity. But disunity and division will result in deletion of any and all diversity and identity. Intuitively, this tactic leads to only one worldview, the one condoned by elitism, wherewith individuality will be obliterated along with civil rights, and political and economic freedom until ultimately, we regress into serfdom (Hayek, 1944).

Division is infiltrating the church as well, to include infighting within and between congregations and denominations, causing splitting and dissolution. There may be some variance in traditions, expectations, and regulations but these are not reasons to become adversaries. There are more similarities among factions than dissimilarities, and this happens to be the case regardless of religion or political slant, as long as the standard of the highest good is maintained. It is disparaging when people focus solely on their differences and ignore their similarities (ROM 16:17). They look for reasons to disagree or disconnect. Regarding Christianity, there are central doctrines that unite all denominations; sadly, many churches and sects are veering too far from the beaten path and into beliefs, customs, and dogmas that are not only unscriptural but blatantly antichristian. God warned about those who would create dissention in the church or introduce dissimilar doctrines (ROM 16:11; 1 CO 1:10; HEB 13:8–9). Any degree of impurity can contaminate the entire river especially with respect to the Holy Bible and its inerrancy.

This is the gravest threat to biblical theology, the watering down of scripture if not the flagrant retranslation of it. It has resulted in aberrant theologies. There are more denominations now than you can shake a stick at, the majority of which have deemphasized faith and promoted works, whereby the idea of being a "good" person is the prime directive. You can find everything from the preaching of hellfire and brimstone to let's just get along, shall we. After the Reformation, diverse Protestant congregations emerged. While the diversity itself was not counterproductive, separatism later seeped in. Divisions concerning dogmatics and creeds worsened, with digressing positions on tradition, evangelism, worship, human nature, and eschatology (e.g., millennialism, postmillennialism, amillennialism). Some churches chose to take a doctrinal posture on these issues as if they had anything to do with salvation or essential truth.

There has been an introduction of new theologies and practices to meet a growing yen for increased spontaneity and to enhance the experience of worship. After the spawning of Pentecostal and Charismatic sects, emergent denominations became a dime a dozen; new brands and offshoots sprouted. Religions and churches became big business, many of them preaching prosperity over piety as exhibited by their extravagance. Houses of worship became commercialized, like tourist traps, complete with sideshows and staged antics.

There remains a thirst for spirituality; people seeking psychic advisors, faith healers, gurus, enlightened ones, etc., and following anyone with a convincing theory or a claim to the truth. Institutions and leaders purport to accommodate diverse subpopulations and designations in order to be all-inclusive; but they have wandered far afield from the original intent of the Reformation: *sola scriptura*, which is to say, the Holy Bible is the backbone. Consequently, religiosity ends by alienating everyone from the written truth of God's Word, which has cautioned against seeking teachers that repeat only what congregants want to hear (2 TI 4:3–4).

Young people are especially vulnerable. I remember bad influences in my life that didn't appreciate me progressing or prospering, some of whom I once counted as friends. I didn't condescend or disrespect them, but they distanced themselves from me as if our differences were insurmountable. They were departing from the path when we parted ways, supposing I should pursue them to retain our association. When they ceased to be part of my support, they became part of my problem. Had I not discontinued those relationships God knows what might have happened (JDE 1:18–19). They were mere acquaintances at that point; some became addicts, criminals, or antichristian; some died untimely deaths, lost everything, or ended up destitute. A handful of my friends remain whom I consider part of my true family. And people who sincerely try to follow Christ as I try to do, also are part of my family, because I know they will not betray the truth, their Christian faith, or me. It boils down to either following Jesus and his Golden Rule or making your own rules. But rest assured, a minority of elites will be making the rules and imposing them on you if you go that route.

Beware of anyone who follows the ways of darkness, for their minds are clouded with innuendo and illusion such that true wisdom escapes them; whereby their injustices will bring swift and embarrassing reprisal (PSA 7:16; PRO 3;21–23; PRO 4:18–19; JER 13:16, JOH 11:8–10). The Gospel of Jesus Christ is true wisdom and light; those who snub the Godman and his Word are blinded by the darkness and consumed by their sinful flesh. The Bible makes it patently plain that self-centered specialists who ignore God's calling merely playact to be superior. But they are mighty only in their wickedness; they are neither noble nor strong (1 CO 1:23–27). Through the intertwining of lofty dreams, torrents of money, and profusion of words come many vanities (ECC 5:7).

Don't join their club for they are odious and dishonest; they cannot stomach diversity, and they cannot conceive integrity. People who intentionally get in the way of other people are creating a stumbling block for themselves (ROM 14:12–13,20–21), and those who follow them or their path will likewise stumble and fall (1 CO 8:6–13; 1 PE 2:6–8). We are to regard everyone as equally important with ourselves; we are to love them and build them up, not wreck their plans (ROM 14:19).

A person who exalts himself or herself over others eventually will hate those people, and consequently, hate God (TIT 3:3–4; 1 JO 2:8–11). They may feign affection for members of their cause, because evil surrounds itself with its own kind (LUK 6:31–38). Conned into thinking they are for unity because they have found it in a common enemy, they participate in smearing, profanity, and intimidation towards anyone who disagrees. Do you think the bosses have their backs or will let them increase within the organization? Heck no! Neither will they ever go to bat for anyone but themselves. Either way, they will strike out, the whole lot of them. How can they expect to make it home when they can't even make it to first base, unless someone gives them a walk? Their open door will be to a shaft with no elevator; the only way is down and the fall is fast and hard. If you sow seeds of discord, your crop will yield nothing but weeds (DEU 22:9).

We must uproot the troublemakers, agitators, dissenters, bad influencers, and their ringleaders who have no honorable motive in mind, but simply to be celebrated, compensated, empowered, and extolled. Totally out of touch with the real world, they have bought forward a new world order with themselves giving the orders; they will collect their fifteen minutes of fame and expire. The biggest threat to individual, group, or corporate happiness, success, safety, and comfort are parties such as they, who calculatingly attempt to disrupt or smother freedoms. Perhaps their hired hooligans feel deprived of such things and want others to feel deprived; or maybe they feel empowered in their aggression. For many it is the vile sense of controlling another person. For others, it is plain selfishness, the outright refusal to share, though there is plenty enough for everyone. The secular progressives, with their exaggerated political correctness, profess to be grossly offended by conservative-minded people (Carson, 2014). But their super-sensitivity is psychologically unhealthy, not unlike that of factitious disorder, whereby the "victims" present themselves as ill or injured, expecting the secondary gain of attention, sympathy, or compassion. It is pathological when their deliberate deceitfulness becomes second nature to them, not to mention spiritually reviling.

God emplaced diversity for goodness; by the power of his Spirit he gave each and every one of us important but different talents, courses, positions, and possibilities (1 CO 12:4–7). Opponents of diversity are working against God, for they are divided against him and for no good reason. Just as God enables diversity, he also invokes division, for he will divide his people from the rest (EXO 8:23; LUK 12:51). Note that his people make it home, the rest will be banished (MAT 25:31–46). Let us embrace diversity and reject division; let us persist in unity as a nation and stay strong in the power of God's might (EPH 6:10). Let us strive for and fight for the greatest good and stop backsliding into the pit. Too many are fighting for the wrong reward, for a stupid reason, or for an unworthy cause. What they deem diversity is actually division. They are working for the globalists and elitists and against the populists and themselves.

The tragedy is this: the devotees have been duped; they don't know what they are doing or the fateful outcome, because they are oblivious to the truth and too lazy to learn. They have swallowed the poison without performing a thorough inspection or tradeoff analysis. All they can see is the beginning but they have no picture of the end game. Finding gratification at the start they will find dismay at the end. With the pretext of being one of the enlightened, they have allowed their spirits to turn dark and have nothingness to guide them (MAT 6:22–24). Divide and conquer is their slogan. What else could be the aim of those community organizers behind it but greed? They are the only ones who benefit, but that will be short-lived, because the global collapse will begin with them.

There are many catalysts effecting division, separating us from the truth and from one another. The greatest uniting factor is the Gospel of Jesus Christ, but you wouldn't know it by listening to the mass media which would prefer to eradicate anything biblical. The domains listed below are targets of control, with the aim to separate us from God, our inner spirit, and one another.

1. Education: This is the main channel causing division. The impetus grew after the Scopes trial back in 1925, where it was argued in court whether or not to permit the teaching of Darwinism. In that infamous case, William Jennings Brian won the battle, but would lose the war to Clarence Darrow. Public schools won't even propose intelligent design as a viable theory, but you will find evolution taught at all levels. Nowadays, you will encounter no biblical teachings introduced in the classroom outside of religion-centered schools. Funny, because most of the premier universities began with a biblical foundation, to include Harvard, Yale, Princeton, William and Mary, U of Pennsylvania, Georgetown, Columbia, and Oxford; but many have done a complete reversal and dropped their religious platform.

Parents should keep tabs on what their children are being taught. Speak to them about it, discuss it, and clarify it. Especially counsel them about what to expect when they enroll in college. There is a deliberate attempt to persuade youth of a contrary ideology and steer them away from biblical truth (ACT 20:28–30). Not that college is a waste of time, but it is important for students to conduct independent research (sometimes I learned more via independent study than from professors). Educated, informed, and multitalented individuals are the worst enemies of the globalists (Marrs, 2008). Controlling the education system and the curricula is central to their agenda, for they intend to propagandize our youth throughout their schooling (kindergarten through graduate school).

It will be counterproductive for students to speak out against disinformation, however, as that will only invite repercussions from instructors and administrators; it will be like slamming into a brick wall. But students can make a statement by exhibiting an upright character; and they can be prepared to witness to individuals who ask. They also have the right to assemble but may resort to doing so off campus. Parents should teach their children apologetics in the home and motivate them to research this in their spare time. Otherwise, they will not be convinced of the faith in which they were raised when introduced to counterarguments by instructors, who may have themselves departed from the faith (PRO 22:6).

Another issue that deserves mention is the failure of schools to acknowledge diversity. Equality is misinterpreted as giving all kids passing grades, or the same grade; or equal praise whether merited or not; or the same trophy for those with superior versus substandard performance; or unearned reproof. Children ought to learn that equality has to do with their intrinsic value. It's about respect and opportunity; accountability, law, and order. It is recommended that educators be more partial and unequal in the amount of remediation or attention provided to students, because their need is not equal. I have encountered innumerable kids that dropped out of school because they couldn't cut it; or so they thought. Oftentimes it was because they needed more tutoring, or they needed to be held back a grade. Once kids get behind it is near impossible for them to catch up, especially if they are moved ahead before they are ready. The prime objective of schools and school boards is success; they are apt to alter the data to imply a higher graduation rate or argue that a low rate has only to do with regression towards the mean. What they will never acknowledge is incompetency.

Finally, there is an unusually high quantity of inept teachers, administrators, and school boards. But the teacher unions are powerful, making it very difficult to evaluate, remediate, or fire ineffectual teachers, not to mention require them to take periodic proficiency tests. I already touched on the inadequacy and inaccuracy of the curricula, which leave us with high school graduates having an eighth-grade reading level, who cannot do algebra, who do not recognize the founders, and who are unable to name those occupying high public office. Did they stop teaching civics altogether? I have an idea, why don't they make it mandatory to coach pupils in critical thinking and encourage them to rigorously appraise what they are being told?

2. Socialization: Culture, subculture, and counterculture play significant roles in shaping minds and attitudes. Examining history, one will discover periodic culture shifts permeating this country. They were largely influenced by our freedom to speak and assemble; these human rights used to be cherished and were established to promote an exchange of diverse ideas. When the government gets off track, or civil rights are violated, or groups of people become outraged for whatever reason, reparations can be advanced via peaceful, organized protest. Such activism has pioneered positive outcomes, as was the case for the Protestant Reformation in the sixteenth century and the Civil Rights movement in the twentieth century. This was the legacy of Martin Luther King who followed Gandhi's notion that nonviolent protest and passive resistance produce better results than aggression and hostility. Look at the effect that moderate Tea Party activists had on a recent national midterm election.

The leftists feared the Tea Party, maligning, infiltrating, and subverting the movement at every turn (Ingraham, 2017). Why? Because it threatened everything the liberal Democrats stood for (Armey and Kibbe, 2010). The outcome was the Dems lost the House and then the Senate. The Tea Party represented religious conservative-populist ideals held by the silent majority who had begun to break their silence, and that voice resounded loud and clear when the electoral votes were counted. Their political gatherings and representatives were composed, friendly, and orderly; but the media portrayed them as unruly, vicious, and revolting. The only ones subscribing to that nonsense were those putting out the false narrative. Obviously, the cause would not have been a smashing success had they been any of those things, as it would have characterized them as the very political entities they were resisting.

I remember studying Thoreau and Emerson in high school; they advocated civil disobedience. This was during the hippie movement which attempted to promote peace and love while vehemently protesting the war in Vietnam. I also remember four students being massacred at Kent State during such a protest. All of this had a profound impact on the direction of this country, which has become progressively more backwards each decade. Activism has devolved and become regressive; because, all too often an assembly turns into a riot, replete with savagery, attacks on bystanders, and destruction of property. Militant protestors have been turning out in swarms to censor duly invited speakers, preventing them from taking the podium. Hatemongers parade through the streets chanting death to police officers and other detestable obscenity, which itself should be censored. They wear disguises, itself a violation of the law in some regions, emplaced precisely to discourage violence. Disregard of laws has been unenforced as officers are ordered to back off and observe while protesters assault those promoting peace and unity. Mass media hypes the anarchy by portraying rebels as heroes or patriots, thereby invigorating backseat extremists to act out even more viciously. These vermin are the converse of heroes and patriots.

Isn't it ironic the denigrating of our actual champions, as if they must be extraordinary in valor and self-sacrifice, as well as pure as the driven snow? Jesus Christ happens to be the only perfect hero, yet I hear the same maligners diminish and belittle him unremittingly. One of the most revered stars of the Bible was King David, a man after God's own heart (1 SA 13:14; ACT 13:22), who happened to be an adulterer and a murderer (2 SA 11). Should we destroy Michelangelo's famous sculpture of David since he was such a flawed hero?

Name your hero and I will show you a sinner. This holier-than-thou attitude coming from radical, leftist, socialist wimps would be almost laughable, but for the fact that they really believe their pseudo-revolutionary posture is relevant. Ignorance, propagated by a prejudicial education system and biased media, has turned their pliable brains into mush, revealing they know nothing about the glorious history of the framing of America, and the unmitigated hardship our victors endured (the magnitude of which such students of stupidity could never fathom, much less face). So then, who are their heroes? Who do they decree to be above reproach? They don't know so they must presume, identifying only radicals belonging to the scourge of society, or the ones who recruited them to become members of the unruly class. Would they elevate world leaders today or sing the praises of the crooked politicians and government officials of their time, whose impertinent behavior actually illuminates the saintliness of those so-called tainted heroes from American history? Do these disingenuous brats believe themselves qualified to define standards for excellence? Any timid individual who steps up to the plate and selflessly comes to the aid of fellow Americans is a hero in my book, though equally errant as you and me.

One side of the coin reveals individual freedom; the other, doing the right thing, which is loving your neighbor as yourself. We have been decimated by floods, earthquakes, wildfires, and shootings in which heroes have emerged, loving, caring, and doing for others what you would have them do for you. Which type are you, the one to stop and render aid or the one who keeps running? Are you the one who pauses before a statue because it brings to mind the cause for which that individual stood, strove, fought, or died... or the one who brings that statue down? Do you make a spectacle of yourself in stoic protest, or do you humbly and silently do something proactively to right the wrongs you've witnessed?

Beware, my fellow Americans. The First Amendment does not ratify hate speech, riotous assembly, or inventing news. I have seen celebrities, activists, even politicians advocating bloodshed against conservatives, policemen, and heads of state; I have seen white supremacists retaliate and spew their hateful rhetoric as well. These extremists do not represent the mainstream, but pariahs of their particular demographic. Fascists are multiplying like roaches, committing horrific acts of turpitude, even homicide, against others they accuse of being the fascists. In reality, all of these rabble-rousers are anarchists at best, devils at worst. Surely there are fringe elements on all sides of an issue, and undoubtedly, those people do not represent the whole of a particular ideology. But it is the clash of cultures that widens the divide, usually perpetrated by fanatics, psychopaths, and vigilantes among every ideological, theological, and sociopolitical bent. Such has led to the anti-socialization of America.

Another social divide arises when newcomers to our country refuse to assimilate into our culture and insist on maintaining a separate identity other than American. They want everyone to accommodate them but they are the most unaccommodating. This leads our discussion into the realm of identity politics. People vote for people that look like them or talk like them, without scrutinizing a candidate's track record of words, policies, and actions. It shouldn't matter if they are male or female, black or white, straight or gay, Democrat or Republican, rich or poor, or anything else, as long as a person has the right ideas at the right time, and their heart is in the right place (MAT 6:21).

3. Politicization: The trend these days is for those in office to politicize every single item that comes down the pipe. In fact, a popular leftwing tactic is to take advantage of each crisis and create a political football out of it in order to score points against the conservative right, or shove through undemocratic agendas and irrational spending projects. Instead of addressing the actual problem, they magnify ancillary conditions or demands, focus the blame on the other side, invoke stall tactics, and divert attention from real facts or causes. Diversity is not the aim and neither is unity; the aim is to dominate the dialogue instead of coming together to find solutions.

Some people flat refuse to be united in any fashion with those who disagree with them. We fought an entire civil war over such division and may be facing another one soon. We were able to abolish slavery forever in our land, but unfortunately, we were unable to eradicate bigotry and prejudice. This enflamed the pandemonium during the 1960s and into the 1970s when we went from segregation to desegregation, neither of which made sense or worked to settle anything. And though the country has enjoyed decades of ethnic peace without government intervention, we have slipped back into a partisan quagmire of separation, mostly thanks to certain government and political pundits, creating a divide between races as well as all segments of society. Once upon a time the rightwing and the leftwing were able to pass bipartisan legislation, but lately it has been nothing but resistance and obstruction. Wouldn't it be nice if Congress would unite and get something practical accomplished?

Are you up to speed in civics? Did you know that the Democrats were the original land-grabbing racists and segregationists, and still are? At the inception of the party they were mostly white supremacists who were anti-civil rights and pro-slavery (Bartlett, 2008). It was the Republican party that managed to draft and pass bills granting equal rights to blacks, women, and minorities, despite ardent opposition from the Dems. Now the Democrats claim to be the titleholders of civil rights, and masquerade as minority advocates, while painting Republicans as xenophobes and discriminators. In order to make reparations for past sins the Dems offer economic carrots to minorities and illegal aliens. But their motives are more sinister than altruistic, as the objective is always to shift the minority vote to their favor, while making minorities more dependent on the government than on themselves. This itself is demeaning and condescending, forcing the disadvantaged into a lower social class all over again. It is all about garnering "cheap" votes via open borders and sanctuary cities; combating immigration enforcement and opposing voter identification; portraying immigrants as the only people who are willing to pick cotton, avocados, or oranges; and if that doesn't work, it's outright cheating. Not that cheating doesn't occur in all segments of society to some degree, but who actually has your best interest in mind?

Yes, you surely can coax a great many to join the party if there is no cover charge and everything is on the house. Would you call this progress; or is it closer to regress if not control? It certainly does not reflect morality or equality, but superiority. Come to mama little people and we'll take care of you. I would think legal immigrants would be far more interested in the American Dream, whereas perpetual welfare is nowhere near it. Again, ultimate control of the people and the narrative is where this goes, a precursor to globalism by way of socialism.

So, which political party actually holds the moral high ground? Parties do not hold it, people do. We need to select them and deselect the deadbeats. When Congress has a chance to set things right, they seem to shuffle their feet a lot, and barely make it as far as the bathroom. When they finally pass a bipartisan bill, it looks nothing like the contract they made with Americans.

4. Religion: Doubtless, the primary influence energizing the American experiment has been the Holy Bible. I'm sure many today would dispute that fact but study your history (if you can find an accurate history book). It has become inconvenient to depend on God anymore or to cling to faith. The diluting of religion in this country has chiefly come as a result of giant leaps in the fields of science and technology. Though the discoveries and advances opened our minds to unending possibilities, they were misconstrued as being antithetical to religion. The separation of religion from everything else ensued, to include science, government, and culture. This divergence has been amplified with the current fundamentalist-modernist divide, particularly within religion and among evangelicals (Fitzgerald, 2017). A distinct departure from a literal understanding of the Bible has occurred, with the expectation that religion be readapted to oblige scientific theory and progressive thinking.

When it comes to scientific facts there is no disagreement with religious facts. Facts are facts regardless of how they are acquired. Attempts to integrate unproven theories or nonfactual information with the truth will never create a healthy merging between science and religion. Are evolution of man and creation of man compatible? No. Is science and religion compatible? Yes. People of faith have been stereotyped as unschooled, unsophisticated, rural, outdated, narrow-minded, and more. This has heightened since the love generation (baby boomers) sought new ways of discovering and expressing spiritualism. They moved from the faith in which they were raised into eastern philosophies and experiential avenues to illumination, embracing Hinduism, Buddhism (particularly Zen), and Transcendental Meditation, not to mention experimentation with mind-altering drugs. When they were unable to find themselves, they simply turned to secular humanism and that stuck. I for one, broke free of such inanity.

Religion has assumed a new face, having little to do with the worship of God or adherence to his Word. In fact, the term seldom refers to belief and adoration of a supreme being anymore but has a negative undertone that is unchristian. The subject of religion has taken on irreligious connotations, such as God being an invention of humans, Christian rituals and traditions being old-fashioned, backward, or nontheistic, and the practice of religion being irrelevant to one's personal faith or worldview. What is ignored is that religion is precisely the practice of one's faith and the foundation of a belief system, not a wayward description of it (JAM 1:26–27). But in order to respect religious freedom we are now forced to invite any belief system, to include the adulation of oneself, idols, animals, the cosmos, invented spirits, demons, and inanimate objects. Freedom of religion now covers anything that can be construed as a creed, such that nonprofit status is extended to institutions and organizations that are blatantly irreligious and irreverent, while that status is denied to legitimate faith-based groups. Inventors are devising new religions every day, so is it any wonder how the term "religion" has been redefined if not adulterated?

5. *Economics:* Certainly, economic conditions can be a catalyst for division; this especially will be the case during the latter days. Money provides clout and can buy a lot of things, not the least of which is influence, particularly over politicians and the media. Lack of money can produce poverty, unrest, and rebellion. Look at the devastating effects on individual freedom and happiness from economic depression, recession, inflation, stock market fluctuations and failures, unemployment, increased entitlements, government waste, and general uncertainty and fear. Such things cause mayhem and unrest abroad as well, and often lead to wars, not to mention a greater reach towards globalism. But the most devastating effect has been on individual mental health, increasing the rate of suicide and other irrational behaviors.

Many governments are under siege by deprived and oppressed citizens and for good reason. They legitimately doubt their leaders' ability to protect and prosper them. Developing countries are especially vulnerable as the next regime consists of incompetent powermongers with no leadership skills who merely repeat the atrocities of preceding rulers. They are careless with the money and resources, preventing any reforms, repairs, opportunities, or modernization, neglecting the needs of the people, unable to create jobs, and falling behind the rest of the world technologically and competitively. Consequently, the gap widens between the privileged and the impoverished (Bremmer, 2018). Inequality also broadens between classes, subcultures, and ethnic groups, not to mention education and employability. This spells economic disaster and makes a country ripe for exploitation by dictators, maniacs, and opportunists.

Foreign affairs exacerbate the problem, what with the uncertainty associated with broken treaties, nuclear proliferation, regional conflicts, mass migration, unpredictable reprobate leaders, communism, and nations experiencing civil war, unrest, and economic turmoil. And what does America do about that? We invoke economic sanctions to further confound their problems, making us their prime target because in their minds we are responsible for their woes. We intervene militarily, thinking we can democratize them by force, only to radicalize both sides against us. We need to be making allies not enemies. It's okay to back regimes that have their heads on straight. We don't need to be flooding dollars into dilapidated economies, however, especially when their leaders despise the USA. Review the section on Economic Disaster for more on this topic.

6. Conflict. War and civil unrest have broken out around the globe due to all the conditions outlined above. The USA is at war with terrorism, a very enigmatic enemy, not to mention engaging in cold wars with China and Russia. Here in America it looks like civil war is brewing. Nothing divides people more than war. But people can be united by making peace. What religious, political, or sociocultural entity other than a united Christian America would be able to withstand and thwart an evil global empire from taking over? Notice that the weakening of our faith foundation and the collapse of our economy are the very results the globalists seek. If anything, we should declare war against them. Yet, a thorough reading of end times prophecy does not appear to include the USA in any scenario. Could this mean divided we will fall, and subsequently fail? I pray not. But this was the greatest fear of our forefathers, that we would implode from within.

Hence, either we are destined to reunite and regain the moral high ground or God will similarly abandon us, pretty much like everyone else seems to be doing. I would like to see a revival of faith in this country. Though I regard myself as an independent thinker, I judge conventional conservatism to be more aligned with my Christian beliefs than modern liberalism. I cannot deny being invigorated by the novel resurgence in this country of the Christian silent majority. This movement has been positively shaping our country from the beginning, founded mainly on morality and theism, and reflected to some degree in fundamentalism, altruism, pragmatism, and utilitarianism. If I am forced to take sides, I choose inclusivity over separatism, populism over pluralism, nationalism over globalism, democratism over socialism, and constitutionalism over revisionism.

THE ESSENTIALS

Do you want to be on the right side, to know the truth, to act appropriately, to feel blessed? What must a person believe to receive the incomparable gift of eternal life? What do I have to do to become a child of God and a member of his household? How can I be saved? I trust you have at least a passing curiosity in these matters. Don't you have the time to contemplate for a few minutes your fate, your salvation? Or are you too busy for God? I sincerely hope not. I will begin by conveying some of the essential doctrines of Christianity based on two significant proclamations of the Christian faith: *The Smalcald Articles* submitted by Martin Luther (1537) and the *Augsburg Confession* submitted by Philip Melanchthon (1530). These documents proclaimed the position of the Reformation torchbearers. Did you know the world recently celebrated the 500th anniversary of the Protestant Reformation, initiated when Luther nailed his ninety-five theses to the castle church door in Wittenberg Germany on 10/31/1517?

➢ The divinity of God is undeniable; he is eternal, unchanging, the creator and preserver of the universe, humanity, and all things visible and invisible; perfect in goodness, holiness, and justice; absolute in power, presence, and knowledge. God, who is one, exists in three distinct and equal persons: the Almighty Father; the only begotten Son, the Godman Jesus Christ (PSA 2:7; JOH 5:23); and the Holy Spirit that proceeds from both the Father and the Son. The Holy Trinity is clearly spelled out in both Old and New Testaments (ISA 48:16; JOH 1:1,14; 1 JO 5:7–8). There is no other, alive or dead, including angels and saints that should be the recipient of worship, veneration, and prayer but our Triune God (DEU 6:4; MAT 28:19; 2 CO 13:14); anything else would be idolatry and reprehensible to God (MAT 4:10; COL 2:18; REV 22:8–9).

➢ Humans, though created in the image of God, are sinful by nature; that is, we have an evil side where our wicked thoughts become manifested in rebellion (GEN 8:21; ROM 8:7). Sin is an infection or curse that has fallen upon every natural born person (PSA 51:5; ROM 6:11–13); we are conceived in sin and we are culpable for sin (JAM 4:17). Therefore, no individual is able to be justified before God by their own merit or works.

We can be justified only by faith which is a gift of the Holy Spirit, available to anyone who will receive this gift through Christ (EPH 2:8–9). God became a man precisely to show us the way, to be an example of obedience, to provide atonement for our sins, and to raise us into eternal life, as long as we cling to that saving faith (ROM 5:1).

➢ The ministry and teaching of the Gospel of Jesus Christ is the foundation of our faith (ROM 1:16–17; EPH 2:19–27), through which we are sanctified by the Holy Spirit to be conformed into the image of our Lord (1 CO 6:11; 2 CO 6:14–18; 1 PE 2:5). Our commitment and submission are demonstrated through participation in the Sacraments of Baptism and Holy Communion (ACT 2:38–39; GAL 3:26–27; 1 CO 10:16; 1 CO 11:23–29); hearing and study of God's Word the Holy Bible (JAM 1:22); fellowship with other Christians in worship and service (HEB 10:21–25); and witnessing to others who are interested in what we have found in Christ (1 CO 2:14). We are compelled to bear good fruit in devotion to his eminence, not as an attempt to earn his favor (MAT 3:8; JOH 15:8).

➢ The holy church comprises the community of saints, the body of Christ which is held together by him and also lives forever with him (ROM 12:4–5); we edify and are edified by that church and fellow believers. The church is not to be defined or bound by traditions, rites, pilgrimages, vows, fasts, and regulations commanded by people (MAT 15:9). Additionally, certain holidays, festivals, practices, and ceremonies instituted by churches are not compulsory and do not contribute to one's consecration (HEB 10:10–18). This is not to say that an individual must never choose to participate in these activities as a personal act of worship or sacrifice (COL 3:17,23); in fact, it is good to make personal sacrifices to God out of reverence, as a tendering of ourselves, and in tribute to him (ROM 12:1).

➢ Obligations imposed by leaders are not always in conformance with God's Word, however. Firstly, the imposition of celibacy placed upon clergymen is unscriptural (1 TI 3:1–12; 1 TI 4:1–7); it is unnatural and unbinding to refrain from love, marriage, and children when in accordance with the biblical prescription (GEN 2:18; 1 CO 7:2–9). Does that mean God expects us to marry? No, wedlock is a privilege, a blessing, and a responsibility; but it is not for everyone (1 CO 7:8–10). Secondly, it is unnecessary for parishioners to enumerate their sins to a priest, seeing how it is impossible to recount all of your transgressions (PSA 19:12). Does that mean we are not required to confess and repent our sins to God, or confess them to one another? No (PRO 28:13; JAM 5:16; 1 JO 1:8–9), we should appeal to God with a contrite heart by repenting, thanking, and praising him every day (PSA 51:17; MAR 1:15; ACT 17:30–31); we also should seek forgiveness from people we have wronged and likewise offer forgiveness to those who have wronged us (MAT 6:14–15).

- The Protestant Reformation disputed a number of divergent practices which were being imposed by the Catholic church at the time. I urge you to peruse the disputes which Luther raised half a century ago; he objected to many unorthodox practices such as praying to saints, which ran contrary to God's instruction. We are to pray to the Father in Jesus's name, a name which is above all other names (PHP 2:8–11). Do you think God responds to prayers offered in Mary's name? Maybe, but I wouldn't count on it, because Jesus is the only intermediary. Also, the paying of indulgences to bail out people from purgatory is completely improper. Jesus paid for all sins in full, and for all time (HEB 10:10–12). There is no place called purgatory; upon death, the soul either resides with the condemned or with the saved. There is no salvation beyond the grave (PSA 6:5; HEB 9:27); neither is there a doctrine in the Bible that proposes one should pray for the souls of the dead (ECC 9:5; ECC 12:7). Once you die, that's it; your fate is sealed (DAN 12:2; HEB 9:27).
- There is nobody who is God's advocate to the world save Jesus Christ (COL 2:16–23). In short, it is unnecessary to go through an earthly mediator, an angel, or a saint to get to God; our mediator is Jesus Christ himself (1 TI 2:5; 1 JO 2:1). Those who minister, teach, or lead are not to be exalted, though they are sent by God into the mission field to do his work. Ministers of the Word have the authority to proclaim the Gospel, teach the scriptures, administer the sacraments, forgive sins in Jesus's name, bless parishioners in the name of the Father, Son, and Holy Ghost, and perform rites of dedication such as marriage and confirmation. And by the power vested in them and their office by God, they may perform feats greater than these if credit is awarded to God alone (ACT 3:1–20; ACT 4:1–14; HEB 11:17–35). There is not a single soul who can instigate these bonds without the power of the Holy Spirit working through him or her (MAT 19:24–26).
- Though separated from the world, Christians are still bound by the laws of the land (ROM 13:1–7; 1 PE 2:13–14). We are capable of making proper moral judgments, and we are expected to be law abiding. We are

free to make choices, own property, enter into contracts, and hold public office. We can celebrate special occasions, consult physicians and therapists, and do anything else that is lawful and upright. Everything works, if in accordance with the will of God (1 CO 6:12; 1 CO 10:23). It is inadvisable, however, to do anything that runs against God's Word, which is why everyone should read it and digest it.

Nature Versus Nurture

Though possessing aptitudes awarded us by God, we are nevertheless quite the opposite of him; for he is by nature holy and we are by nature sinful. We are allowed to select a path, but only one path leads to God and that is Jesus Christ. The rest of the choices are worldly. It is fair to say that earthly pursuits are not necessarily against God, for our sustenance is provided within nature which God installed for our benefit. Everything we need will be found on the path of righteousness; if we follow Christ, we can achieve our worldly goals and satisfy our natural desires (MAT 6:33). But if we seek to placate our own will we invite disappointment and may become disillusioned.

Because of our sin we defile not only ourselves but also the land where we have prospered (LEV 18:20-28; DEU 7:11–15; DEU 28:9–28; DEU 30:15–20); that is, our sinful nature has become a pandemic to nature herself (GEN 3:17; 2 CH 7:14; JER 3:4–9,19). Corruption is contagious, like the spreading of a bacterial infection, which makes a person sicker and weaker and a health hazard to others. And when governments become corrupt so do the people, and when the people are corrupt so will be the government. If you radiate negativity and depravity that is what you will attract; the reverse also is true, so I recommend being positive and nurturing. Either way, you likely will surround yourselves with likeminded people. By the look of it, the entire planet is becoming tarnished and its leaders shady. Is it possible to reverse the damage and divert the perversion? Well, anything is possible with God; without him the world will come to ruin.

To ensure your kids and loved ones are following the right path, they must be drilled and groomed in the ways of the Lord (PRO 22:6; EPH 6:4). Upon reaching the age of accountability, people must infuse themselves with love, truth, and ethical notions. Otherwise, they will be all the more vulnerable to the lusts of the world. While there is abundance on this planet for everyone to satisfy and sustain, to overindulge or to abuse anything of the physical realm is unhealthy if not life-threatening. Go ahead and use it but do not abuse it, else you may suffer the wrath of nature, or worse, the wrath of God. There are consequences in this life and the next; truly you reap what you sow in both spheres (GAL 6:6–8).

What are we to do, given our sins have condemned us? It's easy really; just love everyone, beginning with God. Remember, love is the ultimate virtue. Love is what saves us (JOH 3:16). Question: what does a child need most in order to grow up of sound mind, body, and spirit? Answer: love. Nurturing and caring are the best methods for rearing children if you want them to flourish. However, there is no guarantee since they too can become entangled in the diversions of the world. Unconditional love like the kind a parent has for his or her child is natural, as well as otherworldly. It is the power of God our Father passed onto all living creatures, which blossom in the presence of love and wilt in its absence.

The two-parent system of one man and one woman is the ideal setup for the raising of children, provided that mom and dad also love each other and model that love in the home. The family is the most solid system by far for promoting morality and achievement regardless of culture. It is easy to see how the breakdown of families has led to the debasement of society. Remove God from the home, the school, and the society and what do you get? You get adultery, divorce, redefinition of matrimony, open relationships, deadbeat dads, moms that exclude dads, same sex parenting, infanticide, abandonment, irresponsible kids, platonic associations, compromising of religious freedom, discriminating against Christians and people of faith, rewriting of the laws to encourage if not promote deviant sexual behavior, addiction, and so forth. Is it any wonder the family has taken the biggest hit? And that has produced a most deleterious effect on societies worldwide.

Research has proven time and again that a nurturing environment produces superior offspring as opposed to a deprived environment. Genetics has very little if nothing to do with one's growth potential. God provides nurturing to every living being (PSA 145:15–16); in like manner, we are to provide nurturing to one another. Without it a person falls into despair until there is nothing to live for. Nature needs fostering as well or it will die. It's a miracle humankind hasn't already destroyed the planet with all the pollution, demolition, and neglect. Companies dump chemicals into rivers and lakes killing them; wildfires raze grasslands and forests due to human carelessness or intention; governments misuse nuclear devices and contaminate the ground and water indefinitely; rain forests have been decimated never to recuperate; animal species have neared extinction or already died out; all these examples are motivated by profiteering and selfishness. The physical domain provides valuable and precious natural resources that must be preserved. Undoubtedly, if we run out of clean air and water, nobody will survive. Since God made us stewards of the planet, we must do a better job cherishing and cultivating it. It boils down to what type are you, self-sacrificing or self-indulgent?

The flesh is never satisfied and many succumb to its wants; it is the wild animal in all of us. Hedonists will find it very compelling; they permit the flesh to govern, forcing the conscience to take a back seat. Don't forget, one will tire of pleasure, and at the expense of true love, relationships, and caring. To indulge the sinful nature is to take no interest in what the higher power is relating. Pursuit of physical gratification reduces character and discipline since sensuality is the sole motivator. But unnatural fun will not enthrall a person for long, so the tendency is to chase increasingly more risqué enjoyments. It's a slippery descent into a moral cataclysm.

There is an age-old battle between the flesh and the spirit (ROM 8:5–9; GAL 5:17; 1 PE 2:11). Recall we are holistic beings, possessing a physical, mental, and spiritual component (sort of like God). If the physical and spiritual are at war, what are they fighting over? Answer: the mind, the soul, the thoughts. You don't want the flesh to prevail in that conflict or you will end up sacrificing your ethics and losing control over your behavior. The purpose of twelve step programs is to get your higher power to govern your thoughts; this is the most effective approach to treating addictions of the flesh (Zemore, 2007).

This is where discipline comes in; with a plentiful supply you can manage an upright disposition, one to be admired and emulated. I bet everyone can bring to mind a most revered and respected man or woman. For me it was my maternal grandfather; everyone liked him as he was a man of faith, patience, integrity, honesty, humility, and godliness. He was not the only one in my life that influenced me to shun the evil and egocentric ways of my generation, but he certainly possessed the character that I strove to emulate (next to Jesus Christ who was his role model as well). Have you a memorable and admirable figure, alive or dead, that you hold in high esteem? If you do, I'll bet he or she was (or is) such a person: disciplined, principled, wise, upright, and esteemed. Such a character is respected by everyone. These are the heroes of the world.

Who would not think highly of a person who dodged a barrage of enemy fire to drag a wounded comrade to safety? We give medals to people like that (read the biography of Medal of Honor awardee, Desmond Doss). We want to be like them: fearless, courageous, and selfless. Sacrificing one's life, is that not the supreme gift? It is not natural to lay down your life for somebody else. Animals don't do it, though they will protect their young and their kind. But you won't see a stag take a bullet for another, for they are competitors to ensure their progeny is prolonged. Whereas any soldier that died to save another will never see his or her progeny. Such love is supernatural and imitates that of Christ; supernatural connotes exceeding nature. Nature itself is not spiritual; it does not possess a spirit, nor is it alive.

Resolved: the ultimate sacrifice is to risk or lose your life to save another (JOH 15:12–13)? Yet people dishonor the military and the police who risk their lives every day to protect us. If these servants disgrace their position, there will be justice for them same as everybody. Yes, there are dishonorable people in every profession and demographic. But those who choose a profession to protect others, despite the danger to themselves, are generally the least likely to compromise their ethics; they certainly aren't doing it for the pay. Yet perpetrators who mock and deride our heroes are hailed and exalted, while those enforcing the law and providing protection are disgraced and ruined. Shouldn't it be the other way around?

And then there is Jesus who died for you and me, for no other reason than love. He is love personified. Do you have any idea the suffering he endured to redeem you from the grave? Never in history has a man been so tortured, humiliated, and burdened. Yet he accepted that fate without reservation (LUK 22:40–44), irrespective of the scorn and ridicule ceaselessly dumped upon him. Who but God would enter such terrible horror and then forgive those who were complicit? By the way, you and I are among the complicit, as well as the forgiven. What a magnificent act of love is forgiveness. The root of the word is "give." Do you forgive others? Have you forgiven yourself? You do know that you have to give it to receive it, I trust (MAT 6:14–15; MAR 11:25–26; LUK 6:37–38)?

The Price of Your Soul

Let's get back to the matter of the soul. First of all, what is it? It is the essence of the self; the source of thought, emotion, and will; the repository of experience, the personality, and the immaterial construct of the mind. The Greek word psyche is synonymous with the word soul, the entity of being. Socrates conjectured that the soul is immortal, invisible, and the mental governor of the body. In Roman lore, Psyche was a princess. Cupid the god of love fell for her, much to the dismay of his mother Venus who was jealous of her beauty. Eventually Cupid would marry Psyche turning her into a goddess. Okay, with mythology aside, it is safe to assume that the soul has been venerated as sacred even among the ancient Romans and Greeks. It is the element of humanity that makes us more valuable than any other creature, for the soul is also an attribute of God (GEN 2:7; EZE 18:4). As a psychologist, I am interested in the study of the psyche, or soul, or mind.

The soul is of great value, which is why there is a war being waged over it. This fight goes on within you and without you. You can win the war outside of you by siding with God, who will fight for you and beside you (PSA 55:18; PSA 86:4,13); because it is his battle (DEU 20:4; 1 SA 17:41–51; 2 CH 20:10–24). And you will fight for him and with him for he is your captain (2 CO 10:3–5; 1 TI 6:12–13; 2 TI 2:3–5). If you open your heart to God, you can win the war inside by the power of his Holy Spirit dwelling in you (ACT 2:38–39; 1 CO 6:19; EPH 6:10–17); combined with your spirit you are able to control your thoughts and avert your flesh from predominating (PRO 23:19; ROM 12:2). Equipped with God's Word you can defeat the enemy that is in the world via that same power of the Holy Spirit.

Lucifer would have you acquiesce to the flesh, in attempt to steal your soul (1 PE 2:11); for he is jealous of humankind and he despises God. Also known as Satan meaning "adversary" he opposes everything that God stands for, to include you and me. Satan doesn't want anyone to be saved including himself. He has fallen from grace and wants to bring down as many people as possible. He is your archenemy. His method is to tempt you into sinning (PRO 21:10); for sin separates you from God (ISA 59:2; TIT 1:15). Since before Adam, Lucifer wanted to be worshipped. Ironic as he was appointed worship leader in heaven but exalted himself, and that got him tossed out of heaven (ISA 14:12–15; EZE 28:14–19). He influenced the first couple to give into him, is still trying to get people to follow him, and will continue this evil mission until the end of the world. But any praise or worship Satan steals from God will be insufficient to satisfy him just like any addiction, and he will perish with it along with those who he enlisted.

There is nothing in this natural world that is as valuable as your soul; in fact, the entire world is not worth the price of your soul (MAT 16:26). The purpose of the salvation of Christ is to save your soul from death and reunite you with God. Without a soul you no longer exist; you cannot reason or hope, or feel (PRO 24:24). If you have been washed by the blood of Jesus your soul has been cleansed of sin, and you can reside in the company of God who is perfectly holy. And God will let you keep your soul (PSA 23:1–3; LUK 21:19; HEB 10:39); otherwise you will lose it (PSA 49:7–8). Either way, it is forever. I ask you: do you want to be free or do you want to be dead?

Do not fear Satan or the purveyors of his evil schemes who can attack and destroy your body. Instead, fear God who will destroy your body and your soul in hell (MAT 10:28); he will allow you to remain divorced from him for eternity if that is your preference (EZE 18:4; LUK 12:19–20). I suggest you connect with God and not disconnect by taking the path of Lucifer. That road leads to obliteration. Besides, you can easily defeat the devil with Christ living in you (JAM 4:7; 1 JO 4:4; EPH 3:16–19). Yes, this is spiritual warfare; I cannot emphasize that enough. And the stakes are life and death, with the fate of your soul weighing in the balance.

That some people choose to fight on the side of evil is beyond me. Let's face it, there is a monster inside each and every person. The monster is released in a variety of ways such as drug addiction, hedonism, oppression, ethnic cleansing, sexual deviancy, enslavement, bigotry, greed, and the rest. Take hatred, for example, which wicked souls elicit as the motivation for malevolence. The classic case is seen in radical Islamism, the proponents of which engage in all of the aforementioned atrocities. These miscreants are as evil as they come. They are misogynous; that is, they disdain women. Take a look at how women are treated under their laws; women are reduced to a class akin to slaves. Not long ago I heard the report about a young Muslim girl who was gang raped; she was charged with adultery and stoned to death. Notice also how they handle captives; they rape, beat, torture, massacre, and enslave them. This is the price countries will pay when they admit thousands of unvetted refugees from hostile nations (mainly Islamic). Many are hellions who enjoy wickedness while claiming blamelessness. They want to be feared, proving they do not possess a godly fear that will humble them into repentance.

A recent suicide shooter was reported to be laughing, texting, and putting his face on social media; he was so proud of himself to be martyred killing innocent Americans. On the night preceding their suicide bombing of the World Trade Center on 9/11/2001, the perpetrators were engaged in all manner of debauchery and promiscuity. Funny isn't it? All those said behaviors are prohibited in Islam, though supposedly reserved for martyrs who die for jihad and arrive in paradise where such mayhem is permitted. What a warped understanding they have of God's realm. Do they really believe this hogwash? Yet it is preached by the mullahs and imams in mosques all over the world. Let me be clear, not all Muslims ascribe to such behavior, so let us not place the same label on all proponents of Islam.

True prophets warned against those who pretend to be godly but are evil to the core (2 TI 3:1–7). These warmongers fancy themselves initiating the final Armageddon as their claim to fame. Demonstrably, the dummies cannot be honoring Islam or God in any way, shape or form. They honor Satan who also seeks world domination, and represent the refuse of humanity. Anyone can be radicalized who has evil intentions and decadent impulses in their heart. And they will use religion, ideology, politics, or relativism as a rationalization to warrant release of the monster inside. Influenced by the devil, occultism, and demonism, they allow the spirit within them to turn dark and ugly (MAT 6:22–23). The light inside can become extinguished if you dabble with the dark side long enough (JOB 18:5–6; PRO 13:9). What do you think the odds are they will be saved and wake up in a garden of earthly delights? Nil, that's what.

Plant your feet on solid ground and build your life on the foundation laid by Christ (1 CO 3:9–14). Don't teeter, as if driving a rattletrap with no brakes, for you can be sure the ride will end in a crash (1 TH 5:1–6; 2 PE 3:10–13). You must prepare now and not wait, presuming erroneously that there is plenty of time. Every indication suggests time is running out (REV 22:7,12,20). If you are vigilant you will not be caught by surprise when the Lord returns (PSA 130:6; LUK 12:36–39). The status of the world is in decline and tribulation is approaching fast; the life-raft will sink before you know it. But you will be saved out of it if you are all in (PSA 63:8; JER 30:7; MAT 24:21–22); if you are almost there you will not make it home.

The commitment must be complete or you will forfeit your salvation and your soul. Many arguments have been proffered concerning whether one can gain salvation and then lose it. Suffice it to say that salvation is forfeited if you have not surrendered yourself to the Lord, for God expects total submission (EZE 18:24). You cannot lose something that you never had. But if you were shown the light of Christ and rejected it, the consequences will be terminal (HEB 6:4–6; 2 PE 2:20–22). When God speaks, whether through his Word or ministers of his Word, some people will hear and listen, some will hear but not listen, some will do neither (MAT 13:2–23; JOH 3:19–21). I implore that you hear, listen, read, contemplate, underscore, and absorb God's Word (JER 15:16; COL 3:16); continue to do so for the duration of your life and you can be sure in your heart that you are saved. If you are unsure, you are not trusting fully in Christ. Are you willing to risk it, or does the doubt bring you to your knees? But how can you be 100 percent sure and never doubt? Only through a saving faith by the power of the Holy Spirit is this possible. You can know things to be true in your heart of hearts even though the physical evidence, however overwhelming, does not remove all possible doubt. But the spiritual evidence is absolute, seeing how it was spoken in God's own voice (DEU 8:3; MAT 4:4; JOH 6:63).

I've heard it said that only good people are worthy of heaven. In a way that is true, because only God is always good and Jesus is God, so he alone among men is worthy of going to heaven (MAR 10:17–18). So, how does anyone make it to heaven since the rest of us are unworthy? We are made worthy solely by the righteousness, witness, and atonement of Christ. Once one receives the free gift of the Holy Spirit given to all who commend their lives to Christ, a change of heart occurs (ACT 8:14–22); and that should result in an overall change in thinking, behavior, and attitude (PSA 51:10–12). Does that mean a person must never sin again or they blow the deal? Thankfully, no it doesn't mean that. We are incapable of ceasing the sin, but we can definitely reduce it. Though we will trip and slip at times, we can improve day by day if we are focused on Christ. Forget about thinking that salvation, having been received, insinuates you can sin with impunity (ROM 6:1–23: JDE 1:4). True contrition, confession, repentance and worship should be offered to God every day to demonstrate your longing to be like Jesus and to live forever with him (1 CH 16:23; PSA 145:2; HEB 12:28–29; 1 JO 1:8–10; REV 4:11). And he will indeed trade his righteousness for your unrighteousness, thereby making you good, cleansed, and deserving via the transformation of your soul (ROM 12:1–3). Clearly, this is not an evolutionary, natural process. Sanctification is spiritual selection.

Humankind hasn't evolved morally, but instead, the human race appears to be devolving. Think about the "unnatural selection processes" that deplorable humans exhibit, like legalized infanticide, euthanasia, genocide, and other murderous acts. It reeks of eugenics, a practice endorsed by Darwin himself to establish the preeminent race, not to mention the likes of Margaret Sanger the founder of Planned Parenthood, who wanted to sterilize black men because she deemed them subhuman. In the USA, we have been slaughtering babies in the womb at the tune of 1.2 million per year; this is the average since the Center for Disease Control began collecting data in 1970. That comes to about 55,000,000 American fetus homicides (includes only statistics on authorized abortions). Can you imagine what the worldwide numbers must be? Assisted suicide and other means of euthanasia of the elderly and terminally ill are legal in some states, and also in Europe where the rate is especially high. Though actual data are scarce, some US states keep track; one nationwide estimate is about 1000 per year, but again, a great many do not get counted. Of course, this does not include people who have chosen to withdraw life support (re: do not resuscitate orders), though this itself does not equate to euthanasia.

It would be impossible to estimate the number of people who have died throughout history due to war. Worse than that, many tyrannical dictators have been the purveyors of mass murder in the millions by waging war against their own citizenry. Extrapolating from numerous sources (try your own Internet search if you like) the following estimates were derived. Mao takes first place with an estimated eradication of over fifty million; Stalin comes in second, as he annihilated some forty million; Hitler is third with an estimated twenty million, followed by Leopold with ten million, Tojo with five, Pol Pot with two, and the list goes on. So, we're talking somewhere in the neighborhood of one hundred twenty million souls or more, murdered to make way for a "superior" race or class. Religion had nothing to do with it, to include the Islamist terrorists roaming the globe committing ethnic and religious cleansing. But they are not the only serial killers running rampant. In some countries it is common to slay the handicapped, deformed, and/or female offspring. Really! Whether you live or die is based on societal preferences? This is outrageous. Would you agree that none of these categories of assassins are superior? The only things they excel at are ignorance, conceit, and meanness. Whatever happened to all men being endowed by our Creator with unalienable rights—such as life? Those who continuously take life, can they be saved? God only knows the hearts of people, but when a sin is done continuously, repentance becomes ineffectual.

The day of reckoning is nigh and everyone will face judgment. But you will not be judged by the balance of your bad deeds versus your good deeds; it will be on the basis of your belief versus your unbelief. You might ask, won't kind and generous people have a better chance of being saved, or won't they receive a greater reward? If they did not believe in God and trust in his only begotten Son, they will lose everything. Yes, your deeds are a reflection of your character; and good deeds should be an answer to your faith once you confess Christ as your Savior. But your deeds neither save you nor condemn you. Salvation is free to all who accept Christ by faith, period. Lucky for you, God will not hold any of your debt against you once you have repented, received his forgiveness, and dedicated your life to Christ. He redeemed your soul with his personal sacrifice, that is how valuable your soul is.

There is still time if you decide now. But don't wait until the last minute or until you are reclining on your deathbed. I'm not saying that people cannot be saved from deathbed conversions, because I recall a certain thief crucified with Christ who joined him in paradise that day (LUK 23:42–43). The main ingredient was and still is to be wholeheartedly sincere in the one true faith. If so, it stands to reason that you have accepted God's offer through repentance and chosen to live from that point onward putting him first in your life, regardless of when you became saved. It's about who you are becoming, not who you used to be. Be careful, for if you do not cling to that faith until your dying day it could slither out of your grasp. Satan would like nothing more than to sway you into foregoing your inheritance in lieu of worldly treasure or pleasure. By all means, do good deeds and be of good character; this may be the catalyst for moving someone else to faith because they were drawn to the light of Christ reflected in you. You can be a player on Jesus's team, bring lost souls to him, and win the crown. Or you can compete in the rat race and never finish it.

Eternity

How long is eternity anyway? It is so long it cannot be measured in units of time. The fraction of time you have lived compared to the age of the universe can be estimated, however, and it is infinitesimally small.

According to current numbers it would be approximately fifty years divided by fifteen billion years (= 0.00000000033); additionally, fifteen billion years compared to eternity is infinitesimally smaller than that proportion. How about the proportion of your earthly lifespan to your eternal life? There would not be enough zeroes to fill this book. Maybe you would rather not be around that long. Ask yourself, given a choice would you opt to be around forevermore or not? For the atheist, the current life is long enough. They must hate their lives because they are unremorseful, supposing contrition followed by repentance to be a meaningless venture. They would deny they possess a soul; but that's okay as they won't for long. How long? Eternity!

Eternity, in human terms, begins when Christ returns. He will either escort you into his kingdom or will dump you into a lake of fire. I don't know about you but this choice is a no-brainer as far as I'm concerned. Naturally, the atheists and agnostics would rather not choose, so the choice will be made for them. They don't believe they have to choose, and that is their prerogative. Do you believe you have a choice? Don't fall for great deceptions that everyone lives forever; that you don't need God and you needn't believe in him either. We are free spirits that can do whatever we want, both in this life and the next, right? Unfortunately, no we cannot do whatever we want in this life for there are consequences. Knowing this, it is dangerous to assume that the next life will have no consequences (ROM 2:6–9; 2 CO 5:10–11)? The purpose of this life is to learn these lessons; the purpose of the Holy Bible is to teach them.

Eternity, in God's terms, never had a beginning; for he is infinite. This universe is finite; it began and it will end someday. Although humans are presently finite beings, we can live with God in a new universe that is nothing like this one (REV 21:1–4), for the rest of eternity. Can you think of anything more marvelous than that?

I suspect you don't really want to go to hell. And is hell forever? Some theologians say yes, some say no. The Bible states that hellfire burns forever (MAT 25:41–46; 1 TH 1:7–10). Does that mean the inhabitants suffer torment for eternity, or that eternal fire destroys completely and for good (JDE 1:7; REV 14:11; REV 20:10–15)? The concept of people living forever in hell seems unlikely given their body and soul is destroyed (MAT 10:28). Besides, Jesus said those who do not believe will be condemned to death (JOH 3:17–18), implying the soul is immortal only for those who live. If you die the second death, it is forever (REV 21:8). As for me, I have no interest in finding out the hard way how long one must endure hell. I don't want to spend a single second of torment in Hades, Hell, the Lake of Fire, Gehenna, or any other place like that—especially when I can abide eternally, in ecstasy, with the Lord of the universe. Those terrorists thinking that they are going where I am going better think twice before contemplating suicide by murder; their reward is the wrath of God, and those who entice converts to do their dirty work will likely get the worst of it (MAT 23:13–15; HEB 10:28–31).

Life without God is a frightful thought. How does eternity in heaven sound? The Bible doesn't say a whole lot about heaven; in fact, there are more passages that discuss hell. Probe these verses that address heaven; it sounds like a great, beautiful, peaceful, happy, fun, and glorious place (see PSA 145:11–12; ISA 64:4; JOH 14:2–4; 1 PE 1:2–5; 2 PE 1:3–4; REV 7:15–17; REV 22:1–5), whereas hell sounds like the opposite (see DEU 32:22–24; ISA 38:18; ISA 66:24; EZE 26:20–21; MAT 25:30,41; LUK 16:19–24; REV 14:9–11). Perhaps you do not trust the biblical accounts of heaven and hell. The only problem with that is, the concept originated from God's Word. And the impression of hell being horrible and heaven being wonderful is pretty much universal, to the extent that practically every culture in the world has a similar understanding. Thus, the Bible is actually the most authoritative and reliable source on such things. And since it is the most trusted source on this topic, it stands to reason it could very well be reliable in a whole lot of other areas. Actually, it is the most solid and credible source of truth known to humanity. Why else do you think the Holy Bible is held in such high regard? Do you know anybody who has not heard of the Bible? What is odd to me is that so many people refuse to read it even though they know it to be the most popular book ever written and will be forever. If you haven't taken a gander at it yet, why not give it a try?

Granted, the Bible is hard to grasp; it takes a lot of work to scratch the surface of the wisdom found therein. But the effort pays off as your comprehension increases and you begin to behold unveiled mysteries that will expand your intellect immensely. Imagine being able to continue to extend your horizons for eternity; and even then, you will have scarcely touched the coattails of God's wisdom. The nice thing about living with him is he will be there to answer every question you will ever have. In this life it is laborious just clearing out the myriad of untruths being tossed at you as interference. That's why we necessitate a source of truth with which to sort it out; and that truth is itself eternal. Everything that originates from God is absolutely true and always will be (LUK 21:32–33).

Scientists cannot explain eternity but the Bible can. Even as I attempt to explain it, I admit that I haven't clarified much. Because our deficient minds have not the capacity to fully appreciate conceptualizations like infinity, perfection, and God's elaborate plan. Such fascinations make more sense the more you get into God's Word, however, because they are understood by the spirit better than the mind (JOB 28:12,28; JOB 32:8). In other words, I think I understand this eternity thing a lot better than I can explain it. If you value learning, you can receive an eternity of it; if you don't then you might not enjoy heaven. Something more difficult than learning is unlearning all the baloney that was dumped on you by those you thought knew what they were saying. God always knows what he's talking about. Truth is like a sword that cuts away the clutter, the interference, the gristle, and the waste (HEB 4:12). Won't it be great when purity of thought will be as unencumbered as freedom of the spirit?

The Real Jesus

In a nutshell, the real Jesus is God. God the Father said that he is the eternal I AM, the Alpha and Omega, the first and the last (EXO 3:14; ISA 41:4; ISA 48:12–13). God the Son said that he is the eternal I AM, the Alpha and Omega, the first and the last (JOH 8:58; JOH 9:9; REV 1:18). Jesus and the Father are both the great I AM (JOH 8:23–30; REV 2:23); they exist forever, from before the beginning and after the end. I AM sent himself to us to be his Messiah, and that witness is Jesus Christ (ISA 43:10–13; ISA 52:6–7; JOH 17:5; HEB 1:8). Jesus commissions those who believe in him to be his witnesses; those receiving the testimony of Jesus's witnesses receive him and therefore are received by God the Father (ISA 46:4; JOH 13:19–20).

I used to watch a television program when I was a youngster; it was entitled *To Tell the Truth* (the show has tried to make a comeback). Anyway, a panel of celebrities had to guess which person was the real deal from among impostors whose job it was to confuse the panelists when answering their questions. After making selections as to who could be the actual inventor, hero, entrepreneur, or whomever, the host would say, "Will the real [so-and-so] please stand up," at which time everyone learned which were impostors versus who was telling the truth. This analogy is spot-on in describing the reality of false prophets, errant teachers, and fake messiahs.

THE ESSENTIALS

There have been countless charlatans impersonating Jesus Christ, as well as gurus proclaiming that they know or they preach the real Jesus; not to mention books that claim the Bible is obsolete which is why their authors have replaced or revised it with their own truth. In order to tell the difference, you need to see and listen to the real Jesus so you will recognize him when he speaks and when he reappears.

Before that happens, there will be innumerable phonies (LUK 21:8; 2 CO 11:13–14; 2 PE 2:1–3,18–20). They will invent sham religions and reinvent scriptures, concocting a perversion of the Bible. Given that truth will have been bartered, anyone following these dead ends will be damned, for such is the work of the devil. I'm describing a well-orchestrated deception and you'd better take caution (ISA 59:13; JER 14:14; LAM 2:14; MAT 7:15–23; COL 2:18), for many will be fooled (MAT 24:11,24). Magicians will perform fabricated miracles instead of proclaiming the Gospel, steering people away from the truth and towards themselves (2 TH 2:9–11; 2 TI 3:13; 2 TI 4:3–4). They will trick people who are ignorant about the technological devices being employed. If you are equipped with knowledge and truth you can test the sewage they are spreading; it will not pass the smell test. You will prove them wrong and expose them as frauds (1 JO 4:1–3; 2 JO 1:7–11). Those equipped with truth are Satan's worst nightmare, for he thrives on deception.

Unmistakably, get to know the Jesus of the Holy Bible of which both Old and New Testaments declare and testify. There are many counterfeits out there proposing attributes, acts, and intentions of Jesus inaccurately. Some purport Jesus was a mere man or angelic being, some claim he was a god or a subordinate god, some allege he was a myth or a conman. To tell the truth, Jesus is God in human flesh. He is equal to and intertwined with God the Father and God the Holy Spirit. Jesus is nothing less than the Almighty, the Creator, the Redeemer, the Judge, and the Messiah (COL 2:8–10). While all three persons of the Holy Trinity have seemingly different functions, responsibilities, personifications, and characteristics, all are equivalent, holy, and united into one deity. Jesus is God who became a man so that we could know him and believe (ISA 43:10–11). He demonstrated the perfect man for all to see; and everyone that sees and knows the Son has seen and knows the Father (JOH 14:6–13). Thus, all of the absolute attributes ascribed previously to Almighty God are ascribed equivalently to Christ. This is why he is worshipped and praised, and why we can approach God, ask for anything in the name of Jesus Christ, and receive it (JOH 14:14).

How can I be sure that Jesus truly is God? Firstly, he said he was God. Ignore those who profess that Jesus never claimed to be God, like Muslim clerics often do. Jesus stated unambiguously that he was God on numerous occasions (EXO 3:14; DAN 7:13–14; JOH 8:52–58; JOH 10:30; JOH 13:13). God also testified that he was sending himself, in the name of his only begotten Son (ISA 7:14; ISA 9:6–7; ISA 42:1,6–7; ISA 44:6; PHP 2:10–11). Thus, the OT and NT avow that Jesus is God and that God is Jesus. Secondly, Jesus came among us to reveal the way to heaven (JOH 14:6), forgive us of our sins (MAT 9:1–8), save and redeem us (2 TI 1:7–10), and bring us from death into life (JOH 5:24). Who but God can do these things? Thirdly, among other amazing miracles described in the NT of which only God could perform, Christ died for our sins and rose again from the dead further proving that he was God. Fourthly, many who met Jesus addressed him as God, Son of God, Lord, and Christ (MAT 16:16; JOH 20:28); while many others despised, taunted, and scorned him for affirming to be God (MAT 26:62–66; MAT 27:38–43). That's why some people love Jesus, and that's why some people hate him, because of who he is not for who he isn't. The Koran alleges that it would be perverse for Allah to have a son, that he would never do such a thing. I don't know about their god, but my God is all powerful. He can do anything; and everything he does is righteous. Besides, why wouldn't God have a Son? Is there a better way to reveal himself to us? Nobody does it better than God. And he is not a stranger, or a distant star, or roaming around outside of the universe somewhere; God is there watching you read, and is loving you absolutely, whether you love him or hate him. If you love him, he will never leave you (DEU 31:6).

Those who say they follow Christ but do not believe he is God have a different Jesus in mind than the Jesus of the Bible. There are many who claim to be Christians but they do not worship Jesus Christ along with the Father and the Holy Spirit. Unfortunately, they do not know their Bible very well; and they certainly do not know Jesus. I believe the scriptures are quite clear about this. Review the passages cited in this section and see if you agree. Will the true Christian please stand up? Will you take a stand for Christ? There is no other like him, you can be sure about that. He will stand by you if you stand for him. He died for you so you can live with him. He purified you so you can be like him. But you cannot be him; and you are not and never will be a god. For there is only one God and there is no other (ISA 45:5; 1 CO 8:6). But you can be adopted by God, and I can think of nothing I would like more. Trying to play God or to be your own god is exasperating, especially when your frailty, impropriety, or higher power kicks in.

To fully understand the real Jesus, it is important to see him as the Lamb of God. The full message of truth presented in God's Holy Word is that of salvation, illustrated in the sacrifice of an unblemished lamb. The tradition of sacrificial offerings began with the first family (GEN 4), whereby the first fruits of one's increase was submitted to God. That sacrifice represented a temporary atonement gift, shown in appreciation for all of God's gifts, and given freely in sincere contrition for sin and disobedience (LEV 4; LEV 17:11; LEV 23:5–12). Sacrifices for sin were, by themselves, insufficient to redeem anyone; and God knew this, which is why his plan of salvation went way beyond blood offerings presented by his people (HEB 9:1–28). Though I previously touched upon the fundamental doctrine concerning the sacrificial lamb, allow me to further expound.

The words of Abraham declared God's plan of redemption most succinctly when he told his son Isaac that God would provide the lamb for a sin offering. If you are unfamiliar with the events that led to this proclamation, read Genesis 17 and 22. God tested the faith of Abraham by commanding him to sacrifice Isaac on a mountain that God would reveal. In obedience Abraham took a few servants and his son and headed out towards Mt. Moriah; upon arrival, Abraham told the servants to hang back while he and his son proceeded. About that time, Isaac asked his father a very poignant question. "Okay Father, you have the knife and the fire and I am carrying the wood for the burnt offering, but where is the lamb to be offered for sacrifice?" Isaac didn't know it was him until Abraham bound him and placed him upon the alter. God had promised Abraham that the world would be blessed through Isaac, and now God was telling him to take his son's life. But in faith, Abraham believed God; he figured, God is powerful enough to raise his son from the dead and fulfill that promise, so he proceeded with God's commandment (HEB 11:17–19). But an angel of the Lord stopped Abraham, and Abraham sacrificed a ram trapped in the bushes instead. This episode is a declaration of the doctrine of grace through faith, which is the New Covenant, whereby Abraham's faith in God's promise was counted to him as righteousness (ROM 4:1–3).

The Passover lamb is another portent of the New Covenant. If you are unfamiliar with these affairs, read Exodus 2, 11, and 12. Pharaoh refused to free the Hebrew slaves after nine plagues came upon the Egyptians, so God sent a tenth and final plague that would wipe out the first born of all living creatures throughout the land of Egypt. However, the firstborn of Israel was spared (like Abraham's firstborn and legitimate heir), when the angel of death passed over the abodes of those who had sacrificed a lamb, painted the door frame with its blood, and eaten the lamb for dinner in accordance with God's instructions to Moses. Thus, the shedding of the blood of the lamb was the only remedy for God's curse over the land, which would fall upon all who did not heed the Word of God. Once their freedom had been secured, Moses introduced the presage of a blood offering that would endure ceaselessly, by reintroducing the New Covenant to the people of Israel (EXO 12:3–13; EXO 24:7–8). That New Covenant is through Jesus Christ.

Jesus was formally declared the Lamb of God by John the Baptist. At the moment John baptized Jesus, the Holy Spirit descended upon him like a dove and the voice of God echoed throughout the valley, "This is my beloved Son in whom I am well pleased" (MAT 3:17). If you are unfamiliar with these events, read Matthew 3 and John 1. Jesus was conveyed to us as the blood offering which would prevail forever. His ministry of grace was officially underway with his baptism, after which Jesus fasted in the wilderness where he was tempted by Satan to give up and give into him. Upon Jesus's dismissal of Satan, and his subsequent return across the Jordan River where John was still baptizing, John declared to all present, "Behold, the Lamb of God who takes away the sin of the world" (JOH 1:29). Immediately, disciples following John began following Jesus, pronouncing him to be the Messiah of God.

You see, this was ordained from the beginning of time, God creating people to be his own, and to be cleansed of their sin to safeguard their redemption. The only method that will atone for sin is offering a pure and spotless sacrifice. Since we are far from pure, we cannot fulfill that requirement. Only God can as he alone is pure and holy. So, he sent himself. He had to suffer and spill his blood for our sin and die in our place so that we could live. And because he lives, so will you if you believe in Christ (JOH 14:19). Anybody that preaches a different kind of Jesus is in error; anybody that believes in a different kind of salvation is condemned. There is only one real and true Jesus Christ, the perfect sacrifice who could absolve sin and conquer death through his own death and resurrection. Don't get this one wrong or it will be the biggest mistake of your life.

The Resurrection

The pivotal moment in Christendom is the resurrection of Jesus Christ. His resurrection is the most vital piece of evidence proving that Jesus is God. Naturally, those denying this decisive event maintain that there is no conclusive evidence. But this simply is not the case; there is an overwhelming amount of evidence endorsing the resurrection (Habermas 1993; Sanders, 1993). Further, contentions made to dispute the evidence are insanely absurd. There are entire books written on this subject that are worth appraising. In the interest of space, I will highlight some of the incontrovertible proof of Jesus's resurrection, as well as the ridiculous attempts to explain it away.

That Jesus was crucified, died, and entombed is not in dispute; even nonbelieving historians will concede these circumstances. The gist of the debate is in explaining the empty tomb. I will begin with a brief assessment of the resurrection attestation. (Review also the archaeological findings reported at the beginning of this book corroborating that the Bible is true, and so also, the resurrection narrative.)

➢ First of all, each of the four Gospels (Matthew, Mark, Luke, John) provide detailed testimony; in particular, they comprise eyewitness accounts of Jesus's ministry, trial, crucifixion, resurrection, and ascension. The authenticity of the Gospels and their authorship has been well established. The New Testament is the most authoritative treatise on the life of Jesus Christ, and unquestionably is the most authenticated and distributed book of antiquity. Keep in mind that Jesus proclaimed to the apostles the exact manner in which he would die, and that he would arise three days later. Evidently, it didn't sink into their minds and hearts until it actually happened, after which they never doubted Jesus's deity.

➢ The risen Christ appeared several times and there were numerous eyewitnesses, over five hundred on one occasion (ACT 1:3; 1 CO 15:3–11). As a result, the incident of his rising spread like wildfire and was thoroughly documented and circulated. To this day we can read all about it. We have manuscript evidence from the first century up until now proving the chronicle of Christ and his resurrection from the dead. Jesus and his memoir have not changed, and both remain alive and well.

➢ The fact that Jesus's followers met their demise for proclaiming his victory over death is noteworthy. These halfhearted souls were in abject fear, thinking it was over and their faith was in vain—until they saw

Jesus alive, beheld his wounds, and spoke and ate with him. This resulted in a major turnaround; with newfound courage they boldly carried the news to remote corners of the globe at great peril. It is highly improbable any one of them (much less all of them) would have given up everything, suffered, endured torture and imprisonment, and/or died a gruesome death in order to perpetuate a meaningless prank. No, they believed it, lived it, and died for it.

➤ Moreover, among those who were converted and became witnesses were Jesus's half-brothers James and Judah, several Roman soldiers and citizens, and even some of the Jewish Pharisees: Paul, Nicodemus, and Joseph of Arimathea to name a few (ACT 15:5–11). These people made a complete turnaround too, because they started out shunning Jesus and oppressing believers. Instead, they became the outcasts and the persecuted because of their faith in Jesus and his testimony; and many were executed for their witness. What changes a person so dramatically and quickly? I think it would take a miracle.

➤ If their intention was to advance a ruse, the disciples certainly would not have planned for women to be the ones to discover the empty tomb and sound the alert (MAT 28:1,5–10), since the testimony of women did not hold much weight in first century Judea (MAR 16:11; LUK 24:10–11).

➤ The early church leaders kept the Gospels and Epistles alive and helped distribute them to the world. Even secular historians recounted the unusual events surrounding the ministry, trial, execution, and alleged resurrection of the one called "Christos," to include the fact that the "cult called Christianity" had continued to flourish long after his death.

➤ The Shroud of Turin and the Sudarium of Oviedo provide forensic proof of Jesus's resurrection (JOH 20:6–7). Some maintain that the shroud was dated centuries after Christ (around AD 1300). This exposes an unfamiliarity with new data ascertaining that the radiometric sample was contaminated by the introduction of new fabric weaved into the shroud to repair it (Benford and Marino, 2002). Other parts of the shroud have been dated as far back as the second century (*ibid*). Its obvious representation of a crucified victim (who looks to be Judean) negates that later date as well, since Romans ceased the practice around AD 300. Further, the discovery of bones from a first century crucifixion victim found in the land of Palestine supports an earlier date for the shroud.
  o Clearly apparent on the Shroud of Turin are puncture marks around the crown of the head indicative of thorns; approximately one

hundred wounds on the back match an ancient Roman whip called a *flagrum*; bruises and swelling on the knee, shoulders, and face indicate the individual fell on one knee, carried a heavy weight on his shoulders, and was beaten in the face; a gaping wound in the side is the size of a spearhead; puncture (nail) wounds on both wrists and ankles pierce all the way through. Not only does this image confirm a unique crucifixion, the wounds mimic perfectly those of Christ which are detailed in the NT.

- Blood stains and streams on the shroud mirror all of the above-mentioned wounds. The blood was tested and is type AB; note that this is the rarest type and is a universal plasma source. How thought-provoking; I mean, doesn't Jesus's blood provide universal donor application? Note further how blood stains on the Sudarium (head cloth) match precisely those of the Shroud, to include blood type AB. This proves beyond a shadow of doubt that these two grave-cloths covered the same head (Bennett, 2001).
- There also are remnants of dirt, plant and pollen material placing the two relics in ancient Palestine.
- The shroud has undergone extensive photographic, forensic, and microscopic analyses by scientists and scholars. Most remarkable is the image on the shroud itself, which cannot be replicated, explicated, or repudiated, despite many attempts. Interestingly, the shroud provides a photographic negative in three dimensions, sort of like a holograph, which is a twentieth century technology. Considering the quantum physics of the shroud, it has been suggested that an extraordinary event like a resurrection created the image, explained by the possible breach of an event horizon (Missler, 2009). Fascinating, isn't it?

Okay, I have made a case for the resurrection being true. If this topic interests you I encourage you to dig further, because there is plenty more proof out there (see Barber, 2020). I will turn now to the dissenting position as it is my intention to present both sides. The problem, unfortunately, is that there exists no proof that the tomb was undisturbed or that Christ remained dead. Those who deny Jesus rising from the dead are prone to deny miracles of any kind, and/or they have not objectively reviewed the evidence. Let's face it, had the Romans or Jewish leaders produced Jesus's dead body there would be nothing to debate. Anyway, you decide whether you can buy into any of the following theories and innuendo.

- The tale most often perpetuated, ever since the day the tomb was found empty, is that Jesus's disciples stole his body. This supposition has a very weak foundation. First of all, one must assume that the disciples conspired to, and succeeded in, overpowering a full cadre of Roman guards armed to the teeth. Typically, sixteen soldiers were assigned to a guard consisting of four four-man teams. Do you think it reasonable to imagine that they were disarmed, or abandoned their posts, or slept while the stone was rolled away and the disciples absconded with the body right under their noses? Normally, a Roman soldier would get the death penalty if found guilty of any of the above infractions. The biblical account says the guards were witnesses to an earthquake, saw the angel(s), observed the empty tomb—and were scared to death (MAT 28:2–4). They hurried into the city and related what they had seen to the chief priests and elders, who bribed them with a large sum of money to lie about what they had experienced. The Jewish elders formulated a ruse that the body was stolen in the night, assuring they would vouch for the soldiers to their superiors (MAT 28:11–15). Incidentally, one can verify that the church leaders knew of Jesus's prophecy about rising from the dead, because that is why they appealed to Pilate to seal the tomb and post a guard in the first place. They wanted to prevent the body from being stolen, hoping to prove Jesus wrong (MAT 27:62–66). Well, he was right but they claimed the body was stolen anyway.
- The next most popular narrative is that Jesus didn't really die. This would assume that despite the beating, flogging, torture, blood loss, and being impaled with nails and a spear, the Romans were unable to kill Jesus. Really? The Romans specialized in torturing people to death; they had it down to a science. That's why a soldier jabbed a spear into Jesus's side, so the centurion could confirm his death prior to removing him from the cross (MAR 15:44–45; JOH 19:31–37). Even if Jesus had lived through it, he would have been in no shape to unwrap himself, get up and walk, much less remove the stone and break out of the tomb, all without the Roman guards noticing. And he certainly wouldn't have been spotted roaming throughout the town, preaching to crowds and dining with friends; he would have been in intensive care.
- Another version along these lines is that the Romans crucified an impostor (or maybe a twin). This is advanced by Islam and reported in the Koran (Surah 4:157–158). I guess somewhere between his arrest and his execution, Jesus and the impostor swapped places, okay? Or maybe

Judas accused the wrong guy who just happened to be hanging out with members of their gang. Or maybe Judas was in on the deception, but why then did he later kill himself? He got what he wanted which was the money; but he felt guilty and gave it back, because he knew he had betrayed a friend and couldn't live with himself (MAT 27:1–5).

- Then there is the yarn about a mix-up concerning which tomb Jesus was laid in. So, the reason they never produced Jesus's body is because they forgot where they put it. Yeah, right. Or how about this one: it was the Romans who stole the body, maybe so they could extort money from the chief priests. Oh, but then they would receive the death penalty for dereliction of duty, probably to be crucified themselves.
- Dishonorable mention goes to the idea that Jesus's disciples concocted the entire episode. That's right, ordinary and largely uneducated men produced a scam that has continued to sucker billions of people after two millennia. Of course, that would necessitate the whole of historical scholarship concerning Jesus of Nazareth also was manufactured.
- My personal favorite is that everyone who witnessed the resurrected Jesus were hallucinating. This would be psychologically impossible, since any one individual's hallucinations will be unique to his or her experience and mental state; there is no possibility for hundreds of people to generate the exact same hallucination at the exact same time. This is a veritable copout, like those proposing Jesus of Nazareth is a fictional character.

Do you believe in life after death? I vote yes. Those advocating an afterlife usually believe in deity; those who do not advocate an afterlife prefer nihilism. If there is an afterlife, would it not apply to every mortal who has lived? I believe it does; though your next life may vary from others in duration and location, as with your current life. The two main camps regarding life after death are resurrection versus reincarnation. I favor resurrection because there is proof that Jesus Christ arose from the dead. I reject reincarnation because there is no proof of anyone coming back as another person or an animal. I believe we all come back once, to be judged (HEB 9:27). One group will be judged not guilty and will live forever with Christ in heaven; the other group will be judged guilty and will die a second death in hell (REV 20:6,14). This is what the Bible teaches, and since it has been repeatedly demonstrated to be accurate, I believe all of it.

Where do people go after death, prior to the resurrection of their physical bodies? It is one of two places; one group goes to Abraham's Bosom in which the saints reside, and the other group goes to Hades where disbelievers reside (LUK 16:19–31). In the end, all people will experience a bodily resurrection to stand in their flesh before God (JOB 19:26); for the latter group it be their final opportunity to cast their eyes upon Jesus (REV 1:7).

What about near-death experiences, in which people describe heaven or hell with seeming lucidity? No natural born individual goes to either destination and returns, because you have to die to get there (JOB 38:17). St. Paul may have had a near death experience complete with vision of heaven; but God forbade him to write about what he witnessed there (2 CO 12:2–5). So those claiming they spent time in heaven and conversed with the dead likely dreamt it; their accounts cannot be trusted. Isn't it possible for someone not to have died but maybe who got a glimpse, you ask? God already has given us a glimpse in his Word. In all likelihood, that picture and place reside in everyone's memory in some form or fashion because God revealed it (ROM 1:19); it is embedded in one's long-term memory.

Nobody has perceived or experienced anything like God's impeccable domain (ISA 64:4; 1 CO 2:9). Neither can they fathom the scope of the lake of fire. But anyone can imagine these settings, and everyone who does will feel a positive or negative vibe, respectively. The Bible provides abstract images of heaven and hell, stimulating the imagination; literature, arts, and media further have embellished these images. So, if you meditate on heaven perhaps you can see the light, and remember passed loved ones, and role play with them; one could likewise imagine hell and experience the darkness and emptiness. I suspect this happens when a person is unconscious, and their life flashes before them in their memory and soul. Perhaps they have unencumbered access to the chronology of their life in that state. And they recognize how they have lived their lives to that point; and they realize they have placed everything on the line. Remember, the spirit is the life force (JOH 6:63) and is our connection to God, as well as to other spirits and living souls. Your intellect, thoughts, and willpower reside in the soul, which you will surrender if you haven't been transformed by the renewing of your mind (MAT 10:28; ROM 12:2).

Imputation

Why is the resurrection so important? Because it is our ticket to life. Christ took upon himself our guilt while simultaneously giving us his guiltlessness. He left the guilt, shame, and sin on the cross before they buried him. He came alive again proving he was exactly who he said he was. And his life gives Christians new life, for we too will rise again. Those choosing Christ will live forever in paradise because they are no longer stained by sin; those who do not will die all over again condemned by their sin.

The doctrine of imputation is another requisite of the Christian faith. To impute means to "ascribe or transmit" something to another. Jesus imputes his righteousness to his people. Imputation coincides with the premise that we cannot earn salvation on our own; only with Christ can we be saved from sin that leads to death. To reiterate, the moment he took our sins upon himself, he willed his righteousness upon us (ROM 5:4–13). You can either receive this gift or reject it. Nobody but Christ is or can be righteous by themselves. No matter how wonderful you are and no matter how many great things you do for others, for society, or for God, you still will be a sinner. Isaiah said it best, "our righteousness is as filthy rags" (ISA 64:6). We are unclean and we cannot help it; and we cannot change it (ROM 3:10). However, we can possess the righteousness of Christ, and that is a righteousness that leads to salvation; and salvation represents redemption from all sins, past, present, and future.

Redemption equates to reconciliation with God our Father when Christ returns for his flock at the resurrection of human beings. Remember, we cannot enter the kingdom of heaven with any impurities. Being purified by the blood of Jesus makes anybody acceptable to God. Without that you are not acceptable to God and you will not be raised to eternal life. Jesus exchanged his purity for our impurity, his perfection for our imperfection, his holiness for our sinfulness. He has given us everything including himself, so that we can be made blameless, incorruptible, and immortal. He imputed upon us his virtue so that we might be made pure, and all we must do is thank him, trust in him, and never turn away from him (DAN 9:9–14; ROM 5:18); in the meantime, the Holy Spirit will continue to make us holy by way of sanctification. In short, the Lord is our righteousness (JER 23:5–6).

It is ridiculous to assume that once saved we needn't focus on doing the right thing, or concern ourselves with others or the will of God, or make an earnest effort to be charitable. If you have chosen to accept the gift, you should respond in kind. But your response is because you have believed; faith should be the motivation. And the rectitude you have received will make you a better person; and this will compel you to act, speak, and think like Jesus. And he will strengthen and preserve you every day (2 TH 3:3–4; 1

PE 5:10). But there are a great many people who assume they are saved because they believe, whereas they have not responded properly. The purpose of Christ is to save; to receive that gift is to receive him into your heart. Being changed from the inside results in a change on the outside. It's not like you can just keep on doing what you were doing before you invited Christ into your heart. Even demons believe and they shake with fear at the remembrance of their guilt and the surety of their condemnation (JAM 2:19), knowing full well they chose their path and ultimate destiny.

"Great," people sometimes say to themselves, "I am set for life; I have nothing to worry about because I believe." Problem is, you must believe with your heart and confess with your lips (ROM 10:9), not just think in your mind that you believe. Again, there should be an outward appearance of any change that occurs inwardly (ROM 10:1–14). I know people that are living in sin. Yes, we all sin, but are you living for sin or living for the Lord? I guess some people have no intention of changing; they carry on in their adultery, drug abuse, deceitfulness, dirty dealings, corrupt business practices; well you get the picture. "I'm saved because I asked for forgiveness, and Jesus said he will forgive us as often as we ask." That would be true if one confesses with authentic contrition and godly sorrow. But if that doesn't influence you to exit the devil's den and spend more time in God's house, something isn't right.

Our returning God's love and caring about others is because he gave his love first (1 JO 4:19–20). We do not earn his love, and we do not perform acts of obedience because we owe him. Those who aver that you must pay penance are misinformed; your debt has been paid in full if you trust fully in Christ. Penance is voluntary, just as any form of sacrifice or giving. For example, it is not mandatory to give tithes in order to make it to heaven, but you will be rewarded if you do (MAL 3:8–10). It is not mandatory that you be baptized, or that you partake in the Lord's Supper, but these are public proclamations of a commitment to the Lord that will keep you headed in the correct direction, progressively conforming you into his image. Paying a fine or performing community service to expiate sins or to reduce one's sentence is not biblical. It is a dodge to suppose that any payment on your part is necessary when Christ already has paid with his life. We respond to his lovingkindness we do not pay for it; it is freely given to all people who desire it. And so is redemption, but you will not be redeemed if you don't want it. If you do you will receive it, after which you will proclaim it and support it.

The result of imputation is being reborn in the Spirit, because you have accepted the transfer of Christ's persona into yourself. When we stand before God, he will see us as he sees his Son, clean, righteous, and honorable. We will have been fully transformed into a picture of Christ, free of sin and pure of heart; and we will live in that elevated condition forever and ever, Amen. In no other religion or worldview outside of true Christianity is this doctrine acknowledged. Survey other faiths carefully to see if the idea of being good-to-go because of your fine deeds resonates. The works we do are of no account as the only work that counts occurred on the cross of Calvary. What we can do is cherish the gifts God gives us, especially the gift of himself: Father, Son, and Spirit; then, share those gifts. He gives you everything you need so you needn't pray for worldly things except that God would open your eyes (2 KI 6:15–18; EPH 1:17–23) and guide your paths (PSA 119:105). When he does, you will see clearly a new direction, and you will beam with joy and walk in peace. If you follow that way faithfully, others will be watching; and if they like what they see they may join you. You will especially want your kids to find their way because they learn by example. If your example is Jesus, they will see him in you, and they will follow you to him. It is easy to talk the talk, much more so than to walk the walk.

Looking Forward

Before looking forward in time, let us take a look backwards. I'd like to start at the beginning, when God was creating the universe. I have pointed out, this creation was for us, so we can thrive and love, and find God. Many have sought God and found Christ and his love, and God has favored them. Though the biblical patriarchs and matriarchs were imperfect, often unsound in their judgment, spiritually weak, and strayed from time to time, those who regained their bearings and returned to God were protected, prospered, and sustained. If they drifted too far, and headed down the path of no return, they experienced calamity and catastrophe. We have seen this pattern throughout our existence—live right and flourish, live wrong and perish. Those who love and follow Christ will be loved by others, and this equates to happiness.

Now let's take a look at the history of the USA. This country was founded on the dogmas of Christianity as outlined in God's Word. The founders knew what would happen if this nation ever compromised those precepts. These men were not outcasts, they were scholars, professionals, philosophers, and patriots; and they were men of great faith in God and in this new nation being launched. They had clear vision, considerable insight, and remarkable foresight (PRO 29:18). They were articulate and thoughtful presidents, senators, congressmen, justices, merchants, and freedom fighters. They risked everything to retain their beliefs and realize their dream of a free society; and they sacrificed much if not their lives or livelihood.

We are losing these capacities, especially our children who are lacking in vision, ambition, and courage. I find it upsetting how the radical extremists have suggested that the founders were despicable and dishonorable men, deflecting from their virtues and values, and reeducating our youth with lies. Is that fair, to disregard a person's accomplishments and focus only on their shortcomings? Who can claim to be without faults and failures? Who is qualified to judge the character of another? Freedom comes with restrictions, but our children are being induced to enjoy freedom without restrictions. How does it profit anyone to denigrate patriotism, bravery, or conscience while ascribing these qualities to degenerates and hooligans?

Ours was a Christian nation from the start (Schweikart, 2011), so have orated the trailblazers, policymakers, educators, and judges who sought to preserve that heritage. Like ancient Israel, the USA may have been God's choice, or "almost chosen" as Abe Lincoln put it. Because of our devotion to God, his hand guided us forward. We must not let go of that hand, like a petulant teen supposing he or she is ready for independence from parents. Distinguish the obvious hand of Providence in the revolutionaries' successful defeat of the British Empire. Intending no disrespect to our friends across the pond, it is the greatest underdog story I have ever read. Notice how the providential arm of God has been evident from the start and how he continuously intervened to perpetuate our beloved land (Medved, 2016; Mataxas, 2016). This fact has been acknowledged by many great men of conscience throughout the annals of our American heritage.

Review the following quotes from some of our noted founders (alphabetized by last name). It is recommended that kids study the history of the American Revolution in general, and these men in particular. Note the contributions each of them made in defining the philosophy of our nation. It should not be forgotten how this country originated and prospered, and how its demise is near if we do not inaugurate these principles once again.

John Adams: *The Christian religion is, above all the religions that ever prevailed or existed in ancient or modern times, the religion of wisdom, virtue, equity, and humanity... The highest glory of the American Revolution was this: it connected, in one indissoluble bond, the principles of*

THE ESSENTIALS

Christianity... Our Constitution was made only for a moral and religious people. It is wholly inadequate to the government of any other.

John Quincy Adams: *In the chain of human events, the birthday of the nation is indissolubly linked with the birthday of the Savior. The Declaration of Independence laid the cornerstone of human government upon the first precepts of Christianity.*

Samuel Adams: *The rights of the colonists as Christians may be best understood by reading and carefully studying the institutes of the Great Law Giver and Head of the Christian Church, which are to be found clearly written and promulgated in the New Testament.*

Fisher Ames: *The happiness of a people, and the good order and preservation of civil government, essentially depend on piety, religion, and morality... Our liberty depends on our education, our laws, and habits. It is founded on morals and religion, whose authority reigns in the heart... We're spending less time in the classroom on the Bible, which should be the principal test in our schools.*

Elias Boudinot: *Let us enter on this important business under the idea that we are Christians on whom the eyes of the world are now turned... Good government generally begins in the family; and if the moral character of a people degenerates, their political character must soon follow.*

Charles Carroll: *I am grateful to Almighty God for the blessings which, through Jesus Christ our Lord, He had conferred on my beloved country in her emancipation... The great, vital, and conservative element in our system is the belief of our people in the pure doctrines and divine truths of the Gospel of Jesus Christ.*

John Dickinson: *Rendering thanks to my Creator for my existence and station among His works, for my birth in a country enlightened by the Gospel and enjoying freedom, and for all His other kindnesses, to Him I resign myself, humbly confiding in His goodness and in His mercy through Jesus Christ for the events of eternity. Kings or parliaments could not give the rights essential to happiness... We claim them from a higher power—from the King of kings and Lord of all the earth.*

Benjamin Franklin: *God governs in the affairs of man... Here is my Creed. I believe in one God, the Creator of the Universe. That He governs it by His Providence. That He ought to be worshipped.*

Alexander Hamilton: *I have carefully examined the evidences of the Christian religion, and if I was sitting as a juror upon its authenticity I would unhesitatingly give my verdict in its favor. I can prove its truth as clearly as any proposition ever submitted to the mind of man.*

John Hancock: *Continue steadfast and, with a proper sense of your dependence on God, nobly defend those rights which heaven gave, and no man ought to take from us... That the kingdom of our Lord and Savior Jesus Christ may be established in peace and righteousness among all the nations of the earth.*

Patrick Henry: *It cannot be emphasized too strongly or too often that this great Nation was founded not by religionists, but by Christians; not on religions, but on the Gospel of Jesus Christ.*

John Jay: *The most effectual means of securing the continuance of our civil and religious liberties is always to remember with reverence and gratitude the source from which they flow... The Bible is the best of all books, for it is the word of God and teaches us the way to be happy in this world and the next.*

Thomas Jefferson: *We all agree in the obligation of the moral principles of Jesus and nowhere will they be found delivered in greater purity than in His discourses... Can the liberties of a nation be thought secure when we have removed their only firm basis, a conviction in the minds of the people that these liberties are of the Gift of God?*

James Madison: *My confidence will under every difficulty be placed, next to that which we have all been encouraged to feel in the guardianship and guidance of the Almighty Being, whose power regulates the destiny of nations. We have staked the whole future of American civilization, not upon the power of government, far from it. We've staked the future of all our political institutions upon our capacity to sustain ourselves according to the Ten Commandments of God... Cursed be all learning that is contrary to the cross of Christ.*

George Mason: *The laws of nature are the laws of God, whose authority can be superseded by no power on earth... That religion, or the duty which we owe to our Creator, and the manner of discharging it, can be directed only by reason and conviction, not by force or violence; and therefore all men are equally entitled to the free exercise of religion, according to the dictates of conscience; and that it is the mutual duty to all to practice Christian forbearance, love, and charity towards each other... Justice and virtue are the vital principles of republican government.*

James Monroe: *When we view the blessings with which our country has been favored, those which we now enjoy, and the means which we possess of handing them down unimpaired to our latest posterity, our attention is irresistibly drawn to the source from whence they flow. Let us then, unite in offering our most grateful acknowledgments for these blessing to the Divine Author of All Good.*

William Penn: *I do declare to the whole world that we believe the Scriptures to contain a declaration of the mind and will of God in and to those ages in which they were written; being given forth by the Holy Ghost moving in the hearts of men of God; that they ought also to be read, believed, and fulfilled in our day; being used for reproof and instruction, that the man of God may be perfect.*

Benjamin Rush: *I do not believe that the Constitution was the offspring of inspiration, but I am as satisfied that it is as much the work of Divine Providence as any of the miracles recorded in the Old and New Testament... The only means of establishing and perpetuating our republican form of government is the universal education of our youth in the principles of Christianity by means of the Bible.*

Roger Sherman: *All civil rights and the right to hold office were to be extended to persons of any Christian denomination... I believe that there is only one living and true God, existing in three persons, the Father, Son and Holy Ghost, the same in substance equal in power and glory... Let us live no more to ourselves, but to Him who loved us, and gave Himself to die for us.*

Joseph Story: *I verily believe Christianity necessary to the support of civil society. One of the beautiful boasts of our municipal jurisprudence is that Christianity is a part of the Common Law.*

Joseph Warren: *May we ever be a people favored of God. May our land be a land of liberty, the seat of virtue, the asylum of the oppressed, a name and a praise in the whole world... It is an indispensable duty which we owe to God, our country, ourselves, and posterity, by all lawful ways and means in our power, to maintain, defend, and preserve those civil and religious rights and liberties for which many of our fathers fought, bled, and died, and to hand them down entire to future generations.*

George Washington: *While we are zealously performing the duties of good citizens and soldiers, we certainly ought not to be inattentive to the higher duties of religion. To the distinguished character of Patriot, it should be our highest glory to add the more distinguished character of Christian... It is impossible to rightly govern the world without God and the Bible.*

Daniel Webster: *If we abide by the principles taught in the Bible, our country will go on prospering and to prosper; but if we and our posterity neglect its instruction and authority, no man can tell how sudden a catastrophe may overwhelm us and bury all our glory in profound obscurity... Finally, let us not forget the religious character of our origin. Our fathers were brought hither by their high veneration for the Christian religion. They journeyed by its light, and labored in its hope. They sought to incorporate its principles with the elements of their society, and to diffuse its influence through all their institutions, civil, political, or literary.*

Noah Webster: *The religion which has introduced civil liberty is the religion of Christ and His apostles. This is genuine Christianity, and to this we owe our free constitutions of government... Our citizens should early understand that the genuine source of correct republican principles is the Bible, particularly the New Testament, or the Christian religion.*

James Wilson: *Human law must rest its authority ultimately upon the authority of that law which is Divine... Far from being rivals or enemies, religion and law are twin sisters, friends, and mutual assistants.*

No doubt, the United States originally stood firmly on God's Word and this is why America heightened, prevailed in wars, defeated tyrants, and averted criticisms of our laws and beliefs. This is not the case in recent decades. We have declined in stature and popularity. We have fought many wars but for the wrong reasons and have not prevailed. We have overthrown dictators, despots, and demagogues to see them replaced with scoundrels worse than the ones we dispatched. We have allowed infiltrators to secularize our society and permitted the weakening of our morals and the subversion of our faith. History does, indeed, repeat itself. How else could historical research receive any credibility as an analytical tool? Therefore, by looking back we sometimes get a glimpse of what might lie ahead. And it doesn't look particularly rosy at this juncture (MAT 24:4–8).

My fellow Americans, do not forget your roots, creed, convictions, and history; these are what made us the greatest nation on earth. The revisionists would disown our Christian heritage and the sacrifices of self for the sake of this republic. They rewrite the history books leaving out critical ingredients, going to great lengths to change our past, and removing any mention or display associated with the Holy Bible. They want to extinguish the memory of the adversities that were overcome to free the slaves, so they take down statues or flags of the Confederacy. It is loathsome to them to acknowledge our faults as well as our greatness. Shouldn't we remember how we got to this place in history? Shouldn't we retain our heritage and our values? We cannot forget how we got here lest we lose sight of where we are going.

Our national treasures and founding documents ought to be reinserted into educational curricula at each echelon of our kid's schooling and into every household. Especially, God commanded us to teach our children the ways, works, and words of the Lord (PSA 78:1–8; PRO 22:6; EPH 6:4). Remember, most forefathers regarded the Bible as the premier primer for tutoring our children. Instruction also must deliver the accurate history of our native land, to remind kids how the fortunes of people, nations, and the world rests in possessing individual integrity and godly faith. This lesson also needs to be instilled in everyone who wishes to become a member of this society.

Collectively, like-minded people can become a force to be reckoned with. Christians could steer this country back towards posterity and protection if we were to reunite as one spirit in communion with the Holy Spirit of God (GAL 6:7–10). Or, would you rather the secularists, globalists, and postmodernists triumph, thereby integrating the USA into a universal society of relativism, materialism, and socialism? Talk about exclusionary; each of these positions are self-defeating. The outcome would be the collapse of morality, economy, and equality, to the detriment of the human race. We once were the spiritual, financial, and military powerhouse of the world. Are we to relinquish these distinctions and assent to a lesser god?

Although the short-term view appears rather bleak, it is not totally hopeless. I estimate that we have maybe ten or twenty years to get it together before reaching the point of no return. What can we do, people ask? The surefire answer is, something else. You may recall Einstein asserting that it is insane to keep doing the same thing while expecting a different result. Since the current course is getting us nowhere a change in strategy is needed. Actually, we need to reverse course completely. We have to cut spending, eliminate useless programs, shrink government, abolish waste, repeal burdensome regulations, enforce laws, end bad politics, quit accumulating debt, stop placating lobbyists and special interests, and the list goes on.

Where then, should we start? Let's start with the principles of the signers of our Constitution and Declaration of Independence, who vehemently opposed taxation without representation, tyranny, obstruction of justice, inequality, immorality, corruption, unfair trade, and abuses of government. They instituted a democratic republic where the civilians were in charge; where voters elected good people to represent them and removed those who were not cutting the mustard. We the people must take our government back, and if that means throwing out the whole lot of them then so be it. But be forewarned, the career politicians will resist with more energy than they ever expended performing their duties; because they don't want to disembark from their cozy little gravy train. It is they who should be on the top of the list to get fired. Please, become involved and educated; know before you vote by investigating the candidates, then cast your ballot. I suggest that you select people who embrace the following priorities: God, country, family.

I would like to propose reforms in areas that would redirect our path, all of which require that the government quits doing what it has been doing and starts doing what it is supposed be doing.

1. Protect and serve: Arguably the principal responsibility of government is to protect our freedoms, including those endowed by our Creator and those granted in the Constitution of the United States. It also is tasked with protecting the citizenry from existential threats. This connotes multiple responsibilities to include maintaining military supremacy; effective law enforcement, border control and immigration policy; homeland, energy, electronics, and cyber security; disaster relief; forging alliances, declaring war, and diplomacy. It also implies a number of services to include intelligence gathering, criminal investigation, tax collection, trustworthy national elections, and infrastructure upkeep. This is not an exhaustive list, nor should it be; the list cannot be unlimited as many bureaucrats would have it. Above all, we need them to keep us safe from harm and danger. That includes retaliating against terrorists and the countries that sponsor them; otherwise the menace will proliferate like jackrabbits.

It is not for the people to serve the government, quite the contrary, we elect leaders to serve us. And if they are using their offices to serve themselves or their coconspirators, it's time for them to take a hike. When it comes to serving the citizenry, the government has failed miserably. The job performance rating for Capitol Hill dropped to a single digit a short while ago. Prior to retiring from office, a former House majority leader wrote the following (Armey and Kibbe, 2010): "Every week we come to town and do things we ought not to do in order to keep the majority so we can do the things we ought to do but never get around to doing." He further declared that "elected leaders fall victim to the incentives being offered." Throwing the bums out just results in a new set of bums. Unfortunately, governments can become monstrosities, especially when garish people with irreverent purposes hang around too long (Paine, 1979).

Our republic allows for progress and prosperity, both individual and national; but this is impeded when those same desk jockeys with their personal ideologies are allowed to linger. Change can be a good thing, notably with respect to leadership. It brings new ideas, solutions, and innovations. Absence of change equates to more exploitation, oppression, class warfare, and status quo. Change does not imply evolution, much less devolution; that is, we mustn't retreat from democracy, capitalism, and republicanism and slip into socialism, statism, and centralization.

The intellects who kick-started this republic regarded public service a civic duty, and an honor not a career. A good neutralizer would be to pass a term limits amendment to the Constitution, holding elected officials to a total of twelve years of service. Eliminate their lifetime retirement and medical packages. These reforms might also reduce partisanship and obstructionism. If Congress refuses to get together it will be up to individuals and states, which could make a big difference in determining how we are to be governed henceforth. I address this idea further in the Drain the Swamp paragraph.

2. Fiscal responsibility: Pork barrel politics has to go, along with those who love to spend other people's money, while throwing caution and our tax dollars to the wind. Deficit spending, what a concept; stop that nonsense! And while you're at it, quit borrowing money to pay for garbage we don't need. Discontinue all sunset programs that have expired without proper legislation to refund them; eliminate corporate welfare and big business bailouts; cease from picking industry favorites, making speculative investments with our money, swaying markets, and otherwise interrupting the flow of free enterprise. Get out of the real estate business and sell off properties that perpetually remain empty. Forbid all non-appropriated spending and reign in so-called discretionary expenditures; liquidate slush funds, hush funds, and stipends. Crack down on tax cheaters and remove them from office. Monitor entitlement programs to prevent waste, abuse, fraud, and excess. Discontinue ridiculous research projects (approximately

$400K was allocated to see if Swedish massages would benefit ailing rabbits). Estimates of government waste run higher than the deficit. If you want to offset tax cuts while lowering the deficit, here is an easy way to do it: junk the costly and ineffective programs. It doesn't take a Rhodes Scholar to identify projects where almost nobody benefits, costs are exorbitant, the programs are unfeasible, there is insufficient research cited that warrants the project, or the purpose is outrageously stupid even to a moron.

Transfer all seized property and assets immediately to the US Treasury and return all recovered funds and unspent money to the treasury. Place money into a special account to replenish funds depleted from Social Security. Simplify the tax code, abolish loopholes, and limit deductions. Write laws that can be read and studied, that address one issue along with the recommended funding. Don't slip irrelevant procurements into a bill that have no bearing whatsoever to that piece of legislation. Oh, and limit the bill to a minimal number of pages. Furthermore, require government officials to enforce laws already on the books before trying to change them incessantly.

Be reasonable. I expect the administrators would never be so reckless with their personal finances. Balance the budget for a change and submit a Constitutional amendment to ensure future administrations are bound to continue the practice. Compel legislators to cut spending. This is the only way to balance the budget. Arguments that it is not possible because the money has been procured, or the law would have to be amended, or the infighting would interrupt normal order, or whatever—this is a bunch of hooey. The reason they don't is because they haven't the gumption. It might be unpopular with certain constituencies or special interests. It could jeopardize their cushy nest, which is padded with your cash. Consequences should be levied upon those who refuse to wield the fiscal axe judiciously; in other words, toss the weaklings out. Maybe then they will realize the need to normalize their own financial situation. Anyone with half a brain knows that budgeting one's money ensures there is enough for everything with some left over for anything. If lawmakers don't care about streamlining the economy it's because they aren't spending their own money so it doesn't affect their pocketbooks. When a person doesn't care they are not inclined to act. We should ensure that, if they care about their jobs, they'd better care about us and get busy, or else.

3. Equal representation: First of all, obey and uphold the Constitution; don't redefine what it says, because our framers got it right from the start. Enforce the laws equally and without prejudice, to include applying them accordingly to our very leaders and authorities who think they are immune from prosecution. Which is more important, passing laws or obeying them? Make the penalty fit the crime and oblige everyone who is convicted to pay that penalty. There must be a deterrent compelling people to think twice before breaking the law, especially our lawmakers.

Employ the three branches of government as intended using the checks and balances system. There should never be a unilateral action that excludes the body responsible for that decision. To illustrate, Congress declares war, ratifies treaties, and passes laws; the President is the commander-in-chief of the armed services, and he submits treaties and political appointments for confirmation; the Judiciary interprets laws and treaties, and enforces the Constitution. How hard is that; can it be spelled out more plainly? The entire Constitution including twenty-six amendments is shorter than most bills, you know. I have a complete copy that I can carry in my shirt pocket.

Pass good laws and regulations and repeal bad ones. This should be straightforward; revise or rescind those laws and regulations that inhibit growth, violate rights, kill jobs, jeopardize citizens, destroy the planet, or discourage businesses from forming or continuing. Regulators especially need to get a handle on the worldwide web and remove sites and patrons that promote illegal acts, deviant sex, terrorism, foreign propaganda, etc. Such atrocities do not constitute protected speech or any civil right.

4. Resource development: Our country has substantial resources to sustain us indefinitely. No doubt, our reserves of oil, gas, coal, and shale are extensive; if we ever were to run out, it likely would be after we already were using alternative energy sources which are more economical and efficient. Why pay foreign governments a penny to supply things we already have? Capitalizing on our untapped reserves would not just meet the demand, but would grow the economy, increase commerce and trade, and create jobs as well. This can be done without harming the environment. Assist the private sector in developing economical, safe, and productive ways of tapping into our resources to include natural resources above and below the ground.

We should go back to making our own materials and cease farming it out to third world countries, especially essential needs such as pharmaceuticals. Producers that cut costs to make the items cheaper also cheapen the quality of those products, and make us dependent on foreign governments. We probably can do it better; and that makes it last longer, saving money in the long run. That's where the government might be able to participate, by granting funds for viable research and development ventures (not for pet projects or kickbacks). We don't really want the government to perform research and development; that is not their area of expertise. Maybe some guidelines will be necessary, but we certainly do not need the bureaucrats running the show when it comes to resource development and industry.

Reduce the tax burden on corporations and small businesses so prices will go down appreciably on products and goods. Why should Americans be paying the highest tax rates in the world for minding our own business? A good start would be scaling back rules that hinder free-enterprisers from innovating. Incentives should be provided and penalties levied to discourage companies from moving overseas. Sure, we can trade; let's export our surplus and import only what we need. Ensure that free trade is a certainty and not a misnomer; free trade, by definition, must be equitable (i.e., fair). Let's invest in foreign resources that advance us and our allies, and renegotiate deals when equity wanes.

Further, limit the release of billions of dollars to foreign governments, especially those that hate us. If they are our friends, they will back us up too. If they want to be a part of our team, they can pay their way. If they need and ask for our help, let's help them; when they get back on their feet, they can find a way to reciprocate. If they despise, attack, or plot evil against us, cut them off. Especially we should avoid interventionism and imperialism. Unless national security or law enforcement is the purpose, stay out.

5. *Downsize:* The government is too big and their reach is too far. In violation of their mandate, administrators bail out banks and companies that are "too big to fail" while the government has become "too big to succeed" (Armey and Kibbe, 2010; Schweikart, 2011). There are justifiable reasons to warrant establishment of governments. For good reason, our forefathers preferred limited government. Keeping government's grubby hands to themselves was an imperative.

There are many things governments don't do well, like build airplanes and railroads. The feds do not need to stick their noses into every public and commercial enterprise. We don't need their involvement in agriculture, land management, education, labor, housing, transportation, manufacturing, banking, healthcare, insurance, energy, religion, Wall Street, global enterprises, and the politics of other countries. Obviously, our government should stay out of a great many things, too numerous to mention here.

Imagine the savings if some departments were scaled back or eliminated. Additionally, those agencies that are actually useful could be streamlined by reducing personnel via attrition, eliminating duplications of effort, and narrowing overall direction and reach, thereby making them cost-effective, and focused on their true mission.

Almost everything is done better by the private sector, wouldn't you say? The feds blow it when they commandeer things not granted them in the Constitution. We hear promises after promises, and emplace the people granting them into Congress to make good on them, and they take years to get it done if it ever gets done at all, which would take maybe weeks if we the people did it ourselves. Take the welfare system, which is awash with waste and corruption. It is well-established that private citizens are more apt and able to care for the underprivileged or disadvantaged than is the government. Farm out some of these responsibilities to the private sector and realize the immediate savings.

6. Drain the Swamp: You have heard this cliché repeated a time or two, haven't you? The swamp, establishment, career politicians, shadow government, deep state, whatever you call them—well they need to leave. Congressional newcomers who are aware of the charade, and actually want Congress to return to regular order, are being throttled. Those who object to the status quo, the pay to play, the influence peddling, and the crony capitalism become the recipients of scorn, exclusion, restrictions, and opposition during bids for reelection (Buck and Blankschaen, 2017). It is all about protecting one's turf, not about protecting America or Americans. It's about lining their pockets not improving the economy. It should really be about enabling all residents to flourish and not just them.

Let's eject those immoral, repugnant, promiscuous, substance abusing, foul-mouthed, self-serving legislators who violate more laws than they pass. Dismiss lobbyists, fire politically charged employees, impeach dishonest jurists, prosecute leakers of classified information, and send criminals in government to prison. Make representatives pay their own way, stop giving them an allowance, they make enough money; and prohibit them from accepting gifts or political favors of any kind. Let's get rid of egocentric, self-aggrandizing officeholders; they are the real denizens in the swamp (Bolling, 2017). Jesus warned us about these tricky double-dealers (LUK 16:1-15). The current trend is hiding ill-gotten gain by enriching their inner circle, retaining proxies, commissioning foreigners, and forming insider trading associations (Schweizer, 2018). We should confiscate such assets and transfer them to the US Treasury in lieu of jail time, after they are immediately terminated without pay.

Crack down on illegal campaign contributions. Rigorously enforce campaign finance laws, and levy additional reforms and restrictions. Abolish the receiving of contributions from lobbyists, government contractors, anonymous donors, criminal enterprises, news outlets, and foreign entities. Force candidates to return unspent campaign donations after the election or to confer them to the US Treasury, fining them dollar for dollar when they use the money for personal benefit. Prohibit them from fund raising while on company (taxpayer) time. Make them spend more time at the office in DC and less on vacation.

Leadership roles are not deserved unless they are earned. That is, promotions must be based more on merit than tenure. The elevation of politicians who have been in Congress forever is counterintuitive and counterproductive. The power they wield is licentious and gratuitous. Good leaders empower, they don't overpower. They extend an open hand, not raise a clenched fist. Lending a hand does not mean push, jerk, squeeze, or smack, but point, lift, uphold, and assist. If you want a perfect example of a leader, take a look at Christ. If you want a dismal example of a leader, you can find a few doozies on Capitol Hill who have been there as long as I can remember.

7. Reinstate Morality: We have a Bill of Rights that is obstinately being stomped on or reworked. Religious freedom is unbalanced, speech is censored, bearing arms is frowned upon, and state's rights are circumvented. Institutions are redefined, ethics are nonexistent, laws are relaxed, and scandals are rampant. It seems that all of our freedoms are being "modernized." Turn loose of my liberties and focus on your jobs for a change. We hired you to combat corruption and put the criminals in jail. We must coerce leaders to be responsible, transparent, and accountable, or get lost. Never forget, morality, liberty, justice, and faith are not mutually exclusive and they are the pillars of our society. Lose any one and the system collapses; and all four pillars seem to be wobbling noticeably.

Summary: Are you forward looking? Can you see a future of blessings or debacles? Do you envision buildings or ruins? You have some control over this, you see. But if you just sit in the bleachers and observe, your team will get trounced. As will you, because you're betting your life on the outcome of that game. You can see what's coming by assessing the condition of the road that took us to where we are now. It has been a major diversion from the road we started on. The route this country is taking is going downhill fast; and we are gaining speed towards a dire cataclysm ahead. Haven't you seen the signs: slow, detour, bridge out, dead end? We should put on the brakes and make a U-turn now. If the rest of the world doesn't like it, well too bad. We have been an independent and sovereign nation from the beginning. Do you want to give that up and let some bureaucrat in a foreign country dictate your fate? I would rather go down fighting for this country than assimilating into the new world order, which will lead to ruin. If that is where you want to go, you may proceed without me.

Then there is the final journey to cogitate: an elevator going up, or the escalator down. As a Christian, I do not fear the end as I already have made plans for a trip to paradise. Like most voyages, it is necessary to book your reservations in advance. You do want to know where you are heading before you walk the plank, I trust. Watch your step and follow the light, or darkness will hide the way. If you board the wrong train you cannot exit, ever.

There is great joy to be had in this life when you contemplate the heavenly rewards God wants to give to you, among them honor, power, and glory. He made us below the angels but in heaven we will be above them (1 CO 6:2–3; HEB 2:5–8). Does anybody deserve that? No. But such are the blessings of God and an indication of how special we are to him. Am I looking forward because I desire the power and the glory? No, I'll be joyful just to be with the Lord. There will be work to perform, and it will be fun; and we will be empowered to accomplish everything God wills. We also will have opportunities for fellowship, praise, song, and celebration. You bet I'm looking forward to happiness, fulfilment, and peace. Well guess what. We can have these things here as long as we stay on the right path, and implore the Almighty to head our government.

Revival

Is there hope? There will be hope until the moment Christ arrives (ACT 3:18–21). How far off will be this sacred event? Well, nobody knows; but he is coming soon (HAB 3:2; REV 22:20). In what state of affairs will he find the world? That will be up to us, the United States, in my opinion. After all, the world usually follows our lead. Lately, we are not leading but following the ways of the world. God told Israel to humble themselves, pray, seek his face, and turn from their wickedness, and he would forgive them and heal their land (2 CH 7:14). What happened when they did not heed that advice? The exact opposite; they continued the downward spiral and that resulted in them getting drawn into the habits of their neighbors. Dear friends, we must abandon our pride and humble ourselves (ISA 57:15; ZEP 23); get on our knees and pray fervently for revival (HOS 6:1; LUK 18:1); come to God's throne and worship him with reverence and awe (ISA 58:1–2,8–9; 2 TI 4:3–4; JAM 4:8–10); and not simply ask God for a handout. And in response to his lovingkindness, let us modify our direction, our ways, and our priorities (PSA 80:19; ISA 55:6–7).

Authentic revival is exhibited in a complete turnaround. It is not a temporary condition or a diversion. And the result will be the transformation of the hearts of individuals, the church, and the nation. Then we will be ready for the day when Jesus comes again—which will prompt a revival and restoration that will be every bit as significant and transformational as his first appearance. But we cannot wait until then; we need to execute a monumental restoration before he returns. The impact will reverberate throughout the world. If the world continues to sink at the current rate, Christ will be here before you can whisper his name. There is only one conceivable reason that he has not yet come: the chance for many others to be saved. When the scales are totally out of tilt, there will be no reason for him to wait any longer. Restore the fundamentals of Christianity into hearts and minds, and into the soul of our nation; or we will be weighed in the balances and found wanting (DAN 5:17–28). And you will bear witness to our beloved country imploding from within (REV 18:9–10).

A trend towards radical liberalism is taking hold with tragedy at its core. They have adopted a double standard whereby human rights are unequally respected, although liberals used to be champions of human rights. These people are terrorists in their own right, funded by wealthy globalists to infiltrate politics, media, education, and other institutions that once espoused diversity, freedom, truth, and civil rights. Proponents of globalism endorse deviancy, protect hate speech (or redefine it when it is more convenient), and elevate likeminded politicians, celebrities, demonstrators, and special interest groups over law and order. They watch from a distance and hold back the arm of the law, with the intention of letting the children play and vent. Property is damaged and people are injured but nobody is answerable. They want to weaken our Constitution while growing government exorbitantly. Problem is, the Constitution, which governs those elected to government and to whom authority is relegated to enforce that Constitution, is ignored if not debased. It gets back to the lust, greed, and pride problem.

Meanwhile, hypocritical crybabies are making life a nightmare for everyone else, plotting some sinister revenge whenever they don't get their way, or they get overruled, or they are not reelected. When they object to another opinion, they whine and pout. They setup safe places where grouches can be immune from free speech, where they are issued puppies, security blankets, and coloring books. The objective is to guarantee that common people have no voice, ensure conservative pundits are targets of censorship and brutality, and influence inquisitive and pliable brains using exploitation and indoctrination.

This will affect Christians most of all, as well as other people possessing a devout faith in God, because the instigators want to outlaw organized religion much the same as communist regimes have done. No surprise, as the persecution of Christians was prophesied two millennia ago by Christ himself (MAT 5:10–12; LUK 6:22–23; JOH 15:18–21; REV 2:10–11). You have witnessed it time and again both here in America and especially overseas. The suffocating of Christianity will accelerate a downfall that might happen in your lifetime if you consent to the sickness spreading. We can postpone it by bonding together with Christ as our head and God's Word as our foundation. This was the modus operandi of the founders; let's adopt it again and decree a Christian caucus, emerging in force during each election.

Again, I would proffer the words of C.S. Lewis on how Christians can have a political impact on the course of this nation (adapted from *Meditation on the Third Commandment*, 1941):

> The Christian Party must either confine itself to stating what ends are desirable and what means are lawful or else it must go further and select from among the lawful means those which it deems possible and efficacious and give to these its practical support... I think it means a world where parties have to take care not to alienate Christians, instead of a world where Christians have to be loyal to infidel parties... There is a way—by becoming a majority. He who converts his neighbor has performed the most practical Christian-political act of all.

Everyone needs to be regenerated, turning away from sin and towards God (JER 31:18). We as a nation need to be rejuvenated; to join together, hand in hand, and get this train back on track. Hopefully, our beloved country will survive; without a conversion it cannot. In the words of Benjamin Franklin, "We must all hang together or most assuredly we shall all hang separately."

Fate

The fate of the world is doom, sooner or later. Humans will be judged individually, and many will fade away; and our world will cease to exist. When will this take place? God only knows, but there is no time to waste. In the meantime, the fate of this nation is priority one. America has been blessed by God and appointed to be a shining light on a hill (MAT 5:14); it is the light of freedom represented in the Statue of Liberty. People all over the globe have come here to find liberty, escape tyranny, or both. But the light is flickering.

I have written at length about what I call the four pillars of fate (Barber, 2016). Once again, they are morality, liberty, justice, and faith; our nation was established upon these principles. Parallels were evident between the American Declaration of Independence and the French Declaration of Rights; both signified struggles against tyranny, not just for a nation but for the world, and both provoked a revolt in favor of freedom (Paine, 1979). Alexis de Tocqueville was enamored with the American Revolution because it was a more principled cause, and therefore had an immensely more profound impact than the French Revolution. During his study of our democracy, he proposed that "nations cannot establish liberty without morality nor morality without faith" (see Tocqueville, 2000). I have added "justice" to his list. If any of the four supports falter, our self-governing system cannot be upheld.

You will find these four fundamental virtues in the Holy Bible because they are assigned by God. I am convinced God had a hand in the forming of America, considering his countless interventions which have saved and preserved this republic since its inception. The primary miracle for humanity always will be the resurrection of Christ, who is the foundation that holds the four columns erect. Remove the foundation and the building collapses. The framers were guided by these biblical tenets in their quest to "form a more perfect Union, establish Justice, insure domestic Tranquility, provide for the common Defense, promote the general Welfare, and secure the blessings of Liberty" (*Preamble to the Constitution*).

Tocqueville postulated that a lapse in morality could be the weakest leg when he wrote, "If America ceases to be good it will cease to be great," and "Everyone feels the evil, but no one has courage and energy to seek the cure"

THE ESSENTIALS

(*ibid*). Portentously, he may have declared our downfall. Morality is knowing what is right and doing what is right. It is based on God's law and is demonstrated by our adherence to it. But morality would be meaningless if there was no liberty. What good would it be to know the right thing if you were not free to choose the right thing? And what good would it be if you had the freedom to choose but had nothing to choose between? Further, morality would be ineffectual if there were no consequences. Clearly, doing right generally yields positive results, and doing wrong yields negative results. Even if we were not endowed by our Creator with intrinsic value, we would learn right and wrong very quickly via knowledge of results. You see, unpleasant outcomes are universally despised whereas success and happiness are universally valued. Thus, you cannot have morality or liberty without accountability, and that requires justice. None of these can survive in the absence of law enforcement, because freedom implies rules. There are some things we are free to do and some we are not free to do, because we have a lawful code. Violating rules leads to punishment, whereas obeying rules generates favor. Bottom line: if you act irresponsibly you can and should be penalized for your actions; in fact, you should expect it.

Once again, liberty, morality, and justice are interdependent. These concepts come from the Lord and are clearly outlined in his Word; they have been instilled in humankind, and even in nature to some degree through the laws of cause and effect and non-contradiction. God produced superior beings capable of apprehending these principles, allowing us to choose rightly and adore him. If you deliberately do the opposite beware, for the arm of justice will come upon you (PSA 7:16; OBA 1:15).

Incredibly, the Lord will find you not guilty regardless of your mistakes if you believe in his promises. This is the doctrine of justification by grace, through faith in the redemption earned for you by the atonement of Christ. Faith is indispensable, for without it you could neither believe in God's love and Christ's atonement, nor morality, liberty, and justice. Our forefathers were men of faith; they believed in this system and it worked. Regimes that do not adhere to these tenets have a citizenry of languid souls who possess no hope, no future, and no direction. Their system of beliefs is unfounded because the populous is not free to choose anything, especially religion. How can they find the truth if it is kept from them? Only by faith in God will they find it; and they can expect persecution as a result. So, they merely exist and await the inevitable end. The Mayflower pilgrims sought the freedom to believe and to choose, with the judiciousness to hold themselves answerable to one another and ultimately God, instead of wayward rulers.

Why do you suppose this nation is referred to as a nation of immigrants? Because everyone's ancestors came here from somewhere else, looking for freedom, truth, purpose, and hope. They fled oppression; they despised having choices dictated to them; they did not believe their governments had their best interests in mind; they were held back from becoming all they could be; and they were mistreated, even murdered for beliefs contrary to the ruling party. In a way, this also is a planet of immigrants; because it is a temporary residence for everybody. A more permanent residence awaits us all; and you get to choose which one you prefer to spend eternity in. No doubt, you have pondered your future more than a few times in your life, whether in the near term or the long term. If you are seriously worried about your future you might want to reconsider your direction. Fate is a state that is predestined, depending on which road you take in life.

Governments and leaders often try to deny liberty, shun morality, pervert justice, and destroy faith. But they cannot, because God instituted these virtues and gave them to the human race. If they are forgotten, a most terrible fate awaits. When you see your government attempting to remove any or all of these jewels, you should not flee, because you will not encounter them elsewhere. You must not freeze or you will get steamrolled and squashed. No, the only option is to fight if you want to keep them. Our forefathers knew this all too well. And they fought and they won, because God was on their side. If God is on your side, the enemy has no chance; case in point, when David slew Goliath (1 SA 17). The devil is the real enemy and he has no chance either (JOH 12:23–32). Whether you win or lose the war will depend on whose side you take; if you pick God's, you win.

When leaders defy what God has ordained, they are bound to lose in the end. Lose what, you may ask? Everything that's what! The ship will sink and you will go down with the losers if you do not admonish them and try to lift them into the lifeboat (EZE 3:18–21). I have seen many bureaucrats engaging in unadulterated idiocy. Who in their right mind thinks it is okay to disregard ethics, facilitate corruption, multiply debt, pursue evil schemes, attack dissenters, engage in promiscuity, weaponize government institutions, and selfishly disregard or even despise the aspirations, feelings, and labor of others?

America is great because we started out a self-governed people with tall moral standards. People capable of governing their own behavior are vastly more apt to create a more perfect union. Freedoms of religion, speech, the press, assembly, and bearing arms center on personal responsibility. America has been the most successful nation to make that idea work. We don't need to be told what to do, we know. The reason the framers were able to pull it off is because the electorate and those elected to represent them held these values close to their hearts. If either the government or the citizenry abolishes these parameters we will fail. In fact, if we lose any one pillar in the edifice, this nation will tumble.

Do you want to go down along with the rest of those perpetrating a globalist society? They are just like the ancient Mesopotamians who began to erect a temple to heaven. While being joined in their resolve, it was toward an evil and contentious ideal in the eyes of God, who confounded their language (GEN 11:1–9). There remained no alliance, only disunion and scattering. Today's globalists are bargaining for a restoration of Babel, but it will be a regression. The forming of a worldwide pact is being disguised as a harmonious assemblage of tongues and nations. The lesson of Babel is that this strategy is not workable. For it is not parity they pursue because their creed is greed; and those who follow get cheated, only to succumb to subjection. The masses will be unaware of what is really taking place until there is no way out of the pit. The subversive undertaking will surely flop as it competes with God; that is why globalism always fails. The Bible refers to this forthcoming affair as a restoration of Babylon, an empire that thrived on greed and world domination (REV 17—18). Do you see the parallels?

Babylon took captive God's chosen Israel (2 KI 24), their reward for defiance and apostasy (1 KI 11; 1 KI 18). Will this happen to the USA in the future due to our defiance of God and renunciation of our faith? Americans have witnessed a comparable whittling down of our moral backbone. Jesus warned that the times preceding his return would be like Noah and Lot (LUK 17:26–30). Israel morphed from a nation zealous for God into one of idolatry. America has pushed God aside in favor of money, self-indulgence, vulgarity, unrestricted sex, sacrificing babies in the womb and other forms of mass murder (ROM 3:10–18). History does repeat itself (see Cahn, 2017).

Speaking of which, note the marked similarities between President Reagan's ascendency and that of President Trump (Ingraham, 2017): the populist message (America first), tough foreign policy stance coupled with beefing-up the military (peace through strength), opposition to the establishment and its elitism (which fostered animosity from both political parties), lowering taxes (which actually increased revenue), bad press from the media (in response to the wide support and influence of conservativism). Those who hated these presidents were proponents of leftism, progressivism, globalism, relativism, multiculturalism, secularism, atheism, materialism, and paganism while rejecting the Holy Bible and the Constitution of the United States. Given lessons from history, which of these two clashing postures will most likely accelerate the fall?

Personally, I don't want any part of the new world order. Will you choose to be a secularist or a constitutionalist; a populist or globalist? Or will you just run and hide? While leaving Independence Hall, Ben Franklin was asked what the Constitutional Convention had accomplished. He replied, "A republic, if you can keep it." I for one would like to keep it. How about you? If we lose it, the scenario just described comes next. And that will be followed by an even more bleak outcome.

The End

Many religions propose an end time that will usher in the extinction of humankind and/or the demolition of the planet. Scientists also believe in the eventual demise of planet Earth. While the universe may be fine-tuned for life, the law of entropy will prevail in due course. That is, there will come a time in which the conditions in this solar system will cease to nourish human life. But the sociopolitical climate will probably destroy us first; because evil causes self-destruction. It could happen anytime between now and whenever. Any number of circumstances could destroy our world, but only one could save it—the hand of Providence (see Medved, 2016). And any number of developments could accelerate the end.

- ➢ The sun is heating up and that will eventually fry us, but it would take up to seven billion years according to some cosmologists.
- ➢ The fine tuning of the cosmos can support humans for a finite window of time which should conclude after about ten to twenty millennia.
- ➢ Artificial intelligence may render humans obsolete, with machines taking over the world, like an old *Star Trek* episode. Perhaps the entirety of humanity would have nothing to do but loiter in a state of perpetual intoxication only to die addicted. That end is highly speculative.

THE ESSENTIALS

- We could overpopulate the planet and everyone would starve to death (possibly the reason dinosaurs didn't make it); that would take a century or more. Or the reverse could happen and homo sapiens expire due to zero population growth from infanticide, sterilization and infertility, and unnatural sexual acts. That should take a century or less.
- We could destroy the ecology due to pollution, extinctions, wastefulness of our resources, inattention to deteriorating living conditions, disregard for the conservation of our air and water, or just plain avarice. We would last maybe fifty years with any combination of those developments.
- A cataclysm like a gargantuan volcanic eruption, asteroid or comet impact, or deadly parasite or superbug pandemic might take us out after a few decades. A perfect storm of pestilence, disease, famine, natural disasters, war, and murder could take us out in seven years; this calamitous scenario can be found in the book of Revelation.
- The deployment of any weapon of mass destruction be it radiological, biological, or chemical could suffice in initiating the end in five years. Whereas a nuclear exchange could wipe out every living species, and that could occur overnight. This seems a conceivable scenario given the rise in nuclear proliferation, especially among rogue nations indicating they are anxious to bomb us.
- Jesus could return and bring his people home—and recreate everything. That will happen in the twinkling of an eye (1 CO 15:52).

Okay, we really don't know when, but only that it won't last forever. It will last until Jesus returns and that could ensue any second (MAR 13:32; 1 TH 5:1–3; REV 3:2–3). But death is not the end, except when it comes to the material world. Or do you think humankind can continue indefinitely down here? Not even the scientists believe that. In a contemporary speech at Oxford University (11/17/2016) the late Steven Hawking said humans have one millennium at best to find another place to live.

By the look of it, Jesus's return might happen before the other circumstances listed above can transpire (REV 1:19). If you want to better understand the end times it will be necessary to study several books in both the OT and the NT; studying the book of Revelation alone will give you an incomplete picture. But if you put it all together it is not a stretch to assume this momentous end might occur before your very eyes. To spark your interest, below are reviewed some of the signs suggesting a time of gloom and doom preceding the Lord's second coming. For a comprehensive review, read Isaiah, Jeremiah, Ezekiel, Daniel, Joel, Micah, Zechariah, the four

Gospels, 1 and 2 Thessalonians, 2 Timothy, 2 Peter, and Revelation; but keep in mind there are many other books and passages from the Bible that address the latter days and the Second Coming of Christ (Barber, 2020).

- ➤ A falling away from the faith will escalate, because the people seek worldly means of getting satisfaction while ignoring God. Christians will be persecuted, insulted, abused, silenced, and executed. Churches will close their doors and those that remain will see a drastic reduction in congregants and financial support. The church will endure profound persecution from the outside and corruption from the inside.
- ➤ False doctrine will be preached across the globe; even Christianity will be refashioned to accommodate humanistic views. Religion will become a scam. There will be an increase in occultism, demonology, and Satanism; this could go so far to include animal and human sacrifices. People will be coming out of the woodwork claiming to be Jesus. There will be a great yearning for the truth but it will not be found unless you have an unaltered Bible.
- ➤ Hostilities and warfare will befall us all, and the wars will not stop but multiply. We will behold a global bloodbath. Earth will be contaminated with radiation and other types of poisoning. Dead bodies will be scattered or dumped in hollows. And all the while the kingpins will be talking about peace. Servitude, oppression, materialism, and global economic failure will burgeon.
- ➤ Lawlessness, immorality, hate, and sexual perversion will be rampant, worse than ever before. It will be a very evil time and generation, with those in power being the worst of the worst, eradicating any semblance of godliness and religiosity. The bosses will assemble a final evil empire to rule the planet in completion of their global reach; they will succeed, but not for long.
- ➤ Geological, natural, and ecological disasters will abound to include pestilences, diseases, and savage beasts (including human); shortages of food and water, and worldwide famine; earthquakes, tornados, volcanos, hurricanes, tidal waves, floods, wildfires, you name it. The earth itself will appear to be in pain akin to the travail of childbirth (MAT 24:8; ROM 8:22; REV 12:2). Astronomical events will signal the end is near; in addition to earth pangs, the heavens also will be shaking (MAT 24:29).
- ➤ People will despise their lives, and pray, not for salvation but for death (REV 9:6).

With any luck, you might get brought out of it alive, or maybe not. And when it ends there will be a new beginning, if you're on the winning team. If you were on the wrong side there will be another, more devastating end. What do you think? Will it be over soon? Do you want it to be over? Are you looking forward to it? Regardless, it will catch everyone by surprise (ECC 12:9; MAT 24:44). The real lesson is, this will not be the ultimate end.

The table at the end of the chapter provides an overview of the events of the Great Tribulation and associated end-of-times prophecies. It is not intended to be a precise scheme of things but represents a popular breakdown of the signs. Given the variety of interpretations being circulated, the table embodies a consolidated model of prevailing patterns among the various theories.

Included are assorted perspectives regarding the rapture, tribulation, resurrection, and millennial reign. None of these views can be considered the golden fleece of eschatology. So, take it all with a grain of salt. Remember, the primary objective is to get a sense for what is yet to come, the most important of which is who is coming, namely Jesus Christ.

The table reflects the millennialist viewpoint; it is based upon a literal interpretation of the thousand-year (millennial) reign of Christ. It also holds that the first resurrection occurs prior to, and the second resurrection occurs right after, the thousand years. Both are considered physical resurrections, one for the just and one for the unjust. While perhaps the most widely accepted position, it is not the only viable theory. Personally, I do not support or endorse any one theory. For instance, the amillennialist viewpoint also has merit. It interprets the thousand years as symbolic of an era. This position holds that the millennial reign occurs during the period between the first and second comings of Christ. In that scenario the first resurrection occurs upon one's death; it is a resurrection of the spirit. The second resurrection is of the body and occurs upon the return of Christ. Regardless of one's viewpoint, the judgment is the last thing that occurs for every individual prior to their arriving at their final destination.

Three popular but differing views of the rapture also endure as indicated in the table. The most commonly held position is the pre-tribulation rapture; it maintains that the saints are taken up into heaven to be spared a seven-year tribulation here on Earth. Other positions hold that the rapture occurs either midway or at the end of the great tribulation, suggesting that the chosen of Christ will have to undergo some or all of that terrible time.

The book of Revelation introduces the seven seals, which begin with the four horsemen of the apocalypse. The seventh seal ushers in the seven trumpets, which are associated with certain calamities that appear to characterize the tribulation period. The last trumpet ushers in the seven bowls (or vials) of wrath poured out upon the wicked souls remaining in the end. Many theologians expect a period of seven years of tribulation; some associate it with the seven seals, some associate it with the trumpets, and some associate it with the vials of wrath.

You may wonder why there are so many different explanations of end-time events. Well, God clarifies things he wants clarified and other things he deliberately holds back (1 CO 12:6; REV 10:4). If he wanted the signs to be unmistakable, they would be; but I think it would give too much away. Personally, I don't believe it necessary for ministers to take a stand on any one theory, especially while addressing their flock from the pulpit. It is better to be preaching the Gospel of Jesus Christ since it is the center of salvation. This is not to say that ministers should never preach about the Revelation of Jesus Christ, as long as the message is clear—Jesus is coming soon and you had best be ready. Whatever manner in which the final events transpire, it is irrelevant to eternal life. God provides signs to remind everyone that we could be in the end times now; either way, we still need to be watchful and vigilant. Please, don't wait until the last minute to commit to the Lord Jesus for time might be running out.

When we go on vacation, we often take a roadmap; but we do not plan every day and night in advance because we want there to be spontaneity and surprise. There has to be some mystery concerning the future, otherwise people would just wait until then to make up their minds. Be assured, there is no reason to wait until the trip has begun to make plans, because the end can come before the sun rises tomorrow. And that finale can occur as a result of your death or Christ's return, whichever comes first. Therefore, the study of eschatology should bring to mind the signs preceding Jesus's coming. They will awaken you to the reality that he is coming soon just like he said at the close of the book of Revelation in his last words to humanity. The correct response is, "Amen, my sweet Lord, please come" (REV 22:20).

The basic questions and answers that you should always be mindful of are as follows. Is God? Yes, God is! Can I? I can do all things through him who strengthens me (PHP 4:13). Did Jesus Christ rise from the dead? He is risen indeed (MAT 28:5-6), alleluia! Praise and thanks be to our Triune God!

THE ESSENTIALS

THE GREAT TRIBULATION AND THE END OF TIMES		
False prophets proliferate	White Horse of Apocalypse	Pre-Tribulation Rapture
Antichrist arrives on scene		
Rebuilding the temple		
Corruption of the church		
Wars and rumors of wars		
Pestilence and disease		
Lawlessness and disorder		
Synagogues of Satan		
Final empire of evil	Red Horse of Apocalypse	
Global economy, society		
Sealing of 144,000		
Mark of the Beast		
Gog and Magog		
Persecution of the faithful		
Fake miracles		
Gospel sent to the world		
Worldwide famine	Black Horse of Apocalypse	Mid-Tribulation Rapture
Abomination of Desolation		
Two witnesses prophesy		
Beast comes back to life		
Worst of times		
Economic collapse		
Four punishments		
Global war		
Mass death, martyrdom	Pale Horse of Apocalypse	
Natural disasters abound		
Depleted resources, rations		
Poison water, air		
Heavenly signs, wonders		
Stinging creatures		
Cavalry of 200,000,000		
First Resurrection		Post-Tribulation Rapture
Armageddon		
Vials of Wrath		
New Babylon falls		
Judgment		
Millennial Reign		
Second Resurrection		
Second Death		
ETERNAL REIGN OF CHRIST AND HIS CHOSEN		

This table does not represent an agenda since the order of events is subject to variation.

REFERENCES

The primary reference for this book has been God's Word, the Holy Bible.

Adler, M. (1952). The Great Ideas: A Syntopicon of Great Books of the Western World. In *Great Books of the Western World. Vol.2.* Chicago: Encyclopedia Britannica.

Alinsky, S. (1971). *Rules for Radicals*. New York: Vintage Books.

Amato, P. R. (2005). The impact of family formation change on the cognitive, social and emotional well-being of the next generation. *Future of Children, 15*(2), 75–96.

Armey, D. and Kibbe, M. (2010). *Give Us Liberty: A Tea Party Manifesto*. New York: HarperCollins.

Austin Institute for the Study of Family and Culture (2014). www.austin-institute.com

Bagley, C. and Tremblay, P. (2000). Elevated rates of suicidal behavior in gay, lesbian, and bisexual youth. *Crisis: The Journal of Crisis Intervention and Suicide Prevention. 21*(3), 111–117.

Barber, A. V. (2016). *Faithbook for Christian Counselors*. El Paso, TX: Special Delivery Press.

Barber, A. V. (2020). *Fundamentals of Christianity: A Bible Study and Guide (Fourth Edition)*. El Paso, TX: Special Delivery Press.

Barber, A., Korbanka, J., Stradleigh, N., and Nixon, J. (2003). *Research and Statistics for the Social Sciences*. Boston: Pearson Custom Publishing.

Bartlett, B. (2008). *Wrong on Race: The Democratic Party's Buried Past*. New York: St. Martin's Griffen.

Behe, M. J. (2006). *Darwin's Black Box: The Biochemical Challenge to Evolution*. New York: Free Press.

Benford, M. S. and Marino, J. G. (2002). *Textile Evidence Supports Skewed Radiocarbon Date of Shroud of Turin*. Originally presented at Worldwide Congress (Sindome 2000) in Orvieto, Italy. www.shroud.com/pdfs/textevid.pdf.

REFERENCES

Bennett, J. (2001). *Sacred Blood, Sacred Image, The Sudarium of Oviedo: New Evidence for the Authentication of the Shroud of Turin*. San Francisco: Ignatius Press.

Bible Archaeology Society (2018). *Biblical Archaeology Review*. www.biblicalarchaeology.org.

Bolling, E. (2017). *The Swamp: Washington's Murky Pool of Corruption and Cronyism and How Trump Can Drain It*. New York: St. Martin's Press.

Bremmer, I. (2018). *Us Vs. Them: The Failure of Globalism*. New York: Penguin.

Buck, K. and Blankschaen, B. (2017). *Drain the Swamp: How Washington Corruption Is Worse than You Think*. Washington, DC: Regency.

Byrd, R. C. (1997). Positive therapeutic effects of intercessory prayer in a CCU population. *Alternative Therapies in Health and Medicine, 3*(6), 87–90.

Cahn, J. (2017). *The Paradigm: The Ancient Blueprint that Holds the Mystery of Our Times*. Lake Mary, FL: FrontLine.

Carson, B. (2014). *One Nation: What We Can Do to Save America's Future*. New York: Penguin Group.

Carter, B. (1974). *Large number coincidences and the anthropic principle in cosmology*. IAU Symposium, 63.

Chakraborty, A., McManus, S., Brugha, T., Bebbington, P., and King, M. (2011). Mental health of the non-heterosexual population in England. *British Journal of Psychiatry. 198*(2), 143–148.

Clarke, D. (2017). *Cop Under Fire: Moving Beyond Hashtags of Race, Crime, and Politics to a Better America*. New York: Worthy Books.

Comfort, R. (1993). *The Evidence Bible*. Gainesville, FL: Bridge-Logos.

Corsi, J. R. (2018). *Killing the Deep State: The Fight to Save President Trump*. West Palm Beach, FL: Humanix Books.

Craig, W. L. (2010). *On Guard*. Colorado Springs: David Cook.

Darwin, C. (1859). *On the Origin of Species by Natural Selection, or the Preservation of Favored Races in the Struggle for Life*. London: John Murray.

Davies, P. (2007). *Cosmic Jackpot: Why Our Universe is Just Right for Life*. New York: Houghton Mifflin.

Dawkins, R. (1996). *The Blind Watchmaker: Why the Evidence of Evolution Reveals a Universe without Design*. New York: W. W. Norton.

Dembski, W. (1998). *The Design Inference*. New York: Cambridge University Press.

REFERENCES

D'Souza, D. (2015). *Stealing America*. New York: Broadside Press.

Erikson, E. H. (1968). *Identity: Youth and Crisis*. New York: Norton.

Fagan, P. F. (1995). *The Real Causes of Violent Crime: The Breakdown of Marriage, Family, and Community*. The Heritage Foundation. www.heritage.org/research/reports.

Fitzgerald, F. (2017). *The Evangelicals: The Struggle to Shape America*. New York: Simon and Schuster.

Freud, S. (1928). *The Future of an Illusion*. London: Hogarth Press.

Friedman, M. and Friedman, R. (1980). *Free to Choose: A Personal Statement*. New York: Houghton Mifflin Harcourt.

Geisler, N. and Bocchino, P. (2001). *Unshakable Foundations*. Minneapolis: Bethany House.

Geisler, N. and Turek, F. (2004). *I Don't Have Enough Faith to Be an Atheist*. Wheaton, IL: Crossway.

Gorka, S. (2016). *Defeating Jihad: The Winnable War*. Washington, DC: Regnery.

Greenleaf, S. (1874). *The Testimony of the Evangelists: The Gospels Examined by the Rules of Evidence*. New York: James Cockcroft.

Gunderson, L. (2000). Faith and healing. *Annals of Internal Medicine*. *132*(2), 169–172.

Habermas, G. R. (1993). *The Historical Jesus: Ancient Evidence for the Life of Christ*. Joplin, MO: College Press.

Haisch, B. (2006). *The God Theory*. San Francisco: Weiser Books.

Hammond, P. (2010). *Slavery, Terrorism, and Islam*. Cape Town, South Africa: Xulon Press.

Hawking, S. (1996). *Life in the Universe*. www.hawking.org.uk/lectures.

Hayek, F. A. (1944). *The Road to Serfdom*. University of Chicago Press.

Hitchens, P. (2010). *The Rage Against God: How Atheism Led Me to Faith*. New York: Harper Collins.

Hodge, D. R. (2006). Spiritually modified cognitive therapy: A review of the literature. *Social Work, 51*(2), 157–166.

Horowitz, D. (2014). *Unholy Alliance: Radical Islam and the American Left*. Washington, DC: Regnery.

Hubble, E. (1929). *A Relation Between Distance and Radial Velocity Among Extra-Galactic Nebulae*. Proceedings of the National Academy of Sciences of the USA. *15*(3), 168–173.

REFERENCES

Hook, J. N., Worthington, E., Davis, D., Jennings, D., Gartner, A., and Hook, J. P. (2010). Empirically supported religious and spiritual therapies. *Journal of Clinical Psychology, 66*(1), 46–72.

Horowitz, D. (2014). *Unholy Alliance: Radical Islam and the American Left.* Washington, DC: Regnery.

Hoyle, F. (1983). *The Intelligent Universe.* London: Michael Joseph.

Ingraham, L. (2017). *Billionaire at the Barricades: The Populist Revolution from Reagan to Trump.* New York: All Points Books.

Jeffrey, G. (2003). *Creation: Remarkable Evidence of God's Design.* Colorado Springs: WaterBrook Press.

Keller, W. (1956). *The Bible as History.* New York: William Morrow.

Kelly, G. (1955). *The Psychology of Personal Constructs.* New York: Norton.

Koenig, H. G. (2012). *Religion, Spirituality, and Health: The Research and Clinical Implications.* New York: ISRN Psychiatry.

Koenig, H., Hooten, E., Lindsay-Calkins, E., and Meador, K. (2010). Spirituality in medical school curricula: Findings from a national survey. *International Journal of Psychiatry in Medicine, 40* (4), 391–398.

Larson, J. S., Swyers, J. P., and McCollough, M. E. (1997). *Scientific research on spirituality and health: A consensus report.* Radnor, PA: Templeton Press.

Levin, M. R. (2009). *Liberty and Tyranny: A Conservative Manifesto.* New York: Threshold Editions.

Levin, M. R. (2015). *Plunder and Deceit: Big Government's Exploitation of Young People and the Future.* New York: Threshold Editions.

Levin, M. R. (2017). *Rediscovering Americanism.* New York: Threshold Editions.

Lewis, C. S. (1946). *The Great Divorce.* New York: HarperCollins.

Lewis, C. S. (1947). *Miracles.* London: G. Bles.

Lewis, C. S. (1952). *Mere Christianity.* London: G. Bles.

Lofgren, M. (2016). *The Deep State: The Fall of the Constitution and the Rise of a Shadow Government.* New York: Viking.

Lincoln, A. (1838). *The Perpetuation of Our Political Institutions.* Speech given at The Young Men's Lyceum in Springfield, IL.

Locke, J. (2002). *The Second Treatise of Government.* New York: Dover (first published in 1690).

REFERENCES

Luther, M. (1943). *Dr. Martin Luther's Small Catechism*. St. Louis: Concordia.

Marrs, J. (2008). *The Rise of the Fourth Reich: The Secret Societies that Threaten to Take Over America*. New York: HarperCollins

Marshall, I. H. (1982). *Luke: Historian and Theologian*. Grand Rapids: Zondervan.

Metaxas, E. (2015). *Miracles: What they are, why they happen, and how they can change your life*. New York: Dutton.

Metaxas, E. (2016). *If You Can Keep It.: The Forgotten Promise of American Liberty*. New York:1 Viking.

McDowell, J. and Wilson. B. (1993). *A Ready Defense*. Nashville: Thomas Nelson.

Medved, M. (2016). *The American Miracle: Divine Providence in the Rise of the Republic*. New York: Crown Forum.

Meyer, S. (2013). *Darwin's Doubt: The Explosive Origin of Animal Life and the Case for Intelligent Design*. New York: Harper One.

Meyer, S. (2009). *Signature in the Cell*. New York: Harper One.

Missler, C. (2009) *An Easter Surprise: A Quantum Hologram of Christ's Resurrection?* www.khouse.org/articles/2009/847.
  (see also www.shroud.com/books.htm).

Moore, N. G. (1996). Spirituality in medicine. *Alternative Therapies in Health and Medicine*. 2(6), 24–29.

Mundt, P. (2007). *A Scientific Search for Religious Truth*. Austin: Bridgeway Books.

Nagel, T. (1997). *The Last Word*. New York: Oxford University Press.

Oakes, K., Allen, J., and Ciarrocchi, J. (2000). Spirituality, religious problem-solving, and sobriety in Alcoholics Anonymous. *Alcoholism Treatment Quarterly, 18*(2), 37–50.

Paine, T. (1979). *The Rights of Man*. New York: Dutton (first published in 1791).

Paley, W. (1802). *Natural Theology: Evidences of the Existence and Attributes of the Deity, Collected from the Appearances of Nature*. Philadelphia: John Morgan.

Pew Research Center (2015). *America's Changing Religious Landscape*. www.pewforum.org.

Penzias, A. and Wilson, R. (1965). *People and Discoveries*. www.pbs.org.

Perloff, J. (2002). *The Case Against Darwin: Why the Evidence Should Be Examined*. Burlington, MA: Refuge Books.

REFERENCES

Polkinghorne, J. (2005). *Exploring Reality: The Interaction of Science and Religion*. New Haven, CT: Yale University Press.

Proctor, C. and Groze, V. (1994). Risk factors for suicide among gay, lesbian, and bisexual youths. *Social Work. 39*(5), 504–513.

Propst, L., Ostrom, R., Watkins, P., Dean, T., and Mashburn, D. (1992). Comparative efficacy of religious and nonreligious cognitive-behavioral therapy for the treatment of clinical depression in religious individuals. *Journal of Consulting and Clinical Psychology, 60*(1), 94–103.

Ramsay, W. M. (1915). *The Bearing of Recent Discovery on the Trustworthiness of the New Testament*. London: Hodder and Stoughton.

Rana, F. and Ross, H. (2010). *Who Was Adam?* Colorado Springs: NavPress.

Rhodes, R. (2016). *Manuscript Evidence for the Bible's Reliability*. www.home.earthlink.net/~ronrhodes/Manuscript.html.

Ross, H. (2001). *The Creator and the Cosmos*. Colorado Springs: NavPress.

Ross, H. (2008). *Why the Universe is the Way it Is*. Grand Rapids: Baker Books.

Sanders, E. P. (1993). *The Historical Figure of Jesus*. London: Penguin Press.

Schweikart, L. (2011). *What Would the Founders Say? A Patriot's Answers to America's Most Pressing Problems*. New York: Sentinel.

Schweizer, P. (2018). *Secret Empires: How the American Political Class Hides Corruption and Enriches Family and Friends*. New York: Harper.

Spitzer, R. L. (2003). Can some gay men and lesbians change their sexual orientation? 200 participants reporting a change from homosexual to heterosexual orientation. *Archives of Sexual Behavior, 32*(5). 403–417.

Starnes, T. (2014). *God Less America: Real Stories from the First Lines of the Attack on Traditional Values*. Lake Mary, FL: FrontLine.

Strobel, L. (1998). *The Case for Christ: A Journalist's Personal Investigation of the Evidence for Jesus*. Grand Rapids: Zondervan.

Sunderland, L. (1988). *Darwin's Enigma: Fossils and Other Problems*. Santee, CA: Master Book Publishers.

Sun Tzu (2017). *The Art of War*. London: MacMillan.

Tocqueville, A. (2000). *Democracy in America*. New York: HarperCollins (first volume published in 1835, second volume in 1840).

United States Debt Clock. www.usdebtclock.org.

Wallace, J. W. (2013). *Cold Case Christianity*. Colorado Springs: David Cook.

Wallace, J. W. (2015). *God's Crime Scene*. Colorado Springs: David Cook.

Wikstrom, D., Oberwittler, K., Treiber, B., and Hardie, B. (2012). *Breaking Rules: The Societal and Situational Dynamics of Young Peoples' Urban Crime*. Oxford, UK: Oxford University Press.

Wollack, E. J. (2012). *Cosmology: The Study of the Universe*. NASA. http://map.gsfc.nasa.gov/universe.

Wycliffe Global Alliance (2016). *Scripture and Language Statistics*. www.wycliffe.net/statistics.

Yarwood, M. A. (1998). When clients seek treatment for same-sex attraction: Ethical issues in the 'Right to Choose' debate. *Psychotherapy, 35*, 248–259.

Zacharias, R. (2007). *The Grand Weaver*. Grand Rapids: Zondervan.

Zacharias, R. and Vitale, V. (2017). *Jesus Among Secular Gods: The Countercultural Claims of Christ*. New York: FaithWords.

Zemore, S. E. (2007). A role for spiritual change in the benefits of 12–step involvement. *Alcoholism: Clinical and Experimental Research, 31*(S3), 76–79.

Zuckerman, P. (2006). *The Dead Sea Scrolls Shed Light on the Accuracy of Our Bible*. www.probe.org/the-dead-sea-scrolls.

INDEX

Abbreviations, iv

Abortion, 86, 254

Absolutes, 32, 87, 108, 226–227

Absolution, 224–229

Accountability, 83–88, 168

Adoption, 83, 177, 228

Alliances, 100–101, 141–145, 152

Anarchism, 10, 98, 131

Apocalypse, 150–153, 297

Apologetics, 1, 234

Archaeology, 17, 18–22

Armageddon, 150, 252, 297

Astronomy, 25, 28–29, 197–206

Atheism, 10, 33, 49, 56–57

Beginning, 28, 30, 64, 166, 174, 182, 198–199, 203

Beliefs, 9–15, 95, 123, 272

Bias, 111, 210, 215–219

Biology, 26, 30

Causality, 1, 3, 30, 31–33, 40–41, 111–112

Christianity, 12, 15, 35–36, 47–49, 120, 129–135, 154–157, 243–246, 272

Church, 129–130, 151–152, 171, 191, 230–231, 244

Citizenship, 79, 132, 140, 272–276

Comfort, 51–54, 77, 148

Commandments, 75, 139, 274

Communion, 77, 171, 186, 244, 277

Condemnation, 72, 78, 123, 153, 161, 262, 270

Connecting, 170–173, 191, 194–195, 202, 228–229

Conscience, 39, 60, 69–71, 86, 96, 125

Constitution, 10, 129–131, 168, 272–277, 278–283

Corruption, 80, 88–91, 222, 246, 283–284

Cosmology, 25, 28–29, 198–200

Covenant, 156, 171, 186–187, 192, 261–262

Debate, 15–17, 113, 206–211, 263–267

Decisions, 36–37, 92–95, 121, 212–215, 227

Definitions, 3–14, 38, 41, 77, 108, 125

Destiny, 163, 165–167, 175, 213, 215, 270

Differences, 196–197, 201–202, 211–212, 229–231

Direction, 117, 213–214, 229, 285–287, 290

Disaster, 40, 145–149, 294

Discernment, 39, 57, 60–62, 115, 224

Discover, 17, 110, 113–118

Diversity, 229–235, 238

Division, 127, 144, 229–235, 238, 241–242

DNA, 26–27, 33, 37, 200–201, 206–209

Economy, 10–14, 140, 145–149, 241–242, 281

Education, 85–87, 101–102, 234–235, 277

End of Times, 141–145, 242, 292–296, 297

Entitlement, 147, 161–164, 172, 241, 279

Equality, 75, 78, 139–141, 168, 212, 227, 235, 239

Eschatology, 152, 292–296

Eternity, 34, 228, 255–258

Evidence, 1–2, 15, 16–32, 35, 56, 112, 118–124, 157–159, 215, 263–265

Evil, 39–41, 57–64, 75, 145–151, 149, 294

Evolution, 26–27, 32, 118–120, 205–208

INDEX

Exclusion, 47–51, 106, 224

Exceptional, 27, 200–202, 212

Experience, 67, 117–118, 211–216, 267–268

Facts, 3, 15, 23, 24, 56, 107–113, 159, 219, 240

Faith, 15, 35–36, 41, 43–44, 110, 115, 163, 183–184, 240–242, 243–246, 255, 261, 288–292

Fate, 78, 243, 251, 288–292

Fear, 66, 97, 133, 148, 150, 172, 251

First Fruits, 185–188, 261

Forgiveness, 41, 221, 224–225, 245, 249

Founders, 79, 131, 139, 168, 271–277

Freedom, 124–129, 167–170, 228, 241, 272, 288–291

Genesis, 29–30, 202–206

Geography, 26

Geology, 25–26, 210, 294

Globalism, 11, 80–81, 90, 98, 127, 145–147, 162, 241–242, 286, 291–292

God, 1, 9–14, 15–16, 31–56, 57–58, 61–78, 97, 106–107, 114–117, 122–124, 132–133, 138–141, 154–157, 160–161, 170–173, 176–177, 181–188, 191–195, 203, 221, 224–229, 243–246, 258–262

Gospel, 154–160, 194–195, 243–246, 258–264,

Government, 10–14, 79–83, 140, 145–148, 272–286

Hate, 49, 161, 178–179, 232, 260, 294

Heaven, 41, 47–48, 165–167, 175, 194, 253, 257–258, 267–268

Hell, 194, 256–257, 268

History, 16–22, 157–159, 271–272, 276–277

Holy Bible, 15–17, 54–56, 157–159, 240, 277

Holy Spirit, 53, 154–155, 170–172, 182, 184, 191, 221, 243–245, 250

Holy Week, 23, 185–188

Humanity, 39, 62, 196, 201, 211–212, 250, 292–294

Idolatry, 75, 139–140, 193, 240–241, 243

Imputation, 268–271

Information, 108, 111, 121, 206–211, 215

Intelligent Design, 33, 111, 206–211

Invisible, 29, 37, 114, 250

Islam, 97–100, 131–134, 142, 154–155, 188, 251

Israel, 19–22, 141–144, 150, 156, 185, 291

Jesus Christ, 48, 55, 154–161, 170–173, 176–177, 185–186, 224–229, 243–245, 258–271, 296

Judaism, 141–142, 155, 185–188

Judgment, 41, 50–51, 71–74, 82–83, 152–153

Justice, 58–59, 62–63, 74–79, 83–85, 219–220, 288–290

Killing, 59–60, 75, 98–99, 156, 169, 261, 266

Koran, 47, 49, 131–134, 154–156, 260, 266

Lamb of God, 76–78, 185–186, 261–262

Laws, 18, 30, 40–42, 69–71, 199, 220, 280–281

Legacy, 68, 89–91, 147

Liberty, 75, 167–170, 288–290

Life, 1, 26–27, 32–33, 115, 117–118, 160–161, 164–167, 194–195, 209, 256

Logic, 2–9, 31–33, 49

Logos, 56, 221, 226

Love, 16, 41, 63, 70, 95, 97, 133, 174, 195, 224, 247, 249, 270

Lust, 65–66, 90, 95

Lying, 122, 128, 183, 219–222

Medicine, 27, 115

Miracles, 33, 42–48, 297

INDEX

Morality, 39–41, 60–62, 124, 284, 288–290

Murder, 49, 51, 59–60, 75, 133, 169, 254, 291

Nature, 32, 40, 42–43, 246–249

New Testament, iv, 17, 23–24, 45–47, 154, 157–159, 263, 272–276

Old Testament, iv, 17–21, 45–47, 75, 154, 186–187

Paleontology, 29, 118–119

Passion, 68, 95–96, 159, 187

Passover, 76–77, 156, 185–188, 261–262

Personal, 52–53, 176–181, 244

Physics, 28–30, 42–46, 227–228, 265

Political Correctness, 93, 124–130, 233, 287–289

Politics, 9–14, 27, 127, 131, 238–240, 272, 282–284

Prayer, 35, 43, 115, 173, 180, 191, 245

Presence, 38, 53, 63, 181–182, 191–195

Progressivism, 13, 80, 135–137, 233, 240

Proof, 2, 16–17, 31, 157–159, 197–202, 263–267

Prophecy, 16, 54–55, 150–152, 294–297

Randomness, 33, 42, 117, 181, 206–211

Rapture, 144, 295, 297

Reality, 12, 58–59, 107–108, 221, 224

Redemption, 41, 47, 261–262, 269–270

References, 298–304

Religion, 9–14, 47–49, 106–107, 116–117, 120–121, 154, 240–241

Research, 85–86, 112–115, 118–119, 217, 219, 247

Resurrection, 23, 45, 48, 55, 158–159, 171, 263–268, 295, 297

Revival, 285–288

Rights, 124–129, 135, 168, 230, 272–276, 284, 286

Sacrifice, 76–77, 261–262

Salvation, 47, 73, 182, 221, 225, 253, 261, 268–269

Sanctification, 77, 244, 269

Science, 24–30, 56, 106–107, 111–118, 205–209, 215, 240

Second Coming, 47–48, 150, 188–189, 286, 293–295, 296–297

Service, 173–176, 244, 279

Sexuality, 86, 91–97, 124, 145, 165, 247, 294

Signs, 150–153, 188–191, 223, 292–297

Sin, 39–41, 62–65, 69–70, 73, 75–78, 261–262

Singularity, 44–45, 111

Sociology, 27, 235–238

Soul, 37–38, 245, 250–257

Special, 196–202, 224, 285

Substitution, 76–77, 163–164, 268–271

Suffering, 39–41, 62, 151

Swamp, 80–82, 126–127, 148–149, 283–284

Temptation, 64–68, 72, 250

Terrorism, 97–105, 143–144, 242

Testimony, 17, 23, 156–159, 186, 219, 263–264

Theism, 14, 24, 49–50, 215

Tolerance, 50–51, 131–132

Tribulation, 149–153, 295–297

Trinity, 170–171, 181–185, 194–195, 227, 243, 259

Truth, 2–3, 56, 106–113, 160–161, 195, 219–224, 258–259

Tyranny, 135–141, 254, 278, 288

Uniqueness, 48, 196–202, 209, 211–215

Universe, 28–30, 38, 44–45, 197–211

War, 59, 97–107, 131–135, 242

www.ingramcontent.com/pod-product-compliance
Lightning Source LLC
Chambersburg PA
CBHW060508300426
44112CB00017B/2585